ACCREDITATION IN TEACHER EDUCATION ● ITS INFLUENCE ON HIGHER EDUCATION

ADVISORY COMMITTEE

ACCREDITATION
IN TEACHER EDUCATION

ITS INFLUENCE
ON HIGHER EDUCATION

JOHN R. MAYOR
Director of the Study

WILLIS G. SWARTZ
Assistant Director

NATIONAL COMMISSION ON ACCREDITING
Washington, D.C.

FOREWORD

Of the many issues in the accreditation of colleges and universities, none has been more vexatious, complicated, and difficult of resolution than those related to the accreditation of teacher education. No field of accreditation has continuously required more attention on the part of the National Commission on Accrediting than teacher education; no field shows a greater lack of consensus among educators as to the proper approach to accreditation; and in no field have the issues of accreditation been argued as intently both within the educational institutions and among the numerous laymen concerned with the quality of education.

In the belief that it could be of some assistance in reaching a socially sound resolution of these issues, the National Commission has sponsored a Study of the Influence on Higher Education of Accreditation in Teacher Education with the assistance of a generous subvention from the Carnegie Corporation of New York. In sponsoring this Study the Commission has proceeded on the principle that it should be conducted in a completely autonomous manner with the Director possessing freedom of action and independence of judgment. The most objective and unbiased analysis is required to assist in the eventual attainment of a mutually satisfactory agreement for the various national and regional groups concerned with the issues. I fully expect that the report of this Study will help to make it possible for the proper solutions eventually to be developed to resolve the many questions in the accreditation of education for teachers.

The National Commission was exceedingly fortunate to obtain the services of Dr. John R. Mayor who was granted leave from some of his responsibilities as Director of Education for the American Association for the Advancement of Science. As Director of the Study, Dr. Mayor has exercised judgment and perception supported by a breadth of knowledge and a conscientious recognition of the importance of his responsibilities. His current position in an esteemed national organization not directly involved in the education of teachers and his background as a former professor of mathematics and of education made him a logical choice for this most difficult assignment. The Executive Officer, Dr. Dael Wolfle, and the Board of Directors of the American Association for the Advancement of Science were generous in permitting him to conduct the Study and to do so in facilities that the Association made available.

Dr. Mayor was assisted by Dr. Willis G. Swartz, who has served on a full-time basis while on leave as professor of government and formerly dean of the graduate school at Southern Illinois University. Dr. Lyle H. Lanier, vice president and provost of the University of Illinois, has unselfishly given of his time and advice as chairman of the Advisory Committee whose membership intentionally comprised individuals with different backgrounds and markedly different points of view on the subject of accreditation. This Committee was urged to offer its advice and opinions freely. The National Commission is grateful to Dr. Lanier and his colleagues for the advice that they have generously given to Dr. Mayor and his staff, and it wishes to record the fact that the Committee is in no way considered responsible for the report.

The National Commission wishes also to record its appreciation for the cooperation that the officials of all the organizations concerned with the accreditation of teacher education extended, in many cases making their records and files available on a confidential basis.

In view of the widespread interest in this report, it was agreed, when plans for the Study were developed, that copies of the report would be publicly available at the time they were presented to the National Commission on Accrediting. The Commission is pleased that this plan has been followed in the distribution of this significant report.

WILLIAM K. SELDEN
Executive Director
National Commission on Accrediting

PREFACE

It is understandable that the problem of accreditation in teacher education should have been as troublesome to the National Commission on Accrediting as William K. Selden has suggested in the *Foreword*. The education of teachers is a social function that brings sharply into focus deep-rooted conflicts of educational values and institutional interests—both within and outside the field of education. Furthermore, society's control of this function is probably a matter of greater concern to more diverse individuals, groups, and institutions—within and outside the field of education—than is the case for any other profession.

In the light of this unique character of teacher education, the National Commission wisely decided to choose the members of the Advisory Committee for the Study reported in this volume in order that the Committee would include individuals of widely divergent institutional backgrounds and "markedly different points of view on the subject of accreditation." At the same time, and fortunately, that decision virtually prescribed that the Committee's role would be strictly advisory, and that it should not be expected to reach consensus as to the conduct of the Study, the analysis of the findings, the conclusions, or the recommendations. Had this general frame of reference not been established, the Study almost certainly could not have been completed within the relatively short time available; and, if completed as a Committee task, the final report might well have included little more than unevaluated factual material, with generalities of slight significance for the advancement of teacher education.

Freed from the necessity to reach consensus upon a group report, members of the Committee were able to devote more time to articulating their conflicting views on teacher education and accreditation, and to suggesting divergent approaches to the appraisal of the impact of accreditation in this field on higher education. We hope that the resulting dialectical process performed, on the whole, a useful advisory function for John R. Mayor and Willis G. Swartz. They obviously could not have followed all of the advice that was so freely given; but perhaps their balanced overview of this complex problem partly reflects their reaction to the Committee discussions in the context of the wealth of information assembled as the Study progressed.

Whatever the attitudes of the individual members of the Advisory Committee toward the accreditation of teacher education may have been—or whatever their views concerning the conclusions and recommendations presented in this report may be—I am pleased, on their behalf, to commend Dr. Mayor and Dr. Swartz for the thoroughness and objectivity with which the Study was conducted.

The contributions of this Study will lie in (a) the delineation of the complex interrelations among the educational, professional, and governmental interests concerned with teacher education, (b) the clarification of the issues and developments related to the major controversies over national accreditation in this field, and (c) the comprehensive inventory of the effects of accreditation of teacher education—at state, regional, and national levels—on institutions of higher education. In the light of this impressive systematic analysis, all of the groups concerned should be able to work more constructively toward their common goal: the improvement of the quality of education in the schools, through better education of prospective teachers.

LYLE H. LANIER
Chairman
Advisory Committee for the Study

TABLE OF CONTENTS

PART III. Conclusions

Chapter

Appendices

ACKNOWLEDGMENTS

It is a privilege to acknowledge the generous support of the Carnegie Corporation of New York, which made this Study possible by means of a grant to the National Commission on Accrediting. While the Study has been conducted independently of the Commission, appreciation is expressed to the staff of the Commission for supplying information on accrediting agencies upon request, and to William K. Selden for his sympathetic understanding of the difficulties of the undertaking and his encouragement and patience as the report of the Study was prepared in final form.

The members of the Advisory Committee named by the National Commission on Accrediting and listed on the back of the title page of this report are hereby absolved from any responsibility for the report or its recommendations. The full responsibility for the report in all of its parts is borne by the Study staff. Special thanks are expressed to members of the Committee who, in five meetings held between December 4, 1963, and February 15, 1965, and through correspondence, have given thoughtful consideration to plans under way and have made many suggestions which have led the staff to fruitful investigation, or have prevented them from pursuing a nonessential venture, or making too many unwise decisions on procedures.

In most visits to colleges, one staff member has been accompanied by a consultant. Professor John A. Brown of the University of Delaware, Professor Edwin B. Kurtz, Jr., of the University of Arizona, and Mr. Kenneth W. Medley, Associate Editor of *Nation's Business*, have provided valuable assistance as consultants.

Professor Victor A. Hicken of Western Illinois University conducted a special study of quality measures of college programs which became the basis of Chapter 9 of the Study. Professor Donald J. Dessart of the University of Tennessee conducted a catalog survey of teacher education programs of 95 colleges and universities to which reference is made in Chapters 1, 11, and 13. Additional information on the survey is given in Appendix VI.

Valuable assistance has been provided by members of the National Association of State Directors of Teacher Education and Certification in visits to their offices, in special conferences, and in submitting answers to one lengthy questionnaire to which directors from all 50 states replied, and to other questions addressed to them by letter.

Generous cooperation has been provided for the Study by the staff members of the National Council for Accreditation of Teacher Education, the National Commission on Teacher Education and Professional Standards, and the American Association of Colleges for Teacher Education, as well as by many members of those organizations. The Study has been strengthened by the participation of more than 100 individuals in conferences of representatives of special groups of colleges and universities and of professional organizations, and of several hundred in interviews during visits to states and colleges. Helpful conferences have also been held with many other educational leaders. These have included: James B. Conant; Theodore A. Distler, formerly of the Association of American Colleges; Edgar Fuller of the Council of Chief State School Officers; Manning M. Pattillo and Donald M. Mackenzie of the Danforth Foundation; Robert Poppendieck of the U. S. Office of Education; T. M. Stinnett and Ray C. Maul of the National Education Association. Quite a large number of other persons have read early drafts of chapters of this report and made many valuable suggestions.

All of the many persons who have assisted us have given generously of their time and counsel in their desire to contribute in this way to the improvement of higher education and of teacher education. The authors' debt to them is herein acknowledged.

Appreciation is also expressed to the officers of the American Association for the Advancement of Science and of the Department of Mathematics and the College of Education, University of Maryland, for their willingness to relieve me of regular responsibilities in order to devote one-third of my time for 15 months to this Study.

At the beginning of the Study, Willis G. Swartz was appointed assistant director of the Study. Dr. Swartz, on leave of absence as Professor of Government of Southern Illinois University, where he also was Dean of the Graduate School for 14 years, has given full time to the Study since February 1, 1964. In working on a full-time basis with a director who has been on a one-third time appointment, Dr. Swartz has carried a major part of the work in visits to campuses, in searching the literature, and in writing the report. The Study, and whatever it may accomplish, would clearly have been impossible without his calm, objective, and scholarly approach to the work. He has demonstrated selfless dedication to his assignment, recognizing fully the potential contribution that the Study might make to the improvement of higher education, of teacher education, and of accreditation.

For whatever shortcomings the report may contain, apologies are offered. It has been a stimulating, sometimes trying, undertaking. At the conclusion of the work, wisdom gained would dictate that some things be done differently, but it has seemed of critical importance to complete the report within the original schedule of 15 months because of pressing issues which call for attention. The Study represents a determined attempt to add understanding to a highly controversial subject, and in so doing to contribute to the development of programs for the education of teachers, which must be of the high quality that the educational needs of our time demand.

JOHN R. MAYOR

INTRODUCTION

The Study of the Influence on Higher Education of Accreditation in Teacher Education has been sponsored by the National Commission on Accrediting and supported by the Carnegie Corporation of New York. The National Commission appointed the Director and Assistant Director, named an advisory committee composed of highly respected leaders in higher education, and has served as the fiscal agent for the Study. The Study has been conducted independently of the Commission. This report of the Study has been prepared as a report to the National Commission on Accrediting (NCA), and also has been made available to the public.

Since 1956, the national agency for accrediting teacher education in the United States has been the National Council for Accreditation of Teacher Education (NCATE). In addition, most of the states either accredit or approve teacher education programs of institutions of higher education within the states and, in some instances, in other states. Between national and state accreditation of teacher education, general institutional evaluation and accreditation are conducted by six regional accrediting associations. Thus, there are three levels of accreditation of teacher education: national, regional, and state. This Study is concerned with accreditation at all three levels and its influence upon higher education.

Almost from the inception of accreditation of colleges and universities, accreditation of teacher education has been a controversial issue. There are a number of complicating factors peculiar to accreditation in teacher education, and contributing to a difference of opinion on whether there should be national accreditation in this area, such as:

1. Programs in teacher education are offered by more colleges and universities (1,173) than any other professional field of study.

2. Teacher education is dependent upon or related to more facets

of a total institutional program than any other area of specialized accreditation.

3. There are philosophical differences regarding the best way to prepare teachers.

4. The liberals arts groups which have played a leading role in the regional accrediting associations have tended to question whether national accreditation of teacher education is needed.

5. There are some who ask if teaching is really a profession, and, if so, if it is sufficiently homogeneous at all levels to justify the existence of a professional accrediting agency.

6. There is a greater diversity of specialization within teacher education than is true of any other professional field of study.

All of these divisive elements and influences have made it difficult to achieve a consensus on the organization, and the standards and procedures to be employed in the accreditation of teacher education. When NCATE was formally recognized by the National Commission on Accrediting in 1956, it was agreed that the new agency would be reviewed in 1960 jointly by NCA and NCATE. In 1960 it was recognized that some modifications and improvements were desirable, but because NCATE had been in operation such a short time it was decided to delay action and permit further study until "no longer than the end of 1963." In the spring of 1963 and again in the spring of 1964 NCA drew up a series of guidelines for improving the structure, operation, and financing of NCATE. While changes have been slow in coming, NCA has recognized that NCATE has been making a sincere attempt to respond to the recommendations. In the meantime, a new Federation of Regional Accrediting Commissions has been organized, patterns of accreditation in the states have been changing, more learned societies have been taking an active interest in teacher education, more teachers colleges have become general colleges, and new studies of teacher education have been reported.

As a result of many complicating factors, confusion over accreditation in teacher education is found in all segments of education. This confusion must be removed in order that there may be a clear understanding of the important needs for further improvement in the education of teachers, and just what role, if any, and at what levels (state, regional, national) accreditation may serve as one of the means of assisting in this improvement. In order to remove the confusion, there is need for a clear understanding of the influence which accreditation in teacher education has been and is exerting on higher education. The purpose of this Study is to bring clarity to this basic issue.

The report is presented in three parts. In Part I background information is provided on the history of, procedures in, and issues or problems related to accreditation in teacher education. The influences of this accreditation are described in Part II. Finally, observations and recommendations are given in Part III.

PART I

ACCREDITATION IN TEACHER
EDUCATION

Part I of the Study provides a frame of reference for Parts II and III. It describes the nature and scope of the Study, traces the development of accreditation in higher education, and discusses the important problems and issues in accreditation. It begins with a brief description of the Study itself (Chapter 1), followed by the evolution of accreditation and its significance in higher education (Chapter 2). Next come the development of state accreditation (Chapter 3), regional accreditation (Chapter 4), and national accreditation in teacher education (Chapter 5). Chapter 6 attempts to give an objective portrayal of the controversies that have revolved around national accreditation in teacher education for the past decade. The remaining chapters in Part I deal with some of the special issues and problems associated with accreditation in teacher education. Chapter 7 describes a number of special problems related to accreditation in teacher education. Chapter 8 explains the problems associated with graduate-level accreditation. Chapter 9 discusses the question of using quantitative or qualitative criteria in evaluating teacher education programs and institutions.

Anyone already familiar with the background material covered in Part I may elect to bypass Chapters 2 through 9 of the report and proceed directly to Part II.

CHAPTER 1

NATURE AND SCOPE OF THE STUDY

T HE EARLY 1960's have given rise to a spirited debate over accreditation in teacher education. The controversy derives in part from the fact that accreditation in this setting and in a broad nontechnical sense connotes regulation or control, and the fact that teacher education relates directly or indirectly to the daily lives of possibly three-fourths of the American people. As a consequence, many adult Americans have acquired strong opinions as to just what kind of training is best for those who teach our youth. Although accreditation of teacher education has developed along state, regional, and national lines, the focal point of the controversy has been national accreditation. It is true that there have also been strong differences of opinion over accreditation on the state and regional levels, but it is only natural for such differences to receive less nationwide publicity and popular attention than issues on the national level.

SCOPE OF THIS STUDY

Dealing as it does with accreditation in teacher education,* this Study does not embrace accreditation of the entire field of higher education. At the same time it is necessary to realize that teacher education is so broad in scope that it relates to a very large segment of the total spectrum of higher education. What is referred to as "professional teacher education" is an important, but a relatively small, portion of what may properly be included under the broad term of teacher education. What is commonly known as "general education," usually consisting of those courses in the freshman and sophomore years required of most or all degree candidates, is an important segment of teacher education. Those academic departments in which secondary school teachers of subject matter specialize are likewise included under

---

* By teacher education is meant education of teachers for elementary and secondary schools.

teacher education. Then, too, practically all graduate students in subject-matter areas are at least potential candidates for teaching positions,
hence they may relate to teacher education. Or, to approach it nega-
tively, about the only phases of higher education not related to teacher
education are those training people for professions other than teaching,
such as dentistry, law, medicine, and pharmacy. Such professional fields
as agriculture, business, home economics, and industrial arts are only
partially excluded.

This is a study of *accreditation in teacher education* on the *national, regional,* and *state* levels. On the national level as a study of present and past influence this means that it is primarily a study of the one
professional agency dealing with the accreditation of teacher education,
namely, the National Council for Accreditation of Teacher Education, popularly known as NCATE. A detailed study and evaluation of
NCATE is particularly appropriate at this time by virtue of the widespread publicity given to this organization in recent years. This publicity was highlighted in the reaction which emanated from NCATE accreditation visits to Carleton College, [1] a "prestige" liberal arts school,
and to the University of Wisconsin, a "prestige" state university. [2]
Are the criticisms of NCATE well founded? Are they valid? Or are such
criticisms a byproduct of widespread misinformation and misconcepts
on the part of many of NCATE's critics? This Study hopes to provide
at least some of the answers to these and other questions concerning
NCATE.

On the regional level this is a study of accreditation in teacher
education with respect to the six regional accrediting associations.
These are the Middle States Association of Colleges and Secondary Schools, the New England Association of Colleges and Secondary
Schools, the North Central Association of Colleges and Secondary
Schools, the Northwest Association of Secondary and Higher Schools,
the Southern Association of Colleges and Schools, and the Western Association of Schools and Colleges. [3] The largest of the regional associations, North Central, embraces no less than 19 of the 50 states, extend-
ing from West Virginia on the east to include Arizona on the west. The
smallest regional association, in terms of the number of states included,
is the Western Association with only two states—California and
Hawaii. The other four associations fall between these two extremes
in size.

On the state level, this Study embraces the accrediting or approving
activities of the 50 states now comprising the American Union. [4]
These 50 states represent 50 different and varying approaches to
the schools and colleges located within the borders of the states.
The various state patterns go from the one extreme of New York
and California, where there is a highly centralized state concern
for higher education, to the opposite extreme of states like Idaho and
Montana, which have virtually transferred their "accreditation" authority to the regional and national accrediting agencies. These variations

make it extremely difficult and dangerous to generalize other than to note the complete lack of uniformity.

Finally, this is a study of the effects of *national* or *special, regional* or *general,* and *state accreditation in teacher education upon higher education* in the United States. To what extent has accreditation of teacher education on the three levels influenced such aspects of higher education as college and university administrative structures, budgetary policies, and physical facilities? What have been the effects on student admission and retention standards and policies? On experimentation and research in teacher education? On the employment and retention of staff members in teacher education? On the public support of higher education? The answers to these questions constitute the very heart and core of the Study.

DEFINITION OF TERMS

This is a study of *accreditation.* It is not a study of *certification* nor of *licensure*—although all three are closely enough related to cause a great deal of confusion, not only on the part of the public generally, but even among educators. For this reason it is important at the outset to clarify the meanings of these important educational terms.

William K. Selden defines accrediting as "the process whereby an organization or agency recognizes a college or university or a program of study as having met certain predetermined qualifications or standards." [5] An earlier definition by G. F. Zook and M. E. Haggerty describes "accreditment" as the "recognition accorded to an educational institution in the United States by means of inclusion in a list of institutions issued by some agency or organization which sets up standards or requirements that must be complied with in order to secure approval." [6] By means of accreditation, professional organizations, associations of institutions, and official state agencies make known to the public those colleges and universities, elementary and secondary schools, hospitals, clinics, scientific laboratories, and other institutions serving the public which meet required standards of quality determined by the accreditation agency.

Lucien B. Kinney defines *certification* in teacher education as "a process of legal sanction, authorizing the holder of a credential to perform specific services in the public schools of the state. Its widely accepted purpose is to establish and maintain standards for the preparation and employment of persons who teach or render certain nonteaching services in the state." [7] Certification practices have evolved in each state independently. Accordingly, the national pattern is one of great variety. Hence any generalization should recognize the wide range of practices.

Licensure may be defined as the legal process by which those in professions other than education are authorized by the state to practice their professions before the public and to charge a fee or salary for the professional services rendered. It is a government responsibility whose function is to protect society from malpractice by incompetent individuals.[1]

Accreditation, as the term is commonly employed in education, is conferred or granted by professional organizations, associations, or institutions, or by an agency of the state, and applies only to *institutions* or *programs* within institutions. *Certification* is granted solely by the *state* and is given only to *individuals.* *Licensure* is conferred by a state board or commission and applies only to *individuals.*

ACCREDITATION OF HIGHER EDUCATION IN THE UNITED STATES

This is a study of accreditation at the level of higher education, or education beyond the secondary school. Any reference to elementary or secondary education has been made only as it relates to accreditation on the college or university level.

The historical background and evolution of accreditation in the United States is described in Chapter 2 of this Study. Due partly to their unhappy pre-Revolutionary relations with England, partly to their frontier environment, the early Americans developed a deep-seated fear of, and prejudice against, centralized national authority. And these fears and prejudices were no stronger anywhere than in religion and education which at that time were closely related. Consequently, in the formulation and adoption of the Constitution of the United States, care was taken to provide for separation of church and state and to make certain that the legal control over education was defined as a residual power of the states. [8]

When in the late nineteenth century the rapidly proliferating high schools and colleges required some form of regulation and the states seemed to be only partially able to provide the necessary controls, American ingenuity gave birth to the unique mechanism known as voluntary or self-regulation of educational institutions. Under this system of regulation, professional accrediting organizations and associations of higher educational institutions have sprung up as expediency dictated. Broadly speaking, these voluntary accrediting agencies fall into two categories: (1) regional accrediting associations which evaluate the over-all or general institutional program and (2) professional associations, each of which centers its jurisdiction

---

[1] Kinney (p. 14) defines licensure as "the generic term applying to admission to any profession." It is "the process by which a profession controls the quality of its membership and thus determines its efficiency as a profession . . ." (p. 131). "Education presents the anomaly of a profession without licensure. Certification, which has generally been accepted as licensure, was not designed for this purpose, and is not effective in serving it" (p. 131).

around the particular professional training program in which it is involved.

METHOD OF PROCEDURE IN THE STUDY

The collection of information on which the Study has been based has been carried out by:

1. Visits to colleges and universities; the state departments of education; school administrators, teachers, and officers of the state education associations in selected states.
2. Visits to selected colleges and universities in other states.
3. Conferences with staff officers in the offices of the six regional accrediting associations and with the Chairman of the Federation of Regional Accrediting Commissions of Higher Education.
4. Examination of NCATE files and follow-up to determine subsequent action by institutions.
5. Conferences of representatives of multipurpose universities, state colleges, liberal arts colleges, and institutions of higher learning in the western states, held in Washington, D. C., Palo Alto, and Chicago.
6. Conferences of representatives of the staffs of learned societies, of professional education organizations, and of nationally recognized leaders in teacher education.
7. Special studies on state practices, quality measures, and characteristics of teacher education programs.
8. Extensive analysis of the literature.

In the Study, campuses of 60 institutions of higher education in 15 states have been visited. These include 11 public and 7 private universities, 22 state colleges, and 20 liberal arts colleges. In the campus visits, conferences were held with the president when possible, with deans of liberal arts and of education, with faculty members, and in some instances with students. Often in visits to a college or university, conferences were arranged with school personnel living in the vicinity of the campus. These included: school administrators, teachers, and sometimes members of the state Teacher Education and Professional Standards (TEPS) commissions. Among other things, school administrators were asked whether in employing teachers they were inclined to prefer graduates of NCATE-approved institutions over graduates of other institutions.

Instead of visiting the most populous states (as was done in the Conant investigation of the education of American teachers), [9] it was thought best to select at least one state from each of the six regional association areas. In 13 states, conferences were held with representatives of the state departments of education relative to accrediting and certification policies and practices. These states were Connecticut, Florida, Georgia, Illinois, Iowa, Kansas, Kentucky, Louisiana, Michigan, Missouri, New Jersey, North Carolina, and Utah. Institutions of higher education were also visited in California, Maryland, and Minnesota.

In gathering evidence of the impact of the regional associations the records and publications of the associations have been examined, as well as monographs and articles relating to regional accreditation. In addition, personal visitations have been made to the central offices of all six regional accrediting associations, and their staff members have been interviewed. Also interviewed have been officers of the recently formed Federation of Regional Accrediting Commissions of Higher Education. [10]

Throughout the Study, the participating team has enjoyed the full cooperation of NCATE, including free access to the NCATE files, and has taken full advantage of the opportunity to examine the files of institutions involved in NCATE relationship. It was believed that one of the most fruitful means of determining NCATE's influence, good or bad, on colleges and universities would be to examine the records of those institutions which had experienced difficulty in obtaining full NCATE approval. Just what conditions or special requirements were laid down by NCATE as prerequisites for full NCATE accreditation? Were these conditions reasonable, constructive, and beneficial? Or were they whimsical, arbitrary, and unduly restrictive? Changes toward meeting these conditions by the institutions concerned might be interpreted as appropriate, though inconclusive, evidence of NCATE's influence.

Among the most helpful of the activities of the Study were the seven conferences with representatives of special groups of institutions of higher education and of professional organizations listed above under items 5 and 6. The seven conferences were:

> State Colleges, May 18, 1964, Washington, D. C.
> Multipurpose Universities, May 25, 1964, Washington, D. C.
> Colleges and Universities of the Western States, July 13, 1964, Palo Alto, California
> Learned Societies, September 24, 1964, Washington, D. C.
> Liberal Arts Colleges, October 5, 1964, Chicago, Illinois
> Leaders in Teacher Education, November 16, 1964, Washington, D. C.
> Professional Education Societies, November 17, 1964, Washington, D. C.

The participation in these conferences included more than 100 persons from 36 states and the District of Columbia. In all, staff members from 17 public and 11 private universities, 26 liberal arts colleges, 26 state colleges, and from Teachers College, Columbia University, and George Peabody College for Teachers attended one of these conferences.

Including the annual national meeting of the National Association of State Directors of Teacher Education and Certification (NASDTEC) and other special conferences with NASDTEC members, persons from as many as 45 of the states, the District of Columbia, and Puerto Rico were reached in conferences or by visits.

In addition to the privilege of participation in their annual meeting held in Louisville, June, 1964, other valuable assistance has been provided by members of the National Association of State Directors of Teacher Education and Certification. They gave freely of their time in conference, in submitting answers to a questionnaire to which directors from all 50 states responded, and to other questions addressed to them by letter.

Because standards of accrediting agencies emphasize quantitative aspects of programs, a special study was made of the literature, evaluation instruments, and promising research in the area of qualitative measures which might offer possibilities for use in accreditation. A catalog survey was made of a 10 percent random sample of 962 colleges and universities offering teacher education programs. Tests of equality of means of variables in undergraduate programs of NCATE- and non-NCATE-accredited institutions were determined and applied.

RELATED LITERATURE

There is an abundance of literature on the general subject of accreditation, and the volume tended to increase noticeably in the late 1950's. These include Lloyd E. Blauch, ed., *Accreditation in Higher Education;* [11] Roy J. Deferrari, *Self-Evaluation and Accreditation in Higher Education;* [12] Alvin E. Morris, *A Critical Analysis of Types of Quantitative Data Requested by the Professional Teacher Education Accrediting Agency and the Six Regional Accrediting Agencies;* [13] John F. Nevins, *A Study of the Organization and Operation of Voluntary Accrediting Agencies;* [14] and William K. Selden, *Accreditation, A Struggle Over Standards in Higher Education.* [15] More recent publications are Sam P. Wiggins, *Battlefields in Teacher Education,* [16] James B. Conant, *The Education of American Teachers,* [17] and James B. Conant, *Shaping Educational Policy.* [18]

Earlier works of significance are G. F. Zook and M. E. Haggerty, *The Evaluation of Higher Institutions* (1936), [19] and Fred J. Kelly, et al., *Collegiate Accreditation by Agencies Within States* (1940). [20]

FOCUS OF THE STUDY

This Study does not pretend to be a complete and thorough coverage of all phases of accreditation. Nor is it a study of accreditation in higher education. It is not even a study of accreditation of teacher education in all its phases. Rather, it is a study of the effects of the accreditation of teacher education—not all effects, but only those pertaining to higher education.

Since limitations of staff, time, and money did not permit exploring thoroughly all the possible ramifications of even the highly restricted subject as defined, an attempt has been made here to cover the main core of the topic and to supplement it with suggested areas or tangents which seem to merit further investigation.

REFERENCES

1. James D. Koerner, *The Miseducation of American Teachers* (Boston 1963), pp. 234–241.
2. Lindley J. Stiles, "Wisconsin vs. NCATE," *School and Society*, 91, No. 236 (Summer 1963).
3. John F. Nevins, *A Study of the Organization and Operation of Voluntary Accrediting Agencies* (Washington, D. C., 1959), *passim*.
4. Lloyd M. Blauch, ed., *Accreditation in Higher Education* (Washington, D. C., 1959), Chapter V.
5. William K. Selden, *Accreditation, A Struggle Over Standards in Higher Education* (New York, 1960), p. 6.
6. G. F. Zook and M. E. Haggerty, *The Evaluation of Higher Institutions*, Vol. I., *Principles of Accrediting Higher Institutions* (Chicago, 1936), p. 18.
7. Lucien B. Kinney, *Certification in Education* (Englewood Cliffs, 1964), p. 3.
8. John McCormally, "The Root of Opposition to Federal Support," *Educational Digest*, XXIII, No. 4 (December 1961), pp. 32, 33.
9. James B. Conant, *The Education of American Teachers* (New York, 1963).
10. Chapter 4, p. 39 of this Study.
11. Lloyd E. Blauch, ed., *Accreditation in Higher Education* (Washington, D. C., 1959).
12. Roy J. Deferrari, *Self-Evaluation and Accreditation in Higher Education* (Washington, D. C., 1959).
13. Alvin E. Morris, *A Critical Analysis of Types of Quantitative Data Requested by the Professional Teacher Education Accrediting Agency and the Six Regional Accrediting Agencies* (Detroit, 1959).
14. John F. Nevins, *A Study of the Organization and Operation of Voluntary Accrediting Agencies* (Washington, D.C., 1959).
15. William K. Selden, *Accreditation, A Struggle Over Standards in Higher Education* (New York, 1960).
16. Sam P. Wiggins, *Battlefields in Teacher Education* (Nashville, 1964).
17. James B. Conant, *The Education of American Teachers* (New York, 1963).
18. James B. Conant, *Shaping Educational Policy* (New York, 1964).
19. G. F. Zook and M. E. Haggerty, *The Evaluation of Higher Institutions* (Chicago, 1936).
20. Fred J. Kelly, et al., *Collegiate Accreditation by Agencies Within States*, United States Office of Education, Bulletin No. 3 (Washington, D. C., 1940).

CHAPTER 2

ACCREDITATION IN HIGHER EDUCATION

ACCREDITING BODIES in the United States, other than instruments of the several states, are classified as voluntary agencies. They are lacking in the essential legal authority to compel institutions of higher learning to become accredited. In other words, colleges and universities, at least in theory, are free agents in determining whether or not they will seek accreditation. Be that as it may, a majority of educational institutions, including high schools, feel a strong compulsion to become accredited. So strong is this compulsion for some that accreditation is regarded almost as a matter of life or death. Denial of accreditation will sometimes arouse deep resentments in both the institution and the community.

ACCREDITATION: AN AMERICAN PHENOMENON

A significant feature of American education has been the lack of central or Federal control. In sharp contrast, most European countries have ministries of education which exercise direct control over universities and other units in the educational system. Under our Federal system, the jurisdiction over education is reserved to the several states, which thereby have authority to charter and regulate both public and private institutions of higher learning. By not choosing to exercise a large part of their potential authority over higher education, states have permitted colleges and universities generally to organize and develop in an atmosphere of almost complete autonomy. The natural result of such a *laissez faire* policy is a wide variation among higher institutions in the character and quality of their programs. It was in an effort to bring a semblance of order out of an increasing variation among institutions that a practice known as accreditation was devised. This phenomenon is peculiar to the United States; it has no counterpart in other nations.

11

NATURE OF ACCREDITATION

Accreditation as applied in education is the recognition accorded to an institution that meets the standards or criteria established by a competent agency or association. Its general objective is the promotion and assurance of high quality in education programs. The standard procedure employed in accreditation involves four steps: (1) establishment of standards or criteria; (2) inspection of institutions by competent authorities to determine whether the institutions meet the established standards or criteria; (3) publication of a list of institutions that are judged as meeting the standards of criteria; and (4) periodic reviews to ascertain whether accredited institutions continue to meet the standards or criteria. Institutions which are accepted by an accrediting agency or association as meeting its standards or criteria are said to be accredited or approved.

PURPOSES OF ACCREDITATION

Service to the Public. Accreditation serves the public by supplying the layman some guidance on institutions he may wish to patronize. This is particularly important in selecting an institution to attend, or to designate as the beneficiary of grants or gifts.

Accreditation is made effective through public pressure on institutions to conform to the standards and criteria established by accrediting agencies.

Institutional Improvement. A hoped-for result of accreditation is for institutions to improve their programs by providing for them standards or criteria to strive for. Administrators, faculties, and governing boards, in learning the extent to which their institution does not measure up to the specified standards or criteria, are provided with a strong incentive for institutional improvement. The self-study which many institutions are required to make in preparation for an accreditation team's visit usually has a salutary effect. Some accrediting agencies emphasize improvement more than minimum standards and thus are often helpful in stimulating improvement, even in an institution of very high quality.

Facilitating Transfers. A basic purpose of accreditation is to facilitate the transfer of students from one institution to another. Such transfer is rather extensive. Some of it is horizontal, students transferring from one level in an institution to the corresponding level in another; but most of it is vertical, students complete courses of study in an institution and then move to other institutions for more advanced or professional study. Admissions officers make practical use of the judgments of accrediting agencies in evaluating student records.

Raising Standards of Profession. An important objective of accreditation is to raise the standards of education for the practice of a profession. Almost every profession has adopted accreditation as a means of suggesting how its practitioners should be prepared, and, as necessary, of enforcing its ideas.

Information for Prospective Employers. A basic purpose of accreditation is to inform those who employ graduates of an institution, or who examine its graduates for admission for professional practice, about the quality of training the graduates have received.

SIGNIFICANCE OF LISTS OF ACCREDITED INSTITUTIONS

Each accrediting organization from time to time issues a list of the institutions it has approved or accredited. Just what does it mean for an institution to be named on a list of accredited institutions? Here are some of the answers given to this question:

1. It means that the institution has been evaluated by competent persons interested in maintaining academic standards and has been found to be doing an acceptable job of what it is set up to do. Accreditation thus attests a minimum level of academic quality and integrity of an institution to all who may be concerned with it or interested in it.

2. The inclusion of an institution on a list of accredited institutions does not mean that it is as good as any other on the list. Most such lists include institutions of different types and of widely varying quality, but all have met certain minimum quantitative and qualitative requirements.

3. An accredited institution, as already pointed out, usually has an advantage over a nonaccredited institution in the transferability of its credits. It cannot be assumed, however, that an accredited institution will accept automatically and unconditionally academic credits earned in another accredited institution. Each institution is free to determine for itself just what credits it will accept from another.

4. General accreditation of an institution carries many other benefits. The pre-professional work done in an accredited school usually qualifies a student for admission to a professional college provided he has studied the subjects prescribed by the professional school to which he seeks admission. Too, a student who has graduated from an accredited four-year college may ordinarily be admitted to a good graduate school provided his undergraduate record meets the admission standards of the graduate school in question.

MOTIVATIONS IN ACCREDITATION

In the light of the advantages associated with accreditation in higher education, and even though some see disadvantages, it is not surprising that a premium is placed by institutions of higher learning on the achievement of accreditation, both institution-wide and in specialized programs, such as in teacher education. Indeed, the various motivations or pressures for accreditation have become so strong as to raise serious questions about the truly voluntary nature of regional and national accreditation. [1] What, specifically, are some of the motivations or pressures which induce colleges and universities to seek accreditation? Broadly speaking, they are of two kinds: (1) internal—within the institution itself; and (2) external—those which stem from outside sources.

MOTIVATIONS WITHIN THE INSTITUTION

Desire for Recognition. Institutions, like individuals, seek recognition, respectability, prestige. Indeed, these are motivating forces which appear to be as strong for educational institutions as they are for individuals. Like individuals, institutions of higher learning are fully aware of the advantages derived from prestige. A college or university with the necessary accreditation will usually fare better in competing with similar higher institutions for quality students, be they undergraduates or graduates; also in competing for qualified staff members, particularly during the current shortage of applicants in many academic and professional areas. Likewise, an institution seeking public or private funds—grants, loans, or gifts—will ordinarily find accreditation highly advantageous, if not indispensable. For example, several years ago when The Ford Foundation distributed $75 million among liberal arts colleges, none of the money was assigned to non-accredited institutions. This despite the fact that lack of adequate financial resources was in many cases the one most significant hurdle standing in the way of full accreditation.

An institution that is properly accredited can point with pardonable pride to its fortunate status—on the title pages of its catalogs or bulletins, in press releases, in reports to alumni, and in appeals to potential donors to endowment funds, or for special gifts of money or property. All of these considerations tend to loom large in a college's scheme of values. [2] Some colleges or universities denied accreditation have become belligerently defensive in telling the world why accreditation should have been granted, how and why it was a gross injustice to be denied it, and just what were the weaknesses and failures of the accrediting agency involved.

Student Pressure. Undergraduate students, in the absence of institutional accreditation, may feel serious economic handicaps. Federal loan funds may be withheld; corporation grants for student loans may not be forthcoming; scholarship grants from private sources may not materialize. Undergraduates may also be aware of social and professional handicaps or disadvantages. Prestigious honorary or professional organizations will often refuse to authorize chapters in nonaccredited schools. Even national social organizations, such as fraternities and sororities, as a rule will not permit chapters for students attending nonaccredited colleges. Students wishing to pursue graduate study may experience difficulty in gaining admission to reputable graduate schools as well as in competing for graduate scholarships, assistantships, or fellowships. [3] Students seeking employment following graduation may find themselves at a disadvantage in competing with graduates of accredited institutions. In the undergraduate's or graduate's pattern of values, all these considerations may rate high. As a result, students will tend to throw their individual or collective influence in favor of accreditation.

Alumni Pressure. Alumni will tend to support anything that enhances the prestige and glory of their alma mater. This may mean charters from prestigious honorary organizations, such as Phi Beta Kappa or Sigma Xi; eligibility of their women graduates for membership in the American Association of University Women (AAUW); championship football or basketball teams; or it may mean accreditation. Alumni are acutely aware that their individual prestige is related to that of the institution from which they graduated. In recent years, important professional associations have begun to restrict their membership to graduates of accredited institutions. In professional education, for example, the very important American Association of School Administrators (AASA) since January 1, 1964, has limited new memberships to graduates of programs at the graduate level accredited by NCATE. The American Association for Health, Physical Education, and Recreation has moved in the same direction. [4]

Faculty Pressure. The entire faculty is likely to feel very deeply about the importance, even necessity, of winning the approbation of the regional accrediting association. Hence, all the combined weight the faculty can muster may be brought to bear on the administration to strive for regional accreditation at nearly all costs. In addition, various segments of the faculty may concentrate on promoting accreditation by the particular professional body whose basic interest is identical with that of the segment concerned. A school or department which wishes to launch a new undergraduate or graduate program may believe that accreditation of the school or of the program itself is essential for the program's success. Potential staff members, who may be needed, are likely to refuse to accept a position in a nonaccredited institution.

Pressure from Placement Officials. Not to be minimized as an internal force for accreditation are those college or university officials vested with the responsibility of helping graduating seniors and alumni find suitable employment. Realizing, as they do, that accreditation of their college or university is an important selling point in marketing their graduates to prospective employers, placement officials will naturally do anything within their power to hasten and strengthen the institution's thrust toward academic or professional accreditation. This feeling is shared by department chairmen and college deans whose professional reputation often depends upon the professional success of their graduates.

Motivating Forces Outside the Institution

Accrediting Agencies. Sometimes accrediting agencies themselves are charged with trying to pressure educational institutions into seeking accreditation. In the area of teacher education this means NCATE.

Some people apparently are convinced that NCATE is not above using pressure on teacher education institutions to ask for accreditation. This NCATE has stoutly denied, [5] and no evidence of pressure by NCATE has been found by those conducting this Study.

Professional Organizations. Occasionally, interested professional organizations may give active encouragement to institutions to become accredited. In the field of teacher education two such organizations are the National Commission on Teacher Education and Professional Standards (NCTEPS or TEPS) and the National Association of State Directors of Teacher Education and Certification (NASDTEC). Both of these organizations are constituent members of NCATE. A third organization also a constituent member of NCATE which might be included is the Council of Chief State School Officers (CCSSO) composed of state superintendents of schools.

The enthusiasm of TEPS for national accreditation stems basically from the conviction that national professional accreditation of teacher education is essential to the successful building of a public image of teaching as a true profession, which apparently is a major objective of TEPS. [6] Consistent with the above, in visits to the states evidence was found of considerable support for NCATE from state education associations and state TEPS commissions. A state TEPS commission is appointed and supported by the state education association in a relation analogous to that between NCTEPS and NEA. Furthermore, in most states there are close and harmonious working relationships between the state department of education and the education association of the state. Thus, the state education associations and their affiliated TEPS commissions are generally strong supporters of a program of state accreditation of teacher education programs.

Nearly all state teacher education and certification officers, who constitute the membership of NASDTEC, very much want national accreditation to succeed. Their interest in NCATE is readily understandable and entirely legitimate. It makes available to them an opportunity to grant certificates to out-of-state teachers on a basis of reciprocity. In 1964, 27 states were granting provisional certification to teachers from other states who were graduates of NCATE-approved institutions.[1] Without such reciprocity, the state certification officials might find it necessary to examine the transcript of each out-of-state applicant for certification, and to do so without first-hand knowledge of the institution or teacher education program from which the applicant

---

[1] W. E. Armstrong and T. M. Stinnett, *Certification Requirements for School Personnel in the United States* (Washington, D.C., 1964), p. 17, gives 27 as the latest figure. These are Alabama, Colorado, Delaware, Florida, Georgia, Indiana, Iowa, Kansas, Kentucky, Maine, Maryland, Minnesota, Mississippi, Missouri, Nebraska, North Carolina, North Dakota, Oklahoma, Oregon, Rhode Island, South Dakota, Tennessee, Texas, Utah, Vermont, Washington, and West Virginia. NCTEPS, *Milestones in Teacher Education and Certification* (Washington, 1964), lists 28 states including Arizona, Illinois, and Pennsylvania, but not Kansas and Minnesota (p. 12).

for a certificate was graduated. The certification officials often feel uncertain of their evaluation of credits from an institution unknown or little known to them.

The chief state school officers recognize the assistance that national accreditation can give to their staffs in teacher education. They view national accreditation as providing national leadership and support in their formulation and enforcement of higher state standards. National accreditation may also be of assistance to them in meeting political and group pressures to which as state officials they are too often susceptible. At the same time, as the possessors of the only legal authority over accreditation, the states and their educational agencies are in a good position to exert pressure in behalf of NCATE accreditation in higher institutions within the state.

The Council of Chief State School Officers reaffirmed its confidence in NCATE in a resolution passed at its annual business meeting held on November 19, 1964. The resolution dealt with responsibilities of the states and contained the following reference to national accreditation:

> The interstate mobility of teachers makes accreditation of teacher education programs and institutions national in character, and makes state and national official, educational, and professional cooperation especially important and necessary.
>
> In accord with these principles, the Council approves the reorganized National Council for Accreditation of Teacher Education as an effective vehicle for such cooperation. It urges all who are concerned with the improvement of teaching to assist in making the results of its accreditation services available to the legal agencies for education in the states, where accreditation data serve as one of the criteria for legal certification.

IMPACT OF THE CONANT REPORT

Not to be overlooked in a consideration of pressures in the general area of accreditation, and particularly that of teacher education, is James B. Conant's *The Education of American Teachers.* [7] A distinguished scientist, university administrator, statesman, and diplomat, Dr. Conant was the author of several earlier monographs on various phases of American public education. [8] For a man of Conant's tremendous personal prestige, any public pronouncement on a matter of general popular concern was bound to be listened to and to be pondered carefully. Therefore, when he leveled his verbal guns at the existing machinery for training the teachers of our children and youth, his comments and his recommendations were soberly and thoughtfully received.

An analysis of Conant's "report" on the education of American teachers has been interpreted by some as an indictment of the entire American system of accreditation. Although he refers specifically only to the regional associations and the one professional agency which

deals with the national accreditation of teacher education, his arguments against any accrediting authority beyond the state level might be
interpreted as being applicable to all national accrediting bodies. [9]

Since Conant's book deals primarily with the training of American
teachers, the author directs his critical analysis to accreditation in
teacher education. He admits two theoretical advantages of national
accreditation of teacher education: first, as a form of national recognition, it can help to establish uniformly high standards; and, second, it
can facilitate the free movement of teachers from state to state. He
then proceeds to discount these advantages by pointing out the wide
variation in the application of NCATE standards and the limited
acceptance by the states of NCATE accreditation as a basis for
certifying out-of-state teachers. According to Conant, some state
departments insist that their standards "are obviously much higher
than those of NCATE," and he points out that NCATE standards,
particularly in respect to institutional structure, are applied in such
a way that "distinguished colleges and universities were offered only
provisional NCATE accreditation while obviously poor or mediocre
institutions were given approval." [10]

In an address before the annual meeting of the American Association of Colleges for Teacher Education (AACTE) in Chicago on
February 19, 1964, Conant was even more outspoken in his condemna-
tion of national accreditation and NCATE in particular. He asked
whether any voluntary, untrained team of professional educators, in
the short space of a three- or four-day visit, could possibly produce even
a reasonably accurate or valid evaluation of the institution's teacher
education program. He concluded his indictment of NCATE with these
significant remarks: "To put it bluntly, I would recommend to any
faculty group or college president who asked me, that the institution in
question refuse to receive a NCATE visiting team." [11]

Following Conant's address before AACTE on February 19, the
Chicago Sun-Times, in a leading editorial bearing the caption "NCATE
Is on the Rocks," predicted a general rebellion on the part of colleges
and universities against NCATE and the professional educators. [12]

In his book, Conant urges sweeping changes in both NCATE and the
regional associations. He recommended that:

> The governing boards of NCATE and the regional associations
> should be significantly broadened to give greater power to (a)
> representatives of scholarly disciplines in addition to professional
> education, and to (b) informed representatives of the lay public.
> NCATE and the regional associations should serve only as ad-
> visory bodies to teacher-preparing institutions and local school
> boards. They should, on the request of institutions, send in teams
> to study and make recommendations concerning the whole or any
> portion of a teacher education program. They should, on the re-
> quest of local boards, evaluate employment policies. They should
> provide a forum in which issues concerning teacher education and
> employment are debated. [13]

The fact is that most existing accrediting agencies are regarded by many as too narrow in their representation. It is claimed by some that NCATE representation is broader than most accrediting bodies and that actually NCATE's vulnerability may be that teacher education institutions are not given enough representation.

What would be the impact of the second recommendation if put into effect? Those who are defensive of NCATE and the regional associations insist that a purely advisory status would be the "kiss of death" for all voluntary agencies now engaged in accreditation. Their *raison d'etre* would be taken away. They would soon "wither on the vine." Whether such a dire prediction is well-founded is a matter of personal opinion.[2] Presumably, those critical of voluntary accrediting agencies either would not care, or else would hope that this might be the case.

Both admirers and critics of Conant have expressed admiration and amazement at the apparent breadth and depth of his grasp of the complex pattern of American education. At the same time, attention has been called to what appear to the critics to be important areas where Conant seems to be uninformed. For example, in recommending almost complete freedom and autonomy on the part of all "legitimate" colleges and universities in formulating and administering their teacher education programs, it has been asked if Conant realizes that more than one-third of the states have no adequate legislation governing the chartering, licensing, or operation of private institutions of higher learning.[3] In some states a charter fee of $5.00 permits the organization of a higher institution with "no strings attached." As a result, in some states "diploma mills" are handing out degrees, including in some instances Ph.D.'s, with little or no academic preparation. [14] It is said by some that, under the Conant plan, such institutions would be free to formulate their own teacher education programs. Conant states that by "legitimate" he is excluding "diploma mills," and he did not recommend that the state relinquish all control; rather that the state restrict its scrutiny to the conditions of, and personnel in charge of, student teaching.

What has been the impact of the Conant pronouncements on teacher education? It is too early to predict what the ultimate effect will be. Certainly, Conant has succeeded in provoking widespread discussion—

---

[2] It is interesting to note that John F. Nevins, A *Study of the Organization and Operation of Voluntary Accrediting Agencies,* makes a somewhat similar recommendation. pp. 316, 317.

[3] One state department of education official reported that in his judgment there were 25 or more "diploma mills" operating in his state, and that his department could not touch them. He said his department had tried for more than 10 years, without success, to push a bill through the state legislature dealing with the problem. The legislators apparently were not particularly interested and there was organized opposition from the private colleges which were instinctively fearful of state control. R. H. Reid, author of a 1959 dissertation on "diploma mills" (Columbia University), recently estimated that there are more than 400 such "mills" currently operating in the United States, twice as many as in 1959. *Washington* (D. C.) *Post,* February 14, 1965.

which he has insisted was his prime objective. A plethora of newspaper and magazine articles and reviews followed on the heels of the release of the "report" to the public. A few states are reported already to be contemplating steps designed to activate at least some of the Conant recommendations.[4]

THE ACCREDITING AGENCIES

RISE OF ACCREDITING AGENCIES

The accrediting function in higher education, as understood today, was first exercised, beyond the state level, by regional associations, most of which were originally established to improve relations between secondary schools and higher institutions and to improve college admission standards and requirements. These regional associations (described in Chapter 4 of the Study) began in New England, then developed in the Middle Atlantic states, in the North Central states, in the Southern states, and ultimately in the Western states. In most cases, the accreditation of colleges by these associations did not follow immediately upon their founding. The New England Association, as the most extreme example, was organized in 1885, but did not become an accrediting agency until 1952. As among the first accrediting bodies to be established, the regional associations adopted the practice of accrediting general institutional programs.

Early in the present century, steps were taken to establish procedures for accrediting professional schools and programs. Beginning with medicine in 1910, accrediting bodies were established for dental education (1918), legal education (1923), engineering education (1936), and pharmaceutical education (1940). Today, there are more than 25 professional accrediting agencies operating in the United States, of which 23 are recognized by the National Commission on Accrediting.

From 1910 to 1948, the Association of American Universities (AAU) was engaged in accrediting activities on a national scale. It was concerned initially with conditions under which students might become candidates for higher degrees in American universities or might receive advanced credit in one institution for work done in other institutions. The assumption of accrediting responsibilities by AAU stemmed from a policy adopted by German universities of admitting for graduate study only graduates of AAU member institutions. Recognizing the injustices involved in such a policy and after trying unsuccessfully to persuade the U. S. Bureau of Education to classify American colleges and universities, AAU began to publish a list not only of AAU members but also of other colleges and universities certified as of equal standing. In 1948, AAU announced the termination of its undergraduate accrediting program in order to devote its energies more exclusively to graduate work.

---

[4] Reference is made here particularly to New York and Massachusetts.

The American states, by virtue of their statutory responsibilities for certifying public school teachers, were compelled to face up to the necessity of judging the quality of the educational programs of both public and private institutions of higher learning. Although the Board of Regents of the University of the State of New York began accrediting functions in 1784, most of the states did not begin accrediting schools and programs until after 1910, and then in most cases limited their activities to the approval of teacher education programs preparing teachers for certification. Broadly speaking, some of the accrediting responsibilities of the states have been shared by the state departments of education and the state universities or special state commissions.

THE NATIONAL COMMISSION ON ACCREDITING

Alarmed by the proliferation of professional accrediting agencies, several associations of higher institutions combined in 1949 to establish the National Commission on Accrediting as an over-all coordinator of accrediting agencies.

The National Commission on Accrediting has two types of members: (1) constituent members and (2) institutional members. The constituent members are: American Association of Junior Colleges (AAJC), Association of American Colleges (AAC), Association of American Universities (AAU), Association of State Colleges and Universities, National Association of State Universities and Land-Grant Colleges, Association of Urban Universities (AUU), and State Universities Association (SUA). Colleges and universities which belong to any of the associations named as constituent members may become institutional members of NCA upon accepting the constitution and bylaws of NCA. The membership dues are levied in accordance with a formula related to the size of enrollment. On November 1, 1964, there were 1,288 institutional members of NCA.

The Board of Commissioners of the National Commission on Accrediting consists of 42 members, six each named by the seven constituent members of NCA. All but one of these are presidents or chancellors of institutions of higher education. The two principal responsibilities of NCA are to restrict the number of professional accrediting bodies and to improve the standards and procedures of existing agencies.

EXTENT OF ACCREDITATION

So great is the pressure for regional accreditation that approximately 85 percent of the degree-granting institutions are now on the approved lists of the regional associations. There is equally strong pressure for accreditation by some of the professional accrediting bodies, such as dentistry, law, and medicine, with the result that practically all institutions offering these programs are accredited in their professional fields.

Despite numerous pressures for NCATE accreditation, only 443 out of 1,173 teacher education institutions are presently on the approved list. It should be noted, however, that close to 70 percent of those entering the teaching profession are graduates of NCATE-approved institutions.[5]

From this discussion, it is evident that accreditation has come to play an important role in American higher education. Theoretically voluntary above the state level, so much significance has come to be attached to regional and certain types of professional accreditation that there may be some question regarding its true voluntary nature. So far, the pressure of national accreditation in teacher education is less compulsive than in some of the other areas; nevertheless, it is significant that more than two-thirds of the new graduates in teacher education are graduated from NCATE-approved higher institutions. At present, the national accreditation picture is complicated and confused by the large number of accrediting agencies, their wide variations in standards and procedures, and their overlapping jurisdictions.

REFERENCES

1. John F. Nevins, *A Study of the Organization and Operation of Voluntary Accrediting Agencies* (Washington, D. C., 1959), pp. 249, 250.
2. William K. Selden, *Accreditation, A Struggle Over Standards in Higher Education* (New York, 1960), pp. 4, 5.
3. *Ibid.*; AACTE, *Sourcebook on Accreditation of Teacher Education,* p. 19.
4. A. Lloyd Pulliam, "Form and Substance in the Accreditation of Teacher Education," *Liberal Education,* XLVIII, No. 4 (December 1962), pp. 496, 498; William K. Selden, "Accreditation—What Is It?" A.A.U.P., *Bulletin* 42:629, 630 (Winter 1956).
5. AACTE, *Sourcebook on Accreditation of Teacher Education,* p. 19.
6. Pulliam, *loc. cit.*
7. James B. Conant, *The Education of American Teachers* (New York, 1963).
8. *Slums and Suburbs* (New York, 1958); *The Parent, the Child, and the State* (Cambridge, Mass., 1959); *The American High School Today* (New York, 1959); *Education in the Junior High School Years* (New York, 1960).
9. Conant, *The Education of American Teachers,* pp. 21–23, 69, 70.
10. *Ibid.*, p. 22.
11. James B. Conant, *The Certification of Teachers: The Restricted State Approved Program Approach.* The fifth Charles W. Hunt Lecture, American Association of Colleges for Teacher Education, 1964, p. 14.
12. Chicago *Sun-Times,* February 21, 1964, p. 23.
13. Conant, *The Education of American Teachers,* pp. 69, 70.
14. Lloyd M. Blauch, ed., *Accreditation in Higher Education* (Washington, D.C., 1959), pp. 23, 24; Nevins, *op. cit.,* p. 316; Selden, *Accreditation,* pp. 26–81.

[5] As of the summer of 1964, the traditional state universities in 45 of 48 states (not including Alaska and Hawaii) were on the NCATE-approved list. The three not included were the universities of Delaware, Rhode Island, and Washington. All three were reported to be seeking NCATE approval.

CHAPTER 3

ACCREDITATION IN THE STATES

STATE ACCREDITATION and state certification, although fundamentally different in nature, are in practice very closely related. In fact, state accreditation of teacher education programs involves the approving of curriculums leading to state certification of teachers. Or to put it differently, the reason the state accredits or approves teacher education programs is largely in order to control the quality of those to be certified for teaching. For this reason, the chapter dealing with accreditation in the states will also involve a discussion of state certification.

THE ADMINISTRATION OF STATE ACCREDITATION

In all states except Alaska and Hawaii, the state departments of education have direct or indirect statutory responsibility for certifying public school teachers. What do they do? Because of the interrelationship between certification and accreditation, the authority to grant teaching certificates explicitly carries with it the authority to accredit or approve teacher education programs. Twelve of the 50 states report that no division of the state government engages in the accreditation of higher education. These are Alaska, Hawaii, Idaho, Massachusetts, Mississippi, Missouri, Montana, Nevada, New Mexico, North Dakota, Oklahoma, and South Dakota. Actually in only three of these states (Hawaii, New Mexico, and North Dakota), is there no agency responsible for some form of institutional approval.[1]

The agency of the state government which generally has responsibility for state accrediting is the state board of education (21 states);

---

[1] A questionnaire sent to the state directors of teacher education and certification provided information upon which a large part of this chapter is based. Replies were received from all 50 states, although some questions were not answered by all respondents. See also Theresa Birch Wilkins, "Accreditation in the States," in Blauch, *Accreditation in Higher Education,* Chapter 5.

but the department of education has this responsibility in 12 states. In five states (Georgia, Kansas, Maryland, Michigan, and Wisconsin), the chief state school officer is charged with performing this function. In Idaho and Montana the state boards of education accept the accreditation of regional and professional associations.

The earliest state agency that was given the responsibility of state accreditation in higher education was the Board of Regents of the University of the State of New York [2] established by the legislature in 1784. Subsequent legislation authorized the University, through the state education department, to register curriculums of higher institutions, both domestic and foreign. This registration process is the official system of state approval of curriculums offered by higher institutions and it resembles rather closely the accrediting process followed by regional accrediting associations. Among the other state agencies which moved early into state accreditation of higher education were the Iowa State Department of Public Instruction (1846) and the Utah State Department of Education (1896). Other states were Washington (1909), Virginia (1912), and Maryland (1914).

The terminology used in the state accrediting process varies from state to state. Twenty of the 50 states employ the term "accredit" to their particular method of giving status to higher education institutions and programs beyond the initial chartering. Twenty-five states use the word "approve." Some states recognize the terms "accredit" and "approve" as being synonymous; other states use them for different purposes. Many states reserve the term "accredit" for the voluntary accrediting agencies and designate their own function as "approve." Connecticut and Wisconsin use the term "approve" to apply to courses or fields, and "accredit" to institutions. Other states accredit the entire program of junior colleges, but approve degree-granting institutions for specific purposes. The New York Board of Regents calls its accreditation or approval of curriculums "registration"; Vermont uses the term "certify." In Illinois and Mississippi, the term used is "classify."

What steps are involved in the state accrediting procedures? Thirty-five states reported that one step is the establishment of criteria for evaluating institutions or programs. Thirty-seven states indicated that they send teams to inspect institutions. Thirty-three states publish a list of accredited or approved institutions. Thirty-four states reported making a periodic review of accredited institutions in the state. Twenty-six states reported using all four steps. Ten states reported accrediting through the bachelor's degree only; nine through the master's degree; five through the sixth year; and 23 beyond the sixth year. When asked how often the schools are reevaluated by the state, 15 states reported five years; 16 reported "indefinitely"; two reported annually; and the rest varied between one and 10 years.

It is evident that there are no accepted standards or procedures

---

[2] The New York State pattern is described later in the chapter.

which are followed by all states in the selection of institutions to be recommended for approval by their respective state boards of education or state education agencies. The requirements for placing institutions on the list of accredited or approved institutions, therefore, differ from state to state. The significance of being on a list likewise differs from state to state. Many of the lists are tentative, while others are fairly stable. The meaning of a list usually falls under one of the following three categories:

1. *All colleges and universities on the list are approved institutions of higher learning.*

   If an institution is approved for anything, and if it offers the courses required for certification, then it may prepare teachers.

2. *All colleges and universities on the list are approved for teacher education.*

   A listed institution may prepare students for any teaching position for which a certificate is issued, provided it offers the courses required for those certificates. Here, as in category 1, the state is approving the institution instead of its program.

3. *Colleges and universities on the list are approved for specific programs.*

   Each institution listed must have separate approval for each program it offers for such positions as elementary school teacher, secondary school teacher, home economics teacher, or school administrator. Here the state approves programs as well as the institution offering the programs. [1]

ELEMENTS DETERMINING THE CONTENT OF TEACHER EDUCATION PROGRAMS

Important among the elements determining the content of teacher education programs are the standards established by the state in the use of the approved-program approach to state certification of teachers. In 1964, 40 states reported using this approach to some degree. Twenty-seven of them reported the program in general use; the remaining 13 states were using the approved-program approach in some degree. Just what is the approved-program approach? It "refers to certification of an applicant largely on recommendation of the preparing college that the applicant has completed a program in a special field or area which is approved by the state department of education. This implies that the particular program has received prior approval and that certification is automatic upon recommendation of the institution." [2]

Usually the teacher education institution is given a free hand in formulating programs for state approval. The institution will, of course, be aware of state standards if state standards have been formulated. In some states the state department works closely with an institution while a new program is being developed. Since the state can withhold approval, the state is able, if it wishes, to be quite influential in program formulation. Under the approved-program approach, the state department knows what a candidate for certification has had in his preparation for teaching. New York State, therefore, does not even require the transcript of a graduate of an approved program.

Another important element in determining the content of teacher education programs is the teacher education advisory council on the state level. Forty-eight of the 50 states report having some form of advisory machinery on teacher education and certification. Missouri and Rhode Island are the exceptions.

Of the 48 advisory bodies 22 are called councils and 20 are labeled as committees. In five of the states (Maryland, Oklahoma, Vermont, Wisconsin, and Wyoming), the state TEPS commission serves as an advisory body. In five states (Colorado, Florida, Illinois, New Jersey, and Texas), there is a state board of examiners. California has a professional standards commission. Five states (California, Hawaii, Illinois, Kentucky, and Oregon) reported having two advisory bodies, one legal and the other extralegal. In all but 10 cases the advisory bodies are extralegal, established by action of the state board of education rather than by legislative action. The 10 legal advisory bodies are in California, Colorado, Florida, Illinois, Indiana, Kentucky, New Hampshire, New Jersey, Oregon, and Texas. The advisory groups range in size from eight to 225, with the median size 21. In recent years, some of the states have revised their councils to provide for the representation of liberal arts faculties. [3]

In the questionnaire, to which all 50 states responded, the states were asked to list "factors which determine the content of teacher education programs in your state." In addition to state standards for the approved programs and recommendations of state advisory bodies, the states frequently listed state department leadership as exercised through conferences, sometimes state-wide, and visitations. NCATE standards were factors on the list of quite a number of the states although earlier questions about the influence of accrediting agencies had been answered.

Other factors listed most frequently were:

> *Student needs.* There are various methods both of learning what student needs are and of translating them into educational policy. The instruments involved may be committees of which representatives of the schools are members, student organizations, questionnaire studies, and visits to schools combined with all-institutional committees or school of education action.
>
> *State certification requirements.* Teacher education institutions almost invariably embody in their programs the requirements laid down by the states for certification.
>
> *Interests of the administrators and staff members of departments and colleges of education.* Within the framework in which they operate, those holding positions in the college or school of educa-

tion are free to experiment with new programs. A faculty member may change a course he teaches, or faculty committees may plan course and program revisions.

The factors listed next most frequently were:

Successful examples of other states. Both states and teacher education institutions try to be alert in observing experimental programs and policies in other states. These programs and policies may be communicated from one state to another through professional organizations, professional publications, or by means of the public press. If a new program or policy appears to be advantageous or successful in one state, there is a natural tendency for other states to follow suit.

National and state professional organizations. Professional teachers organizations, such as NCTEPS and AACTE, with their state counterparts, exert considerable influence upon state policies and indirectly upon institutional policies. NEA student organizations are also influential in state education policy considerations. Several of the states listed state organizations and not national organizations. The student organization was listed as frequently as any other.

All-institutional teacher education committees. In some institutions these committees determine educational policy and in others they are largely advisory. Generally they are encouraged to initiate recommendations to other faculty groups or administrators.

Self-study committees on campuses of teacher-training institutions. Self-study committees are established to study the strengths and weaknesses of the institutional program and recommend any program changes that seem desirable.

Learned Societies. The increasing influence of national learned societies, such as the Modern Language Association, the Mathematical Association of America, and the American Association for the Advancement of Science, was noted by eight states. Reference was made to their recommendations on teacher preparation, and of work of the national groups and their affiliated state associations with state departments and faculties of institutions.

One, two, or three states also listed among factors determining teacher education programs: follow-up studies of graduates; demands of the consumer; financial limitations; experimentation; acts of the legislature.

STATE CERTIFICATION

In 1964, authority to determine requirements for teachers certificates and to issue, re-issue and revoke them was almost completely vested by legislative authority in the respective state departments or boards of education. However, in the laws vesting authority in the state education agencies, certain requirements are retained in the legislature. These requirements usually pertain to age, citizenship, health, loyalty oaths, and special course requirements, such as in the state history and constitution. Six states (California, Colorado, Illinois, Indiana, Nebraska, and North Dakota) reported that their legislatures retain some additional measure of certification authority with other agencies. In most of these states large cities or state colleges have what amounts to autonomy in issuing certificates. [4]

As of January 1, 1964, a total of 45 states and the District of Columbia were reported by Armstrong and Stinnett (*Certification Requirements,* p. 4) to be enforcing the degree requirement for regular certificates. Five states (Montana, Nebraska, North Dakota, South Dakota, and Wisconsin) were reported as not enforcing the degree requirement at present. This is a significant gain since 1950 when only 21 states were requiring degrees for elementary teachers and 42 for high school teachers. Twelve states [3] reported the use of proficiency examinations as part of the certification process. West Virginia reported an interesting experiment of using the National Teacher Examinations to certify graduates of liberal arts institutions who had had no professional training. (See Chapter 9.)

Conant, in *The Education of American Teachers,* has denounced the specificity of state certification requirements as a "bankrupt" process and the issuance of literally thousands of emergency certificates each year as a "national scandal." He advocates the elimination of all state requirements other than student teaching and graduation from a legitimate preparatory institution. [5]

Since some states import a large number of new teachers from other states, they are confronted with a serious problem of how to certificate such people. (See Appendix V for data on certification of out-of-state personnel.) All states require out-of-state applicants for state certification to be graduated from a teacher education institution accredited by the state in which the institution is located. Thirty states require both state and regional accreditation.[4] A number of states and the District of Columbia specify state and regional or state and national accreditation,[5] but since NCATE will not accredit without prior regional accreditation this amounts to requiring state and regional accreditation. Twenty-seven states grant automatic *provisional* certification to out-of-state graduates of NCATE-approved institutions.[6] *No state grants certification exclusively to NCATE graduates.*

---

[3] Colorado, Delaware, Florida, Georgia, Kansas, New Hampshire, North Carolina, South Carolina, Utah, Vermont, West Virginia, and Wyoming. Armstrong and Stinnett, *Certification Requirements,* report only six states (Colorado, Delaware, Kansas, South Carolina, Utah, and Wyoming), p. 16.
[4] Alabama, Alaska, Arizona, Arkansas, California, Colorado, Delaware, Florida, Georgia, Idaho, Indiana, Iowa, Kansas, Louisiana, Maryland, Minnesota, Mississippi, Montana, Nebraska, Nevada, New Mexico, New York, North Dakota, Oregon, Pennsylvania, Rhode Island, Utah, Vermont, Washington, and Wisconsin.
[5] Connecticut, Illinois, Kentucky, Maine, Massachusetts, Michigan, Missouri, New Hampshire, New Jersey, North Carolina, Ohio, Oklahoma, South Carolina, South Dakota, Tennessee, Texas, Virginia, West Virginia, and Wyoming.
[6] Armstrong and Stinnett, *Certification Requirements,* give the number as 27;

Conant has strongly questioned the use of NCATE accreditation as a basis of reciprocity in certification. He says that such a policy gives "quasi-legal status" to NCATE and tends to enhance the power and influence of "the establishment" over teacher education. [6] The following comment has been made as a rebuttal to Conant's argument:

> The use by states of national accreditation as the basis for reciprocity seems to engender more bitterness among institutions than any other factor relating to NCATE. By this reaction they appear to disregard or overlook several considerations. In the first place, states generally use NCATE accreditation to expedite reciprocity and not as a basis of excluding graduates of other institutions from certification. And they seem to overlook the fact that most states in past years have used regional accreditation to expedite reciprocity in the same manner. . . . [7]

It might be mentioned here, too, that in professions other than teaching, such as dentistry, law, and medicine, states use accrediting by the national professional accrediting agency as a basis for reciprocity in licensure.

Seventeen states grant reciprocity in certification through regional compacts. One is the Northeastern States Reciprocity Compact with 11 states (New England states plus Delaware, Maryland, New Jersey, New York, and Pennsylvania). The other is the Central States Reciprocity Compact (Iowa, Kansas, Missouri, Nebraska, South Dakota, and Wisconsin). Two regional compacts which existed in the past—the Southern States Compact and the Ohio Valley Compact—apparently are no longer active, and the Central States Compact appears to be falling into disuse. [8]

Recently two states (Florida and Kentucky) may have started a new trend in certification by enacting professional practices laws. These acts are "designed to vest with the teaching profession certain responsibilities in regard to certification and the revocation of certificates." [9] Professional practices commissions are established to develop criteria in such areas as: (1) ethics and professional performance; (2) admission to and continuation in professional service; (3) transfer and assignment of teaching personnel; and (4) contractual obligations.

The purpose of such legislation is to raise the professional standards of the teaching profession. This is done in a variety of ways:

1. By spelling out what constitutes good professional conduct both inside and outside the classroom.
2. By describing the obligations of the employer to the teacher particularly in regard to termination of services or transfer of assignment.
3. By explaining the obligations of the teacher to the employer particularly in regard to breaking a contract.

NCTEPS, *Milestones*, gives 28 as the number; NCATE's 11th annual list of approved institutions (1964–1965), p. 24, lists 28 institutions.

4. By defining what constitutes "due process" in any termination of contract. The important thing is that a good professional practices act protects alike the teacher, the employer, and the public.

It will be interesting to see how many other states will follow suit and how rapidly.

EXAMPLES OF STATE ACCREDITATION PATTERNS

California

A discussion of state approval of teacher education programs would not be complete without special reference to the unique pattern of state accreditation in California. In this state, the accreditation of teacher education is a joint operation between the State Board of Education and the Western Association of Schools and Colleges. Procedures and standards for accreditation have been developed jointly and joint surveys or accrediting visits are conducted by the two agencies. In these joint activities the California State Board of Education is represented by the Accreditation Committee of that body. On January 1, 1964, a new "Licensing of Certificated Personnel Law" for teacher education of elementary and secondary teachers became operative in California. The new program requires a fifth year of college or university postgraduate education and in general places much more stress upon subject matter in the preparation of teachers. The new law makes necessary the re-examination of the teacher education programs by all California colleges offering them.

Under California's unique education pattern, the University of California, which together with its many branches covers the entire state, is largely independent of state control other than through its dependence upon state financial support. There is also a state-wide system of some 18 state colleges which operate under their own board and chancellor, and there are 72 junior colleges each with a local governing board but all functioning within the policies of the State Board of Education. The private colleges and universities in California are relatively few in number, but appear to exert an influence in state education policies far out of proportion to their number and enrollment.

In the 1964–1965 NCATE list of accredited colleges and universities, eight out of the 18 state colleges were included. Four or five of the others have only recently been opened. The teacher education programs of the University of California at Berkeley and at Los Angeles were also accredited. The University now has seven other campuses, but again several of these are only recently opened and the branch at San Diego will not offer teacher education.

The State of California does not have state standards, except for the certification requirements of the state board. A representative of the state department stated that the standards of NCATE may be used as the starting point for the development of state standards. The State

Department of Education recognizes that the more agreement there is between the state standards and NCATE standards the less will be the burden of accreditation on the colleges and on administration in the state department. For these reasons, the influence of NCATE on teacher education in California appears to be increasing.

No evaluation of transcripts of applicants for a certificate is required if the applicant is a graduate of a state-approved program, but this comprises only about one-fifth of the new teachers each year. All out-of-state applicants (about 40 percent of the new persons certified each year) and all others from California are certified only after transcript evaluation.

In identifying differences between California and the other states, one needs to consider the strength of the system of state-supported higher education, the strength of the state colleges which produce a great many new teachers each year, the strong leadership provided by the State Department of Education, the more rigid requirements for certification established by law, the large number of teachers prepared out of state, and the fear expressed by staff members in a number of the colleges that education is too much in politics.

Kentucky

In Kentucky as of January, 1964, there were 24 degree-granting institutions in the Armstrong-Stinnett list of Approved Teacher Education Institutions. These included the University of Kentucky and the University of Louisville, five state colleges, and 17 private liberal arts colleges. All are accredited by the state and all but one by the Southern Association. Nine are NCATE accredited—the six state-supported institutions, the University of Louisville, Asbury College, and Berea College. Quite a number of the remaining are attempting to qualify for NCATE accreditation. A Council on Public Higher Education has been established by state law, and the Council has the assistance of an Advisory Committee on Teacher Education.

Kentucky has enjoyed strong leadership from the State Department of Education, largely by persuasion and rarely by compulsion. The State Director of Teacher Education and Certification, a former president of NASDTEC, has participated in many national conferences and committees on teacher education and through her office has kept the colleges of the state up to date on recent trends in teacher education. She has worked closely with the national agencies generally considered to be affiliated with the National Education Association, but also with national academic groups as well, as a member of the Advisory Board of the NASDTEC-AAAS Studies and as a speaker at a number of the conferences sponsored by the Committee on the Undergraduate Program of the Mathematical Association of America. Kentucky has been unusually successful in maintaining active participation of academic professors in the state in the development of state standards for teacher education.

State standards and procedures for accreditation in Kentucky follow the NCATE pattern, but in the Kentucky approved-program approach, the state goes further than NCATE in providing guidelines for the preparation of elementary and secondary teachers in academic subjects. The guidelines have been prepared by representatives of the academic and education departments of the colleges and universities of the state. In visits to Kentucky colleges and universities, to the Kentucky Education Association, and in a conference with the chairman of the state TEPS commission, there was highest praise for the leadership of the state department.

There was also a great awareness of NCATE, a desire for NCATE accreditation, and little criticism except in a college that had been given provisionary accreditation and on the part of one professor of history who had incorrect information about the Wisconsin situation. Little credit was given to the regional accrediting association for influence on teacher education.

Kentucky, a state with limited financial resources, has obviously profited from strong state leadership in teacher education. At the same time, the state seeks assistance frequently from national agencies, both in professional education and academic areas.

Michigan

A Michigan law enacted in 1935 delegates to the State Board of Education the authority to establish requirements for the certification of teachers. The same board approves programs of Michigan institutions for teacher education purposes. A body known as the Michigan Commission on College Accreditation accredits institutions of higher education in the state. This commission is an extralegal body consisting of the state superintendent of public instruction and representatives of various types of higher institutions. The commission accredits all institutions that are accredited by the North Central Association, as well as any other colleges and universities that meet established criteria. The procedure of institutional accreditation involves an inspection by a visiting team, the publication of a list of accredited institutions, and a periodic review or revisitation.

An approval of an institution for teacher education purposes is continuing unless the State Board of Education finds some reason to withdraw such approval. The law actually specifies that institutions of higher education shall be subject to re-examination annually, but the State Board of Education normally requires only an annual report for this purpose. Ordinarily, a revisitation would not occur unless complaints about the teacher education program had been received or some problem had been identified by the Division of Higher Education and Certification.

The power of the State Board of Education to establish requirements for teachers certificates allows the Board by implication to approve teacher education programs. This enables the state to employ the approved-program approach to state certification. In most cases, the requirements of the institution embodied in the approved programs exceed the minimum requirements of the State Board of Education. In such instances, the institution is expected to require its students in teacher education to meet its requirements before recommending an applicant for certification. At no time is a teachers certificate issued without this recommendation.

Regional or NCATE accreditation is required by the State Board of Education as a basis for certifying applicants from out-of-state institutions, except that an applicant from an institution which is approved for teacher education in his own state, but is not regionally or nationally accredited, may validate credit by obtaining unconditional admission to an accredited graduate school or six semester hours of "B"- average graduate credit. There is no awareness that national or regional accrediting agencies have ever tried to exert any influence on certification policies or procedures in Michigan. However, one institution interpreted recommendations of NCATE to run counter to state certification requirements in certain areas. The only practical choice for the institution, of course, was to conform to the state requirements.

Since the State Certification Code in Michigan is reasonably flexible, higher institutions are permitted and encouraged to adopt experimental programs in teacher education, provided such programs have the approval of the State Board of Education. As a result, numerous experimental programs have been and are in operation in teacher education institutions in the state. A "block plan" of student teaching has been widely adopted without formal requirement as a practical means of doing directed teaching in an off-campus setting.

In Michigan, the proportion of teacher education students who receive their training in public higher institutions is mounting each year and it is widely assumed that this trend will continue. In 1964, there were 10 NCATE-accredited institutions in the state. Of these, seven were public institutions and three were private. Generally speaking, Michigan is a state in which teacher education institutions are given a great deal of freedom and autonomy from state control. The state educational leadership cannot be categorized as aggressive or domineering.

New York

More than 180 years ago the state legislature in New York created a unified system of education known as the University of the State of New York.[7] This is not to be confused with the State University of New York which is an operating unit of the New York State Education Department. The state constitution established the University of the State of New York as a separate, nonpolitical, corporate entity and as

---

[7] Acknowledgment is herewith given to Ewald B. Nyquist, Deputy Commissioner of Education, New York, for material on both New York State and the Middle States Association.

a sort of fourth branch of government. Headed by 14 regents and with the State Education Department as its administrative arm, this unique organization is the oldest continuous state educational administrative agency in America. Actually, it comprises all the public and private colleges in the state, as well as public, private, and parochial schools, museums, historical societies, and libraries. The campus of the University may truly be said to be the state itself.

The University of the State of New York is the oldest formally organized accrediting body in the United States. It is officially recognized by the United States government as a nationally recognized agency for general accreditation. By virtue of its early entry into accrediting, the State Education Department (as the executive arm of the University) has had a wide influence on the Middle States Association as well as on several state education departments in the development of their accrediting programs. As an accrediting agency, the State Education Department accredits programs both inside and outside of the state, as well as in foreign countries.

Accreditation (or "registration" as it is called in New York) may be granted either for general purposes or for professional licensing or certification purposes. It is possible for a single program such as agriculture to have both accreditations. A program registered for general purposes means that the program is approved for various civil service, Federal, and pre-professional preparation objectives.

A questionnaire, similar to that of the Middle States Association, is sent to the college and asks for basic data on the curriculum, the student body, the faculty (competence and background), library resources, laboratory and field work facilities (including student teaching or internship), admission procedures, and graduation requirements. This is followed by a visit of one or two representatives of the State Education Department (usually one generalist and one specialist). As a legal governmental body, the New York State Department accredits only in terms of minimum standards.

Conant and others have written about the unusual strength and high-quality leadership of the New York State Education Department, which derives from the high-level members of the Board of Regents, the financial support, the strength and size of the staff, and the services given by the department to the educational institutions of the state.

SUMMARY

The four examples described above illustrate the varying patterns of state accreditation among our 50 states. At one extreme, there is the New York State system, with its state-wide controls over all levels of education through the unique agency, the University of the State of New York. Centralized in a different way is the California pattern with its four educational "empires": the almost completely autonomous University of California with its numerous branches in different stages of maturity; the 18 state colleges with their significant role in general education; the system of 72 junior colleges; and the powerful State Board of Education with its dominant role in state licensure. Next, there is the Kentucky pattern characterized by strong and enlightened state department leadership. Finally, there is Michigan with its decentralized pattern of state educational administration.

There appear to be two forces operating in the states—one promoting a higher degree of cooperation and standardization; the other moving in the direction of greater differentiation and particularism. The first is exemplified by the organized efforts of state certification officers (NASDTEC) and the chief state school officers (CCSSO) to agree upon common standards and policies. The second is exemplified by special state requirements for certification which constitute a stumbling block to reciprocity and cooperation among the states. Under such circumstances, the road to commonality among the states in standards and procedures for purposes of accreditation and certification appears to be a long and arduous one.

REFERENCES

1. W. E. Armstrong and T. M. Stinnett, *Certification Requirements for School Personnel in the United States* (Washington, D. C., 1964), p. 151.
2. *Ibid.*, p. 21.
3. *Ibid.*, pp. 11–13.
4. *Ibid.*, p. 9.
5. James B. Conant, *The Education of American Teachers* (New York, 1963), pp. 51, 54.
6. *Ibid.*, p. 69.
7. Armstrong and Stinnett, *op. cit.*, p. 17.
8. *Ibid.*, pp. 16, 17.
9. *Ibid.*, p. 10.

CHAPTER 4

THE REGIONAL ACCREDITING ASSOCIATIONS

HISTORICAL DEVELOPMENT

THE PARTITIONING of the United States into six unequal subdivisions, which ultimately became areas or regions for the general accreditation of educational institutions, covered a period from 1885 to 1924. The six regions and their dates of establishment (in chronological order) were New England (1885), Middle States (1889), North Central and Southern (1895), Northwest (1917), and Western (1924). It should be noted, however, that the dates when the regions were formed and the dates when formal accrediting activities were begun are widely at variance. For example, New England was the first regional organization to be established (1885), but was the last one to assume formal accreditation responsibilities (1952). The Middle States Association began accrediting colleges in 1921 and secondary schools in 1928. The North Central Association began to accredit secondary schools in 1905 and colleges in 1910. The Southern Association became an agency for accrediting secondary schools in 1912 and for higher institutions in 1917. The Northwest Association began to accredit secondary schools in 1918 and higher schools in 1921. The Western Association became an accrediting body in 1949. [1]

The Middle States Association was an outgrowth of a meeting in 1887 of representatives of several liberal arts colleges in Pennsylvania for the purpose of trying to resolve a growing number of questions related to college admission practices. When institutions in nearby states expressed interest, the scope of the initial meeting was expanded, and what had begun in 1887 as the College Association of Pennsylvania became in 1889 the College Association of the Middle States and Maryland. In 1893 the membership was broadened to include secondary schools and the organization became known as the Association of Colleges and Preparatory Schools of the Middle States and Maryland. In 1923 the name of the organization was changed to the Association of Colleges and Secondary Schools of the Middle States and Maryland,

36

and in 1931 the present name, Middle States Association of Colleges and Secondary Schools, was adopted. [2]

The New England Association of Colleges and Secondary Schools received its initial impetus in the 1880's from a small group of secondary school administrators who were disturbed by a lack of uniformity among New England colleges, and who recognized the need for a better relationship between the colleges and preparatory schools. At that time the admission requirements were characterized as chaotic and the general situation in higher education as anomalous and inefficient. With the support and encouragement of President Charles W. Eliot of Harvard University, a preliminary conference of 51 delegates was held on October 16, 1885. By 1893, the Association was well established. The original name of the New England Association of Colleges and Preparatory Schools was changed in 1914 to the present title of the New England Association of Colleges and Secondary Schools. [3]

The North Central Association, like Middle States and New England, was organized to meet problems resulting from the rapid expansion of secondary schools at the close of the nineteenth century. Two problems were particularly pressing: (1) established colleges, faced with applications for admission from graduates of a variety of secondary schools, lacked adequate bases for judging the qualifications of the applicants; and (2) the phenomenal growth of secondary schools had led to the establishment of scores of new colleges, many of which appeared to be of such inferior quality as to be little more than secondary schools. The North Central Association of Colleges and Secondary Schools was established in 1895 to set standards for evaluating the programs of secondary schools and colleges, and thus to bring a semblance of order into the educational system. [4]

The organization of the Northwest Association coincided with the beginning of American participation in World War I. It was created at a time of rapid development in both secondary schools and colleges with accompanying lack of uniformity at each level and with inadequate understanding on the part of secondary schools and colleges of their common problems. The first meeting of the Association was held on April 5, 1917, with an initial membership of eight "higher schools" and 25 secondary schools in the four northwestern states. The official name of the organization is the Northwest Association of Secondary and Higher Schools. Early emphasis was upon the formulation and adoption of standards and upon better understanding and working relations between high schools and colleges in the area. [5]

The Southern Association of Colleges and Secondary Schools was organized in 1895 by six charter institutions. The three recognized purposes of the Association were: (1) to organize southern schools and colleges for mutual assistance and cooperation; (2) to elevate the standard of scholarship and bring about uniformity of entrance requirements; and (3) to develop preparatory schools and eliminate preparatory work from a college's program. The Association has been plagued throughout most of its history by problems arising from school segregation, and more recently from school desegregation. Because of a broadening in function, the name of the Association was changed recently to the Southern Association of Colleges and Schools. [6]

The Western Association was carved out of what was assumed to be a segment of the Northwest Association. At least, some of the schools in California had already affiliated with the Northwest Association when the initial steps were taken to create the Western Association. The youngest and last of the regional associations to be organized evolved from a meeting of the Southern California Conference Colleges on April 19, 1924. Following the conference, six Southern California institutions formed the Southern California Association of Colleges and Universities. The declared purpose of the new organization was to develop a spirit of cooperation among all western educational institutions and between the Association and all local, regional, and national organizations and associations having similar interests. In 1931, the Association expanded its membership and adopted the name, "The Association of Colleges and Universities of the Pacific Southwest." As membership spread into Northern California, complications arose with the Northwest Association and continued for several years. In 1942, the name of the new Association became the Western College Association, and later the present name, "Western Association of Schools and Colleges," was adopted. [7]

It will be noted from these brief sketches that all the regional associations were created by the same general circumstances. One important factor was the explosion of secondary education which in the short span of two or three decades had given birth to a host of secondary or preparatory schools without any effective controls or regulations to assure a reasonable standard of quality. This was followed almost immediately by a similar proliferation of colleges. It was largely to provide the necessary standards and controls that the regional associations were created. Since the problem developed in different sections of the country at different times as the population expanded southward and westward, the establishment of the regional associations paralleled the population expansion, starting in New England, the area of earliest population and educational expansion, and terminating in the area west of the Rockies.

By 1964, 1,550 universities, colleges, junior colleges, and technical institutions had been accredited by the regional associations, or two-thirds of all the post-high school institutions listed by the U. S. Office of Education. For two apparent reasons, there were many common elements among the regional associations. One was the common set of circumstances which brought the regionals into operation. The other was the time sequence in which the regional associations were created. This permitted the later associations to adopt numerous features of the earlier associations. At the same time, as special problems developed in each region, variations in policies and procedures made their appearance.

In an effort to encourage a higher degree of coordination among the regional associations, the practice of holding informal conferences developed among the associations' executive secretaries. In 1964, these informal conferences were formalized and strengthened by the creation of the Federation of Regional Accrediting Commissions of Higher Education. Although the executive secretaries of the regional associations were instrumental in establishing the new Federation, the constitution of the new organization provides that representatives of the associations in the Federation are to include members of their college and university commissions. It is not intended that the Federation will become an accrediting agency; rather it "codifies and develops general principles and procedures for institutional evaluation and accreditation toward the establishment of a national consensus for regional application." [8]

ELEMENTS COMMON AMONG REGIONAL ASSOCIATIONS

SIMILARITIES IN PROCEDURES

The regional associations agree that the aim or purpose of accreditation is to improve education; in other words, the regional associations see accreditation as a means to educational improvement. In all of the regionals, the task of accreditation is delegated to commissions—a higher commission for accrediting colleges and universities, and a secondary school commission for high schools. Each commission sets the standards for accreditation and evaluates the institutions in the light of such standards.

Although the standards vary from region to region, the new Federation of Regional Accrediting Commissions has brought about agreement on minimal standards that institutions of higher education must meet to be eligible to be considered for accreditation. These minimal standards relate to such aspects of the college or university as chartering, organization, length of operation, admission requirements, and the institution's principal programs being based upon the liberal arts and sciences. The Federation has also agreed that each of the higher commissions should establish a category of "candidates for accreditation." In all regions, the allowable time in candidacy is limited.

Five of the six regional associations expect an institution under review to undertake a major self-study. The sixth association (New England) in 1964 was developing comparable requirements. Most of the associations regard the self-study primarily as a means of institutional improvement and only secondarily for providing information to the visiting team and the association. It is assumed that the self-study will require between six months and two years to prepare. The self-study is expected to include a report for the commission of the institution's organization and operation.

Among specific questions asked of the institution are those pertaining to the institution's purposes or objectives, the responsibilities of the administrative staff, the institution's income and expenditures, faculty salaries, faculty education and experience, teaching loads, enrollment, extracurricular activities, provisions for student health, the success of alumni, and the institution's present and planned facilities. Several of the commissions ask about the relation between the various characteristics of the institution, plans for changes within the institution, and the institution's strong and weak features.

Most of the associations provide for a representative to visit and counsel the institution at the beginning or during the self-study. In most of the associations, members of the commission participate as members of the visiting team. Several of the associations provide a list of suggestions to team members for use in their visit to the college or university under review. In these suggestions, visiting team members are encouraged to confer with administrative officers and faculty members, to visit classes and with individual students to ascertain the educational climate of the institution, together with its integrity and success in achieving its objectives. The associations exchange with one another their lists of experienced team members.

The associations are in agreement that the chairman of the visiting team is responsible for writing the team report from the comments submitted by individual team members. It is also agreed that the team should not reveal to the institution the nature of its recommendations to the commission concerned. Most of the associations expect the team to report on the extent to which the institution has complied with the association's standards for accreditation. Usually, the chairman of the visiting team is present when the team report is reviewed by the commission or subcommittee of the commission. The action taken by commissions in institutional accreditation decisions may be accreditation with or without qualifications, deferral, or denial. All six associations permit a dissatisfied institution to appeal an unfavorable decision on accreditation, although there are some variations in appeal procedures.

In all regional associations new members are accorded the same status and privileges as older members. All association members—new or old—have the same obligations to the association: (1) to maintain membership standards; (2) to improve academic effectiveness; (3) to submit information when requested; (4) to invite a revisitation when requested; and (5) to inform the commission of any major changes in academic programs. Since 1957 all of the commissions have attempted to revisit and reevaluate member institutions at least every 10 years. Without exception, the associations do not require member institutions to obtain accreditation of their professional programs; however, the commissions take into account a report of adverse action by a professional agency.

TOTAL INSTITUTIONAL ACCREDITATION

Since the regional associations were among the earliest accrediting agencies to be established and because of their early concern with the general standards and quality of secondary and higher institutions, they quite naturally assumed the prerogative of accrediting the total institution, rather than a particular program or group of programs. This function of, or responsibility for, general or total institutional evaluation and accreditation has characterized the regional associations to the present day. In their general evaluation, the regionals ask each institution under review to provide detailed reports on over-all administrative structure, admission and graduation requirements, the curriculum pattern, the provisions and requirements for general education, the requirements for majors and minors, the size and preparation of the faculty, teaching loads, adequacy of the library, and of the general physical facilities. As will be noted later, this information is still required, but within a different framework.

Gradually, however, the emphasis shifted. This change in emphasis manifested itself in three ways: (1) in less emphasis upon minimum standards; (2) in greater emphasis upon stimulation to institutional improvement; and (3) in new areas of association activity.

With approximately 85 percent of existing four-year degree institutions on the regionals' approved lists, the associations found themselves with less need or opportunity to apply minimum standards in accreditation. [9] At the same time, some of the regionals' zeal for a weeding out of new or established institutions of marginal or submarginal qualifications appears to have mellowed. The associations in some instances give an impression of being more tolerant and sympathetic toward the struggling college beset with financial difficulties. When a private institution under review appears to be borderline, or even below minimum standards, it has a good chance of being granted provisional accreditation or probationary status on the assumption that the institution will be able to overcome its difficulties. Then if, at the expiration of the provisional or probationary period, the college still appears deficient, one or more additional periods of grace might be permitted. This has led to assertions that the standards of the regional associations have become lower than they should be, and that institutions which should not be permitted to operate at all sometimes are allowed to "limp along" indefinitely.[1]

STIMULATION TO IMPROVEMENT

A second manifestation of the shifting emphasis on the part of the regional association is the discarding of the specific *quantitative* standards or measurements in accreditation and the substitution of so-called

---

[1] The North Central Association has recently taken steps to "raise its sights" in evaluating submarginal or borderline institutions. There is no inclination, however, to revive the concept of specific minimum standards.

qualitative measurements—or broad, general criteria. [*10*] Under the new technique, these questions are asked: (1) Does the institution have clearly defined, appropriate, and controlling objectives? (2) Has it established the conditions most likely to lead to the accomplishment of its objectives; does it in fact appear to be accomplishing them to a substantial degree, and can it continue to do so? [*11*] The same informational questions are asked as before, but the information is interpreted in this framework. In case the association cannot see a reasonable relationship between a college or university program and its objectives, the institution may be placed on provisional or probationary status, or possibly even lose its accreditation entirely.

Of course, it may be that the changing of regional association standards has sometimes been interpreted as a lowering of regional standards by those who have not understood the new techniques. Under the new approach, for example, a college might deliberately have low admission standards in order to be of maximum service to deprived or underprivileged minorities. In such case, the regional association might not deny accreditation to the institution with low admission standards, provided there is a clear relationship between the admission standards, institutional philosophy, and the academic program.

Along with the broader criteria for evaluating a college or university, the regional associations in their relations with member institutions place a major emphasis upon stimulation to improvement. [*12*] This is done partly through a new approach to the institutional self-study. As indicated earlier in this chapter, the regionals have come to regard the self-study report as being directed to the institution itself, rather than to the commission or the visiting team. Thus directed, the self-study brings into focus the deficiencies present in the institution's structure and program and, by implication at least, the best means of correcting those deficiencies. Likewise, the members of visiting teams are instructed to advise and counsel the college or university under review how it might improve its organization, procedures, or program. Finally, the commission's report to the institution stresses areas of possible improvement.

NEW AREAS OF REGIONAL ACTIVITY

With a major part of the degree-granting institutions already accredited, the regional associations have turned their attention to several of the newer areas of accreditation. One such area is the mushrooming junior college movement; another area is provided by the proliferating specialized schools, many of them on the sub-professional or technical level; a third area is the rapidly expanding number and variety of graduate programs on the fifth-year, sixth-year, and doctoral levels. New and unique problems challenge the ingenuity of the regional associations in some of these categories. Here are situations which in some respects resemble those which confronted the regionals in the early decades of their operation. For example: What constitutes good and acceptable standards among the specialized schools?

VARIATIONS IN PROCEDURES AND FUNCTIONS AMONG THE REGIONAL ASSOCIATIONS

Under the new category of candidacy for accreditation, the associations have no common time requirement. Three of the regional association (Middle States, Northwest, and Southern) apply candidacy only to newly organized institutions. Likewise, the number of members on visiting teams varies with the size and type of the institution under review. Two of the associations expect the team to consist of two, three, or four members; a third usually expects seven; a fourth appoints between three and 10; and a fifth, between five and 12. Where joint visitations are held, the addition of representatives from professional associations may raise the total to as high as 70. Several years ago, the North Central Association inaugurated a program of giving special training to promising institutional evaluators.

In organization and procedures, the higher commissions of the regional associations vary both in size and function. The commissions vary in size from eight to 50 members, with the Southern Association having the largest number of members. In the Middle States and Western associations, the commissions actually make the accreditation decisions; in the other four associations, the visiting committee recommends to the annual meeting of the association for formal action. There is considerable variation among the associations in the actual steps involved in accreditation. In the Middle States and Western associations, accreditation involves two steps; in North Central and Southern associations, there may be as many as four steps involved (visiting team, subcommittees of commission, executive committee, and finally the commission itself). [13]

Generally speaking, the regional associations employ different categories in classifying institutions. The Middle States has no classification; New England recognizes four categories: colleges, teachers colleges, specialized institutions, and junior colleges; North Central has two categories: colleges and universities, and junior colleges; Northwest and Southern have similar categories: colleges and universities, junior colleges, specialized institutions. The Western Association recognizes two categories of senior colleges, four-year liberal arts colleges and universities, four-year specialized institutions; and three categories of junior colleges (junior colleges, specialized two-year institutions, and business schools).

The associations have different methods of handling institutional program changes. The Middle States Association allows the new program to operate two years before evaluating it. When a junior college wants to become a senior college, the Southern Association insists upon a major reevaluation of the institution. In the event of a major program change, North Central requires a review of the entire institution.

The regional associations also differ rather widely in their procedures for reevaluation or reaccreditation of a member institution. The Middle States, Northwest, and Southern associations usually employ essentially the same procedures as in an original evaluation for accreditation. The North Central and Western associations permit a simplified report covering changes since the previous evaluation, the implementation of previous recommendations, and any plans pending for institutional changes.

An examination of regional probation policies reveals a similar variation. The Middle States, New England, and Northwest associations confidentially may require an institution under investigation to show cause why it should not be dropped from an association's list of accredited colleges. The Southern Association employs a system of public or announced probation. The Western Association has confidential (non-public) probation. The North Central employs both public and confidential probation.

In assessing the costs of an evaluation or reevaluation, the regional associations attempt to charge only necessary costs, but follow different procedures in ascertaining and distributing costs. The Middle States, North Central, and Western associations charge fixed fees for different types or sizes of institutions or different numbers of visiting team members. These fees vary from $75 for a small, single-purpose college up to $2,400 for a large, complex university. The Northwest and Southern associations assess an institution the direct costs of the evaluation.

Three of the associations do not provide honorariums to their visiting team members; another provides $100 per day; while a fifth provides $50 to team members and up to $325 to the team chairman. Charges for reevaluating member institutions are generally the same as for evaluating applicants for membership, an exception being that one association charges member institutions $100 less than applicants for membership.

Some of the regional associations prefer to hold joint visitations with professional accrediting bodies. Beginning in 1946 the Middle States invited professional agencies to visit concurrently with its own evaluators. In such instances, the regional and professional representatives participate in some common interviews and conferences, but examine their special areas of interest separately. The professional representatives submit a report for inclusion in the comprehensive report to the institution. The Northwest, Southern, and Western associations definitely favor and encourage this type of joint visitation; New England employs it occasionally. Since 1954, North Central has used the "Generalist Plan" in professional accreditation visits. Upon the institution's request, a college or university administrator will be named as a consultant, not as a team member. The other associations sometimes employ the Generalist Plan.

Among the occasional but highly important services rendered by regional associations, mention should be made of some associations who provide yeoman service to higher education by standing four-square against a serious threat to the autonomy or integrity of their member institutions. These threats have taken several forms: (1) excessive subsidization of, or excessively low standards for participation in, organized athletics; (2) political interference by state authorities in state college or university affairs; and (3) the offering of advanced degrees by unqualified institutions. There have doubtless been numerous instances where no action was taken by regionals when one of the above situations had developed. Occasionally, an institution which was suspect would successfully defy the regional association. More often, in the case of athletic abuses, other agencies would step in and at least give the impression of "cleaning house."

In the early decades of regional accreditation, there was considerable criticism and opposition to some of the associations' regulatory activities. Educational institutions, after enjoying complete freedom of action, resented an outside agency telling them what to do and what not to do. Sometimes when adverse accrediting decisions were made, there were threats of court action. However, when this actually happened, the decisions were uniformly in favor of the associations. [14] The decisions were based on the assumption that accrediting associations are purely voluntary agencies; no institution is required to seek accreditation. By the time regional accreditation had become a practical, if not a legal, necessity, the theory of voluntary choice had become firmly established.

THE REGIONAL ASSOCIATIONS AND TEACHER EDUCATION

Relations With the States

The variations among the six regional associations are revealed in their dealings with the various state departments of education. The New England Association has maintained complete independence from state departments in accrediting private schools. On the contrary, early in its accrediting procedure the Middle States Association established a close relationship with state departments of education in its area. In 1951 the Middle States adopted a policy of including a member of the New York State Department of Education on each committee evaluating a higher institution in the state. In 1952 the same policy was extended to New Jersey and Maryland. Now it applies to other states in the area.

The North Central Association in 1898 expressed its approval of a bill in the Illinois legislature providing for state supervision over degree-conferring institutions. After 1916, the Association sought to secure legislation in various North Central states governing the character of degree-conferring institutions. The Southern Association in 1917 supported the right of the state to control state educational institutions; however, in 1954 the Association expressed concern over the increase of regulatory measures imposed by state governments over public institutions of higher learning. The Northwest Association has worked closely with the states in the certification of teachers. Since 1952, the Western Association and the State of California have worked jointly in accrediting functions. The state department is concerned with certification, but cooperates in evaluating teacher education programs. The Association and the state department also cooperate in the evaluation of junior colleges.

The regional associations, from time to time, have involved themselves directly in such aspects of teacher education as academic and professional preparation, teacher loads, and certification.

TEACHER QUALIFICATIONS

The New England Association in 1890 recommended that inexperienced teachers should be brought into contact with experienced teachers. In the same year, the state legislatures in the New England states were asked to provide scholarships for the training of teachers. [15] The North Central Association at its second meeting (1896) resolved that freshman students in secondary or higher schools should not be entrusted to inexperienced teachers. [16] The Northwest Association in 1929 promulgated the policy of having all teachers teach only in their major or minor fields. [17] From 1902 to 1925, the North Central Association required all high school teachers in the area to have at least the equivalent of graduation from a college belonging to the North Central Association. [18] In 1916, North Central specified 120 semester hours of college work, including 11 semester hours in education, as the standard in teacher preparation.

The Middle States Association in 1923 recommended as a standard for teacher education the completion of a four-year college course, together with either professional training or experience. [19] The Southern Association in 1926 resolved that teachers in secondary schools should have at least 12 semester hours in education. [20] The Northwest Association in 1929 raised the minimum requirement for high school teachers from 12 to 15 semester hours in education. [21]

The regional accrediting associations now require for secondary school teachers a bachelor's degree from an approved college or university. A certain number of semester hours in professional education are also required. The Northwest Association in 1947 fixed 16 semester hours of professional education as minimum for secondary school teachers. Since 1950, the Northwest Association has required the administrative head of a secondary school to have a master's degree or the equivalent. [22] The North Central Association has had a similar requirement, but until recently had not adhered strictly to it in accrediting secondary schools. [23] The North Central and Southern associations both require 15 semester hours in education.

TEACHER LOAD

The regional associations have been concerned for many years with the teaching load on both the secondary and college level. This concern is based on an assumption that the teaching load is a factor in a good education program. In the early decades of the present century, most of the regional associations specified five daily periods of classroom instruction as the maximum for secondary school teachers. In the depression years of the 1930's, the rule was modified to permit six or more daily periods of classroom instruction.

A recognized factor in teacher load is size of classes. The regional associations have therefore attempted to place a maximum limit on the size of secondary school classes. In 1922, the Northwest Association placed a limit of 30 for each class and 150 per teacher per day. By 1925 the total had changed to 160 pupils per day and 35 pupils per class. [24] The North Central Association has permitted no more than six periods daily, including the time spent in supervising study halls and in co-curricular activities. Some of the other regional associations have a similar policy with the provision that the limit may be exceeded in emergencies.

CERTIFICATION OF TEACHERS

As a rule, the regionals have not concerned themselves with the certification of teachers. In 1924, however, the Northwest Association attempted to secure reciprocity with the other regional associations in the accreditation of colleges and in the recognition of teachers certificates. [25] A decade later, the Northwest Association adopted the regulation that all normal schools and teachers colleges be approved for the certification of teachers by the state accrediting agency in their respective states before seeking accreditation from the Northwest Association. [26] The other regional associations in this instance did not follow the example of the Northwest Association.

TEACHER EDUCATION PROGRAMS

Through their contributions to the improvement of higher education, the regional associations undoubtedly have had an important indirect impact upon teacher education in institutions which offer teacher education programs. The direct impact has not been great. The regionals, as a rule, have treated teacher education as one element in the total institutional evaluation. When teacher education has been of minor importance in the total institutional program, an institution with strong academic departments but weak in professional education would normally receive full accreditation. On the contrary, an institution with a strong teacher education emphasis, if strong academically and weak professionally, might be given provisional accreditation or denied it altogether. If an institution is a single-purpose teacher education type, the regionals consider that they should accredit it (or deny accreditation) for teacher education. Otherwise, no more attention is given by the regional associations to the teacher education program than to other special programs of the institution.

THE ROLE OF THE REGIONAL ASSOCIATIONS IN ACCREDITATION

William K. Selden, Executive Director of the National Commission on Accrediting, suggested in 1962 that for two reasons the regional associations were becoming increasingly unimportant and had largely outlived their usefulness. One reason was that the bulk of the existing degree-granting institutions were already on the regionals' lists of accredited colleges and universities. The second reason was that accreditation problems, in large measure, had ceased to be local, state, or regional in character but rather had become predominantly national in scope. [27] Two representatives of regional associations were quick to challenge Selden's thesis, pointing out that the regional associations were the only accrediting bodies which examined, evaluated, and accredited the entire institution of higher education. Such a general approach to accreditation, it was argued, must be made by an authorized agency; the regionals were already doing it; therefore the regionals were performing a necessary service and should continue to do so. [28]

Selden's article emphasized the importance of having the regional associations establish more nearly uniform standards, practices, and procedures. His article may have hastened the organization of the new Federation of Regional Accrediting Commissions of Higher Education, with the above objective clearly enunciated. It remains to be seen to what extent the new Federation can succeed in assisting regional associations to adapt to the growing national needs in higher education.

REFERENCES

1. For general sources on regional accreditation, see Lloyd E. Blauch, ed., *Accreditation in Higher Education* (Washington, D. C., 1959); Roy J. Deferrari, *Self-Evaluation and Accreditation in Higher Education* (Washington, D. C., 1959); John F. Nevins, *A Study of the Organization and Operation of Voluntary Accrediting Agencies* (Washington, D. C., 1959). The authors of this Study were given access to unpublished material on the regional associations prepared jointly by the associations and the National Commission on Accrediting.
2. F. Taylor Jones, "Accreditation in the Middle States Region," in Blauch, *op. cit.*, Chapter 6.
3. New England Association of Colleges and Secondary Schools, *Introducing the New England Association* (Cambridge, Mass., 1957).
4. Calvin O. Davis, *A History of the North Central Association of Colleges and Secondary Schools* (Ann Arbor, Mich., 1945).

5. Fred L. Stetson, "Accreditation in the Northwest Region," in Blauch, *op. cit.,* pp. 59–68.
6. Guy E. Snavely, *A Short History of the Southern Association of Colleges and Secondary Schools,* reprinted from the *Southern Association Quarterly,* Vol. IX, pp. 423–549 (November 1945).
7. Mitchell P. Briggs, "Accrediting in the Western Region," in Blauch, *op. cit.,* Chapter 11.
8. From unpublished material referred to in Reference 1 above.
9. William K. Selden and William G. Land, "The Forgotten Colleges," *North Central Association Quarterly,* 35:271–273 (April 1961).
10. William K. Selden, *Accreditation, A Struggle Over Standards in Higher Education* (New York, 1960), pp. 40–42.
11. Jones, "Accreditation in the Middle States Region," in Blauch, *op. cit.,* p. 43.
12. For newer emphases in the North Central region, see Norman Burns' remarks in "The Professor and Accreditation," *A.A.U.P. Bulletin,* 47:146–150 (June 1961).
13. Nevins, *op. cit.,* pp. 261–278.
14. *Ibid.*
15. New England Association of Colleges and Preparatory Schools, *Official Report of the Fifth Annual Meeting* (Boston, 1890), p. 34.
16. North Central Association, *Proceedings of the Second Annual Meeting* (Chicago, 1896), p. 66.
17. Northwest Association, *Proceedings of the Twelfth Annual Meeting* (Eugene, Ore., 1929), p. 9.
18. North Central Association, *Proceedings of the Thirteenth Annual Meeting* (Chicago, 1925), p. 11.
19. Middle States Association, *Proceedings of the Thirty-seventh Annual Convention* (Philadelphia, 1923), p. 123. F. Taylor Jones has pointed out that the College Association of Pennsylvania, in 1887, made a plea for four-year collegiate education for elementary school teachers.
20. Southern Association of Colleges and Preparatory Schools, *Proceedings of the Thirty-first Annual Meeting* (Birmingham, 1926), p. 78.
21. Northwest Association, *Proceedings of the Twelfth Annual Convention* (Eugene, 1929), p. 14.
22. *Ibid.*
23. North Central Association, *Policies and Criteria for the Approval of Secondary Schools* (Chicago, 1958), p. 13.
24. Northwest Association, *Proceedings of the Eighth Annual Convention* (Eugene, 1925), p. 4.
25. Northwest Association, *Proceedings of the Seventh Annual Convention* (Eugene, 1924), p. 12.
26. Northwest Association, *Proceedings of the Twentieth Annual Convention* (Eugene, 1937), p. 13.
27. William K. Selden, "Relative Unimportance of Regional Accreditation," *Journal of Teacher Education,* 13:319–325 (September 1962).
28. A. E. Meder, Jr., "Absolute Importance of Regional Accreditation," *School and Society,* 91:108 (March 9, 1963). Norman Burns of the North Central Association also wrote an article, similar to Meder's, which in 1964 had not been published.

CHAPTER 5

NATIONAL ACCREDITATION IN TEACHER EDUCATION

EVOLUTION OF TEACHER EDUCATION IN THE UNITED STATES

PROGRAMS of teacher education were operational in the United States for more than one hundred years before the creation of any formal machinery for accrediting such programs. Territorial expansion and rapid population growth early in the nineteenth century provided the need and demand for public education, which in turn created a demand for trained teachers to man the burgeoning school systems. The limited number of existing colleges, originally established largely for the training of the clergy, catered mainly to the wealthy minority of the population, hence were not the least interested in the lowly profession of public school teaching. The idea of setting up separate institutions, or normal schools, for preparing teachers was borrowed from Europe. The first private normal school was established in 1823 at Concord, Vermont. The first public normal schools came into existence in the 1830's. Filling a genuine social need and with no acceptable alternative in sight, the normal schools multiplied steadily during the remainder of the nineteenth century. [1]

Not only did the liberal arts colleges refuse to assume the responsibility for training public school teachers, but they also refused to have any dealings with or to extend any recognition to the newly formed normal schools. This policy of social ostracism on the part of liberal arts people led the normal schools to form their own organization in 1855. In 1870 the normal schools affiliated with the Department of Normal Schools of the National Education Association. Ever since then the normal schools and their successors, the teachers colleges, have sought greater academic acceptance.

Denied admission to the family of liberal arts colleges, the normal schools and teachers colleges tried to gain membership in regional associations, only to be rebuffed. [2] As the "ugly duckling" in the education world, the normal schools decided to try lifting themselves "by their own bootstraps." Such reforms were long overdue, for as late as the turn of the century teacher-training programs were below college level, and from the standpoint of liberal arts standards they were less than secondary level. Meanwhile, beginning about 1875, some universities had begun to give some attention to the training of secondary teachers.

Through discussions and other joint efforts, standards of admission to the normal schools were raised, the curriculum was improved, and more attention was given by the universities to the professional education needs of secondary school teachers. Although no attempts were made at this time to establish specific standards in teacher education, in some degree the way was paved for the beginnings of standardization early in the second quarter of the twentieth century.

ACCREDITATION OF TEACHER EDUCATION BEFORE NCATE

Had the regional accrediting associations been willing to assume the responsibility for accrediting teacher education when they first had the opportunity, their own pattern of development would necessarily have been different,[1] and many of the later problems associated with national accreditation might have been avoided. Be that as it may, the American Association of Teachers Colleges (AATC) became the first national accrediting body for teacher education. In 1927 the AATC began to combine accreditation and membership requirements, and in 1928 it published its first list of accredited institutions for teacher education.[2] By virtue of the fact that AATC membership at the time was limited almost exclusively to teachers colleges and normal schools, only these institutions were affected by accreditation; teacher education programs in universities and liberal arts colleges were not directly influenced. Taking its cue from the North Central Association, the AATC classified its members into A, B, and C groups. The principal difference in AATC and North Central standards was the former's inclusion of specific standards relating to student teaching and the laboratory school. [3]

In combining accreditation and membership requirements, the AATC determined the process it used in improving its standards in the evaluation of teacher education programs. As an association of colleges, it was interested in stimulating its members through research, publications, and discussion; as an accrediting body, the Association was interested in raising the standards of the teaching profession by controlling admission to and membership in the Association. Gradually, special studies in such areas as library, general education, and laboratory experience provided more objective means of determining standards in teacher education. By 1940 sufficient progress had been made to justify dropping the A, B, and C classification of institutions.

---

[1] This would have constituted a departure from their policy of general accreditation.
[2] This list consisted of 63 four-year colleges and 10 junior colleges.

The standards employed by the AATC throughout its existence were designed to evaluate the entire institution, since the institutions evaluated were single-purpose teachers colleges and normal schools. In addition to teacher education in the narrowest sense, attention was given to such important aspects as institutional finance, student health, and academic freedom.

In 1948 the American Association of Teachers Colleges, the National Association of Colleges and Departments of Education, and the National Association of Teacher Education Institutions in Metropolitan Districts combined to form the American Association of Colleges for Teacher Education (AACTE). [4] Thus for the first time an organization was established that was beginning to be representative of the various types of institutions preparing teachers. The one group not well represented at the time was the liberal arts colleges. As late as 1954 there were only 21 liberal arts colleges in the total AACTE membership of 284 institutions.*

As a consequence of the merger of the three associations of teacher-training institutions in 1948, the new organization was in a position to become the national accrediting body for teacher education. Instead of evaluating institutions, the AACTE inaugurated the practice of accrediting teacher education in departments or schools of education. When the National Commission on Accrediting was organized in 1949 to coordinate and improve the activities and policies of the national and regional accrediting bodies, the AACTE was not included in the list of recognized accrediting organizations. One reason for this exclusion of AACTE appears to have been the rumor that a new accrediting body for teacher education was about to be created. [5] Another reason for not recognizing AACTE as an accrediting body was that it combined membership and accreditation. Also the National Commission on Accrediting may have doubted at that time whether teaching was well enough recognized as a profession to have an accrediting body.

ORGANIZATION OF THE NATIONAL COUNCIL FOR ACCREDITATION OF TEACHER EDUCATION (NCATE)

In late 1951 and early 1952, five groups actively concerned with teacher education joined efforts to form the National Council for Accreditation of Teacher Education (NCATE). These five groups were the American Association of Colleges for Teacher Education (AACTE), the Council of Chief State School Officers (CCSSO), the National Association of State Directors of Teacher Education and Certification (NASDTEC), the National Commission on Teacher Education and Professional Standards (NCTEPS, commonly known as TEPS), and the National School Boards Association. It was agreed that, for the

---

* In 1964 more than 200 liberal arts colleges were members of AACTE.

time being at least, the new organization would use the AACTE standards and annual dues. The institutions involved in the merger that were in good standing with the AACTE at that time were to be blanketed into full accreditation in NCATE. [6]

As originally organized, NCATE consisted of 21 members distributed as follows: AACTE, 6; CCSSO, 3; NASDTEC, 3; NCTEPS, 6; and the National School Boards Association, 3. By the time the new organization had been approved by its constituent members and was ready to assume its responsibilities on July 1, 1954, strong opposition was being voiced by dissident institutions and individuals. This opposition, stemming largely from liberal arts institutions, was based on three counts: first, to the extension of professional accrediting into an area which they insisted could be adequately served by the regional associations; second, to the acceptance of the argument that teaching is a profession like engineering or medicine; and third, to the relationship of the certification of teachers with the accrediting of liberal arts colleges by a national professional teacher education accrediting agency. [7]

To understand the liberal arts position in the controversy, it is necessary to have in mind certain important facts in the history of liberal arts institutions. Most of them had never had occasion to deal with any accrediting agency other than their own regional association. Moreover, except for occasional differences, the relationship between college and accrediting association had for the most part been free from tension. Generally speaking, the only professional accrediting body that a liberal arts college might have had dealings with was the American Chemical Society, which included fewer than 100 liberal arts colleges in its list of approximately 300 approved institutions. Moreover, the American Chemical Society limits its attention almost exclusively to chemistry, whereas teacher education—hence an accrediting body dealing with teacher education—covers virtually the entire liberal arts spectrum. Developing as they did in an atmosphere of *laissez faire* and of almost complete autonomy, liberal arts institutions were naturally fearful of what an almost completely autonomous national body accrediting teacher education might do.

As an added factor, liberal arts colleges were aware that in the new NCATE structure, there was no direct provision for liberal arts or subject-matter representation. True, there had been both formal and informal invitations to the Association of American Colleges, a national liberal arts organization, to be represented on the Council (NCATE) and to share the expenses of the new body, with only a negative response on the part of the AAC. This decision was originally based on a policy of the AAC not to be formally associated in accrediting operations, and more recently on a policy of not becoming financially involved in such activities. [8] Be that as it may, the National Commission on Accrediting was sufficiently impressed by the storm of opposition engendered by the organization and plans of NCATE that it refused to recognize NCATE in its original structure as an official accrediting body.

After intermittent negotiations, covering a two-year period from November, 1954, to October, 1956, a compromise settlement between NCATE and the National Commission on Accrediting was reached. NCATE agreed to change its structure in such a way that a majority of its members would come from teacher-training institutions. The representation of the Council of Chief State School Officers (CCSSO), of the National Association of State Directors of Teacher Education and Certification (NASDTEC), and of the National School Boards Associations was reduced from a total of nine to an aggregate of three (from three each to one each). The representation of AACTE was increased from six to seven; and three, presumably from the liberal arts, were to be named on a temporary basis by an *ad hoc* committee convened by the National Commission on Accrediting.[3] The Council (NCATE) further agreed to work in harmony with the general procedures of six regional associations. Agreements between the Council and the regional associations are given in the next section.

In the light of these concessions, the National Commission on Accrediting (NCA) agreed to recognize NCATE as the national accrediting body in the field of teacher education. [9] The reorganization became effective on June 1, 1957. By virtue of the fact that NCATE actually began to operate as an accrediting body on July 1, 1954, its existence as a professional accrediting agency now covers more than a decade. In the first year of its operation, fewer than 10 institutions were visited, partly because few institutions were prepared for a visit, partly because of the mounting opposition from various groups.

In delineating responsibilities of NCATE and AACTE, it was agreed that the latter would continue to provide consultative help as well as research services to member institutions. This would enable NCATE to devote the bulk of its time to the evaluation and accreditation of teacher-training institutions.

At the outset, the budget of the Council was fixed at approximately $45,000, truly a small expenditure for such a potentially large operation; and it remained at about the same level throughout the decade of the 1950's. Since 1960 the income and expenditures of the Council have gradually increased to an amount almost triple that of the original allocation. In 1964 the budget was $138,500, an amount which supporters and critics alike would agree was totally inadequate for the magnitude of the Council's operation. Approximately half of the Council's budget was underwritten by AACTE ($36,000), NEA ($42,000), and AASA ($5,000). The principal other source of support was fees.

This relatively heavy subsidization of NCATE by NEA and AACTE, a department of NEA, is the basis, at least as far as financial support

---

[3] The total membership of NCATE was thus reduced from 21 to 19, with 10 representing institutions of higher learning.

goes, of the charge that NCATE is dominated by NEA as part of a total power structure. [10] NCA has tacitly agreed that AACTE represents the institutions of higher education on NCATE, and the friends of NCATE say that this is recognition that AACTE does not represent NEA since it cannot represent both. Many of the member institutions of AACTE are of course in no other way associated with NEA. The issue of whether NCATE is dominated and manipulated by NEA will be considered in Chapter 17.

Early in NCATE's history the flat membership fee of AACTE was changed to a sliding scale of fees based upon the size of the institution's enrollment. At the same time, NCATE fees for non-AACTE members were based on a sliding scale of $100, $150, or $250 per year depending on the number of programs to be evaluated. Each member institution when visited was to pay a flat visitation fee of $300 for one-category programs (elementary or secondary teachers), $400 for two-category programs, and $500 for three-category programs. In addition, the expenses of the visiting team were to be borne by the institution visited. As of 1964, NCATE income from fees of various kinds was slightly more than half of the total budget.

AGREEMENTS WITH REGIONAL ASSOCIATIONS

One of the first decisions of NCATE was to require prior accreditation by the appropriate regional accrediting association before evaluating an institution's teacher education program. It was also agreed that any institution blanketed into NCATE accreditation without previously having had regional approval would be given until 1960 to become so accredited, otherwise it would lose its NCATE accreditation. In announcing these policies, NCATE was aware of the active opposition to national accreditation of teacher education on the part of various officials of the regional accrediting associations. This opposition stemmed partially from a fear that a national accrediting body in teacher education would encroach on the areas of evaluation already appropriated by the regional associations. [11]

In order to minimize future misunderstandings, formal agreements were negotiated between NCATE and the regional associations delineating their respective areas of evaluation. Accreditation by a regional accrediting association would be regarded by NCATE as adequate assurance of the general financial stability of an institution, the effectiveness of the administration, the adequacy of the physical facilities, the appropriateness of the over-all program, including general education and subject-matter concentrations, the general strength of the faculty personnel policies, the general student personnel program, and the quality of instruction.

This leaves for NCATE "the evaluation of the teacher education program, including the character and appropriateness of the teacher education objectives, the effectiveness of the organization for teacher education, the student personnel policies and practices relating to teacher education, the patterns of academic and professional courses required in the various teacher education curriculums, the quality of the professional education faculty, the adequacy of facilities and re- sources for the teacher education curriculums offered, and the promise of the professional laboratory experience." [12]

One point at which the regional and NCATE evaluations are most closely involved jointly is with reference to the subject-matter aspects of teacher education. The Council must look to the regional accrediting associations to evaluate the qualifications of the faculty, the quality of instruction, and the laboratory and library facilities for the subject- matter courses taken by students preparing to teach. The Council, in turn, determines whether the subject-matter courses taken by prospec- tive teachers provide the kind of subject-matter background needed by teachers. "In other words, the Council evaluates the *pattern* of courses, not the *separate* courses." [13] Here, indeed, is one of the several areas of potential differences of opinion, or even conflict, be- tween NCATE and the regional associations, and the source of much criticism of NCATE by those who believe the standards of NCATE are much too narrow and limited. It should be clear that it is not en- tirely an NCATE decision to limit its accreditation to the professional education part of teacher education programs. NCATE, at least in the beginning, had little choice.

In accrediting teacher education, NCATE does not limit its evalua- tion to the college or department of education, rather the Council in- cludes in its accrediting procedures all teacher education programs. These programs may be in other colleges, as is often the case—in agriculture, in business, in home economics, in music, and in voca- tional or industrial education. In this sense it may be said that NCATE accredits institutions rather than schools or departments. At the same time, NCATE recognizes for accreditation only three categories of teacher education. These are for the preparation of elementary school teachers, for the preparation of secondary school teachers, and for the preparation of school service personnel, such as administrators, super- visors, and guidance counselors. NCATE also distinguishes between undergraduate and graduate programs. The third category is almost entirely at the graduate level.

Within these three categories are a number of specialized groups, some of which at the time of NCATE's creation were taking steps to establish standards and develop procedures for accrediting teacher education in their subject areas. In a deliberate effort to keep all teacher education programs under the jurisdiction of NCATE, the Council invited each specialized group to submit a self-study guide designed to meet the program needs of the group and to recommend a large panel of specialized evaluators for membership on NCATE teams. There were also four of the 23 national professional accrediting bodies recognized by the National Commission on Accrediting, which had marginal interests in teacher education. These four were in the areas of business, library administration, social work, and music. Of these groups, music had already begun to accredit programs in music education. In 1957 the National Commission on Accrediting announced that NCATE should henceforth accredit programs designed for the training of teachers of music, [14] with required cooperation with and references to the National Association of Schools of Music (NASM).

NCATE PROCEDURES

Some of the accrediting procedures of NCATE have already been mentioned. Only institutions accredited by the appropriate regional association and approved or accredited by the state department of education in the state in which the institution is located are eligible for NCATE evaluation. An NCATE visit may be carried on separately or in conjunction with a regional association visit, as determined by the policies of the regional association and the preference of the institution requesting NCATE accreditation. An institution may be accredited for one or more of the three categories: elementary, secondary, and school service personnel. The program or programs to be evaluated may be primarily undergraduate, graduate, or a combination of both.

An institution or category may be given full accreditation, provisional accreditation, or no accreditation. An institution may be provisionally accredited if the program is generally strong but is deficient in some major element of any category in which it is requesting accreditation. If provisional accreditation is granted, the institution is given a maximum of three years to overcome the deficiencies listed; otherwise, it will lose its NCATE accreditation. [15] In its annual published list of accredited institutions, no distinction is made between institutions provisionally accredited and those fully accredited.

THE INSTITUTIONAL REPORT

A college or university desiring to be accredited or reaccredited in teacher education will request from the central office of NCATE two copies of a preliminary application, in which the institution outlines the scope of the teacher education program, indicates the areas and levels for which it prepares teachers, describes the curriculum for teacher education, and reports in quantitative terms qualifications of the faculty for carrying out the program. If, on the basis of the preliminary information, the NCATE staff feels that the institution involved is not ready for a formal NCATE visit, the institution may be advised to postpone its request for accreditation. In such an event, the institution of course is free to go ahead with its plans for an NCATE evaluation.

If an institution elects to go ahead with its application, the institution then receives several copies of the NCATE *Standards and Guide*, together with detailed directions for preparing the institutional self-study and report. At an institution to be visited, rather complex machinery is usually established, consisting of a general chairman, a number of deputy chairmen, and all-institutional committees for assembling the necessary data and ultimately for writing the report. This self-study is regarded as a valuable and helpful experience, indicating to the faculty and administration the strengths and weaknesses of the teacher education program. A self-study may be a time-consuming experience and costly in terms of staff time and secretarial assistance, but little criticism is heard of this requirement except when a self-study is, at about the same time, also required by the regional accrediting association and the state. Then there is legitimate complaint about a duplication of effort.

Some institutions admit a frustrating quandary in preparing the self-study report, whether to be brutally frank in admitting *bona fide* deficiencies or whether it is more expedient to soft-pedal the weaknesses and to emphasize the strengths. Those who choose the former alternative and later receive an adverse decision may assume that NCATE had interpreted their acknowledgment of deficiencies as an admission of not being eligible for accreditation.[4]

Both the self-study report and the institutional evaluation are built around the seven NCATE standards or criteria of institutional functions in teacher education. The standard relating to the organization and administration of teacher education within an institution is illustrative of these criteria. "An organization (1) should assure consistent policies and practices with reference to the different segments of the teacher education program regardless of the administrative units under which they operate, (2) should facilitate the continuous development and improvement of the teacher education program, and (3) should clearly fix responsibility for the administration of policies agreed upon." [16] According to the NCATE *Standards and Guide*, this standard "specifies the principles which govern the organization"; it characterizes "a satisfactory organizational structure without prescribing a pattern." [17] In the words of the former director of NCATE, the Council "believes the organization performs the functions essential to the continuous improvement and integration of the total program of teacher education." [18] "The same underlying principle applies to the other standards of the Council relating to objectives of teacher education, student personnel policies and practices in teacher education, the curriculums in teacher education, professional laboratory experience, and library materials and other facilities for teacher education." [19]

The self-study report, "preferably not longer than 100 pages," is to be completed at least 60 days before the scheduled NCATE team visit. Four copies are sent to the central office of NCATE and at least six

---

[4] This dilemma was explained by a number of institutional heads that were interviewed.

copies are prepared for later distribution as needed and required. A visiting team is then named by the central office of NCATE to spend approximately three days on the campus under review.

THE VISITING TEAM

The visiting team members are selected from a panel of several hundred names submitted by members of AACTE, state departments of education, state education associations, and by professional groups in specialized areas. The size of the visiting team depends upon the nature and number of the programs to be evaluated, and to some extent upon the wishes of the host institution. According to NCATE officials, the institution to be visited has the prerogative of vetoing any name suggested for membership on a visiting team; but there is some evidence, at least in a few instances, that the courtesy was not always extended.[5] Other than for representatives of state departments or state education associations, members of visiting teams are selected from outside the state in which the institution is located.

Unlike the practice of some regional associations, NCATE does not provide orientation sessions for visiting team members. Such orientation, however, is provided for chairmen of visiting teams. As a rule not more than one inexperienced evaluator is named to a visiting team. Many whose names are on the panel of nominees have previously served on former AACTE or regional accrediting teams. When an individual is recommended for the panel of potential visiting team members, the recommendation specifies the area or areas in which he or she is best qualified to serve. A set of printed instructions is given to each visiting team member. Visits of evaluation teams to campuses take place between October 15 and April 15.

NCATE attempts to impress upon its visiting team members that their functions and responsibilities are basically different from those serving on regional accrediting teams. The regional associations, having already accredited approximately 85 percent of their potential membership among four-year institutions, place their major stress on stimulation of improvement. Accordingly, regional team members are encouraged to visit freely with representatives of the host institution, to give advice, to make personal judgments, and in general to be as helpful as possible.

Not so with NCATE. Visiting team members are told emphatically that they are not to "fraternize" with staff members of the host school. They are not to make suggestions; they are not to express oral opinions; they are not to make personal judgments. This also applies to the written report. Since, however, team members are gregarious, and

---

[5] In visits to campuses, some of those interviewed insisted they had had no opportunity to approve or disapprove those assigned to the visiting team.

many of them have served on regional teams, they cannot, at least do not, maintain a completely objective approach to the assigned task. [20]

Each member of the visiting team is ordinarily assigned one or two standards on which to report. He is to take the particular portions of the self-study report assigned to him, and, through conferences with key persons in the administration, through examination of records and any other legitimate means, determine whether the portions of the report assigned to him are complete and accurate. The team member is asked to describe the program as it exists at the time of the visit, to note differences from the institution's report if he detects them, to give reasons for the existence of the program so far as he is able to find out, and to present evidence on results if he can. On the last point he might, for example, say that an institution's admissions policies are producing a high-quality student body.

Each member of a visiting team writes a statement of what he has learned through his investigations and gives it to the team chairman to be worked into the complete team report. A good team chairman will not permit any member of the team to leave a campus until his or her report is completed. Some team members, in view of these procedures, have stated that the duties of NCATE team members tend to be somewhat clerical. This point is one source of criticism of NCATE. [21]

Twelve copies of the report are due in the central office of NCATE within 30 days after the team's visit. The report is read immediately upon receipt by the NCATE staff, and if the information provided is obviously insufficient or appears to be inaccurate the team chairman is asked for additional information. A copy of the report is sent to the institution to be checked for accuracy and completeness of information, and any corrections are inserted in or attached to the copies of the report, which are then sent to each member of the proper section of the Visitation and Appraisal (V and A) Committee.

THE VISITATION AND APPRAISAL COMMITTEE

The Visitation and Appraisal Committee (V and A Committee) consists of 34 members, about one-fifth from the Council membership and four-fifths from outside the Council. As far as possible, the V and A Committee is composed of a balanced representation of the different types of institutions and the different specialties. For reasons of efficiency the Committee is divided into four sections: one that evaluates larger multipurpose institutions and three that evaluate all other institutions of higher learning according to geographic location in the eastern, central, or western states. The several sections meet twice a year.

Each member of the Committee is expected to read all reports before the scheduled meeting of the Committee. Sometimes a section of the V and A Committee has had more cases to handle than the time of the individuals and the group would normally permit in view of their full-time positions in educational institutions.[6] Two members of the Committee are assigned to carry the special responsibility for an analysis of each report and a study of other available evidence in terms of NCATE standards. Copies of their analyses are presented to the Committee for discussion and further analysis during the Committee meeting.

As originally established, the NCATE procedures made no provision for any member of a visiting team to appear before the V and A Committee. Later, this was changed. Now, if the administrative officers of an institution believe that the report is unsatisfactory, or for other reasons, and that the presence of a team member would be advantageous, a team member, usually the chairman, will be invited to appear. Occasionally, if the chairman of the visiting team and the director of NCATE have sensed that an institution might have difficulty in meeting Council standards, a representative of the institution has been invited to appear before the V and A Committee, although the appearance has not always been to the institution's advantage. [22]

Following its deliberations, the Visitation and Appraisal Committee makes a recommendation to NCATE, which takes action on applications at its semi-annual meetings. In the past these meetings have been held in May and August. If the V and A Committee recommendation to NCATE is unanimous, the Council is reported as always having followed the recommendation. However, when the V and A Committee recommendation is not unanimous, the Council decision has not always conformed to the majority recommendations.[7]

COUNCIL ACTION

It was the intent in developing the structure of NCATE to rule out every possibility of pressure or bias in the Council's decisions. This evidently is the rationale behind the three levels of committees. It is intended to provide the Council with an atmosphere of complete insulation and isolation, and hence objectivity in weighing the evidence. For this reason, too, no member of the visiting team is present at the Council meeting. The Council action may be (1) full accreditation for an institution that is judged as meeting all NCATE standards; (2) provisional accreditation for an institution that is considered strong and promising, yet is believed to be deficient in one or more standards; (3) denial of accreditation for an institution that is judged as not meeting the standards; or (4) deferment of action.

The Council attempts to reach consensus on its actions, but may defer action (1) when the information available to it is not sufficient for making a decision at the moment; (2) when the meaning of the in-

---

[6] One V and A Committee member reported that 12 or 13 visiting committee reports was the maximum that could be handled efficiently; but that 15–20 cases were too frequently presented at a single 4- or 5-day meeting. Each member is presumed to have read all of the team reports in advance of the committee meeting.
[7] This impression was given by a member of the V and A Committee.

formation is not clear and the Council is not certain as to the interpretation; (3) when elements in the information available are conflicting and the Council is not able to determine what elements are correct; or (4) when for some reason the Council feels it would be best not to make an immediate and final decision.[8] In all such cases, action is postponed for one year.

If NCATE grants provisional accreditation to an institution in one or more categories of teacher education, the institution is free to accept or reject provisional status. Should it accept provisional accreditation, it is reevaluated at the end of three years by a member of the original visiting team, who reports to the Council on the improvements made in the three-year period. Under such circumstances, the institution must either be given full accreditation or else be denied accreditation. When an institution is denied accreditation, it may either (1) accept this decision and reapply for evaluation and a team visit after two years, (2) ask to have the denial deferred for one year when a reappraisal can be made, or (3) appeal the decision.

After the Council has come to a decision the director officially reports its action to the chief administrative officer of the institution, describes in general terms the strength of the program, and specifies the points upon which further improvements are needed. He does not specify the exact measures the institution should take for achieving the necessary improvements.

An institution may appeal an accrediting decision to an Appeals Board, consisting of five members, appointed by the Council from outside its own membership. Members of this Board are selected not because of their knowledge of teacher education, but because of their courage, their reputation for integrity, and their general standing as educators. No institution has yet appealed to this body.

Should one appeal, the following procedures and policies will apply: (1) the Appeals Board shall select two *ad hoc* members, "well acquainted with but in no way connected with the institution appealing," to serve in that particular case; (2) the institution will prepare a statement of its case for presentation to the Appeals Board; (3) NCATE will make materials at its disposal available to the Board; (4) the Board will hold a hearing in the light of the information available; (5) the Board will make a report of its findings, including recommendations in support of or in opposition to the actions of the Council; (6) the Council will make the report available to the public and will give serious consideration to the recommendations of the Board; (7) the decision in the case is made by the Council exclusively; and (8) the institution concerned will bear the expense of the hearing.

---

[8] NCATE never denies accreditation to an institution at the first meeting of the Council following the institutional evaluation. It always defers action at that time and gives the institution a hearing before the V and A Committee before taking any action either provisional, full, or denial. In other words, an institution is never denied accreditation without a hearing before the V and A Committee.

NCATE accreditation is effective as of September following the academic year in which the institution is evaluated and accredited. Public announcement of accrediting actions is made through NACTE's annual list which is issued in October of each year. An institution is obliged to carry in its catalog the categories and the level for which NCATE accreditation is granted. In case of provisional accreditation, the institution may choose to carry no announcement; the institution is not, however, to give the impression that the total program is fully accredited unless such is the case.

REEVALUATION

The usual interval between accreditation evaluations is 10 years, but more frequent evaluations may be made whenever conditions appear to justify them. In addition, institutions may request interim evaluations for the purpose of adding categories or degrees to their accreditation status. The procedures in reaccreditation are similar to those employed in the initial accreditation, except that a reevaluation for approval of a change of program is more limited in scope than the initial application and evaluation. Interim evaluations initiated by NCATE for the purpose of reviewing a program are conducted by a member of the central office and one other person acceptable to both the Council and the institution. They make a preliminary visit and submit a report to the V and A Committee giving reasons for or against a full-scale reevaluation. The V and A Committee then recommends to the Council a plan of action which may include a full-scale re-evaluation.

NCATE does not require annual reports from accredited institutions, but may from time to time request reports on particular phases and problems of their activities and programs. The Council, itself, makes an annual report to the accredited institutions in which it describes changes in the policies and procedures and makes suggestions relative to them.

MAGNITUDE OF NCATE RESPONSIBILITY

Of the approximately 1,500 degree-granting institutions of higher education in the United States, 1,173 offered teacher-training programs in 1963–1964. More than 850 of these institutions are accredited by the six regional accrediting associations whose approval is a prerequisite for NCATE accreditation. As of September, 1964, NCATE had accredited 422 of the 1,173 institutions and currently evaluates approximately 60 institutions a year for initial evaluation or for reevaluation.

It is estimated that 70 percent of the 175,000 new graduates in teacher education each year are graduated from NCATE-approved schools. This leaves some 750 schools potentially to be accredited, from which are graduated approximately 30 percent of the new teachers each year. Even if it is assumed that many of these institutions will never and should never seek NCATE approval the sheer magnitude of the task confronting NCATE is great indeed.

REFERENCES

1. For a brief discussion of the period see Lloyd M. Blauch, ed., *Accreditation in Higher Education*, pp. 204 ff.
2. William K. Selden, "Basic Issues in Accreditation of Teacher Education," *Liberal Education* (December, 1961). At this time, some of the regional associations had not yet taken on responsibilities of accreditation.
3. Blauch, *loc. cit.*
4. A. E. Joyal, "The National Council for Accreditation of Teacher Education in 1963," published in *Report on the NCATE Conference of One Hundred* (Washington, D. C., 1964), p. 1.
5. Blauch, *op. cit.*, p. 204.
6. Joyal, *op. cit.*, p. 2.
7. William K. Selden, *Accreditation, A Struggle Over Standards in Higher Education* (New York, 1960), pp. 64, 65.
8. AACTE, *Sourcebook on the Accreditation of Teacher Education*, p. 30.
9. Joyal, *op. cit.*, p. 3.
10. James B. Conant, *The Education of American Teachers* (New York, 1963), pp. 16–19.
11. John F. Nevins, *A Study of the Organization and Operation of Voluntary Accrediting Agencies* (Washington, D. C., 1959), pp. 294, 295.
12. W. Earl Armstrong, "Teacher Education," in Blauch, *op. cit.*, p. 206; AACTE, *Sourcebook on Accreditation of Teacher Education*, p. 5; NCATE *Standards and Guide* (1960 Edition), p. 2.
13. Armstrong, in Blauch, *op. cit.*, p. 206.
14. *Ibid.*, pp. 206, 207.
15. *Ibid.*, p. 208.
16. NCATE *Standards and Guide* (1960 Edition), p. 6.
17. *Ibid.*, p. 2.
18. Armstrong, in Blauch, *op. cit.*, p. 209.
19. *Ibid.*
20. Armstrong, in Blauch, *op. cit.*, pp. 209, 210.
21. See below, p. 81.
22. NCATE, *Accreditation in Teacher Education* (Washington, D. C., 1964), p. 4.

CHAPTER 6

NCATE: A FOCUS OF CONTROVERSY
IN ACCREDITATION

THROUGHOUT its 10-year history, NCATE never has been entirely free from criticism. This means that NCATE has had to learn to live with conflict. One may say that all accrediting bodies in higher education are victims of intermittent or sporadic criticisms, as academic, professional, or other groups now and then view with alarm what they believe to be unwise emphases of an accrediting agency or an action or decision relative to accreditation. True, but with NCATE the unfavorable criticisms with which higher education in general and the public are familiar are greater in frequency and in volume. While the criticisms of NCATE may be made in a manner which the critics believe to be constructive and in the best interests of teacher education and of accreditation in general, as the public is made aware of them through news media, the constructive nature of the criticisms has often become obscure. Some prefer to call these criticisms "attacks," but even so, attacks can be made from a constructive view and motivation.

There were outbursts of criticism following the announcement of NCATE's birth in 1954 and the initial refusal of the National Commission on Accrediting to extend recognition to NCATE as an official accrediting body. The reorganization of NCATE's structure in 1956 and its subsequent recognition by the National Commission on Accrediting brought about a period of relative calm until 1960, when NCA had agreed to review the structure and operations of NCATE.

By 1962, the Council increased the number of its accreditation and reaccreditation visits to colleges and universities. The number, if not the proportion, of its decisions to grant provisional approval or a denial or postponement of accreditation, tended to intensify the criticisms. The apparent climax in the criticisms stemmed from the widespread publicity given to the evaluation of Carleton College in 1961–1962 and the University of Wisconsin in 1962–1963. Further encouragement and stimulus to criticism came with the publication in the fall of

1963 of Conant's *The Education of American Teachers.* This was almost 18 months after full accreditation had been given to Carleton College in May, 1962, and subsequent to the full accreditation voted by the Council in May, 1963, to the University of Wisconsin.

The criticisms of NCATE may be listed under three categories: (1) those based on the structure of NCATE; (2) those emanating from NCATE standards; and (3) those growing out of NCATE procedures. Before these criticisms are reviewed in some detail, special consideration will be given to the accreditation of Carleton and Wisconsin.

THE ACCREDITATION OF CARLETON AND WISCONSIN

The NCATE evaluation of Carleton and Wisconsin gave news media an opportunity to build up a story to which great public interest could be attracted. Carleton College is on almost anyone's list of top-level liberal arts colleges. It has a fine faculty and highly selective admission policies. The University of Wisconsin is not only one of the major universities but its output of Ph.D.'s in recent decades has been near the top among all American universities. In the news each was made to symbolize a major group of institutions of higher education reported to have been somewhat distrustful of NCATE from the beginning, namely liberal arts colleges and multipurpose universities.

Although a great deal of publicity has already been given to these episodes, they have been so influential in determining attitudes toward NCATE that further consideration of events relating to Carleton and Wisconsin seems essential to the present Study. Visits to campuses in all parts of the country have revealed that misinformation about what happened at Carleton and Wisconsin is still widespread. Many who spoke of these episodes did not even know that both institutions are now fully accredited by NCATE.

In this presentation of the relations of NCATE with Carleton College and the University of Wisconsin, an attempt has been made to relate the events in as objective a manner as possible. Because of the many conflicting statements which have been publicized objectivity has been difficult to achieve. Also, in trying to cover events and points of view briefly, some objectivity may have been lost. In this presentation there is no intent to point out what agency or institution was right or wrong, wise or imprudent. It is assumed that the motives of all concerned were to protect the integrity and interests of the agency or institution they represented, and to act in a way which would contribute to the improvement of teacher education.

While some aspects of the two episodes are quite similar, as the following sections will reveal, there are some major differences. These are: (1) At Wisconsin, both undergraduate and graduate programs were evaluated; at Carleton, only undergraduate; (2) Carleton officials gave no publicity to their differences with NCATE; Wisconsin officials did; (3) Carleton College followed regular NCATE procedures throughout; Wisconsin did not; (4) unprecedented action by the NCATE executive committee was taken in the Wisconsin case. The two evaluations are considered in the same section, not because of their similarities or differences, but because both controversies focused the attention of higher education on the accreditation of teacher education and served to bring pressure on the National Commission on Accrediting to give special and prompt consideration to a reevaluation of NCATE.

CARLETON COLLEGE

The faculty committee on teacher education of Carleton College made the decision to seek NCATE accreditation in the fall of 1958 and the initial request was submitted to NCATE officers in November of that year. A series of faculty seminars on teacher education had been started as early as 1954. A Carleton official has stated that, in applying for NCATE accreditation, they accepted the premise that national accrediting is both necessary and desirable. The preliminary work, including the preparation of the required self-survey report, was completed by March, 1960. Soon thereafter the evaluation visit was scheduled for November, 1960.

The NCATE team which visited the College was composed of five "professional educators." As has been pointed out earlier in this Study, NCATE depended upon the regional accrediting association's evaluation of academic departments and general faculty competence. While the College might have chosen under NCATE procedures that the team include a generalist nominated by the North Central Association, it chose not to exercise this option. It preferred to have its program evaluated by a team from professional education. The College has never at any time criticized in any way the team which visited the campus.

It was and is the position of the College that the visiting team report was both fair and accurate, describing the College and its teacher-training program in a very adequate manner. This was stated in a communication to NCATE well in advance of the action of the V and A Committee to which, according to regular NCATE procedures, the team report was referred.

The original decision made by the Council in May, 1961, and reported to the College was that "too many elements in the program are below (NCATE) standards to justify accreditation at this time." Again according to NCATE procedures, the College was informed that the decision would become final at the fall meeting of the Council unless the College chose to petition for a review or an appeal.

After the College had been notified, the NCATE action was discussed with the faculty committee on teacher education, and on their recommendation a review was requested. The faculty was not officially informed until the following October, although some learned of the action, as would be natural, from the faculty committee discussion. In the review the College took the position that the report of the visiting team was not fully or fairly treated by the V and A Committee and subsequently by the Council.

Carleton was granted full accreditation by NCATE on May 18–19, 1962, with accreditation effective from the date of the visit by the NCATE team in November, 1960. This effective date supports a view that the change in the NCATE initial decision was not based on changes in their teacher education program.

In fairness to Carleton College it should be stressed here that no evidence has been found of any intentional contribution or encouragement by Carleton officials to the widespread publicity given to the "case." The latter appeared to make every effort to keep the episode from becoming a public issue, to be cooperative and constructive in their dealings with NCATE, and to adhere strictly to established procedures for clearing up a misunderstanding between the Council and an institution under review. The simple truth is that the incident was seized upon by the press for its newsworthiness and by critics of NCATE as a golden opportunity to point out NCATE's mistakes or failures. The first references to the NCATE action in the press came some six months later. The statements in the press and from the platform (not by Carleton people) reached a peak in an article by J. D. Koerner, "Teacher Education: Who Makes the Rules?" in the October 20, 1962, issue of *Saturday Review*.

The College was criticized by some supporters of NCATE for not attempting to "correct the record" when misinformation or misinterpretation appeared in the press. The College administration apparently took the position that such attempts might only serve to call further public attention to a situation which they were trying to work out through proper channels. However, Dean Gilman of Carleton did write a letter to the editor of the *Saturday Review* following the appearance of the Koerner article and also submitted a brief article for publication. The letter was published by the *Review,* but not the article.

A listing of the weaknesses in the teacher education program at Carleton, as communicated to the College by the director of NCATE, serves only to point up the kind of emphases in teacher education which are made by NCATE committees during the period of evaluation, since Carleton was granted full accreditation without making changes in their program. The weaknesses enumerated in the letter from the NCATE office to the College informing the officials of the initial action referred to the role of the institution-wide committee for teacher education, the screening and advising of students for teacher education, the adequacy of the staff in teacher education, the sequence of professional education courses, the provision for professional laboratory experiences, and the "three ways" by which the student teaching requirement could be met.

The Carleton faculty voted to change from a semester plan to a three-term academic year plan the week following the original visit of the NCATE team. The three-term plan does facilitate the scheduling of student teaching. The NCATE office was notified of this decision in February, 1961 (before the initial Council action). Some changes in professional staff were made after full accreditation had been granted.

A fair conclusion seems to be that the Council, between May, 1961, and May, 1962, became convinced of the seriousness with which Carleton College was taking teacher education and their sincerity in a study of teacher education, as demonstrated by the attitude of Carleton officials during the review. Furthermore, the Council acquired through the review an interpretation of the Carleton teacher education program which convinced it (the Council) that the program was sound and consistent with the philosophy of the College. As a result, full accreditation was granted.

In the first data submitted for the review, Carleton criticized NCATE procedures. However, upon being notified that this was irrelevant to the review, the College withdrew this part of its review data. It was not long after, however, that NCATE provided for better communication between the visiting team and the V and A Committee. It can be said with justification that the College's recommendations did have a beneficial effect on NCATE evaluation procedures.

THE UNIVERSITY OF WISCONSIN

The undergraduate and graduate programs at the University of Wisconsin were accredited by AACTE, and Wisconsin, like other institutions, was "blanketed in" as fully accredited when NCATE took over accreditation from AACTE. The Dean of the University of Wisconsin School of Education has stated that the Wisconsin faculty was aware of the criticisms of NCATE and was disturbed by the observation that institutions thinking about applying for accreditation seemed to be most concerned about "What does NCATE want?" However, despite the criticisms and concerns, a decision was made to seek reaccreditation. He further noted that WHAT NCATE WANTS was not considered by Wisconsin in its self-survey. Rather the concern was to analyze and report what Wisconsin wants and does.

An NCATE team visited the University in March, 1962. On August 29–30, the Council voted to approve the Wisconsin graduate programs in teacher education, but deferred action on undergraduate programs for the training of elementary and secondary school teachers. This action was communicated to the University president on September 12. It was further indicated that action on the undergraduate program would be taken in May, 1963, and that the action would be to grant provisional accreditation unless further evidence relating to the standards was presented. In explaining the Council's action, it was stated that the primary reason for deferral in all cases is to provide the fullest possible opportunity for the institution to get its case before the Council before final action is taken. It was made clear to officials of the University of Wisconsin that the normal procedure would be to have their objections to the points raised by the Council presented before the NCATE Visitation and Appraisal Committee in the spring of 1963.

Letters setting forth what was believed to be incorrect information and misinterpretation of the Wisconsin program were sent to the Director of NCATE by the Wisconsin School of Education administration. Also, the Dean made a personal visit to NCATE headquarters in Washington.

After consideration of the report of the August (1962) NCATE action by the Executive Committee of the Wisconsin School of Education, it was decided to challenge NCATE to reassess its own standards and procedures, rather than to comply or to accept provisional status. The Committee recognized that any action by them would become one of public information, since by Wisconsin law representatives of the press may attend all faculty meetings.

The story of the action on the University of Wisconsin evaluation soon became public knowledge. Somehow, as the story was reported in the press, it was made to appear as though NCATE had objected principally to the participation of the liberal arts faculty in the programming of teacher education. Spokesmen for NCATE pointed out that "the Council has never raised any question about the wisdom of having the closest ties between the education group and the liberal arts group. As a matter of fact, the Council has sponsored the movement and has probably done more to foster it than any other individual or agency in the country." [1]

A meeting of the Executive Committee of NCATE was held on November 13, 1962, to consider the Wisconsin "crisis." This was apparently an unprecedented procedure on the part of NCATE. The net result of the Executive Committee meeting was an authorization to the Director to indicate to Wisconsin the Committee's willingness to recommend to the Council the granting of full accreditation to Wisconsin's elementary and secondary programs on the undergraduate level at the Council's May, 1963, meeting. [2] It was pointed out that the Executive Committee's recommendation was in no sense binding on the Council, but that it seemed reasonable to expect that the recommendation would be accepted. Some interpret this action of the Executive Committee as evidence of panic on the part of NCATE officials. Others have interpreted the action as a demonstration of the flexibility of NCATE procedures.

On November 20, Wisconsin's School of Education faculty voted to accept the reaccreditation of the graduate program, to withdraw the application for the reaccreditation of the undergraduate program, and to stand as formerly accredited with regard to the undergraduate program. According to the Dean, the Wisconsin faculty then had the choice of accepting full reaccreditation and "thereby leaving other institutions to deal individually with the growing autocratic power of

NCATE," or to call upon NCATE to correct its weaknesses. The latter choice was made.

In a letter dated January 14, 1963, to the NCATE Director, the Dean stated that no action was indicated for NCATE at the April meeting of the V and A Committee or at the May meeting of the Council, since the application for reaccreditation had been withdrawn. He further stated that the fact that Wisconsin was accredited by NCATE would be mentioned in the School of Education catalog, showing the date of reaccreditation of the graduate program as 1962 and of the accreditation of the undergraduate program as 1953.

Wisconsin's decision to withdraw its application for undergraduate reaccreditation raised some interesting—and "sticky"—questions. Could a college or university submit a formal application to NCATE for accreditation, then after the procedure is virtually completed and the ultimate decision known, yet not officially taken, withdraw the application and thus restore the *status quo ante?* A similar question, yet different, was whether NCATE—after notifying an institution of the decision that would be rendered a year later—could stop the proceedings just short of the decision. These were questions confronting NCATE when the Council met in May, 1963. The matter was discussed for several hours and differing points of view presented.

The NCATE decision to give full accreditation to the University's undergraduate programs was interpreted both by the public and by the University as a defeat of the Council and a victory for the University. The interpretation given by the press was that in the struggle between subject matter and professional education, here was a clear-cut victory for the liberal arts.

Typical of comments in the press was an editorial which appeared in *The Milwaukee Journal*, November 28, 1962. A paragraph from the editorial is quoted:

> In a sense, a conflict between the teachers college concept and the university concept of teacher training is involved. The NCATE believes that those in charge of the teacher-training program should control every phase. The university considers it proper for a future teacher to take history courses under the history department; also to have the full university faculty exercise considerable academic control over the school of education, as over other UW schools and colleges. The university advocates flexible curriculums for teachers, with emphasis on liberal education. ENKATE [sic] stresses teaching methods, with little latitude in curriculums.

One critical issue which was raised in the widespread discussion of the Wisconsin episode was whether any states were refusing certification to graduates of non-NCATE-accredited institutions, and for this reason alone. The news media certainly created the impression that this was happening and with NCATE encouragement. The fact is that NCATE has frequently stated that it did not want states to impose such restrictions. As a result of information obtained in this Study, it is concluded that *no* state has refused certification to an applicant just because he is not graduated from an NCATE-accredited institution.

The reasons for the initial action in the Wisconsin case are given because of the widespread misunderstanding of them. The following were the areas in which improvements were to be made in the undergraduate program in order to qualify for full reaccreditation:

1. The Council does not question the organization which the University has for planning, coordinating, and evaluating the total teacher education program. The question being raised in this regard is the extent to which the present organization is actually bringing about the kind of coordination necessary. The information available indicates that the present structure does not control the teaching majors in the various departments and the academic patterns for those who are preparing to be music teachers. It also indicates that no common general education requirements have been established through this structure and that the students preparing to teach cannot be identified with certainty in the School of Education offices. Unless each department or administrative unit of the University insists on complete autonomy, it may be possible with the present organization to bring about the type of coordination indicated above.

2. Two recommendations are made with reference to student personnel at the undergraduate level. The first relates to the time at which students are admitted to teacher education. It is noted that students in art and physical education are admitted to the School of Education as freshmen; that those preparing to be elementary teachers are admitted at the sophomore level; and all others at the beginning of the junior year. Perhaps it would be possible to give tentative admission to some at the freshman and sophomore levels but final confirmation at the beginning of the junior year. This would provide comparable data on all students admitted to teacher education. The second relates to procedures for admission to teacher education. Apparently applications do not all go to the same committee. For example, music has its committee and home economics has its separate committee. Doubtless this arrangement has some advantages but it also makes for unevenness in the application of standards. It is recommended that policies and procedures be adopted to reduce this unevenness to a minimum or to arrange for one committee to handle all applicants.

3. As already indicated, the general education program seems to be quite uneven from department to department. The low requirements in general education for the fields of agriculture and music are especially noted. There appear to be dual programs for some subject fields; that is, two different ways to prepare for the same school position. It would help to have this situation clarified.

4. The Council regards such facilities as the library, campus school, and the like as fully adequate, in fact quite outstanding,

but the building which houses most of the professional education program is not as good as is generally found in an institution with the standing of the University of Wisconsin. Doubtless
a well-planned building for the School of Education would add
to the quality of the program.

Wisconsin contended that on some points the Council was misin-
formed, that steps were already under way to correct the situation in
agriculture and music, and that the quality of the buildings did not
affect the quality of their programs. It was further emphasized that
there was a difference in philosophy between the Wisconsin faculty
and NCATE on three points: that the existing administrative structure
did not control teaching majors, that no common general education
pattern existed, and that dual programs existed in some fields. These
differences are whether the administrative structure *should* control
academic majors, whether there *should* be a common pattern of general education for all students, and whether there *should* be available
dual programs leading to the teachers certificate.

Supporters of NCATE are of the opinion that the press misrepresented the position and actions of NCATE, and that the publicity
given to the Wisconsin case was harmful to NCATE and to teacher
education. They particularly deplored Wisconsin's failure to follow
regular procedures through which they feel any misunderstandings
could have easily been cleared up. On the other hand, many leaders in
higher education, of course, have applauded the Wisconsin action.

A statement approved by the Wisconsin School of Education faculty,
in October, 1963, expressed appreciation for the May, 1963, decision of
NCATE "which we understand counteracts the original proposed action
by the Council" and regretted that the first action had to be protested
because "the changes specified by the Council in the pattern of control
and operation . . . as well as in curriculums" were regarded as fundamental and contrary to the "philosophy and traditions of this institution." The statement also listed changes in NCATE which were believed
to be necessary.

The criticisms of NCATE made by Wisconsin are included in the
remainder of this chapter.

CRITICISMS OF NCATE BASED ON ITS STRUCTURE

One of the most common criticisms related to NCATE structure is
that there is an absence of any definite constituency to which NCATE
is responsible. True, NCATE has a kind of responsibility to the five
organizations which combined to create NCATE. What this means
in reality is that all five organizations must approve any changes in
the NCATE structure. Naturally to get such unanimity in a relatively
short time is next to an impossibility, as the events of the past year
point up sharply. Likewise, NCATE bears some responsibility to the
National Commission on Accrediting which has the uncertain obliga-

tion of coordinating and improving all the accrediting bodies which it recognizes.

Since the National Commission on Accrediting (NCA) is a voluntary agency to coordinate voluntary agencies, it has to depend upon good will and the art of persuasion to realize any real influence. The significant thing about NCATE's lack of responsibility to a definite constituency is that there is no body (other than NCA, NCATE, or its constituent members) to which people can go to register complaints or to offer suggestions for the improvement of NCATE. The result is that NCA has received many complaints about NCATE, and during its decade and a half of existence has devoted more time to NCATE and the accreditation of teacher education than it has to all the other agencies and areas of accreditation.

As an autonomous body, NCATE within the framework in which it is structured is free to do pretty much as it pleases. It sets its own standards, defines its own procedures, places what interpretation it pleases on both standards and procedures, and renders its decisions without likelihood of having its authority questioned or overridden by a superior authority. In this respect, NCATE did not differ in 1964 from a number of other professional accrediting agencies.[1]

At the time of NCA's formal recognition of NCATE, it was understood that NCATE's structure and finances would be subject to a review in 1960. A preliminary review did take place at the time specified, but since NCATE had been evaluating institutions for such a short time it was decided to delay further consideration until 1963. In view of the mounting criticism of NCATE in 1962 and 1963, it was later decided to re-examine NCATE in all its important aspects. At the 1963 annual meeting, the National Commission on Accrediting reiterated its conviction that "there is a social need for a national organization to conduct an adequate program of accreditation in the field of teacher education with emphasis being placed on improvement in teacher education." [3] NCA emphasized that "the national agency for the accreditation of teacher education must be primarily responsible to the colleges and universities educating and preparing teachers." NCA concluded its resolutions by announcing that NCATE would be reviewed at the 1964 annual meeting in the light of NCA's resolutions. [4]

In 1963 and early 1964, an *ad hoc* NCATE committee met with representatives of the National Commission on Accrediting and separately with representatives of the five constituent organizations of

---

[1] Other autonomous accrediting bodies are in architecture, business, dentistry, libraries, optometry, forestry, nursing, pharmacy, theology, and veterinary medicine. See Appendix III for additional information on professional accrediting agencies.

NCATE. Also, on November 14–15, 1963, the NCATE Conference of One Hundred, composed of representatives of some 50 national educational and other professional organizations and learned societies, was held in Chicago to discuss ways in which national accreditation of teacher education might be improved. NCA, meeting in Chicago on April 17–18, 1964, recognized that NCATE had given indication of progress toward reorganization and agreed to give the Council until the spring of 1965 to complete its task. As additional guidelines to NCATE and the *ad hoc* committee, NCA approved the following principles:

I. That the national agency responsible for the accreditation of teacher education programs in colleges and universities be sufficiently large to include representation from the major groups with legitimate interests in teacher education, such as higher education institutions, learned societies, the teaching profession, those who administer the schools, and the public;

II. That the majority of the members serving on the agency, regardless of its size, be full-time teachers or administrative officers from the full range of institutions preparing teachers;

III. That the operations of the accrediting process by this national agency be conducted in such a manner
(a) that the criteria or requirements for accreditation be developed and proposed for the agency's consideration by the institutions preparing teachers as expressed through an organization or organizations broadly representative of these institutions in consultation and cooperation with other organizations concerned with teacher education;
(b) that the procedures of evaluating institutions for accreditation be developed by the agency itself in accordance with the "Criteria for Recognized Accrediting Agencies" of the National Commission on Accrediting; and
(c) that decisions regarding accreditation be made by the agency alone, relying on an executive committee or such other committees as it may create for initial review and recommendations, with a mechanism for institutional appeal established by the agency itself; and

IV. That the major portion of the cost of the agency be paid directly or indirectly by the institutions preparing teachers. [5]

The question of NCATE structure is a difficult and complicated one. Just who has the best claim to set the standards for teacher education and to administer them? Is it the public which uses or "consumes" the product of teacher education institutions? Is it the principals and superintendents who employ the products of teacher education? Is it the state departments which have to certify that teachers, administrators, and personnel people are adequately prepared? Is it the colleges and universities which prepare the teachers? Or is it a combination of these various organizations and institutions, and if so just what combination?

CONSTITUENT MEMBERS

A second criticism of NCATE based upon its structure is that, as originally constituted and as reorganized in 1955 and 1956, the control of NCATE is heavily weighted in favor of the "establishment" [6] or the "educationists." It is alleged that both the Council and the various standing and *ad hoc* committees are composed principally of non-subject-matter specialists. The Council does not include a representative selected by liberal arts institutions. As pointed out in a previous chapter, [7] the Association of American Colleges had been invited at least twice to be a constituent organization and to contribute toward the financial support of NCATE; but AAC had declined on both occasions. The reorganization which took place in 1955 and 1956 provided for three persons (presumably from liberal arts institutions) to be named by an *ad hoc* committee convened by the National Commission on Accrediting.

Additional "proof" of control by the "educationists" was provided by the distribution of financial support of NCATE. The bulk of the Council's income, other than from fees, came from affiliates of the National Education Association. [8] It is asked why a power and pressure organization, such as some consider NEA to be, would contribute so heavily other than to exercise the control that normally goes with such contributions.

LEVELS OF COMMITTEES

A third criticism relating to NCATE's structure has to do with the three levels of committees or councils involved in NCATE accreditation. [9] Formerly, too, the chairman of the visiting team submitted to the Council, along with the regular committee report, a "secret" report which might be largely at variance with the regular team report. This practice was roundly criticized by schools visited or anticipating an NCATE visit, and was subsequently and wisely discontinued. [10] At the conclusion of its deliberations the V and A Committee submits its recommendation concerning each school under consideration to the Council itself. The Council takes the recommendation of the V and A Committee into consideration, but is not bound to follow it. When the Council deliberates on the action to be taken with respect to a particular institution, no one from the institution or from the visiting team is present, but the chairman of the V and A Committee is always present and makes the report of the committee on the institution concerned.[2]

---

[2] In addition there is a Council member on each section of the V and A Committee. This means that in nearly every case, two of those present at the Council meeting have reviewed all the evidence and have participated in the decision of the V and A Committee to recommend accreditation or the lack of it.

The criticism of the complex structure is that those most familiar with the institution under review (members of the visiting team) have no direct voice in the ultimate decision. They have no opportunity to give initial opinions or judgments relative to the morale of the faculty or students or the general intellectual atmosphere of the institution. Some insist that such subjective evaluations and interpretations constitute the only true means of differentiating between average and superior institutions. By the same token, it is said that those who make the extremely important decisions are the persons likely to be least familiar with the institution under consideration. In other words, a decision upon which hangs an important segment of the academic and professional standing and reputation of a college or university is made by those persons who, in certain respects, are not fully prepared to do so. [11]

CRITICISMS EMANATING FROM NCATE STANDARDS

QUANTITATIVE IN NATURE

One of the criticisms most frequently leveled at NCATE is that its standards or criteria are quantitative rather than qualitative. NCATE, in evaluating an institution, is alleged to concern itself too much with the number of people teaching education courses and the proportion of those with the doctorate; with the size of the professional education library in terms of both space and contents; with the pattern of student teaching and the scope of the laboratory experiences of students in teacher education; and with the physical facilities of the department or school of education. NCATE's retort to these charges, that such quantitative elements are in reality "bench marks" of quality, is not accepted by the Council's critics as valid. [12] These criticisms are made of NCATE, even though it may be recognized that many of the other professional accrediting agencies use data similarly quantitative by nature.

The only really valid criterion for measuring the quality of an institution or of a teacher education program (say the critics) is the quality of the output—the graduates. Defenders of NCATE do not necessarily disagree with this assumption, but they insist that no one has been able so far to devise a reliable instrument for measuring the quality of an institution's output. As in the case of measuring the quality of teaching, the problem is said to be too indefinite and too ephemeral. Nevertheless, because so many critics of NCATE have employed the qualitative argument, it was decided to include in this Study a report on some of the developments in this field (Chapter 9).

ADMINISTRATIVE STRUCTURE OF AN INSTITUTION

A second and related criticism of NCATE standards is that too much emphasis is placed on the administrative structure in teacher education. This criticism comes largely from multipurpose universities which accuse NCATE of trying to straitjacket them with an over-simplified pattern of organization in teacher education. It is alleged that NCATE has taken its cue from teachers colleges, where the general administrative pattern is relatively simple, and is therefore not necessarily adaptable to multipurpose universities in which teacher education programs may be scattered among half a dozen schools and colleges. Officials of Wisconsin, for example, emphasized this point. The NCATE standard on administrative structure, as stated in rather general terms, is quoted in Chapter 10. There also the official interpretation of the standard is given. This interpretation of Standard II of NCATE has been generally taken as requiring one very specific administrative structure without variation as to different types of educational institutions.

The third criticism of NCATE standards is that they are stated in rather vague and general terms, but are rigid and inflexible when it comes to NCATE's interpretation of them. It is argued that such inflexibility in interpretation of standards naturally lends itself to a drab uniformity of institutional patterns and discourages experimentation. [13] Those who attempt to answer this criticism point to the great variety of administrative structures in institutions already accredited by NCATE. There are, of course, also those who criticize NCATE because of the variety.

RESPONSIBILITY FOR ACADEMIC PREPARATION

A general criticism of NCATE, which at least carries an implication of faulty standards, is the charge that NCATE in practice has given full accreditation to academically weak institutions while giving only provisional approval or denying it altogether to institutions of high quality. [14] Some of this criticism may stem from the inevitable variations in the qualities of those who are asked to serve on NCATE visiting teams. A much more fundamental source of such criticism, however, is the fact that NCATE does not examine academic departments involved in secondary education. This restriction was placed upon NCATE by agreement with the regional associations and the National Commission on Accrediting at the time NCATE was recognized as an official accrediting body.

The stated policy of NCATE is not to examine a teacher education institution until such institution is accredited by the state department and the proper regional association. Unfortunately, regional accreditation provides no guarantee that a particular academic department in a fully accredited college or university is even average in quality. The regional associations admit that in their general or over-all approach to institutional accreditation a school that has one or two weak academic departments may be given full accreditation on the basis of general institutional strength. At the same time, it would appear that the public image of a teacher education institution depends much more on the reputed strength of its academic departments than it does on the professional aspects of the program.

NCATE, in its *Standards and Guide,* recognizes its limitations in respect to the accreditation of academic programs:

> The Council regards accreditation by a regional accrediting association as adequate insurance of the general financial stability of the institution, the effectiveness of the administration, the adequacy of the general facilities, the quality of the student personnel program, the appropriateness of the over-all program including general education and subject matter majors, the general strength of the faculty, the faculty personnel policies of the institution, and the quality of instruction. The Council, therefore, evaluates the teacher education program within this setting, including the teacher education objectives, the organization for teacher education, the student personnel program for teacher education, the faculty for professional education, the patterns of academic and professional courses and experiences offered in the various teacher education curricula, the facilities for the teacher education curricula offered, and the program of professional laboratory experience. These factors will be evaluated for the total program offered in the categories for which accreditation is sought regardless of their location in the institution.

What the above policy means is that NCATE is often held responsible for aspects of the teacher education program over which the Council has no jurisdiction or control.

A few years ago representatives of two of the scientific disciplines, as a part of their study of needs of secondary school teachers of these disciplines, examined the catalogs of institutions accredited by NCATE to determine course offerings and staff competence in these disciplines. In quite a large number of instances the evidence was very disappointing to them. But is NCATE properly to blame for this kind of deficiency in an institution accredited by it? Or is it a consequence largely of the present division of labor between NCATE and the regional accrediting associations?

EMPHASIS ON PROFESSIONAL EDUCATION

The restrictions observed by NCATE with regard to academic programs have led many to believe that NCATE is almost exclusively concerned with education courses and the status of professors of education. Since the courses taught by these professors usually are not more than about 20 percent of courses taken in a four-year baccalaureate program, these critics say that NCATE takes much too narrow a view of teacher education. Criticisms in this category often make reference to the fact that professional courses comprise a low-level educational activity, replete with platitudes, unverified assumptions, and pedagogical mumbo-jumbo, all of which make no contribution to the development of good teachers. Disrespect for teacher education in general is readily transferred to the agency which speaks for the program.

Furthermore, these critics of NCATE believe that NCATE is in considerable part responsible for making it necessary for institutions to require teacher education students to give more time to professional courses than is necessary, thus taking the time available to prospective teachers for more substantive courses. They say that NCATE gives direct support to unreasonable requirements in professional education on the part of the states through certification.

NCATE is criticized for inquiring about the salary and rank status of professors of education and their participation in institutional committees and decision-making as having no bearing in the determination of the quality of the teacher education program, and particularly no bearing on the quality of the products of the program. The critics view this as a means of protecting and strengthening the vested interests of the professional "educationists" and of the "establishment."

Many believe that the standards of teacher education are too low and that they must be drastically raised, and conclude that this cannot and will not be done by an agency primarily concerned with the professional education sequence, which is the way they characterize NCATE.

CRITICISMS STEMMING FROM NCATE PROCEDURES

One criticism of NCATE growing out of the Council's procedures pertains to the self-study report required by NCATE of the institution seeking accreditation or reaccreditation. The self-study is said to be too detailed, too much filled with unimportant facts, too time-consuming. Valuable time of faculty members with important teaching and administrative responsibilities is devoted to fact-finding, organizing and writing the report. The preparation of the self-study report indirectly adds a great deal to the cost of accreditation.

A quite different argument is that many times unfavorable decisions by NCATE, and the unhappiness and resentments resulting from adverse NCATE action, stem from inadequacies in the self-study report. [15] It is alleged that if the self-study report were complete and full a favorable decision in some cases might have been given and all the unpleasantness avoided. There is also criticism of the duplication of effort in preparing the NCATE self-study report with that required by the regional associations and many of the states. On the other hand, the criticism is made that the NCATE report should be more like the others so that one report might be used by more than one accrediting agency.

VISITING TEAMS

A second criticism related to NCATE procedures has to do with the quality of NCATE visiting teams. There are several different facets of this criticism. One is that inexperienced and untrained people are asked to serve on NCATE teams. [16] One college dean objected to the fact that members of his staff were invited to serve on visiting teams without NCATE's having sought his advice. He indicated that much stronger persons were available from his staff, but were never invited. It is true (see Chapter 5) that NCATE does not arrange for orientation or briefing sessions for inexperienced team members as do some of the regional associations. NCATE explains that this is due to limited staff and funds for training sessions, and as a partial substitute NCATE attempts to hold briefing sessions for chairmen of visiting teams. Also, as far as possible, NCATE does not name more than one inexperienced person to a visiting team.

Another criticism is that, as a general rule, NCATE does not appoint subject-matter specialists to visiting teams. The reason given for this is that to name team members for each subject-matter specialty would tend to place a heavy financial burden on the institution that is being evaluated. Moreover, as already noted, NCATE depends upon the regional association to certify the quality of training in academic fields.

A third criticism of visiting teams is that under NCATE rules the functions of visiting team members appear to be largely clerical. This is because team members are forbidden to give advice, to make judgments, or to express opinions. In this respect, NCATE teams differ fundamentally from regional associations' visiting teams if not from other professional accrediting agencies. The two approaches are compared—and not favorably with respect to NCATE methods. Professors who have served on NCATE teams have been critical of the restrictions placed on them.

COMMUNICATION

A third criticism of NCATE procedures points up the poor avenues of communication between NCATE and the institutions with which the Council deals. Part of this is said to stem from NCATE's reporting techniques. [18] Colleges and universities insist that they are not adequately informed of NCATE's standards and procedures. The printed materials are written in vague and unclear language. It is said that letters from the central office of NCATE have tended to be brief, terse, and sometimes tactless. Even when an institution is given provisional accreditation, a deferral, or a denial of accreditation the complaint is that reasons or factors in the decision are not clearly set forth.

STIMULATING IMPROVEMENT

A fourth criticism of NCATE procedures is the charge that NCATE in its accrediting functions places too much emphasis on raising minimum standards, not enough on stimulating improvement. [19] Again, this is a conspicuous contrast between NCATE and the regional accrediting associations. The regionals admit that their emphasis on stimulation to improvement stems from their having already accredited approximately 85 percent of their current potential members; NCATE, on the contrary, has accredited only a little more than one-third of the institutions now offering teacher education programs.

At least until NCATE's position in the matter more clearly approximates that of the regionals, the Council's present intention is to continue giving emphasis to minimum standards. Moreover, NCATE has pointed out that the word "accreditation" literally means identifying those institutions which meet prescribed standards and does not necessarily include stimulation to improvement, other than through the self-study and the listing of deficiencies to be corrected. Thus, stimulation to improvement may become a by-product of applying minimum standards.

A closely related criticism is that NCATE in essence has tried to do both—stimulate improvement and establish and interpret minimum standards—and that it can never be accepted or successful until it makes a decision about which is its principal function. Some who have served on V and A Committees, and even on the Council, have stated that when decisions are made the arguments supporting them are based on both purposes and hence are sometimes not clear-cut.

In the fall of 1964 NCATE made a decision on this issue in rewriting its constitution. In the proposed constitution it is definitely stated that the primary emphasis in NCATE accreditation is on minimum standards.

CRITICISMS OF ACCREDITATION IN GENERAL

In addition to criticisms aimed specifically at NCATE, the Council is the actual or potential recipient of criticism voiced by those who oppose all forms or agencies of accreditation. In 1926 Fred J. Kelly listed three inherent dangers in any and all accrediting agencies: (1) standardization endangers public confidence in a profession by limiting the number entering the profession, thereby increasing fees for professional services; (2) accredited schools and departments get a disproportionate amount of funds; (3) accrediting agencies demand a uniformity of educational practice, thus impeding progress. [20]

In 1938 a Joint Committee on Accrediting speaking for several educational organizations listed six specific evils of accrediting agencies:

1. Too many agencies;
2. Too much duplication;
3. Costs of evaluations too great;
4. Too much emphasis upon quantitative and superficial standards;
5. Too much domination by outside groups;
6. Activities which tend to destroy institutional rights and freedoms. [21]

These criticisms, written nearly two decades before NCATE's entrance into the field of accreditation, resemble many of the criticisms presently voiced against NCATE.

Those who are opposed to national accreditation of teacher education say that accreditation has not and cannot guarantee the production of good teachers for the schools, and the existence of national accreditation by which an institution may advertise its endorsement by a national agency leads the public into a false sense of security. National accreditation, these critics also say, places unjustified power in the hands of a few and contributes to the development of an undesirable power structure. While this criticism may be and is applied against all forms of accreditation, those who direct it against NCATE in particular point out the lack of agreement on what constitutes good teaching, the lack of consensus on how to prepare good teachers, the involvement of the states in accreditation of teacher education, the power of the states to certify teachers, and the ultimate responsibility of the local school boards, as reasons why NCATE is the most vulnerable of all accrediting agencies.

These critics say that neither NCATE nor the regional associations can guarantee that a candidate for a teaching job knows his subject and can teach it—the only two essential questions. NCATE approval is said to mean only that an institution has been approved by a group of people, and that this is quite unlike the licensing of doctors or lawyers on the basis of examinations.

In this chapter the first purpose has been to review the criticisms of the structure, standards, and procedures of the National Council for Accreditation of Teacher Education. More attention has been given to the criticisms than the response to the criticisms made by the supporters of NCATE, although on some of the points the response of supporters of NCATE has been included with the hope of clarifying the issue in question. It is hoped and intended that the reader will determine for himself the validity of the criticisms in the light of the information presented in the other 17 chapters of this study.

REFERENCES

1. Letter from W. E. Armstrong to a member of the University of Wisconsin staff, April 24, 1963.
2. *Memo*, January 4, 1963, from W. E. Armstrong to "Collegiate Institutions and Professional Groups."
3. National Commission on Accrediting, *Memo* to Presidents of Member Institutions, "Accreditation in Teacher Education," March 6, 1963.
4. *Ibid.*
5. National Commission on Accrediting, *Reports* No. 14–3, May 1964, pp. 3, 4.
6. For the meaning and use of this term, see James B. Conant, *The Education of American Teachers*, pp. 15, 16. For the meaning of the term "Educationist," see Koerner, *Miseducation of American Teachers*, p. 8, footnote.

7. Chapter 5, pp. 53, 76 of this Study.
8. *Ibid.*
9. William K. Selden, "Basic Issues in Accreditation of Teacher Education," *Liberal Education,* 47:542–544 (December 1961).
10. Koerner, *op. cit.,* p. 236.
11. *Ibid.,* pp. 234–237.
12. NCATE *Standards and Guide* (1960 Edition), p. 6.
13. D. B. Stuit, "Accreditation: Its Problems and Future," *Teachers College Record,* 62:633.
14. Conant, *The Education of American Teachers,* p. 22; Conant, *The Certification of Teachers,* pp. 13–16.
15. Bob Burton Brown, "Issues in the NCATE Controversy," *American Teacher Magazine,* 48:10, December 1963.
16. Selden, "Basic Issues," p. 544.
17. *Report on the NCATE Conference of One Hundred* (Washington, 1964), pp. 40, 41.
18. Brown, *loc. cit.*
19. Selden, "Basic Issues," cited above, p. 545; Stiles, "Wisconsin's Challenge to NCATE," cited in Chapter 5, above. For the NCATE rationale, see W. E. Armstrong, "Regional and Professional Accreditation," *Liberal Education,* 48:234–242 (May 1962).
20. Cited in Roy J. Deferrari, *Self-Evaluation and Accreditation in Higher Education* (Washington, D. C., 1959), p. 262.
21. *Ibid.*

CHAPTER 7

SOME SPECIAL PROBLEMS IN ACCREDITATION IN TEACHER EDUCATION

A NUMBER of the basic problems in accreditation in teacher education have been discussed in the earlier chapters of this Study. Among these are the various problems associated with the organization, the standards, and the procedures in accreditation. For the most part, these are problems common to accreditation at all levels and by all accrediting bodies. In addition to these general problems of accreditation, there are several which are in large measure more commonly associated with teacher education. They include the following:

The magnitude of the problem

The financial problem

The problem of securing the recognition of the profession

The problem of giving status to professional courses

The problem of overlapping jurisdiction in accreditation

The problem of restricting the national accrediting agency's jurisdiction over certain aspects of professional programs

The problem of the proper place of the liberal arts in the accreditation of professional programs

The problem of accrediting specialized areas in the profession

The problem of standards for different types of institutions

As these problems are discussed in this chapter, the subheadings are generally related directly to teacher education.

MAGNITUDE OF THE PROBLEM

This problem stems from two sources: (1) The potential number of institutions and programs to be accredited; and (2) the large segment of the total institutional program involved in teacher education. Out of a total of nearly 1,500 degree-granting institutions in the United States no less than 1,173 are reported as offering teacher education programs. After a decade of active operation, NCATE had an accredited list (November, 1964) of 422 teacher education institutions.[1] For general institutional accreditation, the 1,500 degree-granting institutions are distributed among six regional accrediting associations, averaging 250 for each association. True, the 1,500 institutions are not divided equally among the six regional associations; actually none has any number of institutions of higher education as great as the potential number to be accredited in teacher education.

In contrast with the 1,173 institutions for teacher education, the approximate number of institutions with professional programs or courses in corresponding areas is as follows:

Architecture	75	Law	160
Art	500	Library Science	277
Business	600	Medicine	87
Dentistry	47	Music	235
Engineering	271	Nursing	180
Forestry	28	Pharmacy	77
Journalism	46	Social Work	150
Landscape Architecture	17	Theology	150
	Veterinary Medicine	18	

Most of the accrediting agencies in these areas, including teacher education, also have the responsibility of making periodic reaccreditation evaluations; here again the problem in teacher education greatly exceeds that of other professional or regional agencies.

The second contributing factor to the magnitude of the accrediting problem in teacher education is the broad segment of the total institutional program involved in teacher education. In addition to courses in education and in student teaching, teacher education includes the broad area of general education, most of the subject-matter disciplines, and even parts of programs in agriculture, business, fine arts, home economics, and industrial arts. It is true that, by agreement with the National Commission on Accrediting and the regional accrediting associations, NCATE is not permitted to accredit subject-matter disciplines, but even here the pattern of offerings is examined. Regardless of how the area of teacher education has been restricted, the problem of accreditation in this field vastly overshadows that confronting any other existing accrediting body.

FINANCIAL PROBLEM

Almost from its inception, NCATE has been handicapped by inadequate financial resources. The original budget of $45,000 was in no

---

[1] The 1962 Teacher Supply and Demand Report indicated that approximately 70 percent of the new teachers, produced in 1961, were graduated from an NCATE-accredited institution. A similar report on the new teachers, produced in 1964, will be available in the spring of 1965.

way commensurate with the magnitude of the task confronting the Council. The 1964 budget of $138,500 was still inadequate for the additional activities and services which NCATE was urged to assume. Among these proposed activities and services were orientation sessions for inexperienced NCATE visiting team members, more frequent and more detailed information bulletins to member institutions, and staff visits to campuses of institutions already accredited or requesting accreditation.

In the 1964 NCATE budget, NEA was to contribute $42,000, roughly 36 percent of the total of $138,500; AACTE was allocated $36,000, approximately 31 percent; visitation fees were expected to produce $29,500, just over 25 percent; and the remaining 8 percent, or $9,500, was to come from sustaining fees, state departments of education, and the American Association of School Administrators (AASA). If, as the National Commission on Accrediting and others have insisted, a controlling majority of NCATE should represent the institutions in which teachers are educated, it could also be recommended that such institutions should bear the brunt of the Council's expenses. As of 1964, AACTE, representing teacher-training institutions, contributed less than one-third of the total NCATE budget, while the teaching profession through NEA contributed approximately 36 percent. The $36,000 to be contributed by AACTE represented 18½ percent of the dues collected from member institutions. [1]

According to some estimates a budget of at least half a million dollars would be required for NCATE to sustain the staff and services in keeping with potential and justifiable responsibilities. Financing a budget less than one-third as large as this has proven to be difficult.

RECOGNIZING TEACHING AS A PROFESSION

In every university, and even in the separately established college, there is a conflict between those of the faculty who are members of a discipline and those who are members of a profession. The departments representing disciplines usually comprise a faculty of arts and sciences. . . . It is in these subject-matter areas that much "pure" research is carried on to advance knowledge.

The professional departments usually comprise the professional colleges and schools where the educational objective is more narrowly directed to instruction of students in the technique and skill of applying knowledge to practical problems of everyday life. [2]

The statement just quoted is a generalization which includes all professions, not alone the teaching profession. The latter, however, differs from other professions in that a considerable segment of the population harbors serious reservations as to whether teaching is a true profession. This difference of opinion was illustrated in one of the small group discussions at the Conference of One Hundred, November, 1963, in Chicago. [3] A professor of biology at a large university precipitated the discussion by asking whether teaching is a "profession." A number of the discussants defended, with both fervor and conviction, teaching as a profession. Others agreed that under present circumstances there are at least two reasons why teaching cannot be called a profession. One is the possibility that a housewife might be called from her kitchen at any time to fill a teaching vacancy. The other is that there is no specific body of subject matter that all teachers are required to complete (college teachers are not required to take professional education courses).

Conant reports that "teaching groups and their allies (usually state departments)" insist that all who enter teaching should have completed a prescribed sequence of professional courses, just as lawyers and physicians must satisfy professional course requirements. Conant goes on to say: "In essence, the argument is that public school teachers, in order to be regarded as professionals, must be in possession of some esoteric body of knowledge that sets them apart from those laymen whose general education is equivalent to theirs, or in some cases more extensive. Quite obviously the only esoteric body of knowledge available to distinguish the teacher from other well-educated people is that provided in professional education courses." [4]

In a further discussion of this point, Conant reports that he and his colleagues were told many times that leaders in teachers associations believe:

1. There exists a body of principles that can be taught and which will make an individual a better teacher.
2. The requirement of special training of all public school teachers will serve to attract people of high quality to teaching.
3. Training in professional education serves as a "badge of unity" for members of a teachers association.
4. Specialized training can serve as a protective shield for teachers in dealing with parents.

Conant does not say categorically whether he thinks teaching is or is not a profession; but in his subsequent attacks on the quality of professional education courses, he may have added to the doubt in some minds.

The most cogent expression of faith in teaching as a profession is to be found in the report of the task force on New Horizons in Teacher Education and Professional Standards. [5] Here is also to be found the most determined move to attack the doubters "head on," and to make teaching even more professional. In Chapter 2, the "Teaching Profession" is defined. The chapter begins by recognizing 2,125,000 members of the profession in 1961. These include teachers in public and private elementary and secondary schools, as well as in colleges and universities, school administrators and school specialists, professional staff members in professional organizations, private agencies, and government. A professional is defined as:

An individual who qualifies as a professional, regardless of the particular profession of which he is a part.

A liberally educated person.

Possessing a body of specialized skills and knowledge related to and essential for the performance of his function.

Able to make rational judgments and to take appropriate action within the scope of his activities, and responsible for the consequences of his judgments and actions.

Placing primary emphasis upon his service to society rather than upon his personal gain.

Actively participating with his colleagues in developing and enforcing standards fundamental to continuous improvement in his profession and abiding by those standards in his own practice.

Practicing his profession on a full-time basis.

Engaging in a continuing search for new knowledge and skill.

This is a rather persuasive list, and even though there is no consensus or supporting research for "the body of specialized skills and knowledge," many thoughtful people can find in the *New Horizons* statement sufficient common ground with teachers to recognize teaching as a profession. These people may recognize that many teachers are not very professional; for that matter by this definition, the same might be said of some members of every other profession. However, appealing to the American faith that improvement can be brought about if the resolution is sufficiently great, many see the advantage of now recognizing teaching as a profession.

Most individuals who recognize teaching as a profession regard college faculties as members of the profession. For example, college teachers like to think of themselves as chemists, historians, or linguists, although many of them also consider themselves teachers or educators. The authors of the *New Horizons* report did include college faculty members, and even went so far as to recommend a requirement in "professional" experience for teachers on the college level. Some states require professional education courses for junior college teachers. But the suggestion in the *New Horizons* report of a professional education requirement for college teachers created such indignation that many normally thoughtful people have rejected the entire report and project, possibly without giving the rest of the report the attention it deserves.

The issue of the relation to accreditation of a required sequence of professional courses for members of a profession, and the fact that for college teachers there is no required sequence comparable to that for pre-college-level teachers, is considered by some to be an extremely critical factor. At the moment, there appears to be little likelihood that professional education courses will ever be required of college teachers. However, there is a growing interest in higher education in the development of other ways in which college teaching can be improved and teachers prepared specifically for college teaching.

In accepting NCATE as a professional accrediting agency, the National Commission on Accrediting gave tacit recognition to teaching as a profession. In its efforts to encourage improvement in NCATE, the NCA has hoped to strengthen programs for the education of teachers and the profession of teaching as well. Once teaching has achieved general recognition as a *bona fide* profession, it will still face the common problem with other professions in achieving equal status with the academic disciplines. This in itself is a formidable, though fortunately not an impossible, task.

> The disciplines tend to regard themselves as the elite of the university faculty and to look down upon their professional colleagues. Partly this attitude reflects a belief that professional faculties are too much concerned with technique and method in professional practice and too little concerned with basic knowledge. Partly this attitude reflects a belief that professional faculties are largely composed of poor scholars, that is, of persons with an inadequate mastery of a subject-matter field. It is often pointed out that the great advances in medicine, for example, result from the research efforts of chemists and biologists rather than of doctors. [6]

Needless to say, the professions are not without prejudices of their own. They tend on their part to regard academicians as dwellers in ivory towers who have a completely unrealistic and impractical approach to the hard facts of life and society. Such prejudices are strengthened by irresponsible remarks about the other, by both segments of the academic community.

Fortunately, there is some evidence of improved relations between academicians and professionals:

> In recent years, one of the outstanding developments in higher education in the United States has been the increasingly high degree of collaboration between the disciplines and the professions. . . .
>
> A part of this growing collaboration has come about as a result of the increased competence in a discipline on the part of many professional faculty members. [7]

Many examples may be cited of this growing collaboration. In engineering there is increasing specialization in such academic disciplines as chemistry, mathematics, and physics. As a result engineering is becoming more and more a research discipline. In business there is a growing area of research in economics and social psychology. In medicine there is extensive research in such areas as genetics and physics. In education, there is need of more research in such areas as economics, psychology, public administration, and public finance. Here the confrontation of the academic disciplines and the professional staffs is found on a much larger number of campuses than is the case with any other professional field. Also the cleavage here may be more deep-seated than between academic disciplines and any of the other professions.

The situation in general is that:

> There continues to be an essential difference between the disciplines and the professional schools. The disciplines concentrate upon advancing subject-matter competence in a specialized field of learning. The professional schools concentrate upon advancing the competence of persons to solve practical problems utilizing all available and appreciable fields of knowledge. . . .
>
> The disciplines and the professions are both essential to our concept of higher education in American society, and some means for their fruitful collaboration must be found in each university. [8]

GIVING STATUS TO COURSES IN EDUCATION

Professional education courses are subjected to much criticism. This criticism stems from a variety of sources—from students, from in-service teachers, and from academic disciplines. The most common criticisms relate to their repetitious content, their duplication of material—both on the same level and between undergraduate and graduate levels—and their lack of substance in general. Conant reports that in his visits to campuses, as well as in conferences with administrators, faculty, graduate and undergraduate students, he has found a consensus on the value of the student teaching experience, but on none of the formal education courses required of prospective teachers.

In all fairness it must be admitted that criticisms are sometimes heard about other courses. Among the non-education courses most frequently downgraded are those in psychology, sociology, and some of the other social sciences (more rarely including government and history). The same is true of technical or professional courses in other fields, such as commerce, engineering, or home economics. Here, however, the criticisms are more "spotty" from campus to campus and, when made, often refer to courses taught by certain, but by no means all, instructors on a given campus.

College students in general, as well as those in teacher education, are also critical of other courses in the academic disciplines—in history, literature, mathematics, science, and others—and of the teachers in charge of such courses. But there is a difference. The difference is that it is accepted public judgment, and particularly the judgment of higher education, that history, literature, mathematics, and science are important and worthy of high respect. The student or his parents have paid "good money" to enable him to see and hear the scholar, even though he may not understand him, and despite the fact that the scholar may have little or no interest in the student. It is part of our culture to respect academic courses and scholars, at least while in college. On the contrary, it is not in our culture to respect education courses and surely not sufficiently in our culture to respect teachers, and it might even be said not sufficiently in our culture to respect teaching.

Professional educators are aware of the criticisms of their courses, as well as of student resentment at being required to take them, and as a rule do not try to deny their validity. In professional organizations and circles many voices are demanding that undergraduate education courses be made more substantial and that every effort be expended to develop the field as a sound discipline. As examples, the *New Horizons* report emphasized the necessity for experimentation to improve professional education courses [9] (see Appendix IX), and specific proposals for the remaking of the professional sequences are being developed by the Teacher Education and New Media Project of AACTE. [*10*]

It is significant that experienced teachers frequently report finding more meaning and value in education courses after having had teaching experience. Consequently, one recommendation is that undergraduate courses be kept to a maximum of two, or possibly only one. Efforts to introduce laboratory experiences, school visitation, and pupil counseling at a lower level and as part of the education courses seem to have resulted in some improvement, provided the laboratory experiences are carefully planned and supervised. Too often, because of staff inadequacies in numbers and qualifications, they are not. To some observers education courses offered in fifth-year programs to liberal arts graduates appear to be more satisfactory than those offered at the undergraduate level.

Recently some voices are optimistic about a possible new status for professional education. Observing that we are moving into a time when education will become one of our major occupations, John Walton concludes that "education can and will become one of the most intellectually exciting disciplines in the curriculum of higher education." [*11*] Walton builds his case on analogy with the study of government in the discipline of political science; commerce, under economics; and community organizations, under sociology. In answer to the question of why we do not now have such a discipline, he points out two reasons: Those in education have exhausted their energies in professional training of teachers in arriving at urgent solutions to practical classroom problems, and the reluctance on the part of other disciplines to accept a new discipline about the school and university that might carry more weight than their cherished opinions.

A trend toward acceptance of professional training in England has been pointed out. In 1961 Sir David Eccles, Minister of Education, announced that as soon as conditions permitted all certified teachers in England must have professional training. Harry K. Hutton in an article on "Compulsory Professional Training in England" emphasizes that this is no "precipitate action" and that "it was simply official concurrence in professional and public opinion." [*12*] It was a Conservative Minister who made the announcement and many are waiting to see if Labour will decide that conditions now permit its implementation. England is one of the few countries in which teachers with university degrees are not required to have professional training.

Those who express lack of confidence in accreditation call attention to what they believe are two points of vulnerability in the accreditation of teacher education relative to professional courses as it is currently practiced. One is the emphasis on professional education by the states which frequently implement the emphasis by specific course and credit-hour requirements. The other is the over-emphasis on the professional education sequence by the national agency.

THE PROBLEM OF OVERLAPPING JURISDICTION IN ACCREDITATION

As the American pattern of accreditation has evolved, with three separate levels upon which accrediting machinery operates—national, regional, and state—a resulting problem is overlapping jurisdiction. This problem is not peculiar to teacher education, but there seems to be no question that it is more extensive and a more acute problem in this area. There may be some overlapping of jurisdiction between regional associations and national professional agencies when the regional includes the professional program in its total institution evaluation. There is also some overlapping jurisdiction between the regional association and the state. This is particularly true in those states having general institutional accreditation, but it is also true to some extent in teacher education. In some of the areas served by the regional associations, the problem is relieved to some extent by encouraging or requiring joint visitations or by placing a "generalist" on the professional visiting team. [13]

There are a number of reasons why the problem of overlapping jurisdiction in accreditation of teacher education is more serious: (1) Teacher education programs exist in a larger number of higher institutions than any other professional program; (2) the states are more vitally concerned with teacher education than perhaps with any other professional field of training; (3) there is a definite possibility that conflicting or contradictory decisions or policies will be made; and (4) jurisdictional conflicts may occur at either the undergraduate or the graduate level.

Fortunately there have not been many conspicuous examples of clear-cut conflicting or contradictory decisions in the accrediting of teacher education. One state reported a sharp enough difference between state requirements and what an institution interpreted to be a requirement of NCATE that the institution concluded it could not qualify for approval by both agencies. Since the state represents the only legal authority in accreditation, in case such a conflict occurs, the institution which is caught in the middle would appear to have no choice but to conform to the state requirement. An experience such as this might very well raise doubts in the minds of institution leaders about the value and significance of accreditation.

In Chapter 2 attention is called to a recently passed resolution of the Council of Chief State School Officers reaffirming its belief in the importance to the states of national accreditation. As reported in Chapter 3, there is considerable variation among the states in their enthusiasm for and dependence upon NCATE. For example, those in teacher education in the New York department feel that they "do not need NCATE," while in other states, such as Iowa and Kentucky, NCATE accreditation is held in high esteem.

It would appear at this point that there is much greater danger and likelihood of conflicting decisions in graduate accreditation than there is on the undergraduate level. This is partly because accrediting agencies have moved rather recently into this area, plus the fact that they are tending to move on all three levels—national, regional, and state—at the same time. Already, there have been instances of regional association approval of doctoral programs in teacher education, with a subsequent unfavorable decision by NCATE.

It has been suggested that an agreement might be negotiated between NCATE and the regionals whereby the regional will accredit an institution as qualified to give doctoral work without respect to specific areas or programs, leaving the professional agency to evaluate and approve each program. It is hoped that the recently created Council of Graduate Schools will be instrumental in resolving this problem.

NCATE'S RESTRICTED JURISDICTION

Discussed elsewhere in this Study were the circumstances under which NCATE agreed to rely upon regional evaluation of academic departments in the accreditation of teacher education: qualifications of the faculty, the quality of instruction, and the library and laboratory facilities (see Chapter 5). A number of contradictory reasons have been offered as an explanation of this agreement. One is that NCATE preferred not to evaluate the academic departments, hence asked the regional associations to assume the responsibility. Another is that the regional associations were determined that NCATE would not encroach on what they regarded as their sphere of activity. A third is that the National Commission on Accrediting was convinced that NCATE accreditation of academic departments would precipitate further conflict between academicians and professional educators. Still another reason given is that, when others proposed this restriction, NCATE readily accepted it in the beginning because of the magnitude of the task faced and the Council's limited financial resources.

Be that as it may, the arrangement has been a potent source of misunderstanding and criticism of national accreditation. Under its rules of procedure, the national agency will not evaluate a teacher education institution without its first being accredited by the regional association having jurisdiction over the particular area. It then assumes, without actual rechecking, that in terms of quality any academic departments involved in teacher education are above criticism or at least not in its province to criticize.

This assumption may not be well-founded for at least two reasons. One possibility is that a particular department was recognized as being weak at the time of the regional evaluation, but, because most of the departments were judged to be of acceptable quality, the one or two weak departments were blanketed in under general institutional accreditation. A second possibility is that a particular department was acceptable at the time of the regional approval but in succeeding years the department had deteriorated. It may be that the departmental staff had been depleted by retirement or resignation of staff members and the inability of the institution to attract strong or even competent replacements. Graduates of the teacher education program of such an institution, accredited by both the regional and national agencies including the majors of departments which are weak academically, may be certified by their own state and provisionally by more than half the states through reciprocity. The question is who is at fault under such circumstances for the certification of a graduate in teacher education from an academically weak department. The answer is that, under the present arrangement between NCATE and the regionals, NCATE scarcely can be held responsible for graduates of low-quality departments; yet many critics of NCATE try to pin the responsibility for such an occurrence upon NCATE.

ROLE OF THE LIBERAL ARTS IN ACCREDITATION OF TEACHER EDUCATION

Partly because of its agreements with the regional associations, NCATE in its accrediting functions gives its major attention to, and thus bases its accreditation in considerable part on, the professional education aspect of teacher education. In general, this aspect is also emphasized in accreditation of teacher education by the states. Such emphasis is made despite the fact that at the undergraduate level ordinarily not more than 20 percent of the prospective teacher's program involves professional courses. This attention to professional education on the part of state and national accrediting agencies is a source of considerable concern to many thoughtful people, including laymen, academicians, and those professionally involved in teacher education. However, they should realize that this situation may explain how an institution of higher learning that is weak in the sciences, in the humanities, or in the qualifications of the student body and staff, may still be accredited. Such an institution, sometimes a former teachers college, may have a very strong education program which may quite adequately measure up to accreditation standards, while some of the academic departments are woefully inadequate.

Teacher education and professional education are, of course, not the same thing, as the term "professional education" is commonly used.

For an accrediting agency to appear to be primarily concerned with professional education gives an erroneous view of teacher education to the public, to the schools, and to higher institutions. Staff members of academic departments of higher education are already too willing to leave professional education to the professional educators. For an accrediting team to try to evaluate an institution without becoming acquainted with its fine scholars, its inspiring teachers, its laboratories and libraries is to make a travesty of both teacher education and accreditation. Many consider this restriction on NCATE's jurisdiction to be one of NCATE's serious shortcomings.

Greater awareness of this shortcoming of accreditation in teacher education has resulted from the increased interest in pre-college-level programs and related teacher education on the part of the scientific and other learned societies and of their members. This new and potentially great interest probably started with mathematics and science, when unprecedented major efforts in the improvement of course content by teams of scientists and teachers were made possible by Federal support through the National Science Foundation. Now, with some support in the social sciences from the National Science Foundation, and with more from the U. S. Office of Education, and from private foundations, these efforts are being extended to the social sciences and the humanities. Originally concerned with high school education, these efforts in many cases are being directed to course improvement in the elementary schools and in higher institutions.

Frank Laycock of Oberlin refers to these efforts as "harbingers" of a new relationship between what he calls the two "houses of education in America." Laycock here refers to the scholars and professional educators in higher education. "Happily, in recent years," says Laycock, "there has been increased, if halting, conversation." [14] This new dialogue provides a basis on which the academicians, through their national professional societies, might become involved in the accreditation of teacher education.

Those interested in greater participation by academicians in teacher education, as well as in its accreditation, will welcome the recent changes in the bylaws of the American Association of Colleges for Teacher Education (AACTE). In an effort to provide for a broader representation of its 661 institutional members, AACTE at its 1964 annual meeting amended its bylaws to provide for the official participation in the organization of three representatives (instead of one) from each member institution. One of the representatives is to be a general administrative officer of the member institution (usually the president, except in large multipurpose institutions in which case it is often the dean of the college or school of education). The two additional representatives "shall be persons broadly interested in teacher education and shall be designated so that the teaching fields as well as professional education are represented." This change in organization and policy was partly in recognition of the growing number of liberal arts colleges in its membership and partly in recognition of the all-institutional responsibility for teacher education. The 1964 roster of institutional representatives revealed 22 teaching fields, other than education, currently represented by active participation in the AACTE program.

In addition, the selection of AACTE representatives on NCATE was to be made by mail ballot of the 1,983 representatives of the member institutions. For the 1965 election, the voting was set up in such a way that one of the representatives would have to be from a liberal arts college. The two nominees for this post were C. W. Sorenson, president of Augustana College (Illinois), and Bruce Thomas, dean, Trinity University (Texas). Sorenson is a former professor of geography and Thomas of English.

In one of the conferences held as part of this Study, representatives of the staffs of the national learned and scientific societies discussed the possible roles of their societies in the accreditation process. The conference participants demonstrated a genuine interest in accreditation and a desire to play a role of importance comparable to the role that the disciplines or fields which they represented have in teacher education. There was consensus in favor of the principle of national accreditation, as well as a consensus that the societies should develop cooperation with the state departments of education in a more direct approach to the improvement of teacher education. They applauded the AAAS-NASDTEC studies recently supported by the Carnegie Corporation of New York [15] and the plans which are under way to extend these efforts to the foreign languages and English with the assistance of the United States Office of Education.

The participants agreed that their societies should refrain from an active role in national accreditation of teacher education, so long as existing restrictions on national accreditation relative to subject-matter departments were maintained. On the assumption that these restrictions need not, and in the public interest should not, be continued, the discussants explored ways in which their societies might make constructive contributions to the accreditation process. It was suggested that, in the event achievement examinations were to become a factor in accreditation, the societies might assume responsibility for the preparation of tests in the academic disciplines. They should also have a major part in the development of standards for general or liberal education. Too, their members might take part in accreditation visits, as well as in the committee evaluation of reports, or even be appointed to the NCATE staff, possibly on leave-of-absence appointments. The conference participants also suggested that the societies might be represented on a national accrediting agency in teacher education, either through inclusive organizations such as AAAS or ACLS (American Council of Learned Societies), or by a rotation process in which, for a one-year term or longer, three or four societies might name representatives to be followed in rotation by a similar number of other societies.

The length of the conference did not permit the actual formulation of resolutions. The discussions have been reviewed at this length as evidence of the interest of participants and, so far as they were able to reflect them, of their societies in teacher education and in national accreditation thereof in a positive, constructive spirit of cooperation. This suggests another harbinger of what might be, as well as of things to come.

ACCREDITATION OF SPECIALIZED FIELDS IN TEACHER EDUCATION

In all professional accreditation, questions arise and criticisms are heard about the amount of attention that should be given to specialized fields within a particular profession. Teacher education is no exception. Indeed, there may be greater difficulties here in this respect than in any of the other professions. The questions arise not only with respect to the subject the secondary school teacher will teach, but also within a school or department of education.

There are no fewer than 19 departments in a liberal arts college within a multipurpose university, and there may be as many in a single-purpose college, which offer majors for secondary school teachers.[2] Each of these disciplines is potentially a specialized field in teacher education. In addition, members of an academic department are often members of a national professional society of their discipline which may have a committee concerning itself with the preparation of secondary school teachers in that discipline.

Apart from the academic disciplines, there are agriculture, business education, and home economics (often housed outside the college or school of education), and health education, industrial education, physical education (men's and women's), and recreation (usually found in the college or school of education). Many of these groups also have separate programs for the preparation of elementary teachers and even of junior high school teachers. Thus, there is also an issue of level of instruction. Certification authorities have faced a similar problem with some state departments having met it by issuing more than 50 varieties of certificates. A more recent practice has been to issue fewer kinds of certificates, designating the certificate by level, and then endorsing it for a particular subject or group of subjects. As an example, under this plan a teacher might receive a secondary school certificate endorsed for French or mathematics.

NCATE has separate standards for only one special field—school administration. This is recognized as a field for graduate study, and special consideration is given to it in the accreditation of graduate

---

[2] The following departments should be considered: anthropology, art, biology (often botany and zoology), chemistry, economics, English, French, geography (both social and physical), geology, German, government, history, Latin, mathematics, music, physics, psychology, sociology, and Spanish.

programs. Other fields of education which also are interested in somewhat similar special attention include: curriculum, educational psychology, guidance, higher education, social foundations, special education (blind, deaf, gifted, mentally retarded), and supervision. As an example of the kinds of difficulty which occur, a representative of a non-NCATE-accredited university asked the American Association for Health, Physical Education, and Recreation (an affiliate of NEA) to discontinue the listing of NCATE-approved institutions in its publication by virtue of the fact that NCATE accreditation did not consider health, physical education, and recreation programs. This request was approved at the 1964 annual meeting of the Association (AAHPER).

Consideration of this impressive array of specialties in teacher education comprises a major task for any accrediting agency, or for a cooperative effort among accrediting agencies at the three levels. Yet, so long as no attention is paid to them, there will be some who think that accreditation is inadequate and perhaps unfair.

THE PROBLEM OF STANDARDS FOR DIFFERENT TYPES OF INSTITUTIONS

One of the frequent criticisms of NCATE is that the Council attempts to apply the same criteria or standards and procedures to all three types of institutions of higher learning. These three types are liberal arts colleges, teachers colleges, and multipurpose universities. In elaborating this criticism, critics insist that the criteria or standards applied to all higher institutions in reality are an outgrowth of the single-purpose teachers college concept. Since the number of teachers colleges is decreasing, this concept is said to be largely outmoded. The obvious implication of this criticism is that there are certain basic differences between any two of the three categories or types of institutions, and that these differences justify or necessitate using different standards or criteria in evaluating their teacher education programs.

In response to these criticisms, it is argued that the same basic ingredients should go into the education of an elementary teacher, regardless of the type of institution in which the training occurs. There are said to be more justifiable variables based on the type of school in which the prospective teacher will teach—large or small, departmentalized or non-departmentalized, rural or urban, children from deprived or affluent families—than on the type of institution in which the teacher education occurs. It is recognized, of course, that the type of school in which the teaching will ultimately occur cannot be reliably anticipated, whereas the type of school in which the education of the teacher occurs can be.

INSTITUTIONAL PHILOSOPHIES

Teachers colleges traditionally have emphasized good teaching on the part of the faculty and have placed less emphasis upon research—

basic or applied. In these colleges, departments of education have tended to be the largest and most influential of the departments, the presidents and deans have often been selected from professional education personnel or school administrators, and even the courses in academic departments have been adjusted to the supposed needs of prospective teachers. Most importantly, the staff members have been chosen as persons with a deep interest in teacher education rather than primarily because of their interest in scholarship and research. Actually, as most of the former teachers colleges have become state colleges, these emphases are being replaced by those more traditionally characteristic of a liberal arts college.

Liberal arts colleges have tended to place some, but not necessarily equal, emphasis on both teaching and research. In employing a member of the teaching staff, a liberal arts college is likely to select a good teacher who is research-minded in preference to one who is a good teacher but not interested in doing research. Liberal arts colleges have tended to choose as staff members and administrators persons recognized for, or giving promise of, scholarship and high cultural standards. It has often been considered that courses in academic departments in liberal arts colleges which in any way were "professionalized for teacher education" were courses of low standard.

A large, multipurpose university in selecting faculty members almost certainly places greater emphasis on research achievements or potential than on teaching ability. This is illustrated in the frequently voiced complaint that in a large university good teaching goes largely unrewarded in terms of salary increases or promotions, whereas research and publication are the surest and quickest avenue to professional advancement. This emphasis has existed in the schools of education of multipurpose universities as well as in other colleges of the university. Courses outside professional education are too often planned with primary emphasis on the needs of prospective graduate students. While the existence of graduate programs in education may have an effect upon the undergraduate program in education, the undergraduate courses are less often planned as preparation for graduate study. Indeed, it is said by some that such undergraduate courses are not prerequisite for graduate courses in education because of the overlapping content of education courses at the two levels.

There are some who believe that graduates of teachers colleges are more successful during the first few years of their teaching experience than are graduates of state universities or liberal arts colleges; however, that after four or five years of classroom experience the liberal arts and the university graduates tend to be better teachers. The explanation given is that the major emphasis in teachers colleges is in preparing the inexperienced for his job as a first-year teacher; while at the university or liberal arts college the lesser emphasis given to professional education and student teaching and the greater emphasis to scholarly study paid off after the new teacher had learned "the hard way" through his own experience.

Some of the differences of opinion on what should go into a teacher education program may be due to a difference of objective—namely, preparing the teacher to enter the classroom the first time, or preparing him for a lifetime of scholarly pursuit as well as teaching, which should characterize the professional in teaching. This difference in objective, however, is often not identified as a basis for disagreement.

While there still are philosophical differences among the three types of higher institutions, it is significant that important modifications are taking place. The teachers colleges, in most cases no longer single-purpose institutions, are drawing closer to the philosophy of the liberal arts college. Many of the liberal arts colleges see a place of greater importance for teacher education, perhaps because of the new interest of the learned societies in pre-college course-content and teacher education. Note that the theme of the 1965 annual meeting of the Association of American Colleges was the education of teachers. At the same time, the departments of education in multipurpose universities may be giving only secondary attention to the undergraduate teacher education program and primary attention to graduate programs and research.

If one assumes that these philosophical or "climatic" differences exist among the types of institutions engaged in teacher education, the next question is whether or not they should be reflected in different standards or criteria for each type of institution. Of course, there are differences of opinion on this issue. Many persons representing a variety of fields of special interest suggest that, rather than trying to apply different criteria to each type of higher institution, the more practical approach is to develop and apply standards which are broad enough and flexible enough to be readily adaptable to any and all types of undergraduate teacher education programs.

LEVEL OF PROGRAMS

A second possible accreditation differential among different types of teacher education institutions is that based upon the level of teacher education provided—whether undergraduate only, graduate only, or both undergraduate and graduate. With greatly increased Federal and private foundation support for research in education, and with the accompanying increased prestige for the school of education and its staff among their university colleagues, in a great university like Wisconsin or Stanford, the graduate work and related research are what count in a school of education. And like the department of chemistry or history, the department of education recognizes that its reputation is based upon its graduate, not its undergraduate, program.

Thus a new question arises: Does research in learning and teaching, in guidance and school administration, contribute to making undergraduate courses in education more exciting, and undergraduate programs of teacher education more imaginative and more efficient? The answer should be "Yes." Then does this suggest use of different standards for institutions with graduate work and those without? How shall the four-year colleges maintain high-quality teacher education? It is suggested that they can do this by studying and adapting to what the universities do. This would not necessarily be new. Universities have often claimed that their undergraduate programs set the standards for the smaller colleges in their states; and this claim was heard again in visits to universities as part of this Study. It would only be honest to say that representatives of colleges when asked what factors influenced their programs usually did not mention the programs of the major universities of their state or other states. They did, however, often mention research.

While the presence of graduate programs leading to the doctorate in education—which must necessarily be supported by research—may have an influence on the undergraduate teacher education program, not many individuals propose that a different set of standards be applied in accrediting the undergraduate teacher education program of institutions offering the highest degree in education. Rather, it is proposed that different considerations are necessary in accrediting the graduate programs.

Accreditation machinery in the United States was originally designed for secondary schools and undergraduate colleges. Both were multiplying at a rapid rate with scant regard for uniform or even minimum standards. Today, one of the most spectacular areas of curriculum explosion is in graduate work. Not only is the number of advanced degrees conferred increasing rapidly, but comparatively speaking so is the number of institutions conferring advanced degrees. [16] This proliferation of programs has been encouraged by the Federal government through the fellowship program of the National Defense Education Act, [17] as well as through other forms of Federal support. It is also encouraged by the competition among educational institutions for graduate students, faculty, and prestige. Both faculty and graduate students appear to show a growing reluctance to join a school where doctoral work is not offered. As a result, ambitious and aggressive colleges and universities are tempted to move into advanced programs before they are adequately prepared to do so.

The rapid expansion of graduate work created at least a temporary vacuum in the field of accreditation. All three levels of accreditation—state, regional, and national—have gradually moved into the vacuum thus created. Many of the states as well as the regional associations, in general institutional accreditation, evaluate programs through the doctorate. NCATE and some of the states accredit teacher education programs through the doctorate. As long as the various accrediting bodies act separately and independently in their accreditation procedures, there is always the possibility of conflicting or contradictory actions or decisions.

The Council of Graduate Schools in the United States (COGS) was formed through a federation of several existing regional graduate organizations—notably midwestern, southern, and western. While it was recognized that much good could be accomplished through regional associations of graduate schools, it was also realized that much more might be achieved through a national organization. Particularly to be desired was the establishment of uniformly high standards in graduate work throughout the United States.

At the outset the Council of Graduate Schools did not take an active interest in the accreditation of graduate work. However, a committee on accreditation has now been named to formulate recommendations in this area. While insisting that it does not wish to assume the role of an accrediting body, COGS now quite obviously wishes to have a voice in determining the policies and procedures employed in the accreditation of graduate programs. Up to this point at least, this appears to many to be a desirable and legitimate objective. Other issues related to the accreditation of graduate work will be discussed in the next chapter.

REFERENCES

1. *Report on the NCATE Conference of One Hundred*, November 14, 1963 (Washington, D. C., 1964), p. 23.
2. John D. Millett, *The Academic Community* (New York, 1962), p. 97.
3. *Report on the NCATE Conference of One Hundred*, November 14, 1963 (Washington, D. C., 1964).
4. James B. Conant, *The Education of American Teachers*, p. 26.
5. Margaret Lindsey, ed., *New Horizons for the Teaching Profession* (Washington, D. C., 1961).
6. Millett, *op. cit.*, p. 98.
7. *Ibid.*
8. *Ibid.*, pp. 100, 101.
9. Lindsey, *op. cit.*
10. The American Association of Colleges for Teacher Education, "A Proposal for the Revision of the Pre-Service Professional Component of a Program of Teacher Education," *Teacher Education and New Media Project*, prepared by Herbert F. LaGrone, 1964.
11. John Walton, "Education as an Academic Discipline," *School and Society*, 92: No. 2246 (October 3, 1964), pp. 264–266.
12. Harry K. Hutton, "Compulsory Professional Training in England," *School and Society*, 92: No. 2250 (November 28, 1964), pp. 358, 359.
13. Chapter 4, p. 44 of this Study.
14. Frank Laycock, "Division and Dialogue in the House of Learning," *Saturday Review* (September 19, 1964), p. 59.
15. NASDTEC-AAAS Studies, *Guidelines for Science and Mathematics in the Preparation Program of Elementary School Teachers* (Washington, D. C., 1963); *Guidelines for Preparation Programs of Teachers of Secondary School Science and Mathematics* (Washington, D. C., 1961).
16. *Earned Degrees Conferred, 1960–61* (U. S. Office of Education, Washington, D. C., 1963).
17. "National Defense Education Act," *School Life*, 41:27 (January 1959).

CHAPTER 8

THE ACCREDITATION OF GRADUATE WORK

SOME OF THE PROBLEMS associated with graduate-level accreditation are discussed in Chapter 7. These problems stem partly from the rapid expansion in recent years of graduate work on both the master's and doctoral levels. They are also due in part to the simultaneous extension of state, regional, and national accreditation into this important area with resulting overlapping and at least potential conflicts of jurisdiction among the various accrediting agencies.

GRADUATE ACCREDITATION AT THE NATIONAL LEVEL

National accreditation of graduate programs has expanded as teacher education standards and requirements have risen. For many years, teacher education programs did not extend beyond the bachelor's degree. Then the master's degree programs in school administration, in secondary education, and in counseling became common. More recently, master's degree programs in elementary education and the sixth-year programs—two years beyond the bachelor's—were instituted in teacher education. Today doctoral programs in teacher education are common.

Although most Ph.D.'s in subject-matter fields are potential teachers in high schools or public junior colleges as well as in college and university degree programs, NCATE, probably because of its commitment not to accredit academic departments, has no specific standards to be applied to such programs. This leaves doctoral programs in what NCATE calls "school service personnel" as the principal area of doctoral accreditation. At the same time, the American Association of School Administrators, in deciding to restrict its future membership in the Association to those holding graduate degrees from NCATE-approved institutions, has become actively involved in the formulation of standards and procedures in the accrediting of doctoral programs in school administration. At the Association's request, NCATE has permitted the AASA to help prepare NCATE's *Standards and Guide for Accreditation of Programs for the Preparation of School Superintendents and Principals*. It is in this supplement that most of the NCATE references to graduate programs are given. In Standard II, "Organization for Policy Making, Program Planning and Evaluation, and Program Administration," the supplement states:

> An institution that offers graduate work for school administration should have adequate means for making policies, for planning and evaluating the programs, and for administering the different parts. The graduate programs for school superintendents and principals should operate within the framework of the total institutional graduate program. There should be a policy-forming body which deals specifically, though not necessarily exclusively, with the programs for the preparation of superintendents and principals. This body should perform the following functions:
> 1. formulate policies to govern the programs;
> 2. unify and coordinate the parts of the programs that may be offered or controlled by different administrative units;
> 3. plan the curricula;
> 4. evaluate the programs and the products.

Under Standards V and VI, "Curriculum and Laboratory Experiences," NCATE proposes that:

> The graduate curricula offered for superintendents and principals should be established to the extent necessary to assure competence for the positions involved. Each curriculum should contain a required core including courses both in and outside the field of Education which bear an obvious relationship to school administration. Beyond the required core, each curriculum should provide for variations on the basis of differences in student backgrounds and professional goals. When a student brings to a program an inadequate background in general education or in the field of Education, he should be required to make up the deficiency. Provision should be made for both theoretical considerations and the application of them to problems in school administration.
>
> All divisions of an institution outside the field of Education offering work bearing on school administration should have available for use in this curriculum substantial graduate resources including faculty, offerings, and facilities.

NCATE recognizes that:

> Graduate programs are often less structured than undergraduate programs but the spirit of the Standard applies the same for them. The institution should plan a sequence or pattern of basic courses for each curriculum which all persons in that curriculum should take. If the institution wishes to "tailor" a program to the needs of its students rather than to prescribe it, it must then *assume the responsibility for defining the basis for such tailoring* and *demonstrate that the programs which it tailors have a meaningful structure, that*

they *reach desired and defined ends,* and that they are *organized* and *unified* around clear purposes. [1]

In evaluating doctoral programs in teacher education, other than for school administrators, NCATE uses the same seven standards as in undergraduate programs. These standards relate to:

Objectives
Organization and administration
Student personnel programs and services
Faculty for professional education
Curriculum
Professional laboratory experiences
Facilities and instructional materials

When these standards are employed at the graduate level, they are upgraded accordingly. Also at the graduate level as in undergraduate programs, NCATE depends upon the regional associations to certify the quality of academic departments, curriculums, library facilities (other than in education), and general faculty qualifications.

ACCREDITATION OF GRADUATE PROGRAMS BY THE REGIONAL ASSOCIATIONS

All regional associations have given attention to graduate work, but their concern with it as well as their approach to it has varied considerably. Broadly speaking, accreditation of graduate work by the regionals has been somewhat fragmentary. They consider graduate programs in their self-study and in their visitation programs, but with one exception (North Central) they do so as part of the general review of an institution.

The Middle States Association began evaluating graduate programs in 1956. At that time, a pilot study of member institutions was made and out of it developed a procedure for evaluating such programs. As in undergraduate programs, graduate work is judged in terms of its contribution to the fulfillment of the institution's philosophy and objectives. The Association has decided that large visitation teams are not always necessary and that the higher institutions may work with the Association on a project basis. Graduate study is sometimes chosen for this type of evaluation. When a large team evaluation is undertaken, however, one or two members of the team are designated to give particular attention to the graduate program.

The New England Association has only recently moved into the evaluation of graduate programs. A grant from The Ford Foundation enabled Tufts University to evaluate its graduate program, and thus provide a basis for general accreditation policies for graduate schools in the New England area. The Association ordinarily appoints visiting committee chairmen sufficiently early to enable them in cooperation with the institution under review to select team members who can deal most effectively with the major problems of the institution. Graduate schools may thus receive special attention as needed.

The Northwest Association began the accreditation of graduate programs in 1956. The basis of evaluation is the "Guide for Self-Evaluation and Accreditation," originally developed for undergraduate colleges. The team of evaluators judges the graduate program of the institution in terms of the objectives, purposes, and resources for maintaining such a program. Visiting committees give this area special attention, and in the case of doctoral programs a member of the visiting committee is specially designated to deal with the graduate program. NCATE cooperates by supplying competent team members in those cases in which doctoral programs are limited to the field of education.

The Southern Association began accrediting graduate programs in 1949. In that year, the Commission on Institutions of Higher Education recommended the establishment of a Committee on the Accreditation of Graduate Instruction. When the proposal was not accepted by the Association, the Commission proceeded on its own to formulate standards for graduate programs. Under these standards, the programs are evaluated in terms of the resources of the institution, the nature and quality of the graduate instruction, the nature and quality of research, and the quality of students selected. The Association has instructed senior colleges to notify the Association whenever they intend to enter the graduate field. The institutions are expected to submit evidence that they are legally permitted to offer graduate work and to complete a self-study followed by a visitation before offering graduate degrees.

The Southern Association publishes standards for all areas of its work, and a specific standard (17) applies to graduate work. It states that graduate work should not be undertaken unless the undergraduate base of the institution is carefully laid and financial support unusually strong. Training and salaries of graduate faculty should be above average, teaching loads should be less, and library and laboratory facilities and expenditures should be superior. Advanced degrees should be limited in variety and should meet the best recognized standards. In addition, institutions offering the doctorate should be outstandingly strong. A supplementary statement enlarges on these factors and details minimum standards for master's and doctor's degrees. These cover: admissions; resident and language requirements; requirements for candidacy for degrees; thesis and dissertation requirements; major requirements; and written and oral examination requirements. [2]

The Western Association in accrediting graduate schools and graduate programs has followed a pattern closely resembling that of the Northwest Association. Ordinarily, the graduate program is evaluated at the same time as the general institutional evaluation and is judged in terms of the objectives, purposes, and resources for operating the proposed program. The Association obtains information on the administrative organization for graduate work and some detail on the program. This includes: objectives; course work required in terms of units; residence requirements; credit transfer allowances; requirements for thesis or other creative expressions of scholarship. Information about the training and experience of the faculty and the instructional and advisory load is reviewed. Competence to direct research is also to be reported. Admissions of students, standards of scholarship, examinations, and other means of evaluation are to be reported. For degrees beyond the master's, library, laboratories, fellowships, endowments, and grants are to be reported. Concluding this information there is to be a summary of the institution's main strengths and weaknesses.

The North Central Association, since 1949, has been evaluating graduate programs separately when offered by accredited institutions formerly offering only baccalaureate or master's degree programs. Prior to 1949, graduate programs of North Central member institutions were examined along with general institutional evaluation. The present procedure in graduate accreditation is an adaptation of the undergraduate procedure. Those institutions wishing to begin graduate work or to extend it to a new area or new level are required to make a self-survey. The report of the self-study is examined by the Commission on Colleges and Universities. In evaluating all graduate programs, the North Central seeks to answer three main questions: (1) What is the program designed to accomplish? (2) How is it being implemented? (3) How is it being evaluated? Thus in response to the first question, information on the needs and purposes of the program is expected as well as on courses within the program and on research related to the program. Under the second question, information is required on: faculty, funds, students, curriculum, facilities, research, and administrative organization. The third question requires information on the self-evaluation process within the institution.

If the Commission's impression is favorable, the policy has been to wait until a number of candidates have received the new degree or have been graduated from the new program before a team of examiners is sent to the institution. In 1964, North Central decided to require the team visit and official approval to be made before the new program was to be put into effect. The Commission examines the report of the visiting team and either grants or denies accreditation of the program. [3]

STATE ACCREDITATION OF GRADUATE WORK

There are two types of state accreditation of higher institutions or programs. A large number of states limit their accrediting or approval to teacher education programs or institutions. Where this is the case, the most common pattern is to accredit such programs on any and all levels. Usually this function is exercised by the state department of education. It may or may not be the same agency in the state department which certifies teachers. In accrediting graduate programs, some states model their standards and procedures after those of the regional association. Others take their cues from NCATE. Still others combine parts of both.

A second and smaller group of states accredit general institutional status or the total institution. Where this is the case, the two functions of general accreditation and that of teacher education may be exercised by different divisions of the state department. Under general accreditation, all undergraduate and graduate programs would ordinarily be accredited. Most of the states which accredit Ph.D. programs do so as part of general accreditation.

The State of New York appears to have gone further than other states in the regulation of graduate work. The Educational Assistance Authority of the State of New York requires that graduate students, who receive financial assistance under this program, must be enrolled in graduate work that is approved by the proper officials of the New York State Department of Education. To carry out these responsibilities the staff, under the Commissioner of Education, has prepared a statement of "Regulations of the Commissioner of Education Regarding Graduate Work." The statement includes provisions for a number of factors considered important in judging the quality and adequacy of graduate work. These are: purpose, resources, administration, faculty, library, laboratory facilities, admission of students, courses of study, definition of and employment of full-time graduate students, and advisement.

A brief summary of state accreditation of doctoral programs is given in Appendix V.

ACCREDITATION OF GRADUATE WORK BY PROFESSIONAL ACCREDITING AGENCIES

Of the 23 national professional agencies recognized by the National Commission on Accrediting, few could be considered as being involved in the accreditation of graduate work. In fields such as law, medicine, and theology where work is taken beyond the bachelor's degree, the work is classified as "post-graduate," rather than "graduate." In the arts and sciences, there are two professional associations which have undertaken accreditation. These are in chemistry and psychology. To date, the American Chemical Society has not extended its accrediting functions into the graduate level. The American Psychological Association accredits only clinical and counseling psychology and only at the doctoral level.

Although not always included as part of the graduate school in a university, graduate work is now being given in dentistry, engineering, medicine, and social work. The professional associations in these areas, therefore, have been giving more attention to the problems of evaluation. These are examples of areas in which the graduate accreditation vacuum has been only partially filled.

THE IMPACT OF FEDERAL PROGRAMS [6]

Since World War II, the Federal government has become increasingly involved in programs of various kinds which are designed to utilize the services of top-level universities. The typical kind of activity involves the negotiation of contracts for research of different kinds which are conducted by the staff of the university. The staff includes faculty members, individuals employed by special research centers, graduate students, and others.

The sums going to institutions of higher learning are very large, highly concentrated, and growing in amounts. In 1959–1960 more than $900 million was distributed to educational institutions. That year the 25 institutions with the largest total of Federal grants were awarded totals ranging from $5.8 million to $191 million. Still another 50 institutions each had contracts totaling $1,000,000 or more.

The Federal program, in general, covers the following types of activities: (1) financial assistance to students; (2) funds for construction and other capital improvements; (3) grants and contracts for research and development; (4) grants for specialized instructional programs; (5) specific programs for educating Federal employees and military personnel; and (6) international education programs. The Federal agencies with the most extensive programs are the National Institutes of Health (NIH), National Aeronautics and Space Administration (NASA), the National Science Foundation (NSF), the U. S. Department of State, and the U. S. Office of Education (USOE).

The policy of the Federal government, in the past 50 years, has been scrupulously to avoid governmental evaluation or accreditation of higher education. However, the growing dependence of Federal agencies on universities in the various programs referred to above has led to activities of an evaluative nature. These vary from an agency placing all its research contracts with 43 institutions to the other extreme of formal examinations which involve campus visits and consideration of factors resembling those which go into the regional accrediting procedures. Thus, the evaluation actions may be divided into the two categories: (1) explicit evaluation of graduate institutions and (2) implicit evaluation.

An example of explicit evaluation is the training programs of the National Institutes of Health. In determining whether an institution is competent to administer such activities, committees visit the campus, meet the faculty, examine the laboratory space and equipment, examine the program of graduate studies, and assess the general reputation of the faculty. Particular attention is given to the feasibility of the project submitted by the institution. To assist these and other committees, NIH has developed a comprehensive check-list for campus visiting teams. The National Science Foundation (NSF) employs somewhat similar procedures in its program for providing matching grants for scientific facilities. The U. S. Office of Education in its *Title IV of NDEA* (fellowships) and in Title VI (foreign language centers) employs a simpler version of the same approach.

Under implicit evaluation, a panel of experts may decide whether an individual submitting a project or the institution involved is capable of carrying out the project. Proposals are also submitted by institutions and then a panel evaluates each proposal and considers the qualifications of the institution to carry out the proposed activity. Such decisions are evaluative in character although no records of them are kept.

A common criticism of Federal grants-in-aid is that they tend to help the strong institutions to become stronger while at the same time permitting weaker institutions to become relatively weaker. This results from the policy which permits or encourages the assigning of contracts or grants to the strongest and most prestigious universities.

FIFTH-YEAR TEACHER EDUCATION PROGRAMS FOR GRADUATES OF LIBERAL ARTS COLLEGES

In 1962, there were no less than 183 teacher education programs conducted exclusively for college graduates who previously had not been enrolled in a program of teacher education. Seventy-six percent of these programs came into existence during the decade 1950–1960. Three factors which spurred new programs of this type in the 1950's were: (1) a desire to relieve the teacher shortage; (2) the availability of financial assistance from a foundation; and (3) the growing conviction of university staffs that this was the best way to prepare teachers. The 183 programs included several varieties of specialized patterns, such as programs for internship teaching, intensive training programs, certification programs, programs leading to the Master of Arts in Teaching (MAT), and programs for retired armed services personnel. Some of these programs were initiated in order to build a program of professional preparation on a strong foundation of liberal education. The programs generally were created for young people in liberal arts colleges who had made a late decision to pursue a career in teaching or who had decided to abandon an exclusive career of homemaking.

Of the 183 programs, 45 percent were offered in 58 multipurpose universities; 33 percent were given in 42 liberal arts colleges; 20 percent were offered in 26 teachers colleges; the remaining 2 percent in other professional schools. Within the institutions, 50 programs were housed in the school of education; 33 were located in the department of education; 26 in the graduate school; and 14 in the subject department. Likewise, 159 of the 183 programs culminated in a recommendation for certification, although a professional or academic degree was combined with certification in 86 of the programs. Of the 86 degree programs, 78 were on the master's level and 8 on the bachelor's level.

Of the master's degree programs, 28 schools awarded the master of arts, 15 awarded the master of education, 15 awarded the master of arts in teaching, and 8 awarded the master of science. [7]

In reply to a questionnaire sent to the state departments of education asking specifically about Master of Arts in Teaching (MAT) programs currently in operation (1964), 24 of the 38 states replying reported having from one to 16 MAT programs, aggregating 81 programs in the 24 states. If this astonishingly large number is correct, and if the number of MAT programs was accurately reported in 1962 as 15, the two-year period from 1962 to 1964 has witnessed a four-fold increase just taking into consideration 24 states. In the questionnaire, it was stated that an MAT program is considered to be a formally organized program of at least two semesters' duration to provide preparation for teaching for those who are liberal arts graduates. The term Master of Arts in Teaching, or MAT, appears to be so varied in concept or interpretation that these figures must be accepted with great caution. Furthermore, more than 15 of the programs included in the earlier study probably were of the type identified in this Study as MAT programs. In any case, it seems safe to conclude that programs of the type identified by MAT in the questionnaire are increasing in number and in acceptance.

THE FUTURE OF GRADUATE-LEVEL ACCREDITATION

"The accrediting of graduate work is the most important task that remains to be performed in the accrediting field. What has been done in this area thus far is incomplete and limited. . . . In view of the increasing number of institutions that are offering graduate work, accreditation in this field is one of the leading problems confronting accrediting bodies today." [8]

The Council of Graduate Schools in the United States, at its annual meeting in Chicago on December 12, 1964, recognized graduate accreditation as a legitimate part of general accreditation, performed by the regional accrediting associations, and of special accreditation, performed by agencies representing national professional organizations, such as dentistry, law, and medicine. Presumably a national accrediting agency in the area of teacher education would be included, if recognized and approved by the National Commission on Accrediting.

The Council of Graduate Schools furthermore indicated its readiness to collaborate with the Federation of Regional Accrediting Commissions of Higher Education, or with a recognized professional accrediting body in formulating standards and procedures, and in selecting a panel of qualified people for serving on evaluation teams involved in graduate accreditation. A recommendation, in line with these resolutions, is included in the final chapter of this Study.

REFERENCES

1. NCATE Memo to Institutions Preparing for an NCATE Visit, "Explanatory Materials Interpreting the NCATE Standards," 1964, p. 11.
2. Lloyd M. Blauch, ed., *Accreditation in Higher Education* (Washington, D. C., 1959), p. 66.
3. Interview, April 13, 1964, with Norman W. Burns, Executive Secretary, North Central Association.
4. Blauch, *op. cit.*, pp. 56, 57.
5. William K. Selden and J. Fletcher Wellemeyer, *Memorandum to Committee to Study the Improvement of Evaluation of Graduate Work* (Washington, D. C., 1962), pp. 6–8.
6. *Ibid.*, pp. 13–26.
7. Henry Harap, *Fifth-year Preservice Programs for Graduates of Liberal Arts Colleges*, Health, Education, and Welfare, Office of Education, Teacher Education Series, August 1962, *passim.*
8. Jennings B. Saunders, "Evolution of Accreditation," in Blauch, *op. cit.*, pp. 12, 13.

CHAPTER 9

QUALITATIVE vs. QUANTITATIVE MEASUREMENT OF EXCELLENCE IN TEACHER EDUCATION

QUANTITATIVE AND QUALITATIVE MEASURES

FOR MANY YEARS, accrediting agencies have evaluated institutions of higher education in terms of such quantitative criteria as the following:

Number of Ph.D.'s on the staff

Ratio of staff to student body

Number of books in the library

Number of square feet per student of reading space in the library

Maximum, minimum, and average class size

Faculty teaching loads

Number of square feet per student of laboratory space

Amount of endowment or annual income in relation to the size of the student body

It is reasonable to assume that, up to a point at least, these are indices of institutional quality. However, critics of the system have pointed out that of itself none of the above criteria is a reliable or accurate measure of an institution's excellence. A good non-Ph.D. might be more competent than a second- or third-rate Ph.D. A smaller number of books of quality in the library might be indicative of higher quality than a large number of mediocre books. Too, the frequency and manner in which books are used are significant measures of a library's quality or value. Defenders of quantitative measures have emphasized the obvious advantage of objectivity. There is little room in the use of quantitative criteria for sentiment or subjective impression.

A generation ago the regional accrediting associations discarded to some extent the earlier quantitative specifics except as they relate to broader and more general "qualitative" criteria. Emphasis is now placed on an institution's philosophy and objectives, what is being done to implement its philosophy and objectives, and its capacity to achieve

114

its goal. [1] With more than three-fourths of the degree-granting institutions regionally accredited, emphasis was placed on stimulation to improvement. However, most of the national professional accrediting agencies, including chemistry, dentistry, engineering, law, medicine, and teacher education, have continued to employ quantitative standards, although not necessarily with the same degree of specificity. The evidence seems to indicate that the criteria employed by the National Council for Accreditation of Teacher Education (NCATE) are less specific than those employed by the professional accrediting bodies other than in nursing.[1]

Nevertheless, NCATE appears to have been more severely criticized for depending on quantitative standards in institutional evaluation than any of the other professional agencies. This may be due largely to the fact that people generally are not as aware of the techniques employed by the other professional groups—as well as less concerned—as they are of those administered by NCATE. In voicing their criticisms many have insisted that NCATE should evaluate teacher education in qualitative rather than quantitative terms. Defenders of NCATE retort that to do so is fine in theory, but in practice to try to use this approach would involve some very difficult and frustrating problems, such as (1) just what is meant by quality and (2) how can quality best be measured?

In the past three decades, a variety of schemes purporting to measure the quality of a teacher education institution or program have appeared. Broadly speaking, these involve the measurement of the quality of a teacher education institution on the basis of (1) performance of graduates; (2) observation and testing of institutional qualities; and (3) instruments for preservice testing of prospective teachers.

PERFORMANCE OF GRADUATES

It may be assumed that a quality teacher education institution or program is one that turns out quality teachers; therefore, it would logically follow that an appropriate measure of institutional quality would be one based on the graduates of teacher education programs. It appears that the concept of quality measurement of graduates has inspired a great deal of research in teacher education, with a relatively small amount of success. This research can be grouped into three categories: (1) opinions of employers; (2) follow-up studies (including success in graduate work); and (3) measurement of teaching effectiveness.

Opinions of Employers

It has been suggested that some insight into the quality of a teacher education institution might be gained by surveying the opinions of those who employ graduates of the institution, such as school prin-

---

[1] See Appendix III.

cipals, superintendents, and personnel supervisors. One such recent study seemed to show that small public institutions and large private universities in Indiana have produced the most acceptable teachers.[2]

As part of this Study, a pilot investigation was conducted to see if employers of teachers preferred graduates of certain institutions and to see if they would report their opinions. The following questions were submitted to over 160 employers of teachers throughout the country:

1. In employing teachers in your school system, do you have a preference for the graduates of certain institutions in your area? Yes _____ No _____

2. If your answer is "yes," just what are the qualities of the graduates of such institutions which you think are desirable in teachers?

3. If you care to do so, we would appreciate your listing the names of institutions the graduates of which you prefer.

4. If you care to do so, we would appreciate your listing the names of institutions the graduates of which you least prefer.

Of the 84 replies received, 30 indicated little or no preference for the graduates of any particular teacher education institutions; indeed, some were frank enough to say that, in view of the current teacher shortage, they had been forced to employ whomever they could obtain. Those who specified institutions having good teacher education programs agreed to some extent on this point.

Since the number of inquiries sent out and the number of replies received were so small and since no attempt was made to select the employers on a random sampling basis, no important conclusions can be drawn from the results. It is interesting to note, however, that in the replies all types of higher institutions were included among those mentioned most frequently: state universities; large, multipurpose private universities; state colleges; one teachers college (George Peabody College for Teachers); and liberal arts colleges. Probably it is noteworthy that all six replies from South Carolina listed Winthrop College as a quality teacher education school. Also, there was a surprising degree of frankness relative to colleges and universities reported as having low-quality teacher education programs.

It is encouraging to know that some employers of teachers are prepared to list the names of institutions they consider to have teacher education programs of high quality. If a similar study were to be conducted on a large scale, some account would need to be taken of possible bias on the part of employers. Likewise, it would be desirable to supplement any information thus received with additional opinions obtained from personal interviews with employers. In a personal interview with one employer who had failed to return the questionnaire, it was found that he was quite willing to express opinions orally.

If a reliable rating scale could be devised for employers in rating teacher education institutions on the basis of the success in teaching of the graduates of the institution, the states and other accrediting agencies might find the scale a useful quality measure in the total accrediting process.

FOLLOW-UP STUDIES

Institutional follow-up studies have also been suggested as a source of information concerning the quality of graduates of teacher education institutions. Those who feel that such studies might provide satisfactory data for accrediting agencies apparently assume that most institutions of higher learning keep up-to-date records of the successes and failures of their graduates in teaching positions, and that the institutions would be willing to make such information available to the public. In an attempt to ascertain the extent, nature, and variety of such records, letters requesting information about them were sent to 30 colleges and universities in North Carolina, 21 in South Carolina, and 30 to institutions in other states.

Thirteen of the 81 institutions indicated that records were being kept and some sent copies of follow-up reports. A few of the liberal arts colleges which apparently felt pride in their teacher education programs returned neat and concise tabulations of reports from employers of their graduates. Two small colleges which were listed by employers as producing teachers of high quality were able to produce excellent—though concise—follow-up studies of their former students. Large institutions in general gave the impression that the task of keeping records of this type would be too complex and too cumbersome. A few of the smaller colleges reported the number of their former students currently engaged in graduate study and those who had obtained advanced degrees. A college for women in North Carolina reported that most of its graduates married shortly after graduation, hence no follow-up records were kept.

Those in charge of teacher education programs often discussed the need for and value of follow-up studies of their graduates. However, little evidence was found in the Study that colleges and universities are doing much of significance in this respect.

MEASUREMENT OF TEACHER EFFECTIVENESS

In the past half century there has been extensive research on teacher effectiveness. A. S. Barr, of the University of Wisconsin, was a pioneer and leader in this type of investigation. He concluded that there are three possible methods of measuring teacher quality: (1) the evaluation of a teacher by a trained observer using "accepted" criteria of good teachers; (2) the evaluation of a teacher's effectiveness by his superiors, his fellow teachers, or his students; and (3) the evaluation of a teacher in terms of student gain.[3]

The first two of Barr's possible methods are based on the assumption that there are definable traits in the good teacher and that these can be identified and measured. Just what are these traits? Apparently two basic ones are intelligence and personality. When efforts have been made to be more specific the degree of agreement seems to lessen. Among those which have been listed are: breadth of scholarship, honesty, enthusiasm, magnetism, social understanding, rational behavior, friendliness, warmth of personality, maintenance of order, wholesome relations with students, ability to handle subject matter, sympathetic approach, health, and zeal.

There have been a large number of studies in which a comparison has been made between success in teaching and the factors of training and personal characteristics. One study revealed some correlation between the quality of teaching and grades in student teaching, but little or no correlation between grades in methods courses and good teaching.[4] In another study it was concluded that the teacher most often rated best by students was an individual high in "emotional climate," but there seldom was any correlation between this factor and student gain. Still another study found that holders of degrees in education were better teachers than holders of liberal arts degrees.[5]

"It is not an exaggeration to say that we do not know how to select, train for, encourage, or evaluate teacher effectiveness." [6] This latter statement may be a bit extreme. Perhaps the authors intended to say that there is no agreement based on research on these factors.

What one is left with then are the standard subjective processes of judgment and consensus which may be right most of the time. If a teacher is regarded as incompetent by his supervisors or other responsible individuals, then the chances are that he is incompetent—at least in that situation, at that time, and in those circumstances. If a teacher, on the contrary, is regarded as quite competent by his superiors or by other responsible individuals then that teacher obviously exhibits some of the traits associated with teaching competence. Still, as research has indicated, it is possible that both judgments will be wrong.

A major investigation of teacher characteristics, carried out under the direction of David D. Ryans, was published by the American Council on Education in 1959 as a research study. [7] The research was primarily concerned with the identification and analysis of patterns of behavior which characterize teachers, the development of instruments suitable for estimation of certain behavior patterns, and the comparison of characteristics of various groups of teachers. While no universal acceptable definitions of effective teaching or of characteristics of competent teachers were sought in the research, these investigations do constitute a foundation on which additional research related to these definitions and other critical issues may be based.

In 1964 the U. S. Office of Education made a $266,000 grant to the University of Wisconsin to conduct a study of what is involved when a "judge" evaluates teacher competence. The study is related to the development of better instruments for quality measures which might eventually be useful in accreditation. The Wisconsin project would select and train "observer-judges" from four states. These observers were to include academic staff members, professional educators, public school teachers and administrators, and state education officials. The students to be judged were to come from Northwestern University, Sacramento (California) State College, State University of New York at Albany, and the University of Wisconsin. Those to be observed were to be appraised during their senior year in college and their first year on the job. The objective of the Wisconsin experiment was to ascertain "exactly what is involved when a judge evaluates teacher competence." [8]

OBSERVATION AND TESTING OF INSTITUTIONAL QUALITIES

The method most commonly used in attempts to measure the quality of a teacher education institution or program is that of observation, consisting of an on- and off-campus examination of quantitative or statistical evidence, and by subjective judgment of the fitness of the institution. Obviously, this is the method by which most accrediting agencies now operate. Since this method as practiced is given detailed attention in chapters analyzing the accreditation in teacher education by national, regional, and state agencies, the remainder of this section is devoted to a discussion of recent studies and research not restricted to teacher education, but regarded as holding considerable promise for more general application as well as for application in special areas, such as the education of teachers. These efforts are examples of new attacks on the problem of quality and perhaps suggest that measurement of quality is not as "hopeless" a task as too often has been assumed.

THE PATTILLO-MACKENZIE METHOD OF INSTITUTIONAL EVALUATION

Manning Pattillo and Donald Mackenzie of the Danforth Foundation insist that the accreditation of higher education should take into account both "objective analysis" and the "personal judgment of observers." They also contend that there are certain attributes which are operable in any good college, but which are not susceptible to precise mathematical formulation. These attributes or criteria include seriousness of purpose; the awareness of the distinctive role of the institution; care in the selection of students within the framework of institutional purpose; balance; the atmosphere of intellectual ferment in the college; "perpetual dissatisfaction" with the institution about itself; and the ultimate "effect" of the institution upon the students.

It is obvious that there is a high degree of subjectivity in estimating the quality of an institution according to the Pattillo-Mackenzie criteria. How does one judge an institution's seriousness of purpose? The answer is: "As one visits campuses and talks with faculty and students, he can see marked differences in this respect." How does one judge a college in terms of the selection and retention of faculty members? The answer:

"One must accept the Ph.D. as a partial index and then proceed to examine a faculty's sound scholarship, teaching ability, and personal integrity." How does one measure the level and the intensity of the "intellectual ferment" on a college campus? Pattillo and Mackenzie say it is possible. So far, the Pattillo-Mackenzie criteria are being prepared for church-related, liberal arts colleges. Pattillo, however, thinks that they are adaptable to other kinds of higher institutions.[9]

AMERICAN COUNCIL ON EDUCATION SURVEY

One of the more subjective techniques for institutional evaluation is one which has been applied to graduate study several times in the past. It involves asking a group of scholars to indicate those institutions that have the "strongest" or "highest ranking" departments in the respondent's field of study. Tabulation of the responses has resulted in lists of the "top" graduate schools in each field.[10]

A current survey of this type is being conducted by the American Council on Education's Commission on Plans and Objectives for Higher Education which in the spring of 1964 distributed a questionnaire to 5,300 faculty members in 30 different fields of study. Neither education nor teacher education was included among the fields covered in the survey. Each participant was provided a list of major institutions that had granted the doctorate in his field of study in the past 10 years; he was asked to check one of six descriptions of the quality of the graduate faculty, one of four descriptions of the quality of the doctoral program, and one of three estimates of likely relative change in the next five to 10 years. Nearly 80 percent of those queried replied, and their responses are being analyzed by geographic region of employment, age, academic position, and background. The Commission expects to publish a report on the study in mid-1965. [11]

ASTIN STUDIES

In 1962 Alexander W. Astin of the National Merit Scholarship Corporation, after sampling 335 accredited institutions in a study of 33 variables, arrived at eight assessments for each institution: the first two being the size of the student body and its average intelligence; the other six being the "personal orientation" of the student group. Using the assembled materials in various ways, Astin was able to describe further each of the individual institutions.[12]

In subsequent studies Astin has attempted to determine the effects of these institutional characteristics on the student's aspirations,[13] career choice, [14] and persistence in college. [15]

It was reported that early in 1965 Astin would publish an extensive study [16] based on an attempt to ascertain "the trait measure or dimensions wherein various institutions differ." The extensive compilation had been gathered from questionnaires completed by 127,212 freshmen at 248 colleges and universities. Preliminary reports of results recently appeared in two papers. [17]

The information thus derived has been analyzed into six factors which "seem to represent a meaningful and concise scheme for describing some of the most important characteristics of entering freshmen classes." The six are:

1. Intellectualism: reflects the emphasis on high scholarship and intellectual activities—desire to acquire the Ph.D.—preference for intellectual and scientific activities.
2. Estheticism: past achievements in art and literature—preferences of major fields in art, writing, languages, and music.
3. Status: reflects extent to which students come from relatively high socioeconomic backgrounds; and it also indicates preference for careers in business, law, etc.
4. Leadership: emphasis on competition and verbal aggression.
5. Pragmatism: percentage of students with vocational choices and intended fields of study in engineering, agriculture, physical education, etc.
6. Masculinity: related to vocational interests, impetus to study medicine, law, business, etc.

What Astin has done with the six "traits" is to relate them to various characteristics of the college, such as the curriculum, size, selectivity, and environment. It was found that teachers colleges, for example, typically have student bodies that are low in Intellectualism, Status, Masculinity, and Pragmatism, and about average in Estheticism and Leadership.

OTHER MEASURES OF COLLEGE CHARACTERISTICS

The Pattillo-Mackenzie, the Astin, and the American Council on Education studies have been reported briefly. These studies are part of a contemporary surge in the development of techniques to measure and analyze characteristics of institutions of higher education.

Some of the available testing instruments are designed primarily to measure college environmental factors. Probably the best known of these are the *Activities Index,* the *College Characteristics Index,* the *College and University Environmental Scales* (CUES) and the *College Student Questionnaire* (CSQ).[18] It is claimed that each of these will aid appropriate authorities in a better understanding of types of student bodies and the dominating trait within them. Based on such tests, the colleges scoring high in intellectual climate included: Antioch, Bennington, Bryn Mawr, Goddard, Oberlin, Reed, Sarah Lawrence, Shimer, Swarthmore, Vassar and Wesleyan University. The study in which these colleges were listed showed that colleges scoring high in intellectual climate were also characterized by smaller-sized classes, a larger percentage of Ph.D.'s on the faculties, fewer drop-outs among students, and a higher percentage of the faculty affiliated with the American Association of University Professors. [19]

The College Student Questionnaire, under development at the Educational Testing Service, provides a measure of four different philosophies which may prevail in varying proportions on a college campus. These include: (1) academic philosophy with emphasis on scholarly pursuit; (2) the vocational, emphasizing preparation for livelihood; (3) the college philosophy, emphasizing extracurricular activities as a part of the educational experience; and (4) the non-conformist, in which there is a search for meaning in life.

In summary of the information obtained on observation and testing of institutional qualities, one may state that:

1. Observation of available quantitative and statistical information is an established procedure in accreditation.
2. The Pattillo-Mackenzie approach calls for a greater degree of subjectivity by injecting criteria which are not measurable by a statistical method.
3. Various testing instruments and studies (such as Astin's) add to the growing amount of information available to accreditation teams during institutional evaluations.
4. Recent studies suggest a number of new approaches to obtaining qualitative information on institutions, and illustrate the potentiality of newer research methods.

PRESERVICE TESTING INSTRUMENTS

The third of the proposed methods by which the quality of teacher education institutions or the quality of individuals in teacher education may be measured is that involving the use of preservice testing devices. A considerable number of measurement specialists are optimistic about these measuring techniques.

THE FARR STUDY

In a comprehensive study of testing usage in 443 higher institutions, S. David Farr reported 445 distinct test titles of which 240 could be identified as published tests. The typical number of tests reported per school was four or five, but three schools reported more than 20. No less than 156 institutions reported the use of tests in admission to teacher education; 78 institutions were using tests for degree-granting decisions; and 49 institutions were using tests as one basis for recommending certification. A total of 227 institutions reported using the *Scholastic Aptitude Test* (SAT); 176 were using the *American College Testing Program Examination* (ACT); 144 were using the *Graduate Record Examination* (GRE) Area Tests; 25 were using the *Sequential Tests of Educational Progress* (STEP); 62 were using the *Kuder Preference Record*; and 45 were using the *Strong Vocational Interest Blank*. The *Cooperative English Test* and the *School and College Ability Tests* were also reported as being popular.[2]

---

[2] S. David Farr, "Evaluation and Selection Instruments in Teacher Education Programs," University of Buffalo, CRP Project No. S.005, February, 1964–August, 1964.

The Farr study grew out of an increasing interest in testing on the part of the Subcommittee on Testing in Teacher Education of the AACTE. The effort of the group at the State University of New York at Buffalo, of which Farr is the head, is directed toward research and service activities leading to improved practices in the use of available tests and the development of new instruments for which a need in teacher education is identified. A first step of the group has been to conduct a survey of the present use of tests in teacher education programs. The data reported here from the Farr study are from the survey. A survey instrument was addressed to the 664 member institutions of AACTE. The reports are based on responses from 443 institutions.

The two most frequently used personality inventories as reported in the Farr study are *The Minnesota Multiphasic Personality Inventory* and the Edwards *Personal Preference Schedule.* Sixty-one institutions reported the administration of one of these tests to students preparing to teach and in some cases to the total student body. *The Minnesota Teacher Attitude Inventory* is used in fewer institutions belonging to the AACTE. This test, applied mainly to entrance into the teacher education program, attempts to measure individual attitudes toward children and classroom attitude.

NTE, TEEP, AND GRE

One of the tests most widely used and discussed is the *National Teacher Examinations* (NTE). According to officials of the Educational Testing Service (ETS), which distributes NTE, approximately 7,500 took these tests in 1949; 56,000 took the NTE tests in 1961–1962; and approximately 75,000 tests in this series were administered in 1963–1964. Also according to the same authorities, the percentage of increase in the use of the tests exceeds the percentage of increase of students graduating in teacher education.[3]

The particular uses of the tests appear to be varied and probably exceed the original intentions of the designers. Farr reports, for example, that member institutions of AACTE may use the examinations in one of several different ways. Among the most common usages reported were for program evaluation, certification recommendation, and preliminary to the granting of the degree. Four other purposes were also reported.

There are two parts to the NTE program. The first, the Common Examinations, gives a general appraisal of the prospective teacher's basic professional preparation and his general academic achievement. The second, the Teaching Area Examinations, is offered in 13 different areas and is designed to indicate the student's preparation in his major field. The questions for the Teaching Area Examinations are described by the Educational Testing Service as "objective in character; that is,

---

[3] Interview with Arthur L. Benson, Director of Teacher Examinations at ETS.

for each question five plausible answers are given, and from them the candidate chooses the one he believes is best."

The scores on each of the six "discrete" tests of the Common Examinations are reported separately; although it may be added that a Weighted Common Examinations Total Score is also returned. The total scores for the Common Examinations range approximately from 300 to 900, with the middle half of the candidates scoring from 545 to 655. State and local authorities who use the tests set their own minimum score requirements. Since the Common Examinations are sometimes required as a prerequisite to employment by local school systems, the score needed to qualify may depend upon the available supply of teachers. In fact, the truth in most cases would seem to be that if the supply of available teachers is large the required score tends to go up. The Educational Testing Service provides percentile ranks for the Weighted Common Examinations Total Score. According to a recent Educational Testing Service publication, a total score of 750 would provide a percentile rank of 99; a total score of 600 would provide a percentile rank of 54; and a total score of 400 would provide a percentile rank of two.[4]

Strict security is maintained in connection with the National Teacher Examinations, which precludes any first-hand discussion of testing emphases. There are, however, a number of individuals who are not satisfied with the examinations and who have made their feelings known. James D. Koerner states that NTE "greatly resembles run-of-the-mill standard intelligence and achievement tests. . . ." After examining sample questions of NTE, Koerner complains about their "simplicity," and argues that the examinations "suffer from the fatal handicap of being restricted to testing only what educationists tell ETS they are trying to do in their teacher-training programs." His conclusions, which come at the end of a rather hard handling of the efficacy of the tests, states that the National Teacher Examinations "would be wholly unsatisfactory in the kind of qualifying examinations system I am discussing." [20]

During the fact-gathering period of this Study, a number of educators expressed dissatisfaction with NTE, either orally or as a part of information requested from them by letter. Many of those interviewed felt that the examination was being used in a manner not originally intended, and some felt that it failed to measure facets of character necessary to good teaching. One administrator wrote that he felt NTE was loaded "with biases which we do not share one hundred percent," and that it did not "cover a number of areas which we feel are essential." [5]

Two other instruments which are used by teacher accreditation institutions are the *Teacher Education Examination Program* (TEEP) and the *Graduate Record Examination* (GRE). The first of these (TEEP)

---

[4] Pamphlets supplied by ETS.
[5] Correspondence from a school of education administrator.

is used in ways quite similar to those reported for NTE, including program evaluation, recommendation for certification, and as a preliminary to the granting of degrees. However, Farr reported six other uses ranging from admission to special programs to admission to student teaching.[6]

Educational Testing Service identifies differences between NTE and TEEP. According to ETS, "not only do the test offerings and the scales of scores differ considerably, but also those tests in TEEP which bear similar titles to those in NTE are not equated content-wise or statistically." Further statements of ETS indicate that TEEP is available "only to teacher education institutions for institution purposes"; and although the program "complements the National Teacher Examinations" and TEEP is "fashioned after the National Teacher Examinations" the scores may not be used interchangeably.

TEEP consists of two broad parts:

1. The General Professional Examinations have seven "discrete" tests which are designed to "measure the student's knowledge and understanding of the basic principles in professional education, English usage, and general culture." The seven tests requiring 185 minutes to administer are: Foundations of Education; Child Development and Educational Psychology; Guidance and Measurement; Instructional Methods; English; General Culture I (History, Literature, and Fine Arts); and General Culture II (Mathematics and Sciences).

2. The Teaching Field Tests allow the student "an opportunity to demonstrate certain competencies essential for teaching in a special field." The tests, each with a time limit of 80 minutes, are: Early Childhood Education; Elementary School Education; English Language and Literature; Social Studies; Biological Science; Physical Science; Mathematics; French; Spanish; Industrial Arts; Physical Education; Business Education; and Music Education.

The Graduate Record Examination (GRE) program consists of three separate testing areas: Area Tests, which are "designed to assess the broad outcomes of education in the liberal arts"; the Advanced Tests, which evaluate mastery in selected fields of study; and the Aptitude Test, which is designed as a predictor of future academic success.[7]

Perhaps one of the most significant developments within the GRE program is the increased usage of the Area Tests. Through the Institutional Test Program, these tests may be given in one, two, or all levels of college work, and to a single class in succeeding years. Comparisons of scores obtained in this way with norms provided by the Educational Testing Service presumably give some indication of the development of a particular group of students, as well as the effectiveness of the

---

[6] Farr pre-publication information.
[7] Information provided by ETS.

institutional program. Antioch College and the State College of Iowa, for example, have inaugurated rather refined programs along these lines.[8]

The National Teacher Examinations (NTE), the Graduate Record Examination (GRE), and the Teacher Education Examination Program (TEEP), each provides one kind of measure of individual differences. Some evidence suggests a possible low correlation between the performance of students on one or more of these examinations and the accreditation by NCATE and other agencies of the institutions which they attend. Still, just how much of the information provided by tests may be used for accreditation purposes is difficult to say. The opinion-gathering phase of this Study indicated there are a few college presidents at least who are not averse to the use of NTE in certification and even in accreditation.

Arthur L. Benson, director of the NTE program of ETS, suggests that "one of the possible usages of the various testing devices might be the gathering of supporting data for accreditation purposes." [21]

USE OF EXAMINATIONS BY THE STATES

As stated previously, the uses of NTE are varied. More than 110 school systems scattered throughout the United States encourage applicants for teaching positions to submit scores on these examinations. Forty large municipal school systems *require* applicants to submit test scores. Six states use NTE scores for certification and related purposes. These are Delaware, Florida, Georgia, North Carolina, South Carolina, and West Virginia. [22]

In West Virginia, the use of the National Teacher Examinations grew partly out of a shortage of teachers. In May, 1959, the State Committee on Teacher Education proposed to the West Virginia Board of Education that a plan be inaugurated for the certification of liberal arts graduates who lacked the necessary hours of credit in professional education courses, but who could score well on the National Teacher Examinations. The idea of certifying teachers by examination in lieu of required education courses has been widely discussed, but rarely tried out. Despite some resistance, based apparently on the fear that fewer students would enroll in various teacher education programs in the state, the plan was approved by the West Virginia Board and put into operation. Although the plan attracted relatively few liberal arts graduates, the concept of using NTE on a broad scale took hold. Now the State Board of Education requires all applicants for certification, including graduates in teacher education, to take the examination.

In Florida, the rank of the certificate issued to a teacher depends in part on his NTE Common Examinations score. In the Florida program, there is a vast tabulation of information which will eventually

---

[8] Information supplied by ETS, Antioch College, and the State College of Iowa.

become available to researchers and perhaps to accrediting agencies. Florida state education authorities hope to be able to study the relationship between a principal's ratings and the NTE score with a goal of understanding more about the effectiveness of various teacher education institutions as measured by these test scores inside and outside the state.[23]

Only a small part of the statistical information concerning the use of NTE by various states is available for public use. The states do report, however, that there are wide differences in institutional mean or average scores reported by various colleges and universities. Conant reports, for example, that in one state 75 percent of the senior teacher-training students of two institutions scored less than 500 (the 17th percentile). [24]

Preliminary investigation conducted through the questionnaire study, described on page 116, indicates that some colleges of which the graduates have low NTE scores may also have poor reputations as teacher education institutions; in other words, some supervisory and administrative personnel in that state listed the colleges as having poor teacher education programs. As would be expected, low NTE institutional mean scores are related to the quality of the students admitted to those institutions. Whenever the possibility arises for a comparison of Scholastic Aptitude Test and NTE scores achieved by students of the same institution, the relationship between input and output becomes obvious.

It is evident from the survey reported in this chapter that there is much interest in testing as a part of teacher education programs and the evaluation of them by the institution and by outside agencies. Admittedly, many of the instruments are imperfect. Yet a growing number of persons appear to believe that it is seriously to be questioned whether, in the light of the significant strides in recent years in the field of measurement, testing can be ignored as at least a possible segment of the accreditation process. This applies to the testing of intelligence and knowledge and of personality and attitudes as well as to the testing for an identification of characteristics and atmosphere in a college or university.

Whenever the possible use of tests as a part of the accreditation process has been mentioned, there are of course many who point out drawbacks such as:

1. Any increased use of tests for accreditation purposes would require adequate policing of the entire program (as is true of any objective test). Already, in one of the states using NTE for certification, "ringers" have been caught taking the examination for less gifted friends.

2. There arises the possibility of any college, desirous of establishing an appropriate institutional standing, directing its whole program of instruction toward the achievement by its students of high scores on a particular test.

OTHER CURRENT STUDIES

There are the extensive follow-up studies of high school graduates being conducted under the auspices of *Project Talent* (University of Pittsburgh). [25]

Too, mention should be made of the research project, "The Assignment and Mis-assignment of the American Teacher," conducted by Paul M. Ford for NCTEPS. Of special importance in this study is an effort to obtain an "educators' ranking" of the 12 factors which "limit educational quality." By far the most significant item thus found is the "failure to attract an adequate number of academically and personally talented young people to teacher education programs." [26]

Reference should also be made to the recently completed study by Hazel Simpson of the University of Georgia in relation to NTE scores in that state, and the work of Garth Sorenson and Wayne Gordon at U.C.L.A. The latter two are presently engaged in a study of "quality factors" in teaching.

The Center for Innovation in Education for the University of the State of New York has been described as an attempt to "welcome fresh ideas, and to encourage the trying out of new approaches in schools and colleges, to evaluate the results, and to pass these along to administrators and teachers throughout the state." It has been suggested that the Center may contribute to a better understanding of some measures of quality.

Several studies are being completed under the auspices of the Educational Testing Service. One, the *College Characteristics Study*, is concerned with the selection of desirable student qualities which could lead to variations of admission policies. Another, the *Follow-up Study of a National Sample of High School Seniors*, is designed to "obtain additional interpretative material for PSAT and SAT for students who enroll in college. . . ."

These references to current studies relative to the measurement of quality in American higher education illustrate the challenging and exciting developments in this area. The almost unlimited potentialities of electronic computers and other devices for counting and collating large masses of data are only beginning to be realized. In the future, experimenters and researchers will be far less handicapped than in the past by their own physical and mental limitations. Much more needs to be done, and doubtless will be done in the decade which spans the last half of the 1960's and the early 1970's.

This chapter concludes Part I of the Study of the Influence on Higher Education of Accreditation in Teacher Education. It completes the nine chapters which together comprise the framework for Parts II and III. Here has been traced the evolution of state, regional, and national accreditation in teacher education. Here also has been portrayed the controversy which has developed around the present national accrediting body in teacher education. Finally, some of the problems of accreditation which in large measure differentiate the accreditation of teacher education from the other areas of accreditation in higher education have been presented. Part II will deal specifically with the actual influence or effects of the accreditation of teacher education upon the basic elements in higher education: organization and administration, curriculums, faculty and student policies, finance, and experimentation and research.

REFERENCES

1. G. F. Zook and M. E. Haggerty, *The Evaluation of Higher Institutions*, Vol. I, pp. 91–112.
2. Lloyd S. Standler and W. James Papham, *Preparation and Performance of Teachers* (Bloomington, Ind., 1958).
3. A. S. Barr, *et al.*, *Wisconsin Studies of the Measurement and Prediction of Teacher Effectiveness* (Madison, Wis., 1961), p. 21.
4. Grover Somers, *Pedagogical Prognosis* (New York, 1923); W. E. Charters and Douglas Waples, *The Commonwealth Training Study* (Chicago, 1929); Grover Somers and Douglas Waples, *Teachers for Our Times* (Washington, 1944); Thomas C. Burgess, *Teacher Behavior Ratings as a Criterion of Teacher Effectiveness* (Columbia, Mo., 1953).
5. Barr, *op. cit.*, p. 126; Donald M. Medley, "Experiences with the Oscar Technique," *The Journal of Teacher Education* (September 1923), p. 272; R. L. Turner and N. A. Fattu, *Problem Solving Efficiency Among Elementary Teachers* (Bloomington, Ind., 1960), p. 245.
6. Bruce J. Biddle and William J. Ellena, eds., *Contemporary Research on Teacher Effectiveness* (New York, 1964), p. 11.
7. David D. Ryans, *Characteristics of Teachers: Their Description, Comparison and Appraisal* (Washington, D. C., 1959).
8. New York *Times*, November 8, 1964.
9. Manning M. Pattillo and Donald M. Mackenzie, "What Makes a Good College" (unpublished article issued by the Commission on Church Colleges and Universities, The Danforth Foundation).
10. Raymond M. Hughes, *A Study of the Graduate Schools of America* (Oxford, Ohio, 1925); Report of the Committee on Graduate Instruction, *The Educational Record*, Vol. 15, No. 2 (April 1934); Hayward Keniston, *Graduate Study and Research in the Arts and Sciences at the University of Pennsylvania* (Philadelphia, 1959).
11. Interview with Allen Cartter, Vice President, American Council on Education.
12. Alexander W. Astin and John L. Holland, "The Environmental Assessment Technique: A Way to Measure College Environments," *Journal of Educational Psychology* (December 1961), pp. 308–316; Alexander W. Astin, "Further Validation of the Environmental Assessment Technique," *Journal of Educational Psychology* (August 1963), pp. 217–226.
13. Alexander W. Astin, " 'Productivity' of Undergraduate Institutions," *Science* (April 1962), pp. 129–135; Alexander W. Astin, "Differential College Effects on the Motivation of Talented Students to Obtain the Ph.D.," *Journal of Educational Psychology* (February 1963), pp. 63–71.

14. Alexander W. Astin, "Undergraduate Institutions and Production of Scientists," *Science* (July 1963), pp. 334–338; Alexander W. Astin, "Effects of Different College Environments on the Vocational Choices of High Aptitude Students," *Journal of Counseling Psychology*, in press.
15. Alexander W. Astin, "Personal and Environmental Factors Associated with College Drop-outs Among High Aptitude Students," *Journal of Educational Psychology* (August 1964), pp. 219–227.
16. Alexander W. Astin, *Who Goes Where to College?* (Chicago, Ill.: Science Research Associates) in press.
17. Alexander W. Astin, "Some Characteristics of Student Bodies Entering Higher Educational Institutions," *Journal of Educational Psychology* (October 1964), pp. 267–275; Alexander W. Astin, "Distribution of Students Among Higher Educational Institutions," *Journal of Educational Psychology* (October 1964), pp. 276–287.
18. Robert Pace, *Preliminary Technical Manual: College and University Scales* (Princeton, 1963); George Stern, "The Intellectual Climate in Colleges," *Harvard Educational Review* (Winter 1963).
19. *Ibid.*
20. James D. Koerner, *Miseducation of American Teachers,* pp. 254–256, 258, 261.
21. William K. Selden, "The Place of Accreditation in the Governance of Higher Education," *Annual Report of the Executive Director* (National Commission on Accrediting, 1964), p. 12; Alexander W. Astin and J. L. Holland, "The Distribution of 'Wealth' in Higher Education," *College and University* (Winter 1962), p. 113; Arthur Benson, "The Role of Examinations in the Preparation of Teachers," *Journal of Teacher Education,* Vol. X (December 4, 1959), p. 496.
22. Information supplied by ETS; Moreita Payne Shamblin, "A Study of the Supply of Teachers Licensed Through Scores Achieved on the National Teacher Examinations," unpublished thesis presented to the Department of Education, Marshall University, 1962.
23. *Ibid.* Also information supplied by Florida State Department of Education.
24. James B. Conant, *The Education of American Teachers,* p. 77; information also supplied by various state departments of education.
25. John C. Flanagan, *Project Talent: The American High School Student* (Pittsburgh, 1964); John C. Flanagan, "Explanation of Project Talent," *NEA Journal* (June 1964).
26. P. M. Ford, *The Assignment and Mis-assignment of the American Teacher* (NCTEPS, 1964).

PART II

THE EFFECTS OF ACCREDITATION
IN TEACHER EDUCATION

This is a study of the influence on higher education of national, regional, and state accreditation in teacher education. The influence in most cases is expressed as effects on teacher education, which after all is an important segment of higher education. In some instances an effect on teacher education is associated explicitly with a concomitant influence on higher education but in general the association is considered to be implicit. For example, if accreditation in teacher education has had an influence on institutional organization and structure, on faculty relations, on general education programs, or on research, clearly there has been an influence on higher education.

The inherent difficulty of making certain that a particular change, or the maintenance of the status quo, in teacher education resulted directly from accreditation is clearly recognized. In general, the effects identified in the chapters comprising Part II of the Study are those to which the accrediting agency has made some specific reference in its relations with the college or university. Even in these instances, it is recognized that other factors have probably contributed to the decision or action of the institution. Almost without exception, accreditation is a factor which operates concomitantly with other factors. Yet when it is believed by an institution that accreditation depends upon the correction of weaknesses pointed out by an accrediting agency, or that accreditation may depend upon decisions which the institutional authorities are convinced the accrediting agency will "demand," a decision may be made which otherwise might be delayed or possibly never made. Also, standards of accrediting agencies are often recognized as a consensus of leaders in teacher education (or higher education) and thus carry more weight than the recommendations of a highly respected spokesman or of a report sponsored by a trusted professional society.

At first it was thought to be desirable to make a distinction between direct and indirect effects of accreditation. The latter were identified as those which might manifest themselves while an institution is an-

131

ticipating or preparing for accreditation rather than during or following the actual process. In attempting to do this, the lines of demarcation often become quite uncertain. After all, both the defenders and the critics of accreditation base their cases upon what institutional authorities decide an accrediting agency wants them to do, be it to conform or to experiment, as well as upon what the accrediting agency may actually insist they do.

Occasionally, a college or university which has serious doubts as to whether it merits accreditation will deliberately invite a visiting team to come in for the purpose of spelling out the deficiencies which will need to be corrected for later favorable action by the accrediting authority. The more common practice, however, for a college or university which really wants accreditation, is to try to ascertain in advance of a visitation just what the accrediting agency will want and expect, and thus to make any changes which might enhance the possibility of a favorable decision. To this end, extensive curricular changes may be made—courses may be added, revamped, or dropped; new committees or councils may be established; new administrative positions may be created; admission or graduation requirements may be stiffened; new counseling services may be instituted. As a matter of fact, the period of greatest impact of accreditation may well be the period of anticipation of or preparation for an accreditation visit.

The impacts on higher education of accreditation in teacher education at the national level have been easier to identify, since at any given time only one accrediting agency has been involved, and since the one agency has been primarily if not solely concerned with teacher education. For the past decade the one agency has been the National Council for Accreditation of Teacher Education (NCATE) and before 1954 the American Association of Colleges for Teacher Education (AACTE) which is a successor to the American Association of Teachers Colleges (AATC).

The situation with respect to regional accreditation, however, is entirely different. Here, with few exceptions, teacher education is evaluated and accredited merely as a part of the general institutional accreditation. Teacher education programs on the undergraduate level are not accredited separately; hence, it is impossible to isolate or identify the effects *per se* of the regional accreditation of teacher education. The only alternative has been to identify the effects upon higher education of those regional accreditation policies and to give emphasis to those effects which obviously relate to teacher education.

While some states accredit or approve institutions of higher education, a larger number of them accredit or approve teacher education programs specifically. For this reason, most of the effects of state accreditation on higher education can be expressed as effects on teacher education. The identification of these effects, however, becomes more complicated because there are 50 states and 50 different patterns of accreditation.

The participants in this Study have interpreted their assignment as that of identifying the effects or influences on higher education of accreditation in teacher education—not an evaluation of those influences or effects as to whether they are good or bad, beneficial or injurious, constructive or destructive.

It was recognized that one method of determining the total influence of accreditation of teacher education on higher education might be that of conducting a catalog survey in which two basic questions concerning undergraduate teacher education would be involved. These are: (1) Does there exist a common pattern of undergraduate teacher education programs? (2) Are there any significant differences between teacher education programs in NCATE-accredited institutions and those in non-NCATE-accredited institutions, and what are these differences? The second question, of course, places emphasis on national accreditation.

In conducting this survey, 962 institutions offering teacher education were classified as multipurpose universities, state and teachers colleges, or liberal arts colleges. A 10 percent random sample was selected from each of these categories and the catalogs of the institutions were studied to obtain data relevant to the two questions under investigation. In employing this method, it was realized that catalogs may not always provide a highly accurate description of an institution's actual program and policies; however, it was felt that catalog analyses in conjunction with institutional visitations and other elements in the Study would contribute to more valid conclusions.

The results of the catalog survey are summarized in Chapters 11 and 13, under curriculums and student policies. (Also see Appendix VI.)

Support for the observations made in the chapters of Part II is to be found in Appendix V, Accreditation in the States. Here are reported the opinions of the 50 state directors of teacher education and certification in answers to questions submitted to them about the influence of accreditation at the three levels, state, regional, and national. It is recommended that the reader turn to this section after reading Part II.

The segments of higher education affected most extensively by accreditation of teacher education appear to be those pertaining to a higher institution's organization, finances, curriculums, personnel policies, and exprimentation and research. These are the areas covered by the six chapters which comprise Part II of the Study. Because much of the material in these chapters is based upon confidential sources (NCATE files, personal interviews, and personal correspondence) a large part of the footnote documentation which normally would be included has had to be omitted.

In many instances mention of a specific college or university would be more convincing than reference to a "state college" or a "private university." However, in order to protect the institutions and to avoid making a public issue of the conditions surrounding their accreditation, this has not been done.

In the chapters of Part II examples are given of deficiencies in teacher education programs which have been submitted to institutions by NCATE as reasons for provisional or deferred accreditation or denial of accreditation. These examples were selected directly from NCATE files by the Study staff.

At the end of each chapter is a summary of influences described in the chapter.

CHAPTER 10

STRUCTURE AND ADMINISTRATION

Accrediting bodies, whether concerned primarily with general institutional evaluation or with a particular specialized program or combination of programs, are naturally and necessarily interested in the over-all organizational structure of the institution and with the machinery for administering the institution and its programs. To what extent do the structure and administration reflect the philosophy and objectives of the institution or of the specializations involved? Are the structure and administrative machinery designed for maximum efficiency in operating the institution or the particular program under review? All the while, a basic truth needs to be borne in mind: the poorest structure may work reasonably well with competent and efficient people to operate it; the best machinery in the world will not work well with incompetent and inefficient personnel.

IMPACT OF NATIONAL ACCREDITATION

The primary concern of NCATE in an institution's organization has to do with the machinery for the administration of the teacher education program. In the NCATE *Standards and Guide for Accreditation of Teacher Education*, Standard II, "Organization and Administration of Teacher Education," specifies that:

> The organization (1) should assure consistent policies and practices with reference to the different segments of the teacher education program regardless of the administrative units under which they operate; (2) should facilitate the continuous development and improvement of the teacher education program; and (3) should clearly fix responsibility for the administration of policies agreed upon.

Then, after stating that "because colleges and universities differ in over-all organizational structures, no pattern of organization for teacher

135

education applicable to all types of institutions is prescribed," the following interpretation or implication of Standard II is given:

> An organization will be regarded as acceptable for the development of policies when a single agency is made responsible for coordinating (1) the planning of teacher education curricula, (2) the development of policies that govern the admission of students to teacher education curricula, (3) the development of a system of registration and enrollment which makes it easy to identify all students preparing to teach and can be understood by students and faculty, and (4) the development of policies and standards for the satisfactory completion of all teacher education curricula. Such an agency will be the unit (college, school, division, department) of Education or an interdepartmental committee or council. If it is an interdepartmental committee, its membership will be representative of those divisions within the institution in proportion to their proper concerns for teacher education.

Although they do not specify one particular pattern, these provisions taken together appear to have been interpreted rather generally as an inelastic pattern of organization in which almost exactly the same machinery in administering teacher education was mandatory for all types of higher institutions. It has, therefore, been condemned as an unnecessary and unjustifiable encroachment upon the freedom of the institution to experiment with different types of program operation. It is said that NCATE has tried to force all teacher-training institutions into the same straitjacket of drab uniformity in administrative structure.[1]

In order to consider the impact of NCATE on structure and administration and to analyze the validity of the criticism that NCATE has forced institutions into a straitjacket of administrative structure, attention will be given to four aspects of administration with which NCATE apparently has been most concerned. These are: (1) all-institutional teacher education committees or councils, (2) departments and schools or colleges of education, (3) identification of an individual for administrative responsibility, and (4) single or multiple (usually two) "paths" to certification. All of these aspects relate to NCATE's Standard II.

ALL-INSTITUTIONAL COMMITTEES

NCATE, through Standard II, has induced many colleges and universities to establish closer working relations in educational planning and control between academic and education faculties. This usually has been accomplished through the organization within each college or university of an interdepartmental committee or council. Many persons concerned with teacher education appear to regard the existence and activity of such a committee or council to be generally con-

---

[1] This point of view was expressed at the *NCATE Conference of One Hundred,* in Chicago, November 14, 1963; see pp. 46–48 of *Report.*

structive and beneficial. As in the case of school integration, one can only speculate as to how much time would be required to bring about such a result without strong outside pressure. Also like school integration, there are still some who believe that the achievement of such a result is not worth while if it has to be achieved by pressure on an institution by an outside agency. At all events, in this effect of Standard II of NCATE's *Standards and Guide* is to be found what many consider to be one of NCATE's major accomplishments.

It seems unlikely that any college or university would at this time receive full NCATE accreditation without evidence of the existence of an agency, be it a department, school, committee, or council, which is representative of all segments of the institution's teacher education program. At the same time, it should be noted that teacher education institutions have been accredited by NCATE without an all-institutional council or committee for teacher education. It seems apparent that such institutions have been regarded as meeting Standard II in some other way, such as by bringing representatives of subject-matter departments into the college or department of education machinery. However, any institution seeking national accreditation would very likely set up an all-institutional council or committee in anticipation of an NCATE team visit. This is a view which was never questioned during the conferences held as a part of the Study.

NCATE has also been concerned with the representation on the committee and with its status and functions. Typical of colleges seeking accreditation, one Wisconsin college reported that after an NCATE visit the representation on their committee was changed to include more from liberal arts. A state university in Illinois reported NCATE approval of its council which had the power to establish general education requirements for the college of education and to approve other modifications of existing programs. Yet one dean of liberal arts was unhappy with his institution's method of appointment of the Council. He thought that he, rather than the dean of education, should choose the liberal arts representatives.

Even when an institution-wide teacher education council exists, full accreditation may be withheld pending a clarification of the council's status and authority. NCATE sometimes makes it clear to an institution that the teacher education council must be given authority not only to formulate teacher education policies but also to supervise their execution. An examination of NCATE records reveals numerous instances in which the Council has refused to give full accreditation to a teacher education institution until certain changes were made in the administration of the teacher education program. The administration may be told that institution-wide machinery is needed to plan and coordinate all aspects of teacher education. A specific question may be raised as to the extent to which the academic staff actively participates in the teacher education program. Or the institution may be made aware that successful planning and coordination of professional education is not possible as long as the education offices and laboratories remain scattered over the campus.

NCATE has also influenced quite a number of states to include such committees as part of a "requirement" for state accreditation or approval. In a meeting with the teacher education committee of a state university and the visiting team from the state department of education, the head of the department of mathematics, speaking for the committee, testified to the new interest and participation in teacher education of university scholars, which had resulted from the two-year operation of the all-university committee.

DEPARTMENT AND SCHOOL OR COLLEGE OF EDUCATION

While NCATE's Standard II does not specifically call for the establishment of a department, school, or college of education, it is generally regarded as true that NCATE would hesitate to accredit a state or liberal arts college without a department of education. It has also been assumed that a graduate program in a multipurpose university which does not have a school or college of education would have difficulty in being accredited. One state university offering a doctoral program in education withdrew its application for accreditation because NCATE criticized as disorderly its pattern of administration of teacher education. The university had no school or college of education. A liberal arts college reported that a head of the department of education had been appointed to meet one of NCATE's criticisms. These are examples of influences on administrative structure on which there would not be agreement as to whether or not the changes were beneficial.

In the reference from the interpretation or implication of Standard II given on page 136, note that the reference to the administrative agency of the institution closes with the sentences: "Such an agency will be the unit (college, school, division, department) of Education *or an interdepartmental committee or council.* If it is an interdepartmental committee, its membership will be representative of those divisions within the institution in proportion to their proper concerns for teacher education." The italics are inserted here by the authors for emphasis. These sentences would seem to clearly imply that a teacher education program might be administered by an interdepartmental committee rather than a unit in education.

While the great majority of institutions that offer teacher education programs do have departments of education, there are a few colleges which offer teacher education without such an administrative unit. No record has been found that these colleges have applied for national accreditation nor that they intend to do so. Similarly, there are some multipurpose universities which offer doctoral programs in education which have a department of education but no school or college of education. A notable example is Duke University which is accredited by NCATE. Duke University has a Department of Education which is a department of the Graduate School of Arts and Sciences. The Department offers work leading to A.M., M.Ed., M.A.T., and D.Ed. degrees.

It has been pointed out that the recent NCATE accreditation of Washington University (St. Louis) was a test case in that the teacher education program (graduate and undergraduate) is under the direction of the Graduate Institute of Education which is a unit of the Graduate School of Arts and Sciences. Others would say that the Institute is the equivalent of a department or division of education.

Because of the influence of what institutions believe an accrediting agency will insist upon, one may say that NCATE has had an influence in persuading institutions to hire professors of education and organize units in education.

Critics of what is called the "establishment" point out that it has been willing to stand by and see graduates of liberal arts colleges (without departments of education) cut off from teaching positions in public schools and that state certification officers have pretty consistently taken the position that would force departments and professors of education on such colleges. These critics usually consider NCATE as part of the "establishment."

INDIVIDUAL ADMINISTRATIVE RESPONSIBILITY

In addition to its insistence that a single agency be made responsible for planning and coordinating a school's teacher education program, NCATE has insisted that one individual be made responsible for the administration of the program in teacher education. Standard II of NCATE's *Standards and Guide* puts it this way:

> Responsibility for the total program will be regarded as clearly assigned when some one person is held responsible for the administration of the total program and when that person is in a position to speak authoritatively for the total program. The same person will normally be the one responsible for recommending students for teacher certification.

This emphasis grows out of an awareness that teacher education programs in multipurpose institutions are scattered among as many as a half dozen colleges or schools. Besides education and liberal arts, there may be teacher education programs in schools or colleges of agriculture, business, fine arts, home economics, industrial arts, and music. It is intended that the institution-wide teacher education committee should coordinate all these divergent programs into one overall teacher education program. Ordinarily, someone in the department or school of education is named as administrator of the program. Again, NCATE puts it this way:

> With respect to the administration of the program . . . the principle is expressed that the responsibility should be centralized; that the division of labor should be clearly defined; that administrators should be given sufficient, clearly enunciated authority to be able to implement the policies adopted by the policy forming group; that channels of communication should be open; and that pathways

for action should be relatively free from entanglements which would place unnecessary restrictions on efficient action. . . .

Whether students are enrolled in a college or division of Education or in some other unit is an institutional matter. Wherever they are housed, however, the policies adopted by the institution for its teacher education programs should be equally applied to all. The professional curriculum which the students are committed to pursue, rather than the degrees they will earn or the administration unit with which they are affiliated, should be the major determinant of the policies under which they operate. Again, also, emphasis is placed on the idea that the students will be someone's *primary responsibility* wherever they may be enrolled.

Provisions for reaching students with information about certification requirements or student teaching should be as complete for students housed administratively in Agriculture as for students in a School of Education. . . .

A deficiency in the teacher education programs of some multipurpose universities (including the University of Wisconsin) to which NCATE has called attention has been the relationship between the principal administrator in teacher education, usually the dean of the college of education, with the programs for teachers of music often in the college of liberal arts; of agriculture and home economics in the college of agriculture; of business education in a college of commerce; and of art education sometimes in a school of fine arts. Because of their location in other colleges, these prospective teachers may not have the same program of general education, they may even substitute some courses in their own college for courses in the professional sequence, and the students enrolled in teacher education may be unknown in qualifications, and even by names or the number of them, to the principal administrator.

In one state university the music education program was transferred from liberal arts to education upon the suggestion of NCATE. Again, there is no consensus on whether influence of this kind is to be regarded as a credit or demerit for NCATE. In a meeting on this campus with some 20 persons from education and liberal arts, several members of the education staff called attention to this change as an example of the constructive influence of NCATE. While the dean of liberal arts did not disagree with the worth of the change, he apparently had forgotten that it had resulted in any way from an NCATE visitation.

In the application of the approved-program approach [2] to certification now utilized by many states, under which one institutional official is responsible for certifying that graduates have completed satisfactorily an approved program, and through the insistence by NCATE that one official of the institution be responsible for the administration of teacher education, it appears that almost without exception accredited pro-

---

[2] Chapter 3, p. 25; also Chapter 11, pp. 153, 154.

grams have an administrator with a clearly defined responsibility. NCATE, along with other factors, has had this effect.

"PATHS" TO CERTIFICATION

It is also generally believed that NCATE has frowned upon an institution's having "two or more paths" leading to state certification. This issue arises more commonly with multipurpose universities. While most students who apply for certificates are graduated from the school or college of education, it is possible in some institutions for a student also to be graduated from liberal arts and to qualify for certification by taking electives in education. It has been interpreted that the two "paths" to certification are not in full keeping with Standard II; yet there are institutions on NCATE's accredited list in which this situation is possible. There is little doubt that in other institutions the liberal arts "path" has been eliminated due to anticipated or actual NCATE pressure. Where two "paths" exist, NCATE has recommended that provision be made for a comparative study of the effectiveness of the two "paths."

Thus NCATE has apparently had two kinds of effects on institutions relative to the ways in which students might become certified to teach. In some cases, it has been instrumental in persuading the institution to recognize only one program by which a graduate may become certified for teaching. This program is developed by the agency responsible for teacher education and in many states it is the program approved by the state department of education. In such institutions some kind of regulations are necessary to exclude students not officially in the program from registering in courses required for a teachers certificate, such as social foundations of education and student teaching.

In other cases where an institution has been accredited even though students may complete requirements for a state certificate to teach without being registered in the regular teacher education program of the institution, NCATE has insisted upon a comparative study of the two "paths." The non-program students in these institutions usually are graduated from liberal arts with an academic major and have taken education courses, including student teaching, often without credit toward graduation.

REGIONAL ACCREDITATION

Accrediting agencies on all levels are concerned about certain aspects of an institution's organization and administration. Is there evidence of a rapid turnover in administrative personnel? Is there an evident lack of institutional stability? Are there strong indications of low morale on the part of the administrative staff? Is the institution under the domination of a "dictator"? NCATE, the regional association, and the state authorities may all be concerned about such conditions; but, as a rule, none is concerned enough to do anything toward remedying a "bad" administrative situation. Usually, only when "bad" educational administration has attracted wide public attention is any positive action taken.[3] The result of such reluctance to act on the part of accreditation authorities is that unwholesome administrative conditions are permitted to drag on unchecked and all important aspects of the institution suffer.

A happy exception to the excessive toleration of "bad" college and university administrations was reported by one regional accrediting association. When an accreditation visit was made to a liberal arts institution in the area served by the association, the visiting team found a deplorable situation. Administrative offices were inefficient, the institution's finances were extremely unstable, both faculty and student morale were low. All of the difficulty seemed to point clearly to the head of the institution. After careful deliberation, it was decided to report the committee's findings to the institution's board of trustees. Result: the president was retired and a new president was appointed.

The principal concern of regional associations in the general organization or structure of a higher institution appears to manifest itself at the time of the original accreditation of the school. At this time, a critical look is taken at all aspects of the institution's organization and program. The institution under review is always asked to describe the responsibilities of the administrative staff. Other questions may be raised and pressure may be applied whenever the visiting committee finds something substantially out of line with the normal institutional pattern. If, for example, there is no provision in the institution's structure for a business manager, or for a registrar, or for at least one academic or personnel dean, the institution might be told to correct the structural deficiencies before full accreditation can be given.

On a reaccreditation visit if serious administrative problems are apparent, another close look might be taken at the administrative structure and certain changes insisted upon. Likewise, the regional association in its role of stimulating improvement might suggest or recommend organizational changes believed to be in the best interests of the college or university.

STATE ACCREDITATION

The state's impact upon a higher institution's organization or structure may stem from any one of three sources: (1) from the authority to issue and approve charters for public or private colleges or uni-

---

[3] A spokesman for the North Central Association reported that in extreme cases of administration dictatorship accreditation may be withheld or even taken away. The representative of the Western Association declared that, if there is an administrative problem, "We say in no uncertain terms that changes must be made." The Middle States Association asks the administration, in serious difficulty, if there is any reason not to remove the institution from the Association's list of accredited institutions.

versities; (2) from the authority to accredit or approve teacher education programs or general college status; and (3) from the authority to grant certificates to teachers on the elementary or secondary levels. In actual practice the states seldom concern themselves with matters of institutional organization, except in what the state agency responsible for accreditation believes to be the relation of the teacher education institution to the certification of teachers.

Where states issue charters to public or private higher institutions, there may be a careful or only a casual scrutiny of the institution's organizational pattern. Likewise, where a state accredits the general college status of an institution, it may examine the institution's pattern of organization. Procedures similar to those of the regional accrediting association, which includes the state, are usually followed. One prestigious liberal arts institution reported that full state accreditation was being withheld pending the establishment of a separate college of education.[4]

If the teacher education program of an institution is accredited or approved by the state department for the training of elementary or secondary teachers or school service personnel, the state department will ordinarily issue a certificate to any graduate properly attested by the school as having completed the program in question. In order to fix responsibility for such recommendations, the state will usually insist that one person be designated by the teacher education institution to sign all certification documents. Ordinarily, the person so designated is the dean of the school or college of education or the chairman of the department of education. As with national accreditation, most persons consider this to be a reasonable requirement on the part of the state, particularly where there are several schools, colleges, or divisions with teacher education programs in one institution.

In some states, the standards and procedures of NCATE have had a very considerable impact on state standards and procedures for accreditation of teacher education programs. In these states, state accreditation may depend upon the existence of an active all-institutional teacher education committee or council. Thus at least some of the states, along with NCATE, have had an influence upon the participation of academic professors in determining, in cooperation with their colleagues in education, teacher education policies and programs. In visits to several states the importance of the all-institutional committee in teacher education, and the participation of academic personnel in state-wide conferences and advisory groups, was emphasized by the directors of teacher education more than any other facet of teacher education. Some of the states in which state officials are less enthusiastic about NCATE are also emphasizing cooperation of academic groups in teacher education planning. In these states the

---

[4] This was reported by both the institution and a representative of the state department.

officials would be reluctant to credit NCATE for their interest in this realm.

It seems reasonable to conclude that most state accrediting agencies have had more influence than NCATE in persuading colleges and universities, seeking state approval of teacher education programs, to employ professors of education and establish departments of education and schools or colleges of education, if they wish to offer graduate work.

The impact of the states on institutional policy in permitting the existence of two "paths" to certification is more difficult to assess, and certainly to generalize about, than the influence of NCATE in this respect. If a state certifies a graduate of an institution *only* upon the assertion by the appropriate authority that the graduate has completed an approved program—and this is the practice in some states—then the state has a real impact in this respect on institutional policy and higher education in the state. On the other hand many states, including those which approve teacher education programs and those which do not, will grant a certificate to a graduate who has met a specified list of state requirements. The institutions of higher education find it at least awkward to insist that each graduate must complete a program of teacher education officially approved by the institution. Even in these cases, at least in the sense of *laissez faire,* the state can be said to have an impact on higher education policies.

SUMMARY

It appears that NCATE has clearly had an influence on institutions: (1) in the establishment of an over-all, institution-wide committee or council to formulate and supervise teacher education policies; (2) in the designation of one person to be responsible for the administration of all teacher education programs; and (3) in the re-examination by institutions of their policies in regard to permitting students to satisfy teacher certification requirements without being registered in officially recognized teacher education programs. At least what institutions believe that NCATE wants has had an influence in the establishment in four-year colleges of departments of education and in institutions offering graduate work of schools or colleges of education.

The regional association's general scrutiny of an institution's administrative organization at the time of the initial appraisal of the school, or when the institution is threatened with the loss of accreditation, has had an influence on institutional administration. The regional associations, through recommendations for improvement, have also brought about changes considered to be improvements. The rare cases of the regional association's investigation of an institution, in cases where "bad" administration of the school is widely publicized, have occasionally resulted in a change of administration.

The state's insistence that one person in each institution be named to recommend for certification students who have successfully completed an approved program of teacher education has brought about (or supported) the practice in states where the approved-program approach is used. In some states, usually those which follow the NCATE pattern of accreditation, the state authorities have been instrumental in the appointment of all-institutional committees with responsibility for teacher education in institutions in addition to those accredited by NCATE. The rarely used threat of a state department or legislative investigation of an institution, in the event that the internal affairs of an institution seem to justify or require it, probably has been influential in preventing excesses in administrative malfeasance.

CHAPTER 11

COLLEGE AND UNIVERSITY
CURRICULUMS

THE ACADEMIC and professional programs, in which students receive their cultural and vocational instruction in formal classroom or other college credit-earning experiences, are naturally of vital concern to accrediting bodies. However, the nature if not the degree of this concern varies from agency to agency. The regional accrediting associations traditionally have been interested primarily in the arts and sciences; NCATE is devoted primarily but not exclusively to the professional training programs in education; many of the states are interested in both. In the light of these circumstances, a differentiation is made in this chapter between accreditation of subject-matter programs and those in the broad field of education.

EFFECTS UPON ACADEMIC CURRICULUMS OF ACCREDITATION IN TEACHER EDUCATION

NATIONAL ACCREDITATION

The interest of NCATE in the subject-matter curriculums is two-fold:

1. In the content pattern in general or liberal education; and
2. In the subject-matter requirements for teacher education majors and minors, and in the areas of concentration in elementary education.

NCATE has been manifesting a growing interest in the institution's general education program or courses required of all bachelor's degree candidates. In addition, NCATE as a rule has recommended that an institution have the same general education requirements for all prospective teachers, both elementary and secondary, as well as for teachers of such subjects as agriculture and music. Although NCATE has accredited institutions which did not adhere to this standard, one of the effects of NCATE accreditation has been in increasing the number of hours required in many colleges and universities of general education

146

for elementary teachers, as well as for teachers of home economics, music, industrial arts, and other subjects in which prospective teachers specialize. NCATE has also looked with favor on general education programs which are the same as all-institutional requirements for the baccalaureate. [1]

Most courses offered for general education purposes are offered in liberal arts and sciences departments; hence, according to bilateral agreements between NCATE and the regional associations these courses are supposed to be under the jurisdiction of the regionals. NCATE, however, has realized that the general education program is basic to teacher education; consequently, it is of direct concern to NCATE. Contrary to common belief, NCATE in the past has not shown an inclination to keep the general education requirements low and those in education courses high. In denying full accreditation to some colleges, and particularly to former teachers colleges, NCATE has sometimes listed as a deficiency an excessive requirement of course work in education and too low a requirement in subject-matter courses.

NCATE has depended upon the regional accrediting agency to examine the qualifications of the staff, the nature of course offerings, and the library and laboratory facilities of departments of an institution which offer majors and minors for secondary school teachers and areas of concentration for elementary school teachers. NCATE, however, does concern itself with the balance in a prospective teacher's program in respect to general education, professional education, and major specialization. It also is concerned with the sequence or program of courses in a student's major from the point of view of their suitability as a preparation for teaching. NCATE visiting teams, in general, do not include specialists in academic disciplines, or at best no more than one or two. Thus, they are not in a position to make many judgments regarding the program of major concentration.

However, NCATE does suggest that certain majors appear to be inadequate with respect to number of hours or that students may be permitted too high a degree of specialization. The Council also concerns itself with degrees of uniformity, noting, for example, that it is questionable to require 50 or more hours for a major in music and only 20 hours in mathematics. As a rule, particularly in more recent years, NCATE has encouraged institutions to permit or require a greater major concentration.

NCATE may also concern itself with the selection of courses for a major and may advise an institution that the sequence of courses desirable for a liberal arts major may not necessarily be desirable for the teaching major. This is not in disagreement with recommendations of academic groups which have considered the needs of teachers in their disciplines. While in general NCATE, supported by professors of education and their professional organizations, does not advocate the offering of special courses, even special sections for teachers, the Council has looked with favor on a few of the newer courses which academicians, working with professional societies, have designed especially for teachers both at the elementary and at the secondary level. This is true particularly in mathematics.

In a conference with staff members of academic departments in a private university recently visited by NCATE, one effect of the NCATE visit reported was the introduction of a special course in geometry for teachers. Others in the group also observed that the NCATE visit had focused their attention on the nature of the major for teachers in English, for example, and that some changes had been made as a result of the visit.

NCATE's interest in the academic aspects of teacher education is supported by evidence obtained from the Council's files on teacher education institutions. Here are some samples of deficiencies listed as reasons for withholding full NCATE accreditation:

> The subject-matter requirements in secondary education need to be increased.
> Better balance is needed between theoretical and applied sciences.
> Better balance is needed between general education, professional education, and the area of specialization.
> It appears that secondary education majors are offered in too many areas for the limited financial resources of the institution.
> There should be more hours of academic courses required in secondary education majors.
> General education requirements need to be increased—those on education decreased.
> Thirty hours are not enough in general education.
> No mathematics is presently included in general education requirements.

Some of the deficiencies apply specifically to graduate programs in teacher education:

> Too few subject-matter courses are required in the master's degree programs.
> There is too much education, not enough subject matter in the graduate programs.
> There is too little academic work required of graduate students in elementary education.
> Too few qualified cognate areas are required for the proposed doctoral program in English education.

In visits to higher institutions, examples of changes suggested above have been found and it seems fair to assume that NCATE has had an effect in these ways on teacher education programs and thus on higher education. Word of these criticisms passes freely among teacher education institutions, from institutions to state departments to other institutions, and sometimes brings about such changes before an NCATE visit is scheduled and following the visit. While NCATE does not examine the quality of the staff offering academic courses, the quality or sequence of the courses, or the quality of instruction in those courses, the Council has had an effect on the extent (in percent of hours in the total programs) and breadth of general education, as well as in the amount of specialization, and the appropriateness of courses for prospective teachers. NCATE's influence, relative to academic courses, has probably been greatest in the preparation of elementary teachers and in supporting the present widespread trend in elementary education to less professional education and to more general education, including a degree of specialization, often referred to as an area of concentration, in academic fields, such as art, mathematics, sciences, or social science.

In describing NCATE's influence on academic programs, special reference should be made to the "Supplement to the General NCATE *Standards and Guide,* for the Preparation of School Superintendents and Principals." This supplement was prepared with the assistance of the American Association of School Administrators (AASA). Members of the AASA and others can take satisfaction from the inclusion in the supplement of standards relating to general education and courses outside of professional education. These standards are applied largely to programs at the graduate level.

The "Guide for Developing the Report on Objectives" draws attention to the importance of "courses bearing an obvious relation to school administration (e.g., Economics, Anthropology, Political Science)"; and the "Standard for Curriculum and Laboratory Experiences" includes the statement:

> Each curriculum should contain a required core including courses both in and outside the field of Education which bear an obvious relationship to school administration. When a student brings to a program an inadequate background in general education or in the field of Education, he should be required to make up the deficiency.

These standards bear the date 1960 and four years is a rather short period for measuring their effects. However, they appear to have some potential for bringing about at least a small amount of attention to the area of general education in the preparation of school administrators.

In the catalog survey described in the introduction to Part II of this Study, a comparison of general education requirements was made between NCATE and non-NCATE universities, NCATE and non-NCATE state and teachers colleges, and NCATE and non-NCATE liberal arts colleges, respectively.[1] The subcategories of general education used in the survey were: communications, health and related areas, humanities, sciences, mathematics, psychology, and social studies. Comparisons were made among the six types of institutions for each

---

[1] An NCATE institution is one accredited by NCATE, while a non-NCATE institution is one not on the NCATE list of accredited institutions.

subcategory. In only one instance was there a statistically significant difference between means of requirements of NCATE and non-NCATE institutions. The difference occurred in the area of communications for both elementary and secondary education in the comparison of NCATE and non-NCATE state and teachers colleges:

Category of Institution	Mean Semester Hours of Communications Required in Elementary Education	Mean Semester Hours of Communications Required in Secondary Education
NCATE State and Teachers Colleges	11.6	11.1
Non-NCATE State and Teachers Colleges	17.2	15.0

One observation to be made is that, generally speaking, there is no significant difference between general education requirements in NCATE- and non-NCATE-accredited institutions. One might conclude, then, that NCATE accreditation has had no influence on general education requirements. Actually quite a number of instances were found in the Study in which NCATE caused institutions to increase or broaden general education requirements. The deficiency shown above for one category of institutions may be a result of NCATE's insistence upon a spread in general education requirements.

Of interest also is a comparison of total semester-hour requirements in general education among students preparing to be elementary teachers, those preparing to be secondary school teachers, and those who are to be graduated in liberal arts. The mean range is for purposes of comparison.

Program	Mean Range of Total General Education Requirements in Semester Hours
Elementary Education	47.0–68.5
Secondary Education	46.6–55.7
Liberal Arts	41.0–55.7

In explanation, 47.0 is the lowest mean of total general education requirements and 68.5 the highest mean, among the six types of institutions identified above. One can conclude from this table there is little difference in general education requirements among the three categories of students. Those who assume or believe that general education is sacrificed for professional training in teacher education requirements may be surprised and pleased with the tabulation.

In comparing the specialization requirements in secondary educa-

tion of NCATE and non-NCATE institutions, two significant differences were found: (1) the NCATE liberal arts college mean requirement for a secondary English major was 33.9 semester hours as compared to 30.0 for non-NCATE liberal arts colleges; and (2) the non-
NCATE multipurpose university mean requirement for a pure liberal
arts history major was 34.6 semester hours as compared to 26.6 for
NCATE multipurpose universities. The latter difference may be due to
a greater emphasis on a social science field major than on a history
major at NCATE-accredited institutions, and the former to the introduction of special courses for prospective English teachers.

A comparison of major area requirements for those preparing to
teach in secondary schools and those to be graduated in liberal arts for
the six types of institutions does not reveal as great a difference as is
often believed to be true. The data are given in the following table:

Area of Concentration	Mean Range for Secondary Education Major (Semester Hours)	Mean Range for Liberal Arts Major (Semester Hours)
Art	29.8–38.8	30.2–48.7
Biology	29.7–33.1	30.1–37.9
Chemistry	31.0–34.7	31.7–39.2
English	30.0–35.0	30.0–34.3
French	26.5–30.7	26.2–32.4
History	27.7–34.6	27.7–34.6
Mathematics	27.1–31.3	29.4–34.0
Music	36.0–48.7	38.4–46.1
Physics	29.0–32.5	28.5–38.2
Spanish	25.0–27.4	26.0–32.4

REGIONAL ACCREDITATION

Like NCATE the regional associations have a two-fold interest in
academic curriculums: (1) in the general education program; and (2)
in the requirements for academic majors and minors. In general education or the general degree requirements, the regionals are concerned
with the answers to two questions: (1) Does the general education
program cover all the areas necessary to a well-rounded basic training
for life? (2) What proportion of the total baccalaureate requirements
is given over to general education? No attention appears to be paid as
to whether general education courses are offered as survey courses or as
the more traditional departmental courses. Nor do the regionals interest themselves in the teaching methods employed, whether it is
the lecture method, whether there is provision for discussion, whether
the classes are large or small. In academic majors and minors the concern of the regional associations seems to be the requirements in terms
of quarter or semester hours, rather than in the subject matter taught.
The regionals tend to frown both on too little depth in a subject-matter
specialization and on over-specialization in a major.

In evaluating a higher institution, the Middle States Association wants to know the "extent to which the institution's curriculums provide, emphasize, or rest upon general or liberal education." The New England Association specifies that "a senior college must offer instruction in no fewer than eight major fields in arts and sciences." The North Central Association asks, "Are the curriculum and instructional programs adapted to the goals of the institution?" The Northwest Association wants to learn as much as possible about the nature and quality of the curriculum. The Southern Association in its Standard III states: "The curriculum offerings of an institution should be clearly and accurately described in published materials. Curricula should be directly related and appropriate to the purposes and objectives of the institution, to the ability and preparation of the students admitted, and to the financial and instructional resources of the institution." The Western Association wants to learn as much as possible about the nature of the institution's curriculum. [2]

The current emphasis of the regional associations on stimulation to improvement must be judged as having had an influence on the academic curriculums of institutions of higher education in the ways suggested by the kind of information sought by the several regionals. There are, of course, differences among the regionals in approach to institutions, in rigidity of application of standards, in the amount of attention given to total and specific curriculums. The Middle States appears to have had the greatest effect on higher institution curriculums simply because that Association has given more specific attention to them. Because most four-year colleges are already accredited by the regionals, together with the fact that most colleges welcome a visiting team of "expert" consultants to a campus, few complaints were heard about the regional associations. In the campuses visited as part of this Study, some staff members were of the opinion that the regionals had been highly influential in strengthening academic curriculums of institutions of higher education. Others expressed the view that regional influence had been negligible. There was no noticeable difference by regions except possibly that Southern Association institutions were somewhat more favorable to the regionals.

THE STATES

The interest of state accrediting authorities in college and university curriculums resembles that of NCATE more closely than that of the regional associations. First, the states with their active interest in certification want to know the minimum number of quarter or semester hours of work required for majors and minors in teacher education programs. The concern here appears to be more with *quantity* than *quality*. Second, the states are interested in the general education or general degree requirements of teacher education institutions. Here the states are concerned not only with the total requirement, but also with the general area or division of subject matter, such as English, mathematics, biological sciences, physical sciences, and social sciences. Many of the states specify, as a certification requirement, the minimum number of hours which must be taken in each of the areas listed. Like the regional associations, the states as a rule do not concern themselves with the teaching methods employed in presenting the subject matter, whether in survey courses, lecture courses, seminars, or discussion groups. These are matters in which educational institutions generally have complete freedom of choice.

In addition to their concern for general degree requirements and for teacher education majors and minors, the states in the past half century have shown an increasing tendency to establish specific course requirements in certain areas. Frequently these special requirements are the result of pressures exerted upon state legislatures by special interest groups. Sometimes in states with provision for direct legislation, the requirements may be imposed through the initiative and referendum.

In some instances the special subject-matter requirements have patriotic overtones. Again, the motives involved may be related to personal health or morality. Examples are courses in conservation, in the Federal constitution and government, state constitution and government, health education, physical education, communism, and marriage. One state requires the teaching on all levels—elementary, secondary, and college—of the proper displaying of the United States flag. It is courses like these which, regardless of motive or merit, place a big obstacle in the way of reciprocity among the states in teacher certification. This explains, in part at least, why present provisions for reciprocity in certification grant only temporary or provisional certification pending the applicant's meeting the special state requirements for certification.

If a state issues certificates by "credit counting" and the state requires four hours in mathematics, the teacher education institutions of the state feel obliged to offer a four-credit-hour course in mathematics, even though a three- or five-credit-hour course might be preferred by the department of mathematics. This is an example of one of the dangers from excesses in certification requirements. The wide adoption of the approved-program approach is alleviating this unfortunate kind of situation.

One of the most important of the state impacts on teacher education curriculums is through the approved-program approach to state certification of teachers. Forty of the 50 states are reported to be operating under this pattern of certification,[2] but apparently not all of these have gone all the way. Also, in 50 states a term like the "approved-program approach" can mean many things. Some apparently view it as nothing

---

[2] Armstrong and Stinnett report that 40 states use the approved-program approach (*Certification Requirements*, p. 21). In the questionnaire survey conducted in connection with this Study, 33 reported that they were using this approach to state certification.

more than approval or accreditation of institutions for teacher education.

The usual procedure in program approval is this: The state department will ask the teacher education institution to prepare and submit a curriculum, say for elementary teachers. Sometimes a representative of the state department will collaborate in the formulation of the program —usually not. The program will list the courses and sequences, indicating which courses are to be required and which are to be elective. In some states, the proposals are given careful and detailed diagnosis; in other states, the proposed programs are approved with little more than a cursory examination. Where the approved-program approach is mandatory, the state, if it wishes, is in a position through the simple process of withholding approval virtually to dictate the program and the entire pattern of teacher education in the state. On the other hand, the state can use the approved-program approach to give much more autonomy to the institutions in developing their teacher education programs.

Through working directly with the state department, foreign language specialists, mathematicians, and scientists have been assisting directly in the preparation of state guidelines for teacher education programs. These academicians usually make use of recommendations of national societies of which they are members. The American Association for the Advancement of Science, the Mathematical Association of America, and the Modern Language Association have sponsored the preparation of guidelines (or similarly organized recommendations) for teacher education in their respective disciplines. [3] In the states in which these guidelines are used, and the number of those states is increasing, state accreditation of teacher education has effected the adoption by colleges of academic programs endorsed for their disciplines by national academic societies.

These efforts have been particularly effective in the case of mathematics courses for elementary teachers. The Committee on the Undergraduate Program of the Mathematical Association of America, known as CUP-M, has followed up its preparation of guidelines with state conferences of mathematics teachers held in cooperation with state departments of education. In Kentucky, for example, all eight teacher education institutions visited, with the possible exception of one, had either introduced these courses or were preparing to do so.

Since 1950, representatives of state departments of education and the U. S. Office of Education have been attempting to formulate minimum standards for state approval of teacher education. A report was issued covering four categories of accreditation: (1) procedures to be followed in state accreditation; (2) principles and standards of reorganization; (3) curriculum principles and standards for advanced study. These principles and standards included general education, academic major, and areas of concentration. The original proposal (Circular 351) was issued in 1952; a proposed revision was released for discussion in

May, 1964. This document occupied a prominent place on the agenda of the 1964 annual meeting of NASDTEC (National Association of State Directors of Teacher Education and Certification). As it stands, the proposal is capable of being used with or without the approved-program approach to certification. It recommends close cooperation among state departments, the regional associations, and NCATE. [4]

A very significant aspect of the *Proposed Standards for State Approval of Teacher Education* is the inclusion in it of rather detailed guidelines for majors for secondary school teachers and preparation in academic subjects for elementary teachers. Here again the influence of the academicians and their professional societies is much in evidence. A representative of the Modern Language Association has worked directly with the committee preparing the guidelines, and the committee has made liberal use of the guidelines recently published for the preparation of teachers in science and mathematics. This participation of academic personnel in the preparation of a document for the education of teachers by state directors of teacher education and Office of Education personnel is a landmark in the improved relations between academicians and professional educators. The Proposed Standards promises to be a highly influential document in the next decade.

IMPACT OF ACCREDITATION IN TEACHER EDUCATION UPON CURRICULUM IN EDUCATION

NATIONAL ACCREDITATION

NCATE has concerned itself with three aspects of the professional education segments of an institution's program in teacher education: (1) the course requirements in education, including the content of courses and sequences; (2) the institution's program in student teaching; and (3) the provision made by the institution for laboratory experiences in teacher education.

In evaluating the course offerings in education, NCATE has scrutinized closely not only the minimum quarter or semester hours of work required in education courses, but also the aspects of teacher education covered in each course. If the self-study reveals or if the visiting team discovers serious deficiencies in the education offerings, the institution will be advised or required to "shore up" those weaknesses in the program before full accreditation can be given. One thing NCATE has regarded with jaundiced eye is a lack of evidence that sufficient consideration has been given to the special needs of teachers in terms of the level and nature of the work for which they are preparing. Again, it should be noted that in evaluating the total amount of credit required in education courses, NCATE appears to have shown a greater tendency to insist on a reduction rather than an increase in the requirement.[3]

In the catalog survey, patterns of requirements in professional education were compared for elementary education and secondary education programs. Subcategories of professional education investigated are child development and educational psychology, social foundations, general and special methods, and student teaching. Comparisons of professional education requirements were made between NCATE and non-NCATE universities, NCATE and non-NCATE state and teachers colleges, and NCATE and non-NCATE liberal arts colleges. In only one case a statistically significant difference between NCATE and non-NCATE institutions was found. This difference occurred in social foundations in elementary education in a comparison of multipurpose universities. The NCATE universities required a mean of 4.0 semester hours and non-NCATE universities a mean of 2.6 semester hours.

Again, it may be observed that the impact of NCATE accreditation on professional education requirements, as far as revealed by this survey, could be considered negligible. In relation to professional education, the question may be legitimately raised as to the impact of NCATE standards on state standards and thus on non-NCATE institutions.

Since it is commonly believed to be true that the requirements in professional education are much greater for elementary school teachers than those for secondary school teachers, it is interesting to note that this survey does not confirm the opinion. One might say that these requirements are some greater but not excessively so. The principal difference in range of means for the elementary and secondary levels is in the area of general and special methods.

Program	Mean Range of Total Professional Education Requirements in Semester Hours
Elementary Education	21.3–30.5
Secondary Education	19.0–24.3

However, the requirements in secondary education appear to be somewhat higher than the figures "16 to 18 hours" often quoted. An increase in number of hours required has resulted in recent years from the widespread adoption of a "block plan" for student teaching.

Besides the content and number of courses required in education, NCATE has been actively interested in course sequence. "An institution should plan a sequence or pattern for each teacher education curriculum consisting of the basic subject-matter and professional

---

[3] This was revealed in an examination of institutional files in the central office of NCATE.

education courses which all persons must take in order to complete that curriculum." One institution was denied full accreditation at least in part because a sequence in education offerings was lacking for both elementary and secondary majors. In this connection, NCATE has also been concerned with the best possible synchronization of education courses with observation and student teaching:

> An institution is expected to have a program of professional laboratory experiences designed to make real the concepts that are developed through reading, lectures, discussions, and audiovisual aids, and to help students acquire skill in applying those concepts in teaching situations. For the achievement of these purposes, the laboratory experiences should be closely related in time and nature to the professional education courses of which they are an essential part. [5]

Other examples of NCATE's insistence on changes in education courses or curriculums as a condition of full undergraduate accreditation follow:

> It is doubtful if the limited financial resources justify a program in special education.
>
> A higher requirement is needed in social foundations of education.
>
> Too much work is presently required in social foundations.
>
> Only staff members who have had graduate work in educational psychology or social foundations should be permitted to teach undergraduate courses in those subjects.

Some of the curriculum deficiencies listed by NCATE were directed toward graduate work:

> Too much work (24 hours) in administration is counted toward a master's degree in secondary education.
>
> The guidance program includes too many courses in professional education.
>
> The programs for administration and guidance workers are poorly structured.
>
> There is too much overlap between graduate and undergraduate courses.
>
> Both the faculty and the facilities for parts of the proposed graduate program are inadequate.
>
> Too much extension credit is being counted toward the master's degree programs.
>
> The standards of admission to graduate work are questionable.
>
> Ph.D. candidates who are fully employed should not be permitted to register for 10 hours of graduate work.
>
> There are too few of the graduate faculty who have had experience in supervising doctoral dissertations.

As in the case of academic curriculums, it is reasonable to assume that NCATE has had an effect on professional education programs in the ways suggested by these NCATE admonitions to teacher education institutions seeking accreditation.

It seems clear that NCATE, along with other factors, has been instrumental in bringing about the almost universal adoption of a "block plan" of student teaching experiences. Most observers are of the opinion that no institution would be approved in 1965 by NCATE unless its teacher education program provided for a block of student teaching in an off-campus school. This conclusion will probably not be tested, since it is unlikely that an institution will apply for NCATE accreditation without some such provision.

The NCATE standard for student teaching reads in part as follows:

> The professional laboratory experience should culminate in a continuous period of student teaching so organized as to provide for a wide range of professional activities in which teachers should engage. . . . [6]

In the interpretation of the standard, the following statement occurs:

> While no time block for student teaching is prescribed (except that in the Standard it is clear that two hours a day or less is considered to be too limited an experience), the principle is expressed that the time devoted to it should be of sufficient duration to provide an opportunity to gain adequate insights about teaching. [7]

The term "block plan" is used in many different ways. It is used here, in a broad sense, to include plans under which a prospective teacher is scheduled to teach in an off-campus school (usually a public school) for the entire day for a certain number of weeks, usually six to twelve. In his teaching he is under the supervision of the regular classroom teacher and a supervisor from the college or university in which he is enrolled; he may or may not register for regular classes or participate in a seminar during the student teaching period. A few "block plans" may provide for only a half day in the schools, but this arrangement is apparently looked upon with much less favor. Here again, a literal interpretation of the standards is that NCATE would not require a "block plan"; but institutions believe that they would.

The supplementary set of NCATE standards for graduate programs in school administration, prepared with the assistance of the AASA, has had a considerable influence on education curriculums in school administration. These standards and the application of them appear to be well received by specialists in school administration, and no specific criticism of them has been heard as a basis for the accreditation of programs for the preparation of school superintendents. The interpretation of the Standard on Objectives reads:

> Full range of administrative positions means those positions associated with central administration of a school system (superintendent, assistant superintendent for teacher personnel, assistant superintendent for instruction, assistant superintendent for business management) and elementary and secondary principals. It does not include supervisors or guidance counselors.

Specialists in other special areas of graduate education, such as curriculum and school personnel, feel that the standards for administration result in too much emphasis on administration *per se* in graduate programs in their special fields. Some are quite frank to say that, because of its significance as a precedent, NCATE may have erred in making an arrangement with one of the special groups such as AASA. It was somewhat surprising to find that it is not only the historians, humanists, and scientists who are concerned about the lack of special attention given by NCATE to the preparation of teachers in their disciplines. Specialists in professional education itself are also critical on this point. These include the elementary school principals, the secondary school principals, curriculum specialists, professors of special education, and even the leaders in health education, physical education, and recreation whose programs are found almost exclusively in schools of education.

Not unrelated to the question of accreditation of graduate work in education is the issue, so forcefully brought to public attention by Conant and others, of extension or off-campus courses in education. Such courses are offered and advertised as means of upgrading teachers, and frequently can be taken in partial fulfillment of graduate degree requirements. Some of them capitalize on the broad terminology employed in defining ways of securing increases in salary or promotion in rank. School systems are sometimes not very discriminating in accepting courses for the financial betterment of the teacher, and consequently the consumer may be equally guilty with the institutions of higher education in making possible the availability of low-quality offerings. Naturally generalizations about extension courses are dangerous, since there is great variation in the practice from state to state and district to district. NCATE has questioned extension or branch campus programs when the facilities and libraries seemed inadequate, when programs off-campus appeared to sap the strength of an on-campus program, when the qualifications of the staff are inadequate. Yet it seems obvious that NCATE needs to do even more in this respect as a part of the accreditation of graduate-level offerings and programs.

A commonly held point of view is that NCATE shares with state departments of education, professional education organizations, and others of the so-called "establishment," the responsibility for insisting on a certain pattern of required undergraduate courses in professional education, usually totaling about 18 semester hours of credit. Actually, there is nothing in Standard V which necessarily implies rigidity in course titles, content, or sequence, or total number of hours of credit. The idea expressed in the following statement recurs throughout: "The nature and amount of professional education required for each curriculum should be such as to assure competence for the position to be filled." Nevertheless, colleges and universities requesting NCATE accreditation are likely to be guided as much by a commonly held point of view as by a strict interpretation of the *Standards and Guide.* They can always point to rumors of what NCATE or one of its committees did in the case of such-and-such an institution, and it is apparent that some evaluations have been more rigid than the *Standards and Guide* suggests.

The Regional Associations

The regionals in general do not ordinarily pay particular attention to curriculums in education. Possible exceptions are: (1) the Middle States Association, which appears to be more teacher education conscious than the other regional associations, and (2) the other regional associations in their accreditation of a single-purpose teachers college, which currently they are rarely called upon to do. In evaluating the over-all institutional program, the regional team will ordinarily not give much attention to teacher education programs, particularly if the institution under review is a liberal arts college. If the department of education is weak, as compared with other departments, the institution will most likely be accredited, just as would be the case if an academic department were regarded as weaker than the rest.

When, however, the regional association evaluates an institution in which a large part of the students are in teacher education, the curriculums in teacher education will usually receive more careful scrutiny. In such cases if the teacher education program is rated as weak, the school could not expect full accreditation, regardless of the quality of the academic program. It can, therefore, be said that the regional associations have had relatively little impact upon higher education through the accreditation of programs in teacher education, other than in single-purpose teachers colleges, and this type of institution is rapidly disappearing.

State Accreditation

The states in fulfilling their responsibility of accrediting or approving teacher education programs tend to be more detailed and more specific than either NCATE or the regional associations. The institutions in the state not only may be told the minimum number of hours in education courses to be required, but also may be told the exact courses to be included and the minimum hours in each.

A difficulty arises here in distinguishing between guidelines for accreditation and for the approval of a teacher education program and requirements for certification. The situation is further complicated by the fact that some states waive certification requirements of graduates of state-approved programs; some states would make certain that graduates of approved programs also satisfy certification requirements; still others certify only upon satisfaction of certification requirements, since these states make no use whatever of the approved-program approach.

Since the regional accrediting associations and NCATE have no actual requirements (they have standards which may appear to institutions as requirements) when one speaks correctly of requirements in teacher education, one is referring to state or institutional requirements. State requirements are generally higher in number of hours than institutions interpret regional or NCATE requirements to be. Likewise, the requirements in professional education imposed by the teacher education institutions are often still higher than those of the state, particularly in multipurpose universities and state colleges.

When the state or the teacher education institution has higher requirements than NCATE or the regional associations, the tendency is to interpret this as proof of higher standards. To make this assumption is to fall into the error of confusing quality and quantity, or to equate quality in terms of quantity. It is possible that the higher requirement is unnecessary, hence unjustifiable and excessive, and therefore no evidence of higher standards.[4]

The states as a rule also spell out in detail what the teacher education institutions must provide by way of professional laboratory experiences and facilities for student teaching. Like NCATE, the states attach a great deal of importance to these direct student participation aspects of teacher education. Also, like NCATE, most of the states insist upon the "block"-scheduling approach to student teaching. This, indeed, is considered by many to be one of the most significant improvements in teacher education in the United States in the past 50 years. Undoubtedly, the states have been a strong contributory factor in the acceptance of the "block"-scheduling pattern, and the states are more influential than NCATE because the states reach so many more teacher education institutions. In quite a number of states, the NCATE endorsement of this plan carried great weight in the state's acceptance of it.

Probably the greatest source of criticism of teacher education in general and of accreditation in particular has been the state requirements in professional education for certification. Often it is assumed by the general public that these requirements are higher than they actually are and, as has been noted, the requirements in professional education in public institutions are often higher than the state requirements. Undergraduate students in education often are poorly motivated for education courses. Some may think the courses are state requirements which have been imposed on the colleges and universities, and in turn upon the students by state officials.

While requirements for certification are not requirements for accreditation, they are, of course, closely related to state accreditation. And accreditation, both state and national, must get some of the blame (or credit) for the continuing common pattern of the requirement of some 12 semester hours in undergraduate professional education

---

[4] For an example of this, see Conant, *The Education of American Teachers,* p. 22.

courses, exclusive of student teaching. If state and national accrediting agencies eventually were to approve a number of quite different plans for the professional education of teachers, at first on an experimental basis and later, when and if successful, on a regular basis, the present common pattern might become less common. Thus, one notes a potential effect of accreditation.

SUMMARY

NCATE, the regional associations, and the state departments are concerned with the requirements for academic majors and minors. NCATE and the states for the most part limit their interest to the teacher education program; the regionals are more concerned with non-teaching majors and minors. All three—NCATE, regionals, and states—also want to learn as much as possible about the general education program. The states, in general, spell out the requirements in considerable detail. In addition, the states frequently require certain courses to be taken by all students, or at least those in teacher education. These special requirements tend to relate to patriotism or citizenship, health, and marriage.

The net effect on college and university curriculums of NCATE and state accreditation in teacher education may be summarized as follows:

A change in balance in the over-all institution program of general education, subject-matter specialization, and professional education courses, in many cases resulting in a decrease in emphasis on professional education and an increase in general education and specialization requirements, as well as increased emphasis on general education requirements for elementary teachers and for secondary school teachers of such subjects as agriculture and music.

More attention to course sequences in education, as opposed to increases in requirements in education.

Increased emphasis on a core of professional education as an essential part of the education of teachers, although not in terms of the total number of hours required.

More deliberate integration of education courses with laboratory experiences and with student teaching.

The widespread adoption of "block plans" for student teaching.

A rapid spreading among the states of the approved-program approach in teacher education and certification.

REFERENCES

1. NCATE *Standards and Guide* (1960 Edition), pp. 15, 17.
2. John F. Nevins, *A Study of the Organization and Operation of Voluntary Accrediting Agencies* (Washington, D.C., 1959), pp. 179, 194.
3. NASDTEC-AAAS, *Guidelines for Science and Mathematics in the Preparation Program of Elementary School Teachers* (Washington, D. C., 1963); *Guidelines for Preparation Programs of Teachers of Secondary School Science and Mathematics* (Washington, D. C., 1961).

4. U. S. Office of Education, *Proposed Standards for State Approval of Teacher Education*, A Revision of the 1952 Circular No. 351 (Washington, D. C., 1964).
5. Standard VI of NCATE *Standards and Guide*.
6. *Ibid.*
7. *Ibid.*

CHAPTER 12

FACULTY POLICIES

AGENCIES involved in the accreditation of teacher education recognize the central place of the faculty in determining the quality of the academic and professional programs offered. One important consideration is the adequacy of the training and experience of the teaching staff. Another is the size of the faculty in relation to student enrollment. A third is the geographic origin of faculty members, both as to residence and with respect to training. A fourth is morale of the staff. A fifth is the degree to which the faculty is integrated into the planning and policy-making functions of the institution. A sixth is the degree of involvement of the faculty in research and service activities.

NATIONAL AGENCY

As a professional accrediting agency, NCATE's chief concern with an institution's faculty is that part involved most actively in teacher education. Standard IV of the NCATE *Standards and Guide* "focuses attention on the need for having a faculty adequate in number and competent in preparation and experience to meet the teaching, counseling, and other demands of the teacher education programs offered by the institution." No minimum is set for the size of the staff, rather emphasis is placed on having staff members who have specialized in those areas of work which are taught in education. "An institution should not expect to teach students in specialized and technical fields with a small faculty whose members have only general or inappropriate backgrounds of study." [1]

NCATE is fully cognizant of problems confronting small, privately endowed liberal arts colleges in trying to meet this standard. Naturally, the college's first and prime concern is to provide the strongest possible staff in academic fields. Besides, this is necessary in order to obtain regional accreditation which is an absolute "must" for an institution's long-term operation. Sacrifices in other areas may be made to attract

as many academicians as possible with earned doctorates—and one of
the sacrifices sometimes made is the quality of the staff in the field of
education.

One manifestation of this policy is the employment as teachers of
education subjects people who, as former school principals or superintendents, are long on practical experience, but short on advanced degrees. Sometimes such persons are first employed on a part-time basis
at the college while the school administrator is still employed full time.
Then as the teacher education program grows, and the administrator
approaches or reaches retirement age, he or she is given full-time status.
Sometimes the entrance of school administrators into college teaching
is by way of extension, evening, or summer session classes. Either on
part-time status or as retired administrators, college teaching provides
a bonus or a retirement income. Hence, it is often possible to employ
such persons at a substantially lower salary than the institution's
average salary level. [2]

Such practices have been a concern of NCATE, and, while the
Council recognizes that in some instances high-quality personnel may
be obtained, it tends to discourage these practices and particularly if
several education staff members are obtained in this way.

Many supporters of NCATE take pride in the fact that NCATE has
refused to accredit liberal arts colleges with only one or at most two
staff members in education, if the college has a large number of students enrolled in teacher education or is offering programs for both
elementary and secondary teachers. They consider this one of NCATE's
major achievements. These supporters claim that NCATE has thus
persuaded liberal arts colleges to take teacher education seriously or
to "get out of the business." Probably failure to obtain NCATE accreditation has caused no college to "get out of the business," although failure
to obtain state approval has. On the other hand, NCATE has been
successful in persuading some colleges to offer more restricted programs with small staffs or to increase their staffs.

It must be recognized, too, that some who oppose NCATE most vig-
orously oppose it for these same reasons. They insist that NCATE has
made it necessary for liberal arts colleges to hire professors of education and form a department of education, when graduates of these
colleges might have been successful teachers without so much emphasis
on the professional education aspect of their preparation. These critics
would also claim that NCATE has in this way kept many high-quality
teachers out of the classrooms, when the colleges from which they
were graduated chose not to build up their staffs in education.

In evaluating a teacher education institution, NCATE attempts
carefully and deliberately to ferret out the following information with
respect to the professional education faculty: (1) proportion holding
each academic rank; (2) salary scale in operation for each rank as
compared with regular academic departments; (3) proportion of full-
time faculty members in education holding doctor's degrees, master's

degrees, and bachelor's degrees as compared with the regular academic faculty; (4) teaching loads of the education staff; (5) proportion of courses taught by full-time and by part-time staff; and (6) the specialized field or fields of each staff member in education. [3]

NCATE also encourages the involvement of the general faculty in formulating teacher education policies. This means bringing the academic and professional education faculties into a cooperative relationship which all too often has been lacking. By the same token, NCATE wants to involve members of the professional education staff in the formulation of general institutional policies. Accordingly, one of the questions asked of institutions under evaluation is the number of professional educators on and the number heading institution-wide committees. [4] This insistence on recognition of professional education in the formulation of all-college or all-university policies has had a noticeable effect in some institutions. Sometimes the effect occurs in anticipation of an NCATE visit.

In one of the conferences held as part of this Study, a participant representing a state university preparing for an NCATE evaluation reported that he had been able to persuade the president of his institution to add members of the education staff to several all-university committees, including the committee on general education. The argument used in the case was that NCATE would frown on an absence of education people from important policy committees. Others at the conference gave similar testimony. This is another illustration that the influence of NCATE and other accrediting bodies may be most operative in anticipation of visits.

Sometimes it is possible, through misunderstanding or misrepresentation of NCATE's position or policy, to obtain concessions from the administration. Those responsible for preparing for an NCATE visitation may be able to persuade the president that, in order to obtain accreditation, certain staff members must be added, or certain courses must now be added, or certain committee appointments must now be made. The changes may or may not be important factors in obtaining accreditation, but often these actions antagonize staff members in other departments and create ill-will both toward their colleagues in education and toward NCATE.

NCATE's emphasis upon "fair and equal treatment for education staff members" renders it vulnerable to the charge that the "establishment which controls NCATE" is intent upon protecting the vested interests of staff members in education and to promote those interests. It has been concluded that NCATE exists merely to raise the status of "educationists." In this connection, it seems fair to say that accrediting associations in engineering, business, or chemistry are also interested in the status of teachers in their respective fields. They have, however, not made use of this particular method and there is another basic difference.

Teacher education encompasses such a large part of higher education that many other staff members, in addition to those in professional education, are in reality teacher educators. Therefore the critics suggest that NCATE might be judicious in doing more to promote the professional welfare of the professor of English or history, who may have little or no training in education, but who assumes a responsibility for his department in teacher education. And there is a growing number of these people. Many think that in view of its vulnerability on this point, NCATE would do well to de-emphasize its concern about the status of professors of education.

Some spokesmen for colleges which have had diffculty in obtaining NCATE accreditation, as well as others in higher education, believe that NCATE has been too rigid in the requirement of graduate work by fields of specialization for teachers of education courses. This point of view is justified by some on the grounds that the lines of demarcation by special fields among undergraduate courses in education are not as sharp as in other disciplines and that this is true even at the graduate level. These critics also point to this as just another example of NCATE's effort to add status to a discipline, as well as to its proponents, and that this status could be attained more appropriately by other means. Furthermore, sometimes it seems appropriate to liberal arts faculties that the professor of history or the professor of psychology might teach courses in the history of education or educational psychology to the advantage of all departments concerned. NCATE has discouraged this practice, unless these professors have had graduate work in education. An effect of NCATE's emphasis on specialized preparation in education has been the addition of staff members in education.

The advantage of school teaching experience to the professor of education is also a source of disagreement. Examples have been cited in which a person with school experience, but less qualified in all other respects than a person without experience, has been appointed in education. Some say that this is the reason that the scholarly atmosphere in an education department appears to be less admired by certain groups than that in other departments.

There was no evidence found to indicate that NCATE has concerned itself directly with the quality of the teaching in education, but rather has depended upon quantitative standards as the "bench marks" of the quality of the staff. Since the teaching in courses for prospective teachers should be of exceptional quality (and there would be no disagreement here), critics of NCATE argue that even though other accrediting associations rarely concern themselves with the quality of teaching, NCATE certainly should.

National accreditation has also given some attention to activities of staff members in education, in addition to teaching and counseling students. These activities encompass research and service to the schools. Both kinds of activities are considered "bench marks" of quality. The extent of a staff member's participation in the activities should be given consideration in determining teaching load. A balance among these activities and teaching and counseling should be a factor of greater concern to accrediting agencies than it has been. Some distinction should be made in evaluation of them on the basis of compensation; that is, whether service to the school is done as a professional service or for a consultant fee. In visits to institutions, questions were asked about NCATE's concern with these matters and its possible impact on practices in the institution. The common response was that NCATE encouraged both, and particularly research with graduate programs, but that the impact was not great.

As examples, an examination of NCATE files reveals the following deficiencies cited to support a denial of full accreditation of teacher education programs in various institutions:

> More faculty specialization is needed in education.
> Greater faculty resources are needed in elementary education.
> The education staff is badly overloaded.
> More specialists are needed in science education and in social foundations.
> There are too many part-time people teaching courses in education.
> More doctorates are needed in professional education.
> The education faculty has had inadequate public school experience.

These deficiencies were corrected or steps were taken to correct them, in most cases, in order to qualify for NCATE accreditation, hence such action would be strong evidence of NCATE's influence. It is recognized, of course, that there would be a wide difference of opinion as to which of the above recommended changes would be interpreted as meritorious and which would be branded as deleterious. Such a judgment is not specifically called for in this Study.

REGIONAL ASSOCIATIONS

As accreditors of general institutional qualities, the regional associations are concerned with general faculty policies. There was a time when the regionals emphasized specific data on such matters as faculty teaching loads and class sizes. Exact ratios were worked out relative to teaching loads and the maximum and minimum number of students to be permitted in each class. Nowadays, the tendency is to speak in more general terms. All six regional associations, however, still want to know about faculty teaching loads and faculty salaries.

The regional associations in general collect information from schools under accreditation review relative to the training and professional experience of staff members. They ask for a report on the proportion of the faculty who have earned doctorates. The New England Association specifies that each academic department must have at least one person of professorial rank. This Association also wants information on the "preparation and experience of the faculty." The Western Association wants to know about the preparation of the faculty. The Northwest Association wants to know about both the "training of the faculty" and the "quality of instruction." Five of the six regional associations want to know what provisions have been made for orienting new faculty members into the atmosphere and traditions of the institution.

The Southern Association asks specifically about the training of the faculty, and points out that "instructional techniques and policies should express the purposes of the institution as well as the specific objectives of an individual course. Instruction to be effective must be evaluated continuously, and an institution should be able to present evidence that efforts are being made to improve instruction. Concern for improvement of instruction is a mark of institutional vitality."

Recognizing the dangers of excessive "inbreeding" of a faculty, the regional associations may wish to know the number and proportion of the institution's own graduates on the teaching staff. This problem tends to be especially acute in colleges or universities emphasizing a particular religious or economic philosophy. It is often possible to employ one's own dedicated graduates at a lower salary than would otherwise be possible. Thus, there tends to be the double advantage of "orthodoxy" and "economy."

Almost as important as the avoidance of "inbreeding" is obtaining the broadest possible distribution of staff members geographically. An institution should be careful not to employ the bulk of its staff from the area in which it is located. Like the absence of "inbreeding," a broad geographical distribution of the staff discourages "provincialism" and encourages "cosmopolitanism." As a special aspect of geographical distribution in staff origins, a conscious and conscientious effort is often made to employ graduates of "prestige" schools. In institutional competition, these are highly important "status symbols." Having graduates of "Ivy League" schools on one's staff can be pointed to with genuine pride. The same applies to graduates of prominent foreign universities.

Occasionally, a college or university will adopt the policy of employing on a year-by-year basis distinguished teachers and scholars who have retired from other institutions. This practice is of particular concern to the regionals. This policy is advantageous in many ways to the employing school, as well as to the person who has reached retirement age but is reluctant to abandon his profession. Their reputations may add prestige to the institution and, often because of their broad experience and particularly their achievement in research, they may be a source of inspiration to younger staff members. Because scholars and teachers who are retired from another institution as a rule do not remain in their new positions long enough to supervise a doctoral student through the dissertation stage, accrediting agencies may not recognize them as having top-level status on the graduate faculty. Likewise, if such temporary appointments are extended long enough so that the "retired" professor is teaching several years beyond that possible for his colleagues in the institution, a deleterious effect on faculty morale may result.

In reference to faculty morale, the regional associations, perhaps more than any other accrediting agencies, are concerned with this important aspect of an institution's over-all profile. Is there an excessively high turnover of staff members? Sometimes the basis for such an unfortunate condition is budgetary. The institution's income is such that it cannot compete with similar institutions in terms of salary. At other times, the total income may be adequate with too little proportionally being allocated to faculty salaries or important fringe benefits. Too often an excessive rate of staff turnover is due to bad policies on the part of the institution's administration. The president of the college may not integrate the faculty into the formulation of institutional policies. Sometimes a faculty "exodus" will result from unwise action of a legislature, such as the requiring of "loyalty oaths." The North Central Association asks: Are the conditions of faculty service likely to promote high morale? The Western Association is more specific: Are there "any limitations or restrictions which may be laid on the beliefs and actions of the members of the faculty?" [1]

There is no question but that faculty morale has a vital bearing on the quality of work done in teacher education or otherwise in an institution which educates teachers. Other factors being equal, the quality of work done by staff members varies in direct proportion to the degree of staff morale. And yet, regional associations are extremely reluctant to investigate an institution where there is evidence of a marked deterioration of faculty morale. Only when the situation reaches the level of attracting widespread public attention and criticism is there any real hope of association action. Even then, the hope is a rather faint one. The tenure of college and university administrators is shortened very little by action on the part of accrediting agencies.

STATE DEPARTMENTS

Since most state departments of education accredit or approve teacher education programs and a number of them accredit the total institution, their accrediting policies with respect to the faculty tend to represent a combination of NCATE accrediting policies and those of the regional associations. Some states, in accrediting teacher education programs, adopt more or less *in toto*, the *Standards and Guide* of NCATE. Likewise, in accrediting general college status, the states tend to follow the pattern of the regional association in whose area the state is located.

---

[1] The Southern Association reports that it will not bother with a faculty's instability unless there is a complaint. North Central reports that if there appears to be an excessive turnover of staff the Association may try to determine the reason. The Western Association reports that it has become involved in situations where faculty members have been summarily fired, and has tried to insist at least on "due process."

The state department of Iowa is a good example of a state which follows the NCATE pattern in accrediting teacher education programs. In evaluating the education faculty, the following questions are asked:

1. How many faculty members are giving full time to professional education?

2. How many are part-time in professional education and how much time do they give?

3. What teaching assignments has the faculty carried in the past two semesters and one summer? How well is the faculty prepared for these assignments? What preparations have the part-time persons for their assignments?

4. How well is the faculty prepared as shown by degrees held and professional rank compared with the other faculty members in the same institution?

5. Are there teachers from other institutions or from public schools who teach evening, extension, or summer courses in professional education? If so, how many are there, what do they teach, and who takes their courses?

6. What is the normal teaching load? Are there exceptions? How is supervision of student teaching counted in the load? Is extension teaching done as a part of the regular load with no extra pay, or is it an extra load for extra pay?

7. Do any of the faculty teach evening or extension courses for some other institution? Explain.[2]

When accrediting general institutional status, the states may follow the example of regional associations in asking for statistical information relative to the training and experience of faculty members, the number and proportion of the teaching staff with earned doctorates, the maximum, minimum, and average salary for each rank, and the number and proportion of the institution's own graduates who are employed on a continuing basis as members of the teaching staff.[3]

Many of the states following NCATE's example place emphasis on the importance of the all-institutional committee for teacher education. They have also promoted communication between academic and professional staff through state committees and conferences. Over the past 10 years there has been a very sizable increase in the amount of consultation and advice that state department personnel seek and obtain from academic personnel in higher education. Thus the states have already made an impact on the active role in teacher education planning by professors in academic departments.

The states in general have given more attention to the supervisory staff of the student teaching program than has NCATE. Reference to

---

[2] Taken from a "Check-list of Questions" submitted to an institution seeking state accreditation.

[3] New York State is an example of a state which, in accrediting programs of teacher education, follows a pattern parallel to that of the Middle States Association.

the staff for student teaching was made rather frequently both in campus visits and in the various conferences, perhaps in part due to the fact that the timing of these conversations followed so closely the publication of the Conant report. Full accreditation of a liberal arts college in Kentucky was being held up by the state pending the employment of additional and better qualified persons to supervise student teaching. Colleges anticipating NCATE visits were giving special attention to their staffs for student teaching. Institutions already accredited spoke with pride of their arrangements for student teaching, and the president of one state college stated that the strongest staff member in education was in charge of the program. In addition, this individual was believed to have the greatest potential for research among his staff members.

It seems clear that, whatever other effects the Conant report may have, one result will be the giving of much greater attention to arrangements for student teaching by teacher education institutions, by the states, and probably by NCATE. The states are "close" to both the elementary and secondary schools and to the teacher education institutions, and they are therefore in the most strategic position to give greater weight to student teaching arrangements in accreditation. State accreditation or approval must be given credit for having already had a considerable influence on student teaching as a part of higher education. The states in most instances have insisted on clearly enunciated agreements between the institutions and the schools, on careful selection of the staff, on the adequacy in terms of numbers of the staff, and the amount of a prospective teacher's time given to student teaching.

Quite a number of the states have also been concerned about who teaches the "methods" courses in a teacher education program. They believe that this staff member plays a critical role in teacher education and insist that he should be well trained both in the discipline and in professional education, and should have had teaching experience at the pre-college level. In a number of the states, the directors of teacher education have encouraged joint appointments in education and a discipline, so that the right kind of staff member could be obtained for the methods course in secondary education. Also, in a number of states, staff members in academic departments have become involved in supervision of student teaching through state department encouragement.

State department personnel are sometimes aware of the reputation of college and university members for the quality of their teaching. While they are wisely reluctant to give advice to an institution's administration on the utilization of staff, they nevertheless pass on favorable remarks that they hear, and raise questions about a staff member when they have reason to doubt his classroom effectiveness. Thus, whether or not as a part of their accreditation activities, they may be said to give more attention to quality of teaching than do other accrediting agencies. Instances of the kind referred to here were reported in the visits to states. Some of the state directors expressed the wish that they might find a way to give more attention to quality of teaching.

In states which approve or accredit programs of teacher education, more institutions of higher education are accredited or approved by the state than by NCATE, with the exception of three states (Arizona, Nevada, and Wyoming) in which all state-accredited institutions are also NCATE-accredited. It is sometimes more difficult for a state to reject a college's application, and hence the influence of the state is more likely to be through assisting institutions to improve—or in getting ready for a teacher education program—than in recognition of minimum standards. Many states, however, claim to have persuaded colleges where facilities are limited not to offer teacher education or to discontinue teacher education programs if the college appears unable or unwilling to meet certain minimum standards. The states therefore must be given credit for the elimination of some particularly weak teacher education programs. It must be kept in mind, of course, that a program judged to be weak in terms of the criteria utilized by the state, including a rather strong emphasis in most states on the professional education aspects of the program, would not necessarily be considered weak according to standards determined by others.

SUMMARY

NCATE has had an impact on faculty policies through its efforts to make sure that there is no discrimination against the professional education staff in respect to training, experience, teaching loads, rank and salary, degree of specialization, employment of part-time people, and participation in all-institutional committees; also through insisting upon the involvement of academic disciplines in the planning and supervision of the teacher education program.

NCATE has been a factor in persuading liberal arts colleges with teacher education programs to develop a faculty in education; and in a more strict assignment of staff members in all institutions to teach only those undergraduate courses in subjects in which they have had graduate training.

Regional Associations have concerned themselves largely with the training and experience of the general faculty, the number and proportion having earned doctorates, the avoidance of excessive "inbreeding" in faculty appointments, achieving the broadest possible geographic distribution in staff additions, and the maintenance of satisfactory faculty morale. The regionals have had some impact in these respects on institutions.

With respect to faculty policies the *states* have tended to adopt NCATE standards in appraising teacher education programs and regional association standards in general institutional accreditation.

The above influences or effects may be listed as:

1. A higher proportion of staff members with earned doctorates.
2. More nearly equal salaries as between academic and professional educational staffs.
3. More staff members in departments of education.
4. A smaller proportion of part-time staff members.
5. A higher degree of faculty specialization in teaching fields.
6. A broader geographical distribution of staff members both in origin and in site of advanced training.
7. Some improvement in faculty tenure.
8. Greater importance associated with supervision of student-teaching programs, and improved communication between academic and education faculties in staffing methods courses in particular disciplines.

REFERENCES

1. NCATE Brochure: *Explanatory Materials Interpreting the NCATE Standards* (Washington, D. C., 1964), p. 7.
2. *Ibid.;* Standard IV of NCATE *Standards and Guide* (1960 Edition), p. 11.
3. NCATE *Standards and Guide,* p. 12; *Explanatory Materials Interpreting the NCATE Standards,* pp. 6–8.
4. NCATE *Standards and Guide,* p. 12.

CHAPTER 13

STUDENT POLICIES

THE DEEP and abiding concern of accrediting agencies in student policies stems from the realization that student excellence and welfare constitute the prime concerns of higher education. Unfortunately, not all heads of educational institutions always keep these basic objectives in the forefront of their thinking and planning. They fall into the common American error of confusing quality with quantity, intangibles with tangibles, the intellectual with the physical. Some educators may even be motivated by personal prestige which they believe may be associated with the size of the student body. Unfortunately, too, in public institutions, one of the most effective arguments for an increase in appropriations may be an increase in enrollment. It was largely to combat such distracting forces that accrediting activities were created.

With just what aspects of a school's student personnel policies are accrediting agencies concerned? Basically with admission policies, retention policies, welfare policies, and graduation policies; of these, admission policies or standards probably are most crucial. If only students of high quality are admitted to the institution, the battle is more than half won. On the other hand, it is possible to have a democratic admission policy (give everyone a chance), and then through rigorous retention policies or reasonably high graduation requirements, to weed out the incompetents. In an effort to protect the interests of students, accrediting agencies may also scrutinize provisions for the counseling of students and for student housing, health, and recreation.

ADMISSION POLICIES

NATIONAL ACCREDITATION

NCATE's concern with admission policies relates chiefly to admission to a teacher education program. The central purpose of Standard III of the NCATE *Standards and Guide* is "to direct attention toward the personnel policies of the institution as they relate to students in teacher education programs, toward the end that able students finish the program offered and enter the ranks of the teaching profession." [1] This is the way Standard III is explained:

> The student personnel program and services with reference to teacher education are evaluated in relation to the student personnel program of the institution as a whole. The Standard which relates to student personnel services for teacher education is, therefore, based on the assumption that the organization, the quality of the staff, and such functions as housing, health, and student government have been evaluated by the appropriate regional accrediting association. Only such personnel services as relate specifically to the preparation of teachers and professional school service personnel are covered in this Standard.
>
> The major student personnel responsibilities of an institution with reference to prospective teachers relate to: (1) admission to and retention in teacher education curricula; (2) advising and registration; and (3) records and placement.
>
> An institution should have a plan of selective admission to and retention in teacher education which offers reasonable assurance that only persons of professional promise are prepared and recommended for entry into the teaching profession. Criteria for such admission and retention should be in addition to the general policies and procedures for admitting students to the institution as a whole. Once the student is admitted to a teacher education curriculum, his registration should be such as to identify him as a person preparing to teach. [2]

This section of Standard III ends with this significant interpretation: "Certainly the standards for admission to and completion of teacher education curricula will be greater than the minimum required for students not following professional curricula." Does this mean that a college or university with high admission standards must have a still higher standard for admission to teacher education? This is a point of disagreement. Many defenders of NCATE, including members of NCATE visiting teams, insist that the standard for admission to teacher education must be higher than that of the institution generally. Critics of NCATE assume that this is true and object strenuously to it.

Some defenders of NCATE insist that the differentiation in standards does not necessarily apply to colleges with high admission standards. Some say that the differentiation may apply to special standards of selectivity other than academic, such as personality and vocational aptitude. What NCATE apparently intends here is that in all institutions admission standards for teacher education should be high, and that some special attention should be given to those characteristics regarded as desirable in a teacher, such as "verbal expression and health" and "aptitude for the area or kind of teaching" to which the applicant aspires.

Admission requirements to the institution and to teacher education programs, as listed in institution catalogs, were examined in the catalog survey of 95 institutions of teacher education. In examining the policies for the admission to institutions of NCATE and non-NCATE institutions, it was found that 84 of the 95 institutions in the population required one or two of the following examinations: American College Testing Program (ACT), College Entrance Examination Board (CEEB) tests, or Schools and College Abilities Tests (SCAT). About 70 percent of the liberal arts colleges, both NCATE and non-NCATE, required the CEEB examinations; whereas 25 percent of the state and teachers colleges, both NCATE and non-NCATE, required the same tests. Forty-five percent of the NCATE and 25 percent of the non-NCATE state and teachers colleges required the ACT examinations. The total amount of required high school work varied little from institution to institution, and most institutions have permitted entrance by passing a high school equivalency examination.

In the *admission* of students to teacher education, 71 of the 95 institutions in the population published a grade point average (GPA) requirement. Using a grade A equivalent of 4.00, it was found that a mean GPA of 1.93 was required for *admission* to teacher education in NCATE state and teachers colleges, which is significantly greater than the 1.47 requirement for non-NCATE state and teachers colleges.

Requirements, such as completion of certain course work, passing of speech and hearing tests, and interviews by faculty members, were also required by many schools; but no discernible patterns could be found for comparing NCATE and non-NCATE institutions.

NCATE's concern with the standards of admission to teacher education can be well documented through an examination of the Council's files. Indeed, NCATE's insistence on a strengthening of admission standards in teacher education is shown to be one of the institutional deficiencies most frequently listed by the Council. Sometimes the admission standards are characterized by NCATE as being too low; at other times, the criticism is that the admission standards are "unevenly applied." It may be that the standards as listed are high enough, but there are too many exceptions made to the application of the standards. Or there may be different admission standards for different teacher education programs. NCATE apparently is looking both for quality and for consistency.[1]

During the decade of NCATE's existence, many colleges and universities have raised their standards for admission to teacher education programs. These changes have been brought about by a combination of many factors. Some studies of a decade or more ago which have been widely publicized have shown that students of lowest ability were enrolled in teachers colleges or in colleges of education in multipurpose universities. Just as education courses have a reputation for being "snap" courses on many campuses, too often students in teacher education courses have been looked down upon by their fellow students.

---

[1] The examples cited were obtained through an examination of NCATE files.

Administrators and professors of education have tried to counteract these points of view by raising admission standards of their programs. Their sincere interest in wishing to raise the quality of students who prepare for teaching should not be questioned.

When standards were raised, it was found not only that the teacher education students were of a higher quality, but also that the enrollment in teacher education had increased. These experiences were soon repeated on many campuses. On numerous campuses, the over-all grade point average and the major subject grade point average for admission to teaching are higher than those for admission to some other professional schools or for permission to continue in liberal arts. The attitude of NCATE toward admission requirements has encouraged colleges and universities in general to raise their standards for admission, as well as to strengthen the hands of those where this action has already been taken.

Standards for admission to teacher education are usually expressed in terms of grade point average. There is, however, an increasing trend for teacher education institutions to administer special tests as an essential part of the admission procedure. According to Farr[2] the tests most frequently used for this purpose are the College Entrance Examination Board Scholastic Aptitude Test, the American College Testing Program Battery, the Cooperative School and College Ability Test, the Cooperative English Test, and the College Entrance Examination Board Achievement Tests. Some institutions use personality measures in relation to admission. At least five such tests were mentioned in the Farr survey.

Another fairly common procedure is for prospective teacher education students to file detailed questionnaires setting forth their previous training, work experience, attitudes toward education and teaching. These, along with test scores and transcripts, are used as a basis for interviews on the part of individual staff members or committees, who in turn make recommendations to the admissions office or agency.

While NCATE cannot be given full credit for the initiation or growing popularity of these procedures, it certainly has served as one of the contributing factors. In visits to campuses, and in the conferences associated with this Study, representatives of quite a number of institutions told of their "new" admission procedures, and several reported that while they had always intended to introduce these procedures an NCATE visit or anticipation thereof had finally brought them to culmination.

NCATE's insistence on a policy of uniform standards for admission to teacher education in an institution is a part of NCATE concern, in the accreditation of a multipurpose university, that all teacher education students be responsible to one administrative unit. When prospective teachers in agriculture and home economics, for example, are

---

[2] Chapter 9, pp. 122, 123.

registered in the college of agriculture rather than in the college of education, different admission standards for teacher education students in agriculture and home economics are likely to prevail. NCATE has been influential in bringing about a requirement of registration in two schools in some instances, and the appointment of two advisers for the student, one in subject matter (agriculture or home economics) and one in education.

Also some of NCATE's concern about two "paths" to certification discussed in Chapter 10, is based on the standard that uniform admission policies should be adopted. During lunch at one of the Study conferences, a discussion developed about the danger lest currently popular admission procedures might serve to eliminate from teaching the imaginative non-conformist. Some counselors fear that such a person might have difficulty adjusting to the conformity expected on the part of many communities and by some administrators. It was generally agreed by the professors and deans of education (no academicians were present) that many non-conformists would make excellent teachers. The discussants agreed that great care should therefore be taken in eliminating such candidates from teacher education programs, and further that the teacher education program itself should help such persons adjust to a variety of situations. Again, the above incident illustrates one of the basic fears about accreditation, a fear of conformity in programs which may in turn impose conformity on prospective teachers.

Data provided by the Bureau of Labor Statistics show the production of new teachers, even by 1970, may be considerably greater than the demand in a number of fields, and by 1975 in most fields, except possibly science, mathematics, and foreign languages. (See Appendix VII-D.) If the predicted period of over-supply is reached, there will probably be an even greater emphasis on higher admission standards and a stronger tendency toward higher levels of discrimination in accreditation of teacher education programs.

REGIONAL ASSOCIATIONS

The regional associations are concerned with the institution's general admission policies. The New England Association insists upon graduation from an approved preparatory school as a prerequisite to college admission. The Middle States requires the completion of an appropriate secondary school program or equivalent. The Southern Association asks what the admission requirements are. Under its revised criteria for evaluating higher institutions, the North Central Association judges admission requirements in relation to institutional objectives. If an institution lists as an objective the rehabilitation of students with poor academic records, North Central will not object provided the program is geared accordingly.[3] Not to be overlooked in this connection is the fact that an

---

[3] Interview with Norman W. Burns.

institution's general admission policies have an important bearing on the quality of the teacher education program on that campus.

Another aspect of admission policies in which the regional associations manifest some interest is what might be called the policies controlling the distribution of the student body. This, in turn, may be subdivided into three broad categories: economic, geographic, and intellectual. Other things equal, the regional association would prefer to see the students drawn from different geographical areas rather than solely from the area in which the college is located. The regionals also prefer to see the student body drawn from families of different economic levels. There is some objection, also, to having the students all selected from the same intellectual or scholastic level. In other words, it is desirable, within reason, to have the student body represent a cross-section of society. It should be understood that these considerations appear not to be emphasized sufficiently to dictate an adverse accreditation decision; but they may enter into the counseling that is done to improve the total institutional program.

THE STATES

The concern of the states in admission policies of teacher education programs tends to resemble that of NCATE. This is true particularly in those states which limit their accreditation or approval to teacher education institutions or programs. Those states which also accredit general institutional status naturally tend in this to follow the regional pattern. Because of their responsibilities in certifying teachers, the states are interested in admission standards as they relate to the quality of students entering the teaching profession. Even though a state may give little or no recognition to NCATE, it may attempt to enforce standards for admission similar to those of NCATE.

Among more recently accepted modifications of teacher education programs, second only to the almost universal acceptance of the "block" pattern of student teaching in an off-campus school, is widespread acceptance of "higher standards for admission to student teaching." Along with individual leaders in teacher education, the professional associations, and NCATE, the states should be given partial credit for producing this change. Indeed, when an effect has been produced which begins to appear to be universal throughout the country the state departments almost certainly have played an important role in achieving the result.

In checking the files in the office of one state director of teacher education, reports by colleges were found giving the names of students who had applied for admission to teacher education and subsequently the names of those who had been accepted, together with information as to why certain ones had not been approved. This enabled the state department to ascertain what proportion of those applying had been accepted, also the reason for the rejection of those not approved. This kind of follow-up gives the states an opportunity to be of real influence in the application of admission policies, and to go beyond the acceptance of an institution's grade point average as a guarantee of quality.

In questions asked about the state influence on campuses of eight Kentucky colleges, at least one person on each campus made reference to the state department's insistence on higher admission standards and special admission procedures. One liberal arts college dean was among those who stated that different admission standards for teacher education and liberal arts could not be justified.

What some believe to be a slow but steady trend toward state administration of National Teacher Examinations or similar tests for those seeking certification may seem to point to a lack of confidence, not only in particular programs of teacher education, but also in prevailing admission requirements as an effective screening device in teacher education. Those promoting the use of examinations as one basis of certification would not, however, discourage the use of admission screening. Rather, they would say that the guarantee of a quality product can be made more certain by a combination of careful screening at admission and then testing at the conclusion of a given program. The use of terminal tests actually is likely to encourage the use of admission tests as a kind of pre-test and post-test attempt to measure program quality.

The states have been less concerned than NCATE about problems of registration and admission in different schools or colleges of multipurpose universities. This may be due in part to the fact that, generally speaking, state departments of education are more reluctant to interfere with the state universities. There is frequently a close association between the two state agencies and usually a considerable respect within the state department for the prestige of the university.

Many believe that one of the most critical factors in raising the quality level of those prepared to teach in our schools is admission standards, including both admission standards to the institution preparing the teachers and admission to teacher education programs within the institution. These persons believe that admission standards of some institutions are so low, quality teachers can scarcely be produced in these institutions. They recognize that, although institutional standards are low, admission to teacher education could be made high enough to protect the public interest. But they further emphasize that the grade point average (GPA) at the beginning of the junior year may be meaningless if the general standards of the institution are relatively weak. After all it is generally easier to make an A at a small college with low admission standards than at a similar college with very high admission standards.

Both the states and NCATE have placed some emphasis on GPA in evaluating admission standards, and perhaps have given too much weight to the fact that the GPA required for admission to teacher education is higher than for admission to other programs of the institution. An institutional GPA, after all, is not necessarily a guarantee of quality.

RETENTION POLICIES AND COUNSELING

In Standard III of NCATE *Standards and Guide,* the phrase "admission to and retention in" is used. Thus, NCATE apparently makes a close association between admission and retention policies. In the NCATE files of letters to colleges seeking accreditation, much more reference to "admission" than to "retention" was found and it appears that institutions in general give more specific attention to the development of an admission policy than to a retention policy. In the visits to higher institutions and in conferences involving representatives of educational institutions and organizations, a great many references were made to admission policies and almost none to retention policies. Some way or other both NCATE and the states seem to have created the impression that they have a great concern for admission policies and perhaps that retention policies, if consistent with admission policies, will automatically be taken care of.

Once a student is admitted to a teacher education program, he is generally allowed to continue, provided his grades remain satisfactory and he manages to stay out of difficulties requiring disciplinary action. In some institutions, a disciplinary action which is not serious enough to cause the student to be "dropped" from college may, however, result in his being dropped from teacher education and being refused an official institutional recommendation for certification. This kind of decision is related to the concern about student conformity in teacher education programs reported above.

Quite a number of institutions report that more students transfer into teacher education from other programs than transfer in the reverse direction. This may result in part from late career decisions by the students and in part from their finding themselves unsuited for a particular professional choice they have made. For example, schools of education in multipurpose universities have applications from a sizable number of engineering students desiring to transfer to education in order to become science or mathematics teachers. A factor for some in so doing is a desire to remain in the university after not succeeding as a student in engineering. Those making such program changes may later become successful teachers. No evidence of an effect by accrediting agencies on this practice was found, other than its relation to policies on admission to teacher education.

In a multipurpose institution, the retention standard may vary from one unit of the university to another, depending upon the degree of decentralization or autonomy within the institution.

Perhaps institutional representatives, with whom conversations were held about admission and retention, made less reference to retention policies, because they considered NCATE's concern about counseling procedures to be equivalent to a concern about retention. NCATE apparently expects academic counseling to eliminate many from teacher education who manage to gain admission to the program, but come to be regarded as doubtful prospects of success in the profession.

The paragraph in Standard III which refers specifically to counseling is:

> An institution should have a well defined plan of counseling designed to give assurance that advice to students and prospective students is given by persons of competence; that is, by persons who know the nature and scope of the teaching profession, the problems of the schools, and the resources of the institution available for preparing for the various school positions. [3]

Then in the statement of "Implications of Standard," one finds:

> Advising will be regarded as most effective when it is shared by academic and professional education faculty members with well formulated curricula to be used by them as a basis for guidance.

Here the emphasis is more on the qualifications of the counselor than on retention or possible elimination of poor prospects from teacher education.

Some institutions attempt to satisfy this standard by assigning two advisers to a prospective secondary school teacher—one from his major department and one from the school or college of education. A number of the states, perhaps following NCATE's lead, have also encouraged this practice, especially in multipurpose institutions. Too often, because of heavy counseling loads, the "two-adviser" plan reverts into a practice of one adviser carrying the major load. In general, counseling, no matter how well designed, is a weak spot in an institution with a large enrollment.

In some multipurpose universities, the major department has the responsibility for advising prospective secondary school teachers. This adviser may be a staff member with a joint appointment in education and the academic department. The education department is often more willing to approve joint appointments than the academic departments. At the University of Maryland it is almost a requirement now that a person appointed in secondary education have a joint appointment with an academic department. NCATE and the states deserve some credit for encouraging this practice. Particularly in mathematics, but also in other disciplines in which the academicians have become active in teacher education, the joint or dual appointments have become popular. Among institutions having joint appointments in education and academic departments, some of fairly recent origin, are Emory University, Harvard University, Michigan State University, Stanford University, and state universities in Arizona, Colorado, Delaware, Iowa, Maryland, Michigan, Minnesota, Texas, Washington, and Wisconsin.

While accrediting agencies just before, during, and following an accreditation visit undoubtedly have been effective in promoting more serious attention to counseling, the lack of follow-up makes it possible for the accredited institution to lapse into rather haphazard practices, particularly as enrollments increase and teaching and counseling become heavy. In large institutions a counselor in the dean's office often carries the major load. Some suggest that the most satisfactory solution would be the employment of one or more full-time student counselors to be associated with the chief administrator of every teacher education program.

GRADUATION REQUIREMENTS

Accrediting associations are interested in both quantitative and qualitative requirements for graduation. The New England Association specifies a minimum of 120 semester hours (or equivalent) for the bachelor's degree. The Southern Association asks the institution under evaluation what its graduation requirements are. The Western Association wants a description of methods of grading employed in the institution. The North Central is concerned with the relationship of graduation requirements to the institution's objectives.

NCATE and the states have been concerned that an applicant for a teachers certificate has completed an approved program of teacher education, and that a single administrative officer has the responsibility to recommend graduates for certification. In Chapter 10 on Structure and Administration and Chapter 11 on College and University Curriculums, the influence of NCATE and the states has been reviewed in some detail on these points. The issues of who plans the program of graduation requirements and of who recommends to the administrative officer have been considered.

In comparing the *graduation* requirements of NCATE and non-NCATE institutions by means of the catalog survey, no significant differences were found in the total number of hours required for *graduation* from such institutions. However, it was found that NCATE state and teachers colleges required a mean GPA of 1.96, which is significantly greater than the 1.47 required for non-NCATE institutions in this category.

That NCATE has some concern about the qualifications of graduates is revealed by one item of information requested of the applicant for accreditation as a part of the description of the student personnel plan for teacher education. The item is:

> Present a profile for the last group completing teacher education curricula, showing: (1) rank in high school class (quintile), (2) intelligence test scores (percentile), (3) scores on last achievement or general culture tests administered to the entire student body (percentile), and (4) scores on national or state examinations relating to teaching that have been administered (percentile). All of these except the last item should show comparisons with graduates during the same year not preparing to teach.

This information, while basically quantitative, would give the evaluators of a teacher education program quite a bit of information on the quality of the graduates of the program. It seems probable from accounts of experiences with NCATE reported to participants in this Study that either too much emphasis is placed on the last sentence of the quote above, or that institutions have the impression that here is where the emphasis is placed. Critics of NCATE would say, how else can some colleges not on the NCATE list get there, since it is believed that their admission and graduation standards are low and general institutional quality is not too satisfactory? Is it because teacher education graduates in these institutions compare favorably on test scores with graduates of other programs in their institution, although not so favorably with respect to national norms? This suggests to some that teacher education programs, the graduates of which would not compare favorably with national norms on items (2), (3), and (4), should *not* be accredited by state or national agencies.

At Wisconsin, no student is recommended by the dean of education for a secondary school teachers certificate without the recommendation of the department in which the student has majored. This practice is not an uncommon one. Apparently some liberal arts staff members there gained the impression that this was a factor in the original denial of full accreditation of the undergraduate program in teacher education. An examination of NCATE records, together with conversations with some of those involved, and an examination of NCATE action in other cases gives no evidence that NCATE has any criticism whatever of this practice. NCATE's concern is that there be one person finally responsible for the institution's recommendation. The departments at Wisconsin recommend to the dean, who has the final authority, and the practice has worked satisfactorily there for more than 30 years.

STUDENT WELFARE

The regional associations are the accrediting agencies showing greatest concern for this broad aspect of an institution's program. NCATE and most of the states recognize this to the point of depending upon the regionals to evaluate and certify these important matters. How well developed a program of extracurricular activities exists on the campus? How broad is the spread of the athletic program? What is the degree of intellectual freedom for the students? What kinds of housing facilities are provided? What provisions have been made for student government? What kinds of student counseling service (academic, social, and clinical) are available? What medical or health services are provided? What are the regulations governing student use of the library?

In evaluating an institution, the Middle States Association wants to know whether students are stimulated to continue and broaden their education beyond the point they must reach to earn its credits, certificates, or degrees. The Middle States Association also inquires as to the extent to which the school's objectives seek to inculcate power to form independent judgment, to weigh values, to understand fundamental theory, rather than solely to amass facts or acquire skills. [4]

The New England Association asks about the adequacy of the student guidance and counseling services, as well as of the health services. The North Central wants to know: Is the level of achievement of students consistent with the goals of the institution? Is the student life on the campus well-balanced and educationally meaningful? The Northwest Association inquires specifically about the student activities on campus. The Southern Association asks for details relative to the operation of the athletic program. The Western Association also asks for information on counseling services. [5]

All of these questions have an important bearing upon the total institutional impact both on the students and on the public. Some of these areas are controversial. Other controversial areas, such as on-campus and off-campus housing policies, thus far apparently have not come under the scrutiny of accrediting bodies. Whether or not they should have scrutiny is itself a highly controversial issue.

SUMMARY

NCATE and the states have been largely concerned with admission standards for teacher education, with NCATE insisting that in teacher education "criteria for admission and retention should be in addition to general policies and procedures for admitting students." This has been interpreted generally to mean higher admission standards. The regional associations tend to evaluate admission standards as they relate to institutional philosophy or objectives.

Under retention policies, NCATE is concerned with the elimination from teacher education of those who do not give promise of success in the profession. This can be done automatically on the basis of low grades or by means of personal counseling. The regionals again tend to judge the retention policy of an institution in terms of its philosophy or objectives.

NCATE's concern with graduation policies relates to the desire to certify for teaching only qualified persons. The regionals judge graduation policies on the basis of the school's philosophy and objectives.

Student welfare policies have been left largely to the regionals for evaluation. It is generally treated as a good area for stimulation to improvement, rather than as a basis for granting or withholding accreditation.

The net effect on student policies of the accreditation of teacher education, acting with other factors, has been:

Somewhat higher admission standards, particularly in teacher education (NCATE and the states).

Increased emphasis on counseling services—academic, social, and clinical (NCATE, regionals, and the states).

Somewhat higher graduation requirements (NCATE and the states for teacher education; the regionals for liberal arts).

Additional facilities for student health and welfare (regional associations).

REFERENCES

1. NCATE Brochure: *Explanatory Materials Interpreting the NCATE Materials* (A Tentative Draft), 1964, p. 5.
2. NCATE Brochure: *A Statement of Purposes, Policies, and Procedures* (Washington, D. C., 1960), p. 7.
3. NCATE *Standards and Guide* (1960 Edition), p. 8.
4. John F. Nevins, *A Study of the Organization and Operation of Voluntary Accrediting Agencies* (Washington, D. C., 1959), pp. 165–194.
5. *Ibid.*

CHAPTER 14

COLLEGE AND UNIVERSITY FINANCE

ACCREDITING AGENCIES in general are interested in four aspects of a higher institution's finances; namely, sources of income, degree of financial stability, adequacy of income, and distribution or budgeting of income. The regional accrediting associations are more concerned than NCATE with the sources of income and financial stability. NCATE depends upon regional approval of a college to guarantee that these important aspects of an institution meet acceptable standards. States which accredit or approve the total institution assume a responsibility for approving sources of income and financial stability. On the other hand, states which approve institutions or programs for teacher education only are concerned, like NCATE, with finances largely in terms of adequate salaries and facilities.

The shrinking value of the dollar, the decreasing returns from private investments, burgeoning costs of staff and facilities in the face of swelling enrollments combine to confront virtually all institutions of higher education today with financial problems. To illustrate the extent to which conditions in this area have changed within the past few decades, a brief mention might be made of a $25 million endowment drive promoted in the middle 1920's by a large university. When the aggregate gifts from a quiet mail solicitation had exceeded $30 million, the university was reported to have begun refunding the excess contributions. The mere thought of such an occurrence at the present time would tax the human imagination.

SOURCES OF INCOME

Three-quarters of a century ago men of great wealth sought to immortalize their names by endowing educational institutions. Today they usually find it more advantageous to endow educational and charitable foundations. This is not intended to imply that education is necessarily the loser in this transition. Colleges and universities may ultimately benefit from such foundations in the form of grants-in-aid of various kinds. In addition, a considerable part of the support of a major university today may come from Federal support of research, facilities, staff and student needs. It may not be long until the amount of Federal support or even of private foundation support for a particular purpose and the concomitant fear of Federal or other outside control or influence become matters of concern to some of the accrediting agencies.

In the case of a public or private educational institution, accrediting associations at all three levels might underscore the need for increased funds. This might be done by withholding full accreditation until certain changes are made. It may be that new sources of income will have to be found, that more money must become available from the regular sources, or that a new distribution of funds within the total institutional budget will have to be made. This is a good example of the "leverage" possibilities which may arise from accreditation in obtaining increased staff or facilities on the part of the institution concerned.

In evaluating an institution, both the Northwest Association and the Southern Association ask for detailed information about the school's financial support. [1] This apparently is part of the general information about the college or university to be used in the over-all evaluation of the institution. One state department reported that if a state college or university were asking for an increase in state appropriation and the state department regarded the proposed increase as justifiable, a representative of the department might offer to testify before the proper legislative committee or the budgetary office or commission. It should be remembered, too, that in some states, the state colleges are still under the direct jurisdiction of the state department of education, which naturally and necessarily plays an active role in obtaining state financial support for those colleges.

One concern of accrediting agencies about an institution's sources of income is an awareness that sometimes the giving of money to a college or university becomes a means of controlling institutional policy. Accrediting agencies in general have shown little concern about such effects as these on respectable educational institutions, even though administrators or staff members may resign or be removed because of the pressures.

While there may be some concern about control by sources of income, there is little, if any, evidence that accreditation has faced up to this problem in a way to bring about improvement.

FINANCIAL STABILITY

All accrediting agencies recognize the importance of financial stability in an institution's status and welfare. It is obvious, too, that financial instability normally symptomizes inadequate financial resources. The problem may affect either private or public higher institutions, but it is more likely to occur in privately endowed colleges.

It was such a realization which led the North Central Association to adopt as one of its early standards a minimum endowment of $200,000 for private colleges. This was arrived at by figuring that it would take $200,000 invested at the usual interest rate of 6 percent to pay salaries of $1,500 to a minimum of eight professors. It was soon recognized that this requirement worked a hardship on church-related colleges which received annual cash appropriations from supporting denominations. In 1923 it was agreed that annual contributions to a college would count toward endowment the amount necessary at five percent to produce the said denominational contribution to the college's operating budget. It was later discovered that this solution did not resolve the problem of church-related schools in which members of religious orders contributed all or part of their services to the higher institution. The rule was changed again in 1933 to permit contributed services of faculty to be accepted in lieu of endowment. This, in turn, made it necessary to determine the advanced degree equivalency, hence salary equivalency, of different categories of training for religious orders. [2]

With the revision of North Central accreditation standards in the mid-1930's, specific quantitative standards regulating the minimum endowment of private institutions of higher learning were abandoned. In lieu of such quantitative standards, North Central surveys the financial status of the institution to determine whether it has sufficient financial resources to carry on its program and to achieve its objectives. [3] Since then, the other regional associations have adopted a similar policy. Unfortunately such changes in regional policies have not resolved the basic problem of financial instability. As pointed out at the beginning of this chapter, the shrinking value of the dollar, the declining dividends from investments, the heavy corporation and income taxes, all combined with rising costs, serve as a constant threat to the financial stability of colleges and universities.

Even many of the public institutions of higher learning are having to fight harder each year or biennium for their share of the legislative appropriations. This is one area where competition is increasing, rather than declining.

ADEQUACY OF INCOME

All accrediting agencies are interested in ascertaining whether the income of an institution of higher learning is adequate for its needs. To NCATE, this means adequate for the needs of teacher education. To the regional association, this means among other things adequate for library, laboratory, health, and recreational needs. To the states, this means adequate especially for training people to meet the state certification requirements. To all accrediting agencies, adequate income means putting the institution into a good competitive position in terms of staff salaries and all-round physical facilities.

In other chapters, the needs for teacher education, such as an adequate faculty and broad counseling services as concerns of NCATE, have been discussed. These are related to adequacy of income as is NCATE's concern about physical facilities for teacher education. Under Standard VII, "Facilities and Instructional Materials for Teacher Education," NCATE spells out the teacher education needs:

> Office space, attractive in nature and ample in amount, should be provided to serve the needs of the professional education faculty in planning the professional education program, in counseling the students, and in working effectively with schools and other agencies outside the institution. Classroom space equipped for teaching professional education should be provided within a reasonably concentrated area to meet the needs of the program offered. . . .
> A materials laboratory or center should be maintained either as part of the library or as a separate unit. . . .

NCATE is determined that the facilities for teacher education not be inferior to those for other programs on the campus. The head of an education department in a prominent southern university was sharp in his criticism of NCATE for pointing out the need for redecorating the offices and classrooms in the education building. He insisted that such improvements were not essential to a successful teacher education program. [4] On the other hand, the regional associations might be commended under "stimulation to improvement" for pointing out such a need. Perhaps the difference is due to the fact that criticisms are less objectionable as suggestions for improvement than as a failure to meet minimum standards.

In the Wisconsin case, NCATE was criticized for pointing out that the physical facilities in education at Wisconsin were inferior to those of some of the other schools and colleges of the university. Anyone visiting the Wisconsin campus could scarcely disagree. Many new and modern structures are being built on the campus, as is true of most all large universities.

NCATE has also expressed concern about the ability of many liberal arts colleges with limited financial resources to maintain, at the same time, a high-level liberal arts program and a quality teacher education program. If a college cannot afford to do both, NCATE says with frankness that it simply should get out of the business of educating teachers. [5] Conant says essentially the same thing in declaring that one-third of the colleges should discontinue the training of elementary teachers. [6] However, when as many as half the students in liberal arts colleges are in teacher education, to suggest that the college should get out of the business of training teachers may be equivalent to saying that it should "get out of business" entirely. Such schools under the circumstances, in refusing to give up their teacher education programs, are in reality fighting for their very existence.

Here are some examples of specific deficiencies listed by NCATE in denying full accreditation to teacher education institutions, where the deficiencies relate to inadequacy of income:

It looks as if the school is trying to support too many programs.

The education building is inadequate.

The library holdings in professional education are inadequate.

The facilities in education are generally inadequate.

The periodicals in the library are inadequate.

Specifics like these are capable of being used as a lever to get the funds needed to make the suggested changes or improvements. It is clear that they have been so used both after an accreditation visit and in anticipation of a visit, and in this way NCATE has had an influence in obtaining more adequate facilities for teacher education.

One dean of a state university, requesting not to be identified, spoke of his difficulty in obtaining approval from the administration for an increased budget for teacher education. But after persuading the president of the desirability of NCATE accreditation and the need for budget increases to guarantee full accreditation, the dean found that the president not only approved the request but welcomed accreditation "leverage" in presenting the budget requests to the governing board of the university.

At another state university, the dean of education reported having a new and greater appreciation of NCATE after the university had been denied full NCATE accreditation for excessively high teaching loads in the school of education. Upon reporting this adverse decision and the reasons for it to his fellow academic deans, his colleagues supported his request for a sufficient increase in allocation of university funds to add the needed staff in education—something he had tried unsuccessfully to achieve over a period of years.

At still another state university, the dean expressed no displeasure over an NCATE provisional accreditation. One reason given for the deferment was a totally inadequate curriculum laboratory (lacking in both space and equipment). Because of NCATE's action, he had been able to obtain the space for the laboratory, work had begun on remodeling, and funds had been made available for the needed equipment.

On a visit to a church-supported women's college, the president took the visitors on a tour of the library, which was scattered in rooms from basement to second floor of an old building, to demonstrate why the college was delaying a request for NCATE accreditation until a new library was constructed. She had been advised by state officials to delay a request for accreditation for this reason, and she was using the "need" for accreditation in the solicitation of funds for the new library. This last example illustrates how the state often supports NCATE standards and how it assists a higher institution in preparing for an eventual accreditation visit.

Examples of specific deficiencies, either listed by NCATE in denying or delaying full accreditation or deficiencies similar to them, could be found in many state files. Again this would be true whether or not the state was a strong supporter of NCATE. Since state departments of education are concerned with obtaining an adequate supply of good teachers, they have often been influential in obtaining additional financial support for public higher institutions. Through the pointing out of deficiencies, the states, like NCATE, also have provided a leverage for obtaining funds for private institutions.

While the regional associations have been less directly concerned with support for teacher education, they have placed a great stress on the importance of adequate financial support in general. Through their actions, as well as in anticipation of them, they have, like NCATE and the states, had an indirect effect on the adequacy of college and university financial support. The deficiencies which they have emphasized are suggested by the information which they seek from a college or university.

The New England Association wants assurance that an institution is solvent financially, that its physical plant is adequate, and that it possesses the financial ability to carry out its objectives. [7] The North Central Association wants to know whether the institution has the necessary resources available for carrying out its educational task. [8] The Northwest Association asks about the adequacy of the physical plant, materials, and equipment. [9] The Southern Association wants to know about the adequacy of the physical plant, particularly the library. [10] All of these relate directly to the adequacy of an institution's income.

DISTRIBUTION OF INCOME

Since a college or university ordinarily does not have resources ample enough to finance the requests of all departments of the institution, the administration faces the difficult and unpleasant task of deciding what aspects to nourish and which to "starve," which to stimulate and which to soft-pedal, which to push and which to hold back. NCATE and the state departments of education are concerned primarily with the needs of the teacher education program, and making sure that teacher education programs have a reasonable share of the financial support available. NCATE, particularly, has been criticized on this point by those who believe that NCATE in its concern has too often equated the needs of teacher education with the needs of the department of education. Be that as it may, concern of a professional accrediting agency for the educational program of its profession is not only related to the adequacy of the income of an institution but also to the distribution of income within the institution.

It should be noted that one of the motivations of professional groups, in seeking to establish a professional agency, arises from their desire to assist their members in institutions of higher education to be in a better competitive position in terms of salaries and research facilities.

For example, mathematicians and physicists have been heard to advocate a system of accreditation in their disciplines in order to place them in a better competitive position with the chemists. Reference is made here to the American Chemical Society which has been recognized as an accrediting body by the National Commission on Accrediting. A college or university wishing to obtain approval of the American Chemical Society might even go so far as to build a new chemistry building. It is understandable that the mathematicians and physicists would like to have leverage of comparable effectiveness.

In addition to the problem of fair distribution of income among departments is the problem of the distribution of income among facilities and functions of an institution. This also is a legitimate concern of an accrediting agency. An administration may believe that new buildings constitute a more substantial and permanent improvement than a transitory faculty. A few administrators may view new buildings as a more substantial and permanent monument to a president's achievements than a less conspicuous staff. Consequently, those who control an institution's budgetary policy and emphasis sometimes fall into the error of building buildings rather than an outstanding and scholarly faculty, when there are insufficient financial resources for both. The accrediting associations recognize this and sometimes have identified it as a deficiency, but probably not frequently enough.

The regional associations have long recognized the central importance of a good library; NCATE is particularly concerned with the library facilities in education (Standard VII). Just as the regionals have had an influence on the development of better libraries as an essential element in an institution of higher education, so has NCATE, with the support of the states, had an influence in bringing about greater recognition of the library as an essential element in teacher education. Unfortunately, in both cases, the influence is more quantitative than qualitative. In other words, greater emphasis has been placed upon the number of books in the library than on the quality of the library books or the extent and manner in which the books are used.

Both the regional associations and NCATE recognize the need for paying competitive salaries to the teaching staff. NCATE has been particularly sensitive to the practice in some institutions of paying lower salaries, on the average, to the staff in education as compared with those paid to academicians. There appears to be justification for the statement that the influence of accrediting agencies on salaries, while not spectacular, has been substantial. Over the years, the regionals have applied steady pressure toward an elevation of faculty salaries. At times, they appeared to be the only force working in this direction. The motivation behind this effort was to raise the level of teaching and research. NCATE has apparently had some influence in causing colleges and universities to bring salaries in professional education into line with general institutional salary scales when the two were sharply out of balance.

Accrediting agencies have been concerned with the distribution of income as related to research. In more recent years research has received greater attention both from accrediting agencies and from institutions and many kinds of research have become more costly. The advantages of team research in teacher education, as well as in the sciences, is more clearly recognized, and with the recognition of its advantages is a recognition of a need for increased financial support. Although much of this support may be available from foundations or government, some of it must or should be provided by the higher institutions. Both distribution of income and sources of income as related to research become increasingly difficult problems for institutions. Research in teacher education is the topic of the next chapter.

Two other costly needs of teacher education identified by national and state accreditation of teacher education are facilities and staff for student teaching and facilities for audiovisual instruction. Deficiencies in the area of student teaching are often those which arise largely from inadequate financial support for paying the cooperating schools and their teachers, for employing adequate supervisory staff, and for travel costs. Much of current research in teacher education and teaching is related to the use of audiovisual aids which are often expensive. For example, a plan under which student teachers may see themselves teach via closed circuit television shows unusual promise but many institutions cannot afford to introduce it. Then a problem arises for the institution about using available funds for staff and libraries or for audiovisual aids. If audiovisual aids bring about a revolution in education, as some predict, the problem promises to be more difficult in the years ahead.

The distribution of income within a teacher education program obviously is a critical one for the institution and perhaps should become of greater concern in accrediting. As has been indicated, however, in relation to distribution of funds, the principal impact of accreditation in teacher education thus far appears to be making more funds available for teacher education and in particular for faculty salaries, libraries, and student teaching facilities.

SUMMARY

Institutional finances are largely a concern of the regional associations as part of the general institutional accreditation. Generally speaking, adequacy and stability of income are regarded as more significant than sources.

All accrediting agencies are interested in the distribution or budgeting of the institution's income. NCATE wants assurance that the teacher education interests are adequately served, and particularly that they are not victims of discrimination. Many examples can be cited in which increased funds have been allotted to teacher education programs in order to obtain or maintain accreditation, and in some instances the desire for accreditation seems to have been a critical factor. The regionals are anxious to have competitive salaries paid to the general faculty. All have a concern for adequate library facilities. The basic question asked is whether the financial resources of the institution under review are adequate to carry out its stated objectives. If not, the accrediting agencies insist that the program should be adjusted accordingly.

To gain regional accreditation some colleges apparently have had to strengthen their financial resources. Likewise, in order to gain accreditation, some colleges have had to readjust their budgets, allocating a larger portion to salaries or to improved library or laboratory facilities. An important aspect of regional or state institutional counseling or stimulation to improvement appears to be the assistance given in achieving a higher degree of financial stability on the part of the institution under review.

REFERENCES

1. Summarized in John F. Nevins, *A Study of the Organization and Operation of Voluntary Accrediting Agencies* (Washington, D. C., 1959), pp. 184, 190.
2. *Ibid.,* pp. 213–215.
3. G. F. Zook and M. E. Haggerty, *The Evaluation of Higher Institutions,* pp. 91–143.
4. Edward T. Ladd, "The Proper Place of Accreditation," *Journal of Secondary Education,* 38:5 (May 1963), p. 304.
5. AACTE, *Sourcebook on Accreditation of Teacher Education* (1962), p. 18.
6. James B. Conant, *The Education of American Teachers,* pp. 163, 164; Conant, *The Certification of Teachers,* p. 20.
7. Nevins, *op. cit.,* pp. 165, 166.
8. *Ibid.,* p. 179.
9. *Ibid.,* p. 190.
10. *Ibid.,* p. 184.

CHAPTER 15

EXPERIMENTATION AND RESEARCH

EXPERIMENTATION and research are recognized to be vital elements in a quality institution of higher learning. Since experimentation is an integral part of certain types of research, a definition of the use of these terms is appropriate. The term "experimentation," as used here, refers to the trying out of new ways of educating teachers through different administrative patterns, course or sequence organization, or staff utilization. Some might prefer to call this innovation rather than experimentation. Research, as used here, may involve either laboratory or non-laboratory techniques of broadening the frontiers of knowledge, and includes any search for knowledge which would be recognized as research by a reputable graduate school. It goes almost without saying that the higher one moves in the levels of academic work the more important research and experimentation become.

In this chapter there is some repetition of observations made in the earlier chapters of Part II, since variations in patterns of administration, curriculum, or staff utilization are related to experimentation and/or innovation. Even distribution of financial resources bears a close relationship. Because the degree to which accreditation may or may not stifle experimentation and research is probably the paramount issue in accreditation, repetition for purposes of emphasis seems to be essential.

EXPERIMENTATION

NATIONAL ACCREDITATION

NCATE insists that experimentation in teacher education is looked upon with favor and that, short of financial assistance, it is encouraged and fostered. Defenders of NCATE insist the very fact that a great diversity of programs of teacher education in all kinds of institutions have been accredited by NCATE attests to its flexibility and lack of discouragement of experimentation. Many of NCATE's critics say that NCATE discourages experimentation to the point of stifling it. This controversy stems largely from NCATE's recommended pattern for the administration of teacher education, and its standards, along with the interpretation of them, for curriculum and staff.

It is pointed out by NCATE that the proposed administrative pattern is a recommendation only, and not absolutely mandatory. A similar response is given in defense against the criticism of "rigidity" in interpretation of the other standards. If an institution wishes to conduct a genuine experiment with a different pattern of administering teacher education or of a curriculum, NCATE states it will be welcomed. NCATE, however, may ask for evidence that the different approach is a genuine experiment and not merely a convenient variation from the NCATE norm. [1]

In visits to campuses and in conferences with representatives of higher education, the influence of accrediting agencies on experimentation was rarely mentioned except in response to a direct question. It appears that colleges, in general, do not think of experimentation as being as closely related to accreditation in a positive sense as other facets of teacher education. They certainly do not view experimentation as part of that which they are "required" to do in order to become accredited.

A number of NCATE-accredited institutions are known to have groups of students in experimental sequences of teacher education experiences without fear of NCATE or state disapproval. When small groups of students are involved in an experiment, it can, of course, more readily be accepted as a "genuine" experiment, even though it does not involve careful research controls. In 1960–1962, as part of the activities of the Science Teaching Improvement Program sponsored by the American Association for the Advancement of Science and supported by the Carnegie Corporation of New York, nine colleges and universities conducted experimental studies of new methods for training science and mathematics teachers. The experiments involved modification of professional education sequences. All but three of the nine institutions were or are now accredited by NCATE. No questions were raised at any time by NCATE, nor by the colleges, out of concern for NCATE attitudes toward the experiments.[2]

Early in November, 1964, it was announced that an experimental program was to be instituted in New York State in order to put a part of Conant's theories and recommendations to a practical test. [3] Five institutions of higher education were selected as "proving grounds" for the Conant reforms. The five institutions are: Brooklyn College, Colgate University, Cornell University, Fredonia State College, and Vassar College. These colleges represent a wide range of institutional patterns—a large municipal college, an independent liberal arts college for men, an "Ivy League" university, a state university unit that had been transformed from a teachers college to a liberal arts college, and a prominent women's college. All but Colgate and Vassar are accredited by NCATE. Colgate and Vassar have not applied for accreditation. The experiment is to be conducted with the full approval and cooperation of the New York State Commissioner of Education.

Presumably, the four basic recommendations of Conant would be embodied in the project: (1) placing most of the responsibility for teacher certification on the colleges and universities rather than on the states; (2) making actual performance in the classroom the major factor in certification; (3) shifting a greater part of the on-the-job training burden to local school systems; and (4) making the state authorities responsible for the supervision of the student teaching and on-the-job training. The success of the project might of course be the best way to induce other states and institutions to follow suit.

In colleges in which the plan is used or in others which may later adopt it with a part of the teacher education candidates, there is no reason to believe that NCATE accreditation would be affected, either if such accreditation already existed or if it were sought later. Where the plan involves all prospective teachers, one could not predict if NCATE accreditation could be obtained without knowing more about the plan.

The interest of NCATE in the preparation of the staff of an institution, and the criticisms by NCATE of institutions because a staff member, for example, might be teaching an undergraduate course in social foundations without graduate work in that field, has tended to discourage experimentation in staff utilization.

The problem of adequate staffing of a department of education in a liberal arts college, along with the desire to make the department of education a more integral part of the college staff, led one dean of a liberal arts college to propose the providing of funds to send away a member of the history department and a member of the sociology staff to study the history of education and educational sociology, respectively, so that these men would be prepared to offer education courses. This proposal was not carried out, probably due to lack of funds and possibly also because of uneasiness about NCATE or state disapproval. This is actually a kind of "experimentation" which accrediting agencies might encourage.

A state college was criticized by NCATE for allowing a staff member in music education to teach educational psychology, since he had no graduate work in the latter field. His colleagues testified that his teaching of educational psychology was of the highest quality. Nationally known scholars in the sciences and in the humanities are teaching at major universities without the usual graduate degrees in their fields. While they are recognized as exceptions, such exceptions should also be recognized in teacher education. Too rigid interpretation of staff requirements for accreditation is probably a negative influence on experimentation with staff utilization.

Few colleges or universities are known to have an undergraduate teacher education program without a department of education. Attention was given to this issue in Chapter 10 on Administration. All institu-

tions on the NCATE list of accredited institutions do have an administrative unit in education, and it seems unlikely that an institution
without such an administrative unit would now apply for NCATE
approval. However, the standards of NCATE in this regard do not
clearly suggest that an institution must have a department of education. Indeed the standards imply that a teacher education program
might be administered by an all-institutional committee. Reference is
made here to this question because it contains at least an implication
of restriction on experimentation.

It has been assumed by some institutions that NCATE would look
with disfavor on the development of a graduate program in teacher
education in an institution without a school or college of education.
In Chapter 10 reference was made to a state university, which eventually withdrew its application for accreditation by NCATE because it
interpreted discussions with NCATE representatives to be rather strong
recommendations that a school or college of education be organized
to administer the proposed graduate program. Reference was also
made in Chapter 10 to Duke University which offers graduate programs
in education leading to the master's and doctor's degrees in a Department of Education, which is a department of the Graduate School of
Arts and Sciences. Similarly Washington University (St. Louis) offers
graduate degrees through a Graduate Institute of Education in the
Graduate School of Arts and Sciences. Both are accredited by NCATE.

A fair conclusion seems to be that an institution would find it easier
to supply data in support of its claim to satisfy NCATE standards if
it had a department of education for the administration of its undergraduate program and a school or college of education for the
administration of its graduate program. Thus it can be said that the
interpretation of NCATE standards has tended to discourage experimentation with the administrative units in teacher education, whether
or not this is the actual intent.

A privately endowed university is known to have been given provisional accreditation at least in part because it was not clear to the
accrediting committee of NCATE that the chairman of the department of education had final responsibility for all teacher education
programs and students. The institution is proud of the participation of
its liberal arts departments in teacher education, and apparently is
reluctant to adjust administrative responsibility in any way which
would jeopardize the existing good relations.

In another case, a university, this one tax supported, was compli-
mented for the general strength of its teacher education program and
a newly organized committee on teacher education with responsibilities for coordination of teacher education programs. But accreditation was delayed because of "divided responsibilities between the
School of Education and the College of Arts and Sciences" in planning
the academic and professional curriculums for preparing secondary
school teachers. An academic professor of this institution wrote to the

Director of this Study, seeking information which might be of assistance to the university in meeting NCATE standards without sacrificing the advantages, as he saw them, of the present administrative structure.

Even if not stated explicitly in its standards, some NCATE teams and committees have been too rigid in their expectation of a "straight-line" administrative responsibility between education and liberal arts units in multipurpose universities. While in the evaluations to which reference has been made the institutions probably did not consider their administrative structures experimental, the NCATE concerns as reported tend to make other institutions believe that evaluations in administrative structure may raise problems for them with NCATE.

The development of programs in teacher education for graduates of liberal arts programs has attracted wide attention and, in some segments of higher education, much enthusiasm. These programs which are usually one to one and one-half years in length often are referred to as MAT (master of arts in teaching) programs. They are planned to provide for the student teaching and professional education course experience for high-quality students with baccalaureate degrees in liberal arts, and also for further work in the area of specialization of the participants in the programs. Many of the programs, but not all, lead to a master's degree. In a number of instances these programs are considered to be experimental. Some institutions offering these programs definitely believe them to be the best way to educate teachers. Prestige has been added to the concept of the MAT programs by the high quality of the institutions offering them, by their admission standards, by the foundation support they have received, and in some cases by the reputation of the liberal arts institutions from which students have graduated before entering an MAT program elsewhere.

Whether or not an MAT program is considered to be experimental, the offering of it provides evidence which can be used in resolving an issue which has long been a subject of debate in teacher education. The question is: Does the prospective teacher profit more from professional experience introduced early in his teacher education program and spread out over several years, or when these experiences are concentrated in a final year or more after a broad liberal education and at a time of greater commitment to teaching? While there is probably no one correct answer to this question for all prospective teachers, experiences with MAT programs of the past five years can be very helpful in institutional decision making.

Several institutions recently evaluated by NCATE reported disappointment that the visiting team showed so little interest in their MAT programs. One institutional representative reported that, had he not insisted, the visiting team would not have looked at his institution's MAT program at all. Others reported that, since an MAT program (as the term is broadly used here) is a preservice program not yet offered for a master's degree, NCATE had never made clear to them whether in accreditation they considered the MAT program an undergraduate or graduate program. An inquiry at the NCATE office did not bring forth a clear-cut answer to this question. For these reasons, it is concluded that NCATE has not given MAT programs the attention they deserve, and furthermore that NCATE can be given no credit for having encouraged these programs.

If there has been any impact of accreditation on MAT programs, it has been from the states which are fully aware of their existence. Indeed, in answer to a question about the existence of MAT programs, such a large number of programs were reported by the states that they obviously use the term even more broadly than it has been used in this Study. Some of the states not only have participated in the development of MAT programs but have given specific approval to them and have encouraged students to enroll in them.

At one state college which had been deferred for national accreditation, there was concern over the NCATE criticism that its laboratory school had not been sufficiently utilized for experimentation—the reference here being to experimentation with pre-college curriculums rather than with methods of teacher education. It seemed likely that the college was planning to set up some experimental studies in preparation for the next NCATE visit. The emphasis of NCATE on the student teaching plan of sending prospective teachers off campus does free the campus laboratory school for experimentation. Hence NCATE may directly be encouraging one kind of experimentation. The criticism of this college for not making "proper" use of its laboratory school is not considered an isolated case. It appears that NCATE is definitely encouraging experimentation in laboratory schools.

THE STATES

State department of education officials say they are always glad to see experimentation in teacher education, on the assumption that experimentation is one avenue to improvement, and improvement in teacher education is something very much to be desired. For this reason, state department staffs would like to keep abreast of such experiments, including the findings or results of such experimental operations. Some states, like Michigan, give official status to experiments in teacher education by giving them departmental approval, provided the experimental design in each proposal gives promise of making a worthwhile contribution to teacher education. New York State enjoys a good record in encouraging experimental programs of a number of different kinds, only the most recent of which is the proposed "Conant plan project." (See above, pp. 198, 199.)

In some states the attitude toward experimentation is very similar to and greatly influenced by the attitude of NCATE in this regard. However, even in these instances the state is likely to be more lenient toward experimentation than NCATE, and the college or university less fearful of disapproval, partly because communication is so much better and mutual confidence has already been established. There are, of course, exceptions among the states resulting from greater rigidity in some state departments.

In one of the Studies in Teacher Education, to which reference was made (see page 198 above), the college officials secured approval of the experimental program by the state in which the college is located and by neighboring states in which the graduates of the college often teach. Actually, however, when one of the graduates of the experimental program attempted to obtain a certificate in an adjacent state, the certificate was denied. At least, those in charge of the program at the college in question concluded that this was entirely a result of the rigidity of a certification officer. On the other hand, the certification officer said there had been a misunderstanding of the original agreement.

The adoption of the approved-program approach in a majority of the states should foster experimentation. Indeed that is one reason this approach has recently become so popular. Colleges, in states where the use of this approach is the policy of the state department, often do not take advantage of the freedom that is theirs. One liberal arts college dean in answer to the question, "What determines the teacher education program at your college?" said, "State requirements." While others were not so frank, this answer is not as far from the truth as it might appear. The existence of this kind of situation is one of the principal reasons why professional educators wanted national accreditation and why they seek ways of strengthening it. Do not the faculty members of a college have any ideas about teacher education with which they would like to experiment, even within the framework of state requirements?

Five years ago, more frequently than today, the possibility of certification of teachers by examination in lieu of requirements of courses in education was widely discussed. Most of the states at that time took the attitude, and still do, that if the institution would allow credit, and particularly credit for graduation, by examination—instead of registering in and attending a class—the certificate would be granted. Indeed some states have encouraged such experimentation. New York is one. In Wisconsin the state department gave approval to a plan for meeting certification requirements by examination, including academic as well as education courses, which was initiated by the university and was to be effective at the other colleges preparing teachers as well as at the university. However after the initial publicity, little more has been heard from this plan, except that it has not been very popular, since so many students are not successful on the examinations. The use of examinations in West Virginia has already been reported. (See Chapter 9.) Here again is evidence that a number of the states do encourage and give support to experimentation.

In meetings with the state directors of teacher education over a span of nearly 10 years, many instances of pride of state directors in experimental programs within their states have been noted, and especially if the state department had some direct relationship or at least communication with the experiment. Two factors currently operate to strengthen the favorable attitudes of state officials toward experimentation: (1) the growing conversation between state officials and the academic societies; and (2) the increased Federal support available through the U. S. Office of Education to state departments and colleges, in joint projects or with either one acting alone, for research and demonstration.

Demonstration projects under Federal programs would come under the heading of experimentation as the term is used here. Some state departments are at least discussing possible experimentation in teacher education, initiated and possibly supported by the department with Federal funds in cooperation with colleges within the state.

No safe generalization on the extent to which the states stimulate or stifle experimentation can be made because there are 50 different standards and 50 different answers. It is clear that NASDTEC (National Association of State Directors of Teacher Education and Certification) encourages its members to be flexible in this respect and to give support to experimentation. Yet some state departments appear to remain fearful of the good intent of the experimenters and too cautious about variety.

REGIONAL ASSOCIATIONS

Any interest that the regional associations might have in experimentation would apparently relate in some manner to general institutional improvement. For example, an experiment that would involve selecting students with academically poor backgrounds and concentrating on bringing them up to or above average in academic achievement would probably be regarded with genuine interest by a regional association. The association would have to be convinced, however, that the experiment was genuine, and not merely a "gimmick" for increasing the institutional enrollment or income. An instance of this kind is reported to be pending before one of the regional associations at this time.

NCTEPS AND AACTE

The two professional organizations, both constituent members of NCATE, most concerned with teacher education and together naming 13 of the 19 members of the present Council, have both encouraged and stimulated experimentation with the professional education sequence in teacher education. In so doing, both acknowledge the necessity for improvement while at the same time pointing out the merits of present teacher education programs.

Recent major projects of both groups (NCTEPS and AACTE) have given special emphasis to experimentation with undergraduate sequences in professional education. In 1961, NCTEPS published the *New Horizons for the Teaching Profession* report. [4] In 1964, the new media project for AACTE was in its second year. The positions taken on experimentation by these two projects are reviewed here in order to show the high-level endorsement of professional groups of the need for experimentation and also in support of a point of view that the accrediting agencies probably are much more receptive to experimentation than the colleges believe.

The recommendations on accreditation of the *New Horizons* report are reviewed in Appendix IX. Here our concern is with the report recommendations on the preservice professional education sequence. The report assigns responsibilities for teacher education and accreditation to various groups, including the education associations, state departments, and teachers at all levels. In speaking of college teachers (all college teachers are considered to be members of the teaching profession), the report states: "In sum, the college teacher must work to make the operation of the accrediting agency a force for experimentation, development, variety, not conformity, vested interest, or stale tradition." [5]

Other *New Horizons* statements on the importance of flexibility and experimentation are:

> Great care must be exercised by accrediting agencies to assure that the use of comparative data, the standards for evaluation, and means of assisting institutions in self-improvement do not hamper well conceived experimentation and innovation. [6]
>
> On closer scrutiny, however, the individual who is familiar with current practices in preservice and inservice programs of professional preparation will discover that implementation of the recommendations made here would demand substantial modification in the basic rationale, undergirding current focus of preservice in education. [7]

In May, 1963, the AACTE, under a contract with the U.S. Office of Education (Educational Media Branch) and in cooperation with Associated Organizations for Teacher Education, began a 27-month project to improve the professional sequence in preservice teacher education through the selective and planned use of new media. The project is basically concerned with the use of new media, hence is an extremely important and timely topic for consideration. It is expected that plans and proposals for developing instructional units into multi-media instructional systems will be one of the major outcomes of the project. To achieve this, proposals regarding the restructuring of the organization of preservice teacher education, in order to make full use of the new media, are already in preparation. It is conceivable that the restructuring, which is being attacked boldly and imaginatively, may be a major contribution of the project and may have a very considerable influence on programs which utilize new media as well as those which do not.

In an earlier report (September, 1964) suggestions on the organization of five courses are presented. [8] These courses are given under the titles:

Analytical study of teaching.
Structures and uses of knowledge.
Concepts of human behavior and learning.
Designs for teaching-learning.
Demonstration and evaluation of teacher competencies.

The report also raises questions about the value of student teaching:

> The notion of practice is a far too limited concept for the development of a high-level teaching competence. If it were actually possible to assign all prospective teachers to outstanding experienced teachers, the superimposed effect of imitation or mimicking reduces the possibilities for individual professional growth. A further limitation within this dimension is the random nature of the possible experiences. There is a lack of design and control. [9]

The plans of the project call for a "detailed statement of major behavioral objectives (teacher competencies) of the professional components of preservice teacher education." Later in the current report there is an admission that these behavioral objectives have not been formulated, although the report indicates considerable progress with course outlines.

Presumably the courses eventually will be evaluated in terms of achievement (or predicted possibilities of achievement) of the behavioral objectives by the students who study them. Unfortunately this approach to planning the professional education sequence is too rare. Modern techniques and tools for research make this approach much more feasible than it was a decade ago.

RESEARCH

NCATE's interest in research is two-fold: (1) research that relates to teacher education, and (2) research conducted by members of the staff in the department or college of education. Naturally there is an overlapping of these two categories in that much of the research of professors of education would normally relate to teacher education. In the self-study required by NCATE as part of the accreditation process, an institution under evaluation is asked to list the staff members in education who have been granted leaves for research and study during recent years, and the dates of such leaves. The institution is also asked to describe: (1) the space available for faculty or graduate students for research; (2) any special equipment available for the faculty or graduate students for research; and (3) the amount spent the preceding year for research in professional education by the faculty. [10]

Simply by asking for this information, NCATE presumably can be credited with an influence toward the improvement of conditions for research in teacher education, as well as by education staff members.

A small college, with an unimpressive research record, might conceivably postpone its application for accreditation until such time as it could provide more impressive evidence on this score. In the meantime, steps might be taken to encourage the faculty of the college to become involved in research, or for the college to employ new staff members already committed to research. However, a perusal of the NCATE list of accredited institutions would cause some to question just how much importance NCATE has attached to a college's research record, other than for colleges or universities with graduate programs. For example, Wisconsin's graduate program was approved by NCATE without hesitation. This may well have been, in large part, a recognition of Wisconsin as a major research center in teacher education.

As is proper and to be expected, both NCATE and the regional associations recognize the umbilical relationship between graduate work and research. This relationship exists on any level of graduate work, but particularly on the doctoral level. Therefore, in evaluating graduate programs for accreditation, special attention is given to (1) research facilities—space and general research equipment; (2) special research equipment; and (3) library facilities for advanced student and faculty research—service materials, cubicles, equipment for making and reading microfilm, and funds for employing research assistants. In Chapter 8 additional attention was given to accreditation of graduate work and its relation to research.

NCATE has been successful in discouraging smaller state colleges and universities from offering graduate work in administration. In this the Council has had the full support of the AASA. One of the reasons for the decision of AASA to require graduation from an NCATE-accredited program was to discourage the offering of weak and ill-staffed graduate programs in administration in many state colleges. Almost as soon as they have been approved for the master's degree or higher degrees, these colleges have started offering graduate work in school administration. These programs usually have had few students and have often been staffed by part-time school administrators. Usually research in school administration has been totally lacking in these institutions. Since the larger universities can adequately supply the need for new administrators, the NCATE and AASA move in this direction is viewed by most persons in higher education as a constructive one from the point of view of its resulting in school administrators' being essentially required to take their graduate work in school administration in a university atmosphere of research.

The nature of reports sought by NCATE and the regionals on research appears to be even more completely quantitative than is true of information requested in support of most other standards. Many recognize the need for accrediting agencies to look at the quality of the research, both of staff members deemed to be qualified because of their research and particularly that of students earning the doctorate. Little evidence can be found of a careful examination of the quality of research by accrediting agencies.

Accreditation can be helpful in improving the quality of graduate education by examining space, equipment, and funds available for research, and asking for reasonable teaching loads which are necessary for research, but there is an unfortunate gap when it comes to any attempt to measure quality. There are many who believe that the quality of research in education is open to more question than the quality of research in any other discipline. There are also those who believe that some high-quality research in education is now being done. In this study no evidence was found to suggest that accrediting associations are presently contributing to the spread of a high-quality pattern of educational research.

In answers to the first questionnaire submitted to the states as a part of this Study, quite a number of the states indicated that they were now accrediting or approving graduate programs in education even beyond the sixth year. A second question was addressed to the states to determine if their answers on approval beyond the sixth year were interpreted correctly. From 17 replies to the second inquiry addressed to 23 states, it is indicated that at least 11 states do accredit (or approve) graduate work leading to the doctorate. Again in cases where the state follows the NCATE pattern of accreditation, this practice is extended to graduate work. Most of the states accrediting graduate work depend on consultant assistance from outside the department, usually from the universities within the state, but in some cases from outside the state.

Through accreditation it seems clear that state departments have been influential in persuading some colleges to delay the offering of graduate work until facilities and staffs are more adequate, but their influence in other respects of research is difficult to identify, or to distinguish from the concomitant influence of the regionals or of NCATE.

SUMMARY

All accrediting agencies recognize the importance of experimentation and research in higher education. NCATE's interest is based on the relation of the experimentation and research to teacher education and to graduate work in teacher education. The interest of the states in this respect is largely the same as NCATE's. New York, acting independently of NCATE, appears to have been more active in encouraging experimentation and research than the other states. NCATE may ask if an innovation is a genuine experiment and not just a way to avoid the norm. Either rigidity in interpretation of NCATE standards or stereotype of what institutions believe NCATE wants has tended to discourage innovation in administrative structures and staff utilization.

The regional associations' interest in research and experimentation is through the relation of such experimentation and research to: (1) general institutional improvement; and (2) graduate study. An institution's urge to be accredited for graduate work is a strong motivating force or stimulant to become involved in research. Accreditation has probably had its most limiting effect on experimentation with administrative structure and staff.

The approved-program approach now utilized at least in part by approximately 40 of the states provides more freedom to higher institutions for experimentation. Many states appear to have given more encouragement to experimentation than has NCATE.

From data collected in this Study it appears reasonable to assume that both NCATE and the states view experimentation with teacher education programs in a more favorable light than the institutions of higher education think they do, and thus, contrary to common assumption, actually do not intend to discourage experimentation.

REFERENCES

1. For NCATE's attitude see *Memo* sent to institutions preparing for an NCATE visit, "Explanatory Materials Interpreting the NCATE Standards," 1964, p. 10.
2. "The Professional Education of Science and Mathematics Teachers," *The Journal of Teacher Education,* Vol. 13, No. 2 (June, 1962), pp. 125–139; *Studies in Teacher Education,* a brochure published by the American Association for the Advancement of Science, March, 1960. Colleges and universities participating in the Study were: Bucknell University, Emory University, Hunter College, Oklahoma State University, San Francisco State College, University of Arizona, University of Delaware, University of Hawaii, University of Tennessee.
3. New York *Times* (November 8, 1964).
4. Margaret Lindsey, ed., *New Horizons for the Teaching Profession* (Washington, D. C., 1961).
5. *Ibid.,* p. 123.
6. *Ibid.,* p. 137.
7. *Ibid.,* p. 106.
8. Herbert F. LaGrone, *A Proposal for the Revision of the Pre-Service Professional Component of a Program of Teacher Education* (Washington, D. C., 1964), *passim.*
9. *Ibid.,* p. 63.
10. NCATE *Standards and Guide* (1960 Edition), pp. 13, 23.
11. *New Horizons,* p. 123.

CHAPTER 16

SUMMARY OF THE INFLUENCE ON HIGHER EDUCATION OF ACCREDITATION IN TEACHER EDUCATION

IN THE preceding chapters of Part II an attempt has been made to describe in some detail the ways in which accreditation in teacher education has influenced some of the basic elements in higher education. These basic elements are institutional structure and administration, curriculums, faculty and student policies, finance, experimentation and research.

It should be noted that in describing the various effects of accreditation there is no intention of implying that accreditation is the only factor bringing about the results indicated—or even necessarily the major factor. As pointed out in the Introduction to Part II, there are always concomitant factors involved in the modification of educational structure or policies. These concomitant factors may be so intermingled that it becomes very difficult to isolate or to weigh each separate factor. Included in Chapters 10 through 15 are the effects on higher education to which accreditation in teacher education rather clearly appears to have made some contribution.

Likewise, no attempt has been made, in Part II, to evaluate each particular influence or effect as to whether it has been good or bad, constructive or injurious, or neither the one nor the other. The authors of this report feel that the reader should make his own value judgments in each case.

The reader of this chapter should also bear in mind that the brief outline which follows does not tell the whole story. To get a fuller understanding and appreciation of the influence on higher education of accreditation in teacher education, one should read the entire text of each of the chapters in Part II. It is hoped that anyone reading Chapter 16, without first having read the preceding chapters in this section, will find his or her interest and curiosity stimulated sufficiently to read the more detailed material.

EFFECTS OF STATE ACCREDITATION (each effect probably refers to more than half of the states)

Structure and Administration

1. In the designation of one person in each teacher education institution to be responsible for recommending students for certification.
2. In the appointment of all-institutional committees for formulating and supervising teacher education policies and programs.
3. In discouraging, in some degree, malfeasance in higher educational institutions through the threat of a state investigation.

Curriculums

1. In influencing (in some 40 states) the pattern of teacher education courses and programs through the approved-program approach to teacher certification.
2. By requiring (in other states) specific courses and hours of credit for state certification.
3. In increasing the clock-hour requirement in student teaching.
4. In encouraging institutions to adopt the recommendations of national societies for the improvement of teacher education in science and mathematics, and foreign languages.

Faculty Policies

1. In attaching greater importance to the supervision of student teaching.
2. In developing communication between academic and education faculties and a shared responsibility for staffing methods courses in academic disciplines.
3. In involving members of academic departments in planning teacher education programs in the institutions and at the state level.

Student Policies

In bringing about the development of:

1. Higher admission standards in teacher education.
2. Greater emphasis on counseling in teacher education.
3. Higher graduation requirements in teacher education.
4. In increasing the number of staff members and degree of specialization in departments of education.

Finances

Some states specify a minimum limit on financial resources for chartering a private institution of higher learning and give some emphasis to financial stability, thus eliminating very weak institutions, or preventing them from offering teacher education programs with insufficient financial support.

Experimentation and Research

1. In the active encouragement without financial support of experimentation and research.
2. In providing greater freedom to higher institutions for experimentation through the approved-program approach to state certification.

EFFECTS OF REGIONAL ACCREDITATION

Structure and Administration

1. In bringing about (in some instances) a change in the administration of an institution of higher education.
2. In bringing about (through stimulation to improvement of) structural (as well as personnel) changes in the administration of a higher institution.

Curriculums

1. In the establishment of the same general or liberal education requirements for all bachelor's degree candidates.
2. In giving greater emphasis to academic preparation for secondary school teachers.

Faculty Policies

1. In the appointment of a higher proportion of staff members with advanced degrees, particularly with the doctorate, and with a higher degree of faculty specialization in academic teaching fields.
2. In giving greater attention to the geographical distribution of staff members both as to origin and as to the place of advanced training.
3. In the placing of greater emphasis on academic freedom and tenure.

Student Policies

1. In providing more extensive counseling services—academic, social, and clinical.
2. In the establishment of higher graduation requirements in liberal arts.
3. In providing more extensive facilities for student health and welfare.

Finance

1. In making provision for more adequate financial resources.
2. In the establishment of a higher degree of financial stability.
3. In the payment of higher faculty salaries.
4. In making available additional library facilities.

Experimentation and Research

1. In giving encouragement to experimentation and research through stimulation to general institutional improvement.
2. In insisting upon experimentation and research as a prerequisite to acceptable graduate work.

EFFECTS OF NATIONAL ACCREDITATION

Structure and Administration

1. In the establishment of an over-all institution-wide committee or council to formulate and supervise teacher education policies and programs.

2. In the designation of one person to be responsible for the administration of all teacher education programs in the institution.

3. In the establishment (where they did not already exist in some institutions) of undergraduate departments of education and schools or colleges of education for graduate work.

4. In defining the channels of responsibility in teacher education.

Curriculums

1. In bringing about an adjustment of balance among general education, major specialization, and professional education requirements in teacher education programs.

2. In giving more attention to course sequences in education as opposed to increases in course or credit requirements in education.

3. In increasing the provision for laboratory experience as a part of education courses, and the requirement of more time for student teaching.

4. In designating one "path," in many institutions, through which the institution's recommendation for a certificate may be obtained, and in other institutions, where two "paths" are available, making provision to compare results on an experimental basis.

5. In making possible a higher degree of involvement of academic disciplines in the formulation of an institution's teacher education policies.

Faculty Policies

1. In the employment of fewer part-time staff members in professional education.

2. In the employment of education faculty with a higher degree of specialization.

3. In the employment of a larger number of staff members in professional education.

4. In providing increased staff with specialized preparation for supervision of student teaching.

5. In elevating the status of staff members in professional education through greater participation in institutional affairs and bringing their salaries more in line with those of their colleagues.

Student Policies

1. In provision for higher academic standards, achievement tests, and academic counseling in admission to teacher education.

2. In making available more extensive counseling services, following admission to teacher education.

3. In the establishment of higher graduation requirements (grade-point average and standardized tests) in graduation from teacher education.

Finance

1. In providing increases in library facilities in teacher education.
2. In providing more extensive facilities in education, curriculum, laboratories, and student teaching.
3. In increased financial support for employment of staff members in departments of education.

Experimentation and Research

1. In the encouragement of experimentation and research as they apply to
   a. Teacher education.
   b. The faculty in education.
   c. Graduate work in education.
2. In causing institutions wishing to try various routes to teacher certification to consider them as experimental for purposes of comparing their effectiveness.
3. In causing institutions to conform to more commonly adopted administrative structures and staff utilization.

PART III

CONCLUSIONS

In Part I of the Study of the influence on higher education of national, regional, and state accreditation of teacher education, an attempt has been made to set forth objectively background information on accreditation in general and that of teacher education in particular.

In Part II, an analysis has been made of the observed effects on higher education of accreditation in teacher education at state, regional, and national levels, without giving value judgments on whether these effects are or are not in the public interest.

Part III concludes the Study with some general observations about accreditation of teacher education (Chapter 17) and some specific recommendations with respect to accreditation in this area (Chapter 18).

CHAPTER 17

OBSERVATIONS

IN THIS CHAPTER there are summarized some of the major observations about accreditation, including some assessments of value. An attempt is made to assess the various aspects of accreditation of teacher education, in the light of the past record as portrayed in Part II of the Study. The following division headings are used:

The Present Status of Accreditation

Some Assessments of Accreditation in Teacher Education

Effects of Accreditation by Types of Institutions

Importance of a Broad View of Teacher Education

The Future of National Accreditation

THE PRESENT STATUS OF ACCREDITATION

People who have some knowledge of accreditation in higher education tend to fall into three categories: (1) those who refuse to admit that accreditation has been a constructive force of any significance in higher education; (2) those who admit that accreditation may have been a necessary and constructive force in higher education in the past, but who insist that the usefulness of accreditation is decreasing and that it can have no very useful role in the future; and (3) those who recognize the constructive influence of accreditation in the past and believe that it has an important role in the future of higher education.

Accreditation, like any form of regulation which involves controls and restraints, has never been completely accepted as necessary or desirable by all American educational leaders. It is still regarded by some as an unjustifiable interference with, and encroachment upon, individual and institutional liberty. In this respect, educators and business leaders are alike.

The truth is that both accreditation in higher education and government regulation in business and industry were forced upon our contemporary society by undesirable conditions which had grown up under *laissez faire*. The educational and economic abuses simply should not have been and were not allowed to continue. In both cases, the competitors and the consumers needed to be protected. The remedies alone were different. In business and industry, the Federal and state governments provided the regulations. In education, the controls came partly through state and local authority, partly through "voluntary" accrediting agencies or associations.

Since World War II indications are that more, rather than fewer, economic and educational controls will be needed in some areas in the future. The vast growth in the size of industry, the burgeoning college and graduate enrollments, and subsidies of government for industry and for research are but a few examples. If accreditation is to continue to replace some form of Federal control in higher education, it will have to have support of leadership from the highest echelons of education. One source of this leadership is the National Commission on Accrediting. Another is the accrediting agencies themselves. To function effectively these groups must have the continuing support of higher education and the public which they serve.

Accreditation has become an integral part of the American educational fabric, and is in a way symbolic of the American way of life. At the same time, the proliferating accrediting agencies in the United States symbolize, in some measure, the conditions which brought them into existence. With their overlapping and sometimes conflicting national, regional, and state jurisdictions, and the necessary reports and visitations, it is small wonder that college and university presidents sometimes ask if in accreditation they have created an institution that will ultimately cost them more than the gains from accreditation will be worth. This does not mean that accreditation should be abolished. Rather the activities and functions of national and regional accrediting bodies are in need of closer supervision and coordination.

It was largely to provide such coordination and supervision that the National Commission on Accrediting was set up in 1949. In the 16 years of its existence, the Commission has improved the accreditation picture in several respects:

1. It has eliminated some duplication of accrediting agencies, where more than one agency was attempting to accredit the same area.
2. It has improved procedures of accrediting agencies by persuading some of them to adopt the procedures laid down by the Commission.
3. It has discouraged some additional accrediting agencies from joining the already excessive number of such agencies.
4. It has insisted that any professional group wishing to establish a professional accrediting agency should proceed with extreme care, should justify the agency as meeting a social need, should take into consideration relations with other groups, and should give all facets of the profession proper consideration.

SOME ASSESSMENTS OF ACCREDITATION IN TEACHER EDUCATION

1. In general, state accreditation procedures have been improved in the past decade and the present situation shows potential for even greater improvement through the approved-program approach to teacher education and better communication between state departments and professors of the various disciplines and their state and national societies. The National Association of State Directors of Teacher Education and Certification is providing constructive leadership in advancing these gains.

2. Regional accreditation, through emphasis on stimulation to improvement, has contributed to the strengthening of many colleges, but has not always served to eliminate some of the weakest. There is need for greater cooperation and uniformity among the regionals, which may result from the new Federation of Regional Accrediting Commissions of Higher Education.

3. The greatest weakness in accreditation at all three levels (state, regional, and national) is accreditation at the graduate level. Too many graduate programs in teacher education are being developed in colleges unprepared for them and too many are already flourishing without meeting quality standards.

4. While there is some evidence of cooperation among the agencies responsible for the accreditation of teacher education, more is needed. Accrediting at each of the three levels could thus be strengthened, and the time required for an institution of higher education to prepare for and during accreditation visits would be less burdensome.

5. The procedures and influence of the National Council for Accreditation of Teacher Education have been misrepresented and misunderstood. The absence of accurate information about NCATE has been a source of many of the criticisms.

6. In evaluating the record of NCATE in the accreditation of teacher education, one factor which must be borne in mind continually is that NCATE has undergone a considerable metamorphosis during its decade of operation as an accrediting body in teacher education. Most of the changes very likely have been made to meet specific criticisms of the structure, standards, and procedures of the Council. It seems safe to assume that each stage in the transforming process has made some contribution to the over-all public image of the agency. Therefore, the present public image of NCATE is not a true reflection of the current NCATE organization. The fact is that those aspects of the NCATE organization and operation which have been eliminated or otherwise changed may still be reflected in the present-day public image of the Council as much as, or even more than, the present organization itself. Critics of NCATE still refer to the "secret report" which the chairman of the NCATE visiting team sends to the Council. Reference is still

made in the present tense to the fact that no member of the visiting team is permitted to be present when the team report is discussed by the V and A Committee. Complaints are still voiced against NCATE for permitting a majority of the Council to be representatives of organizations or institutions not involved in the preparation of teachers.

7. NCATE has made mistakes. While its standards are stated in broad enough terms to lend themselves appropriately to application to all types of institutions, its committees have sometimes taken too narrow or too rigid a view of teacher education, and its procedures have sometimes made it too difficult for the Council, in its final decision making, to obtain an accurate view of the philosophy of an institution and how this philosophy is reflected in its teacher education program.

8. NCATE does not differ as greatly from other national professional accrediting agencies as is often believed. None of the agencies has succeeded in basing its accreditation on the quality of the graduates, rather than largely on quantitative standards. With new developments in research related to the quality of education and on instruments for the measurement of quality, all accrediting agencies need to re-examine, and work toward reconstruction of, their standards and procedures.

9. NCATE has had beneficial effects, as well as some undesirable effects, on teacher education and higher education. A decision on the degree to which the beneficial counterbalances the harmful depends in great part on an individual's philosophy of teacher education. As is true of other accrediting agencies, NCATE's influence is probably more the result of what the institutions believe NCATE will insist upon, than what it does insist upon.

10. With reference to the widespread and valid public concern about the rigidity of state requirements for teacher certification, an observation is that national accreditation of teacher education, rather than lending support to this rigidity, perhaps more than any other instrument is in a position to contribute to the lessening of this rigidity. There is evidence that national accreditation has already contributed to an increased flexibility in this area.

11. One of the criticisms of NCATE most commonly heard is that it is controlled by, or is an "organ" of, the National Education Association. This criticism is based in part on the fact that three of the five constituent organizations have their headquarters in the NEA building in Washington and that together these three organizations name 14 of the 19 members of the Council. Besides, two of the three contributed $78,000 out of the 1964 NCATE budget of $138,500. It cannot be questioned that the Council members named by these three organizations are very influential in NCATE decisions, but it could not be substantiated that they speak for, or necessarily represent, the views of the NEA. While the NEA executive secretary, and some of his professional staff, and the president may speak for NEA, few others do.

Indeed it is exceedingly doubtful that anyone can present the views of an organization of nearly 1,000,000 members.

The NCTEPS is a commission of the NEA appointed by the officers of NEA. The six Council members appointed by NCTEPS may, in general, represent the views of NCTEPS, but they do not attend NCTEPS sessions and no evidence can be found that they are "instructed" in any way whatsoever by NCTEPS. The AACTE is a department of NEA, but, like other NEA departments, it acts as a completely independent organization. The Council of Chief State School Officers is not a department of NEA, although its offices are in the NEA building. Representatives of the Council have presented testimony before committees of the Congress which is not in agreement with the NEA position on some particular piece of legislation. CCSSO, like AACTE, is quite obviously independent of NEA.

Members appointed to NCATE by the *ad hoc* committee, with strong academic loyalties, have stated that they have seen no evidence of collusion on the part of Council members representing affiliates of NEA. These experienced members of the Council have stated that split votes are not on the basis of academic versus professional education personnel, and they pay tribute to the sincerity and integrity of their Council colleagues, and express their belief that each Council member votes in terms of his own best judgment as an individual.

12. This Study has revealed a general lack of follow-up studies of graduates (in teacher education and otherwise) of institutions of higher learning. Such studies would provide a basis for institutional self-evaluation and self-improvement. They would also provide useful data for research and eventually for accreditation. *Follow-up of graduates should be given a place of greater importance in higher education.*

13. Based on the projections of teacher supply and demand, made by the U. S. Bureau of Labor Statistics and reviewed in Appendix VII, the predicted surplus of persons prepared to teach emphasizes the need for higher standards in teacher certification and in accreditation of teacher education programs. Furthermore, the caution, given in the projections that the shortage of the past decade will probably persist in some areas, emphasizes the need for reciprocity among the states. The projected surplus of secondary school teachers and the shortage of elementary teachers, and the caution about the shortage of secondary school teachers in certain subjects, emphasize the need for more realistic counseling in teacher education programs.

14. *While progress has been made in the improvement of teacher education during the past decade, sights must be set much higher in the decade ahead. The innovations in school curriculums and in teaching methods and aids call for innovations in teacher education, indeed teacher education should lead the way in innovation. The promise of vastly increased Federal aid for education may make this more possible than is now generally recognized.*

EFFECTS OF ACCREDITATION BY TYPES OF INSTITUTIONS

In Part II, the influences of accreditation in teacher education were reported in terms of structure and administration, curriculums, faculty and student policies, finance, and experimentation and research. These influences were discussed at the three levels—state, regional, and national. In a consideration of the pros and cons of accreditation, it seems appropriate to identify influences of accreditation by types of institution, particularly since the national accrediting agency and many of the state agencies have been accused of basing standards on the teachers college concept of teacher education. In general, the following reference is to national accreditation, which in many states has been a model for state practices, whether or not the state acknowledges this influence. Or, it may be said that national accreditation coming later has been influenced by the practices in some of the states. Since the practices in the states do vary, generalizations about the states are dangerous.

An examination of NCATE standards and of NCATE's application of these standards shows that NCATE has been able to bring about a better balance in general education, professional education, and major specialization requirements in teachers colleges, as well as in former teachers colleges in which the department of education was a dominant factor. This is especially true in programs for the education of elementary teachers and of teachers of special subjects, such as agriculture, art, and music. In some of these institutions, academic majors for secondary school teachers have been strengthened in terms of number of hours and courses (by title) required, but NCATE has contributed little in strengthening academic staffs and course offerings. It seems clear that, in the transition from teachers college to state college or university status, education staff members in too many instances have used NCATE as a threat in trying to maintain a *status quo*. This has been done in the sincere belief that teacher education programs might otherwise be weakened. It has tended to create criticism of NCATE, often unjustified, and given support to the theory that NCATE's best friends are often its worst enemies.

In the case of liberal arts colleges, NCATE has been able to influence them to give greater attention to teacher education. This has resulted in the organization of departments of education, or giving higher status to departments of education, and in the employment of additional staff members in education with specialization in the various fields of education. Some consider this influence to be one of the great achievements of NCATE while others count it as evidence of harmful influence.

The effect of NCATE accreditation on large, multipurpose universities is not so clear. The number of faculty members in schools of education has greatly increased in 10 years, but this is not considered to be as much a result of NCATE accrediting as of increasing enrollments in teacher education programs, the growing importance attached to service to the schools, and the availability of increased funds for support of research. The organization and effectiveness of all-institutional committees has been stimulated in these institutions by NCATE, but NCATE's insistence upon clear-cut administrative responsibilities for teacher education has created friction in some institutions between academic and education staffs, and caused many academic professors to believe that NCATE attempts to remove control from liberal arts departments and place it in the hands of the college or school of education. It is actually very difficult to determine when and if this transfer of control has actually happened. If it has happened, it appears to be in the nature of more reporting and recommending by academic departments to deans of education than previously existed. Where multipurpose institutions have strongly supported their administrative structure on the basis of institutional philosophy, they have succeeded in achieving accreditation with little or no change in this respect.

IMPORTANCE OF A BROAD VIEW OF TEACHER EDUCATION

"Is it possible, as a practical matter, to establish reasonable standards for the accreditation of teacher training, apart from, and independent of, accreditation in subject-matter fields? . . . Is the quality of teacher training so intimately related to the quality of subject-matter education as to make impossible any accreditation of teacher training apart from subject matter?" These thought-provoking questions, raised by a former president of a liberal arts college, emphasize the importance of involving subject-matter groups more intimately in the act of accreditation of teacher education, so that the broadest possible view of teacher education in all of its facets may be maintained by accrediting agencies.

As has been pointed out, the professional education sequence usually comprises no more than 20 percent of the undergraduate program in teacher education. Yet the professional sequence and staff are the center of major attention in an NCATE evaluation, as well as that of many of the states. These accrediting agencies do consider balance among general education, major specialization, and professional requirements, as well as breadth within general education and the suitability of a major for a prospective teacher. But the institutions anticipating an NCATE or state evaluation are most concerned with their provisions for professional education, including administration, staff, student teaching, and physical facilities.

The structure of NCATE makes it difficult to adjust to change, does not give enough control to institutions, and has not resulted in a broad representation on the Council of many groups with a major interest in teacher education, particularly the liberal arts. Because of the nature of representation on the Council, the source of financial support, the restricted jurisdiction of NCATE resulting in emphasis on professional education, the academic groups have not, in general, supported

NCATE. They feel, with considerable justification, that they are not a part of it.

In defense against the criticism that academic groups have only a small part in national accreditation of teacher education, it is often pointed out that the Association of American Colleges (AAC), when invited in the past to become actively involved in NCATE activities, has declined to do so. Fortunately there has been some evidence recently of a change in attitude in this respect. But the participation of AAC, an association of liberal arts colleges, would not provide for representation of the liberal arts personnel of the multipurpose universities and the state colleges. Stimulation of their state and national organizations has made this group, as well as their colleagues in liberal arts colleges, much more concerned about, and active participants in, the improvement of teacher education programs.

In viewing the make-up of NCATE and the various committees in the accreditation process, those responsible for the subject-matter elements in teacher education do not feel confident that, no matter how good the intent, these aspects of teacher education will get their due attention. In conferring with staff members from the liberal arts and other subject-matter departments on many campuses, disappointment was often expressed that they had been completely bypassed in an NCATE or state visitation.

The strongest supporters of NCATE and national accreditation of teacher education are organizations affiliated with the National Education Association, the state teachers associations, and the professors of education in colleges and universities. The philosophy of these groups, so far as they enjoy a common philosophy, is predominant in the standards and procedures of NCATE. The teachers in the schools have supported these groups because they believed them to be the ones who were interested in them as teachers and in the schools. Now that the academicians in the colleges and universities have displayed new interest in education in the schools, in teachers, and in teacher education the loyalty of some of the profession is tending to shift. Now, many teachers are beginning to feel that they have support in the Modern Language Association, the American Institute of Physics, or the American Chemical Society, and that their ties should possibly be closer to these groups than to the National Education Association. This trend makes it more critical than ever that the national accreditation of teacher education clearly represents the philosophy of, and has the support of, the broadest possible segments of groups interested in teacher education.

Most important by far is that all of the aspects of teacher education —liberal education, subject-matter specialization, and professional education—be given full attention and proper balance in the accreditation of teacher education. Greater involvement of subject-matter personnel seems essential for this. It is also important that the "public image" of accreditation in teacher education be improved so that the public can view teacher education as involving almost every aspect of higher education, and in its proper perspective.

In order to provide for broader participation in the accreditation of teacher education, the following methods are suggested as possibilities for the active role of subject-matter specialists:

Appointment to the staff of the accrediting agency, either on a permanent or on a leave-of-absence basis.

Appointment to visiting or other working committees of the accrediting agency upon nomination by academic societies.

Active participation in formulating, reviewing, and modifying the accreditation standards in teacher education.

Assignment of a major responsibility in the preparation of comprehensive tests in subject-matter areas, to be used either as a part of the accreditation process or simply as measures of competence.

Appointment as consultants to state departments of education in developing standards for program approvals.

Enlistment in preparing standards for the preparation of teachers in their disciplines, to be used as guidelines for visiting teams.

THE FUTURE OF NATIONAL ACCREDITATION

It can be assumed that the states, as the only legal authority in accreditation, will continue to accredit or approve programs in teacher education and, in some cases, general institutional status. It seems safe to assume, also, that regional accreditation will be continued, presumably with improvements in both standards and procedures. The list of NCATE influences (Chapter 16) may be interpreted as demonstrating the justification of that organization's existence in the past decade; but it does not necessarily prove the need for its continuation.

The arguments against the continuation of national accreditation are impressive:

1. The problem is too big to be handled effectively on a national basis. There are too many teacher education institutions for one national body to evaluate and accredit, and nearly all parts of an institution are involved in teacher education. This argument assumes that a decentralized approach would be advantageous in this respect.

2. Even with a national set of standards in teacher education, the human factor makes it impossible to have a uniform interpretation and application of those standards. One criticism of NCATE has been that its standards have not been applied evenly.

3. National standards or criteria in evaluating institutions of higher education are generally quantitative in nature and are not necessarily a reliable basis of judgment. Moreover, they

usually emphasize minimal or acceptable quality rather than high quality.

4. National accreditation in teacher education involves too much overlapping of jurisdiction with state and regional accrediting authorities. The over-all accreditation pattern needs to be simplified, and, as one of the newer accrediting agencies, NCATE is the logical one to be eliminated.

5. National accreditation is contrary to the American tradition of local control of education. As far as possible authority should be kept close to the people.

6. Teacher education differs basically from other professional areas; therefore, it is dangerous and far-fetched to draw parallels between them and to suggest accreditation in teacher education because there is accreditation of other professional programs.

7. There is a lack of consensus on what professional preparation should include. Until such a consensus can be reached, it is presumptuous to talk about uniform national policies.

8. National accreditation tends to weaken state departments of education, when actually state leadership needs to be strengthened.

9. National accreditation contributes to the power of the "educational establishment."

10. National accreditation, by promoting uniformity of educational standards and practices, discourages innovation and experimentation in teacher education.

11. The national accrediting agency in 10 years has failed to win the confidence of higher education.

The arguments in favor of continuing national accreditation of teacher education are also impressive:

1. The National Commission on Accrediting has recognized that "there is a social need for a national organization to conduct an adequate program of accreditation in the field of teacher education with emphasis being placed on improvement in teacher education." First enunciated in 1963, this view was reaffirmed in 1964.

2. National accreditation is the accepted pattern in all other areas of professional accreditation. It would be strange, as well as inconsistent, to have a totally different pattern in one area of professional accreditation.

3. National accreditation facilitates reciprocity in state certification of teachers. Twenty-seven or 28 states automatically grant provisional certification to out-of-state graduates of NCATE-approved programs. Reciprocity in teacher certification is a national need.

4. More than three-fourths of the state directors of teacher education and certification believe that national accreditation has

contributed to the improvement of teacher education, and national accreditation has again been endorsed by the Council of Chief State School Officers.

5. National accreditation of teacher education facilitates communication with other national agencies and groups. A common deficiency in accreditation is a lack of adequate exchange of information among the numerous agencies involved. The more decentralized accreditation becomes, the more difficult the problem of communication.

6. National accreditation is one means of avoiding the obvious alternative of governmental control of higher education. With so much Federal support developing in higher education, centralized control through a Federal department of education is a distinct possibility.

7. With the states as legal authorities in accreditation, and the regional associations as representatives of higher institutions, it is logical to have a national agency to represent the teaching profession. The same rationale would apply to all professional areas.

8. Having a national set of standards in teacher education helps the states in their effort to establish and maintain high standards. Such an improvement in state standards is needed.

9. National accreditation would help to offset, as well as to overcome, the present diversity in standards and procedures among both the state and the regional associations. This, too, is needed.

10. National accreditation in teacher education is also a means of overcoming the present excessive diversity in standards and programs in teacher education among institutions of higher education generally. While complete uniformity is not to be desired, it would be advantageous to have a higher degree of uniformity than presently exists.

11. Educational problems have gradually moved in scope from local, to state, to regional, and now to national. The agency dealing with problems of teacher education needs to reflect this transition. Education is a national problem, and the answer for accreditation is national accreditation.

These two sets of arguments appear to produce a paradox: the task of accrediting teacher education on a national scale is virtually an impossible one; yet, there is a genuine social need for national accreditation in this field to be continued. In view of the fact that some 70 percent of new teachers were graduated from NCATE-approved institutions as early as 1961, this problem would seem to be less staggering than statistics would suggest. Moreover, it is entirely proper that the social need for national accreditation should take precedence over the difficulties involved, regardless of the magnitude of those difficulties.

While education, including teacher education, is a responsibility of the states, there is consensus that the states—with possibly a few exceptions—need leadership and support from the national level. National accreditation has already provided this leadership which will be needed even more in the future. While in some ways regional accreditation of teacher education might have advantages, the differences in the quality of education regionally are already much too obvious. Professional accreditation at the regional level might tend to accentuate these differences. The task then becomes one of reorganizing, strengthening, and improving the machinery of national accreditation. A means of doing this is outlined in Chapter 18.

In support of the conclusion that there is a continuing social need for national accreditation of teacher education, attention is called to several of the sources of this need:

1. The large number of teacher education institutions. With the number presently close to 1,200, the probability is that other higher institutions with teacher education programs will be organized in the years ahead. Likewise, institutions which do not now offer teacher education programs are likely to introduce these programs in their future development.

2. The widely varied types of institution currently engaged in the training of teachers. Basically there are the three types: (1) liberal arts colleges; (2) teachers or state colleges; and (3) multipurpose universities. However, within each of these categories there is rather wide variation in organizational patterns.

3. The wide variation among teacher education institutions in standards and requirements, and especially in admission and retention policies. There is a vast difference in the quality of education between the weakest and the strongest institutions and programs.

4. The lack of consensus among both educators and laymen as to what constitutes a good teacher education program, and the need for national definition, broadly conceived, of a quality program for the education of teachers.

5. The advantage of identifying, nationally, the best among the many teacher education programs.

6. The existing limitation of the privilege of teaching in the schools by 50 differing sets of certification requirements often interpreted rigidly in quantitative terms.

All of the above evidence may be employed by opponents of national accreditation in teacher education to demonstrate the physical impossibility and hopelessness of accrediting teacher education on a national scale. Such arguments, however, do not nullify or even reduce the social need for establishing and applying uniformly high standards and requirements in an area so fundamentally important to national welfare as the education of young people.

While the magnitude of the task of national accreditation is not minimized, it is considered to be quite within the realm of possibility.

Financial support of national accreditation will no doubt have to be more than doubled in the next decade, and this increase will have to come largely from the institutions. Cooperation with state and regional accrediting agencies can assist in making most efficient use of the available manpower. The participation of the vast pool of staff members in subject-matter departments, who have never been involved in the accreditation of teacher education at all, will make the job not only more possible, but also of higher quality.

As of 1964 only 36 percent of the teacher education institutions were accredited by NCATE. True, the 36 percent which were NCATE-accredited graduated some 70 percent of the new teachers. Many of those which were not accredited by NCATE were either prestigious liberal arts colleges which felt no strong motivation for NCATE accreditation and with a primary interest in other than teacher education, or else were weak institutions which were fearful of not meeting NCATE requirements. It is not conceived as desirable that every institution offering programs of teacher education can or should become accredited nationally.

The conclusion that national accreditation should be continued is reached with full recognition of the need for improvement and innovation in teacher education in the next decade. It is believed that national accreditation of teacher education, soundly conceived and administered, can do much more to stimulate improvement and innovation in the approximately 1,100 teacher education institutions throughout the country, than it will do to stifle it.

CHAPTER 18

RECOMMENDATIONS

THE STUDY of the Influence on Higher Education of Accreditation in Teacher Education concludes with recommendations designed to improve accreditation in this important area. These recommendations are divided into four categories: Those pertaining to accreditation of teacher education (1) in general; and those pertaining to accreditation of teacher education at the (2) state level, (3) regional level, and (4) national level. For convenient reference, recommendations in category (1) are designated by G; in (2) by S; in (3) by R; and (4) by N.

ACCREDITATION IN GENERAL

OVER-ALL COORDINATION OF ACCREDITATION

Institutions of higher learning are still plagued by the burden of having to prepare for separate accreditation visits by each agency concerned. This accreditation practice is costly in both expense and manpower. Several of the regional associations already have adopted the policy of joint accreditation visits by all accrediting agencies, the approval of which is sought by a particular higher institution. If this were done, some apparently prefer that the regional associations serve as the coordinating agencies. Others profess to see dangers in having one of the existing accrediting bodies serve as the coordinator.

G-1. *There should be one national body or agency, not involved in the function of accreditation, not only to supervise, but also to schedule and coordinate all official accrediting visits to higher institutions.*

Under proper scheduling, there should be a minimum of five-year intervals between accreditation visits. Where two or more accrediting agencies are concerned with the same segment of an institution's program (such as general education, academic specialization, or graduate work), the representatives of such agencies should be encouraged to evaluate jointly, although their report may be acted upon separately.

Such an arrangement should reduce the accreditation costs in time, effort, and money for all concerned. It would be well to put it into effect as soon as possible—before the situation worsens. An agency which might take over this responsibility is the National Commission on Accrediting. The Commission already has general supervisory authority, but to date has not given assistance in scheduling.

BROAD PARTICIPATION IN ACCREDITATION

In Chapter 17, pages 223-225, consideration was given to the critical importance of accrediting agencies' taking the broadest possible view of teacher education and recognizing the responsibility of a broad segment of higher education for teacher education.

> G-2. *In accrediting, a teacher education program should be evaluated in all of its aspects—general education, area of concentration, and professional education—and all agencies and their subgroups or committees responsible for evaluation of teacher education programs should be broadly representative of all segments of higher education having a responsibility for the education of teachers.*

ENCOURAGEMENT OF INNOVATION AND EXPERIMENTATION

In Chapter 15, the influence of accreditation in teacher education on innovation and experimentation was reported. It was concluded that accreditation has served to stifle, somewhat, innovation and experimentation, often because institutions thought an accrediting agency was less flexible than it actually intended to be. Also instances of rigidity in interpretation of relatively flexible standards appeared to prevail.

Both the TEPS Commission and AACTE, two constituent members of the present national accrediting agency, emphasize the need for, and the importance of, innovation and experimentation in programs of teacher education and of research in teaching, learning, and teacher education. AACTE has recently inaugurated Distinguished Achievement Awards for Excellence in Teacher Education and these awards clearly serve to stimulate innovation. The large community of scholars in higher education and of the lay public interested in education feels uncertain about present methods of teacher education and believes that innovation, experimentation, and research by modern procedures are essential. Innovation and experimentation in teacher education, and carefully designed research to support them, are critical national needs for the rest of the century.

> G-3. *All persons with a responsibility for accrediting teacher education should strive to make the operation of the accrediting agency a force for development of new and better ways of educating teachers, rather than a force for the maintenance of traditional, or currently popular, patterns. Flexibility in the administration of pro-*

grams, in all-institutional staff utilization, and in curriculums is essential.

GRADUATE ACCREDITATION

Chapter 8 was devoted to a consideration of the accreditation of graduate work. Some effects of accreditation on graduate work have been noted, but most of the effects summarized in Chapter 16 are more directly related to the accreditation of undergraduate programs. Rather than that there be differences in standards of accreditation for different types of institutions, it has been concluded that graduate work differs sufficiently from work on the undergraduate level to make it desirable that a different set of standards and procedures be used for accreditation of graduate programs.

The one new element that has entered the graduate picture in recent years is the Council of Graduate Schools (COGS). As already indicated, COGS is committed to the improvement of graduate study in the United States. It seems desirable, therefore, to involve COGS in a practical way in the accreditation of institutions with graduate programs.

G-4. *In the accrediting of graduate work (a) standards and procedures should be formulated jointly by the Council of Graduate Schools, the Federation of Regional Accrediting Commissions of Higher Education, and the national agency in teacher education responsible for development of standards for the accreditation in this area; and (b) whenever possible persons involved in evaluating graduate programs for accreditation should be selected from a panel of evaluators named by the Council of Graduate Schools.*

Standards and procedures formulated jointly could also become the basis of accreditation of graduate programs by the states. In order to facilitate this and to utilize the experience of state department of education personnel, the National Association of State Directors of Teacher Education and Certification (NASDTEC) should be invited to participate in the formulation process.

This plan of graduate accreditation would recognize the special and peculiar status of graduate programs as contrasted with undergraduate work. It would also bring into the over-all accreditation scene the Council of Graduate Schools. The visiting team in accrediting graduate work might very well, if it chose, employ the advanced tests of the Graduate Record Examinations as part of its basis of evaluation. Other factors which might be taken into consideration are the training, experience, and research records of graduate staff members; facilities for staff and graduate student research; graduate admission policies; and library and laboratory facilities for advanced study and research. Rather than having standards for different types of institutions, a possibility suggested for consideration by NCA in 1963, it is here recommended that the only difference in standards be by level of instruction, namely, undergraduate and graduate programs.

ACCREDITATION BY THE STATES

Improvement in accreditation practices in the states in recent years has been observed. Listed below are suggestions whereby state accreditation might be further improved. It is recognized that some of these suggestions are already in operation in a number of the states and some of them in more than half of the states. The suggestions are made to strengthen the hands of those states and to give further encouragement to the remaining states to adopt procedures which it is believed would contribute to a strengthening of their services.

S-1. *The states should eliminate partisan politics from state accreditation.* Some states still permit partisanship to enter into the selection of personnel for state departments of education and sometimes into the determination of departmental policy.

S-2. *The states should give increased financial support for teacher education, as a part of a division of higher education in state departments, to provide for more staff of high quality and the employment of consultants,* as qualified experts in evaluating teacher education programs (including experimentation and research) and in counseling higher institutions, as well as in the formulation of state policies. Professional personnel in agencies having a responsibility for accreditation and certification should have training and experience comparable with professional staff in institutions of higher education and salaries commensurate with the quality of training.

S-3. *The states should provide regulations governing the establishment of new institutions of higher learning, in order to eliminate "diploma mills."*

S-4. *Federal and/or foundation support should be sought for NASDTEC-sponsored national conferences on teacher education, and arrangements should be made for greater participation of the teacher education staff of state departments in national deliberation of ways of improving teacher education* as a means of providing national leadership to the states, and from the states to the national level.

S-5. *State departments of education should:*

   a. *provide for the appointment of an advisory committee on teacher education in each state, with adequate representation of academic groups and the lay public, and establish close working relations in each state with academic societies, comparable with relations now existing between state departments and state education associations;*

   b. *make more extensive use of the approved-program approach: (1) with flexibility, in working toward the relaxation of specific course and credit-hour requirements for certification; and (2) with attention to academic majors and staff qualifications in academic departments as a factor in state accreditation or approval;*

c. *give increased emphasis to provisions for student teaching in teacher education programs;*

d. *provide for increased emphasis on quality of teaching in teacher education programs;*

e. *cooperate more fully with regional and national accrediting bodies;*

f. *make arrangements for collecting ratings by school authorities on graduates in teacher education* to be used as one factor in state and national accreditation;

g. *plan for administration of comprehensive tests as a factor to be used in the accreditation of programs by the state and/or national accrediting agency in teacher education.*

REGIONAL ACCREDITATION

The regional accrediting associations should continue to fulfill their dual responsibilities of general institutional accreditation and stimulation to institutional improvement. With the hope of improving the quality of the services rendered by regional associations, the following recommendations are offered:

R-1. *The Federation of Regional Accrediting Commissions of Higher Education should proceed as rapidly as possible with the task of making the associations' policies and practices more nearly comparable for the entire nation.*

R-2. *The regional associations should include on their higher commissions representatives of the scientific and learned societies and of the lay public.*

R-3. *Without necessarily reverting to minimum standards, the regional associations should give more emphasis to minimum qualifications of higher institutions for initial or continued regional accreditation.*

In evaluating institutions for accreditation or reaccreditation, it is suggested that the following aspects be considered:

1. the degree of intellectual ferment on the campus;

2. the institution's financial integrity and stability;

3. the institution's charter and bylaws;

4. the composition and role of the board of trustees;

5. the "image" of itself which the institution presents to the public, and how well its behavior supports this "image";

6. the degree of student participation in institutional policy making relating to students directly, and the general student morale;

7. the degree of faculty participation in the governance of the institution, and the general faculty morale.

Undoubtedly some, if not most, of the above aspects are already covered in the regional evaluations of higher institutions. The seven items are offered as a check-list for regional associations in evaluating their standards and procedures.

NATIONAL ACCREDITATION

In Chapter 17, it has been recommended that national accreditation of teacher education be continued. In order to develop the best possible program of accreditation in teacher education, one which will provide some guarantee that teacher education will produce persons of high quality, the following recommendations are made.

N-1. *The constituent organizations of the national accrediting agency in teacher education should be limited to the American Association of Colleges for Teacher Education (AACTE) and the National Commission on Teacher Education and Professional Standards (NCTEPS).*

The National Association of State Directors of Teacher Education and Certification (NASDTEC), Council of Chief State School Officers (CCSSO), and the National School Boards Association (NSBA) should be represented by one member each on the national accrediting body, to serve in a liaison capacity with full voting rights.

N-2. *Financial support should be adequate to the needs of the national accrediting agency, with the bulk of the support coming from member institutions.*

N-3. *No less than two-thirds of the members of the council or governing body of the national accrediting agency should be persons who are on the staffs of teacher education institutions.*

N-4. *No less than one-half of the members of the national accrediting or governing body should be from the subject-matter disciplines, and at least three of these members should be named by the learned societies on a rotation basis.**

In this recommendation it is intended, for example, that a secondary school teacher of mathematics or home economics, an elementary school supervisor of science or music, or an administrator in higher education who also holds professional rank in a subject-matter department could be counted as representing a discipline. In Chapter 17 page 225, are suggestions for the participation of academic groups in the accreditation of teacher education. In addition to those suggestions listed, academic groups or learned societies might nominate individuals to AACTE and NCTEPS for membership on the national accrediting body. It is especially desirable that a subject-matter representative be included in the staff of the national accrediting agency.

---

* That three members of the Council be named by the learned societies is in agreement with a provision in the revised constitution of NCATE now (March, 1965) before the constituent organizations.

N-5. The standards for national accreditation should be developed by the American Association of Colleges for Teacher Education, as an organization of institutions, working in consultation with other organizations concerned with teacher education, and the standards so developed should be subject to the approval of the accrediting body.*

N-6. Arrangements should be negotiated with the Federation of Regional Accrediting Commissions of Higher Education whereby the accrediting agency for teacher education and the regional associations can collaborate in evaluating the subject-matter departments involved in teacher education.

N-7. Within 10 years, many of the present quantitative standards in the accreditation of teacher education should be replaced, at least on the undergraduate level, by qualitative standards.

This will involve the use of national standardized tests given to all seniors in teacher education. Such tests should be prepared in collaboration with a professional testing agency, such as the Educational Testing Service, and should cover all areas included in a student's teacher education program. In order to accomplish this transition within the 10 years, steps should be taken soon toward the development and experimentation with the necessary tests. In addition to standardized tests, it is recommended that the evaluation of teacher education institutions include a careful checking of the student teaching program and oral interviews with typical employers of the graduates in teacher education of the institution being evaluated. Such qualitative standards should show that graduates of accredited teacher education programs know their subject, that they have some competence in teaching, and that an institution has been producing graduates who are successful teachers.

N-8. A serious reevaluation should be made of the present three-level approach to accreditation in teacher education—visiting team, V and A Committee, and the Council—with a view to simplification of the process and provision for better communication among the three levels.

One ultimate resolution of this problem might be the creation of four regional boards or commissions to apply the national standards formulated at the national level—to evaluate institutions and to make accreditation decisions—with the national body retaining the power to approve standards and to review the actions and decisions of regional boards.

N-9. Provision should be made for the orientation of all who are selected for membership on evaluation visits to teacher education institutions, for service on V and A Committees, or for service on new committees.

---

* This is in line with a provision of the revised NCATE constitution currently (March, 1965) before the constituent organizations.

In view of the desire of the national accrediting agency to give serious consideration to a reevaluation of its structure and financing, procedures and standards, it is recommended that the reevaluation be given precedence in 1965, and even through 1966 if necessary, over its regular accrediting responsibilities.

The recommendation that the constituent organizations of the national accrediting agency be limited to the national organization of teacher education institutions and to a group representing the teaching profession should make it less cumbersome for the national accrediting agency to adjust to changing conditions and to constructive criticisms. Furthermore in a voluntary accrediting agency, while liaison with other groups having a legal responsibility (state or local) to provide the schools with competent teachers is essential, it seems reasonable that these groups should not exercise a "veto" power in the development of the procedures and standards of the voluntary agency.

No recommendation has been made as to the precise number of members of the agency's governing board to be named by the constituent organizations. It seems more important that the criteria enumerated in recommendations N-3 and N-4 be observed. Representatives of teacher education institutions and of academic disciplines can of course be named by NCTEPS as well as AACTE, and undoubtedly would be named by the learned societies.

If national accreditation is to be effective and to receive the support of higher education for which it is to provide governance, institutions of higher education must clearly be represented by a majority of members of the agency. It is recommended that representatives of teacher education institutions comprise two-thirds of the controlling body so that it will be entirely clear that the institutions are in a position to provide the governance afforded by voluntary accrediting, and so that the accrediting will be acceptable to the institutions. No other single change in the national agency holds more potential for winning the confidence and cooperation of institutions of higher education.

At one stage in the formulation of these recommendations, the possibility of recommending that a majority of the members of the governing council of the national accrediting agency be elected by the accredited institutions was appealing. However, when it was noted that all but 12 of the 422 teacher education institutions presently nationally accredited are members of AACTE, when the complications of the voting by institutions and the need for the sharing of the development of standards were considered, it was decided that the election of Council members by AACTE was more feasible and more sound.

The standards for national accreditation of teacher education must be developed, continuously evaluated, and appropriately revised by a common effort of many individuals, agencies, and institutions. The body responsible for this continuous study of standards must be an agency—strong in its own right—which provides, through its meetings, its publications, and its studies and research, a vehicle by which the ideas and criticisms of many persons can be received and acted upon. This in itself is a major undertaking. Since AACTE has always viewed the encouragement of excellence in programs of teacher education as its central purpose, and since AACTE now provides for broad representation of its institutional members on its own boards and committees, this organization seems ideally suited for the responsibility of the development of standards for national accreditation, subject to the approval of the accrediting body.

The magnitude of the responsibility of a national accrediting agency is such that it must seek the assistance of others in its work: the regionals in evaluating academic programs; the states in helping institutions prepare for national accreditation and identifying those institutions which are ready; the Council of Graduate Schools in accrediting graduate work; and the national organization of teacher education institutions in developing standards.

The rationale behind the proposed use of national standardized tests is that this method is used in admission to institutions, admission to teacher education, certification, and admission to a number of professions. In the light of the many uses already made of the tests, plus the many refinements made in recent years, it seems appropriate to use them as part of the process of accreditation. This approach to the accreditation of teacher education should ultimately meet most, if not all, of the important criticisms leveled in the past decade at NCATE standards and procedures.

In place of the former *quantitative* measurements, there would be at least some *qualitative* measurements. In response to the old argument that the only defensible basis for evaluating an institution, or the program, is in terms of the *quality* of its *output*, there would be an evaluation of the *quality* of the institution's graduates in teacher education as part of institutional evaluation.

In response to the old criticism that under NCATE standards and procedures, good institutions were given provisional or no accreditation while mediocre or substandard institutions received full accreditation, accreditation would be based in part on national norms which presumably would be uniformly interpreted and applied.

The authors of this Study believe that the recommendations, N-1 through N-9, provide for a strong national accrediting body which can meet the challenge presented by the magnitude of the task of accreditation in teacher education, and which can obtain and maintain the confidence and support of higher education and of the lay public.

APPENDIX I

THE ROLE OF THE NATIONAL COMMISSION ON ACCREDITING IN THE ACCREDITATION OF TEACHER EDUCATION

The NCA was established only a short time before NCATE was organized and almost since its very inception has been wrestling with the problem of national accreditation of teacher education. This has been the one problem most consistently before the Commission in the past dozen years. Under the constitution of the NCA, the Commission is to "study and investigate present accrediting practices with a view to establishing satisfactory standards, procedures, and principles of accrediting, to correct abuses, and to support the freedom and integrity of . . . member institutions."

Because of the criticism of and opposition to NCATE as originally constituted, the NCA refused to recognize NCATE as an official accrediting agency pending certain changes in the Council's structure. After the institutional representation had been increased, that of professional organizations representing legal officers in public education had been decreased, and after NCATE had agreed not to evaluate subject-matter departments, the new agency was given official recognition by the NCA in 1956. At that time it was agreed that in 1960 NCATE would be reviewed jointly by NCATE and NCA. In 1960 it was recognized that some modifications and improvements in NCATE were desirable, but because the Council had been in operation such a short time it was decided to delay action and to permit further study until "no longer than the end of 1963."

The NCA, at its spring meeting in 1963, agreed unanimously to continue its recognition of NCATE through the spring of 1964 "to enable the Council to make necessary changes in its structure, operations, and financing." To guide NCATE in its planning and deliberations, the National Commission on Accrediting adopted the following resolutions:

1. That the National Commission on Accrediting expresses appreciation for the cooperative and helpful manner in which the National Council for Accreditation of Teacher Education has participated in the current joint review of the latter organization;

2. That the National Commission on Accrediting restates its policy that there is a social need for a national organization to conduct an adequate program of accreditation in the field of teacher education with emphasis being placed on improvement in teacher education;

3. That continued endeavors be made further to improve the procedures employed in the accreditation of teacher education in order that institutions seeking accreditation will be assisted by such an accrediting program;

4. That studies be undertaken leading to the development of standards most appropriate for different types of institutions and for different types of programs preparing teachers;

5. That analysis be undertaken of the financial resources required to support a national program of accreditation of teacher education and that the analysis indicate the most desirable sources for such financial support;

6. That the national agency for the accreditation of teacher education must be primarily responsible to the colleges and universities educating and preparing teachers;
7. That continued recognition by the National Commission on Accrediting of a national agency to accredit teacher education is subject to review at the 1964 annual meeting of the Commission and is dependent upon adequate indications of the attainment of the objectives contained in this series of resolutions; and
8. That the Special Committee on Accrediting in Teacher Education of the National Commission on Accrediting is directed to continue its discussions and undertake negotiations leading to the attainment of these objectives.

At the same meeting, the NCA adopted a resolution opposing any state rule limiting certification to graduates of NCATE-approved institutions.

In its May, 1964, meeting, the NCA recognized that NCATE, "with the cooperation of its constituent members, has been making serious efforts to review its structure, methods of financing, and policies and procedures" in a manner consistent with the 1963 resolutions. In this effort, officials of NCATE had met with representatives of a number of educational organizations in November, 1963, with a committee of NCA in January, 1964, and with officials of the five constituent organizations of NCATE in February, 1964. As a result of these developments the NCA concluded that NCATE

. . . is giving adequate indication of progress toward the attainment of the objectives contained in the Commission's resolutions of March 1–2, 1963. Therefore, the National Commission on Accrediting reaffirms these resolutions and continues its recognition of the National Council for Accreditation of Teacher Education as the national accrediting agency for teacher education in order that it may actually attain the objectives contained in these resolutions.

The Commission affirms, however, that continued recognition of the National Council for Accreditation of Teacher Education beyond the annual meeting in the spring of 1965 will be dependent upon substantial progress toward the attainment *to the satisfaction of the Commission* of the objectives of these resolutions.

To assist in their attainment and to avoid any possible misinterpretation, the Commission hereby states that it will judge substantial progress toward the attainment of these objectives in the spring of 1965 primarily on the following principles:

1. That the national agency responsible for the accreditation of teacher education programs in colleges and universities be sufficiently large to include representation from the major groups with legitimate interests in teacher education, such as higher education institutions, learned societies, the teaching profession, those who administer the schools, and the public;
2. That the majority of the members serving on the agency, regardless of its size, be full-time teachers or administrative officers from the full range of institutions preparing teachers;
3. That the operations of the accrediting process by this national agency be conducted in such a manner
   (a) that the criteria or requirements for accreditation be developed and proposed for the agency's consideration by the institutions preparing teachers as expressed through an organization or organizations broadly representative of these institutions in consultation and

cooperation with other organizations concerned with teacher education;

(b) that the procedures of evaluating institutions for accreditation be developed by the agency itself in accordance with the "Criteria for Recognized Accrediting Agencies" of the National Commission on Accrediting; and

(c) that decisions regarding accreditation be made by the agency alone, relying on an executive committee or such other committees as it may create for initial review and recommendations, with a mechanism for institutional appeal established by the agency itself; and

4. That the major proportion of the cost of the agency be paid directly or indirectly by the institutions preparing teachers.

The "Criteria for Recognized Accrediting Agencies" referred to above contains the following provisions:

1. It is a voluntary, non-profit regional or national agency serving a definite need for accreditation in the field of higher education in which it operates.
2. The agency has an adequate organization and effective procedures to maintain its operations on a professional basis and to reevaluate at reasonable intervals the accredited institutions or programs of study.
3. The agency has financial resources necessary to maintain accrediting operations in accordance with its published policies and procedures.
4. The agency publicly makes available: (a) current information concerning its criteria or standards for accrediting, (b) reports of its operations, and (c) lists of accredited institutions or of institutions with accredited programs of study.
5. The agency secures pertinent data concerning the qualitative aspects of an institution or programs of study and it accredits only those institutions or programs of study which are found upon examination to meet the published criteria for accreditation.
6. The agency reviews at regular intervals the criteria by which it evaluates an institution or programs of study in order that the criteria shall both support constructive analysis and emphasize factors of critical importance.
7. The agency provides a regular means whereby the chief administrative officers of an institution may appeal to the final authority in that agency.
8. The agency provides a means whereby representatives of the National Commission on Accrediting may review and consider with officials of the agency all of its accrediting policies and practices.
9. In the agency's process of recognition for accreditation there shall be adequate representation from the staffs of institutions offering programs of study in the fields to be accredited.
10. In the case of an agency concerned with a particular professional field of study, (a) it is engaged in accrediting programs of study offered primarily by institutions which are eligible for membership in one of the regional accrediting associations, (b) it makes continual and reasonable efforts to coordinate its accrediting procedures and visits with the several regional accrediting associations, and (c) it limits itself in accrediting to those professional areas with which it is directly concerned and relies on the regional associations to evaluate the general qualities of institutions.
11. The agency conducts its accrediting activities in such a way that it:
(a) uses the quantitative information obtained from an institution

only for judging the qualitative accomplishments of the institution in relationship to its own stated purpose;

(b) recognizes the right of an institution to be appraised in the light of its own stated purposes so long as those purposes demonstrably fall within the definitions of general quality established by the agency;

(c) considers a program or programs of study at an institution, including its administration and financing, not on the basis of a single pattern but rather in relationship to the operation of the entire institution;

(d) assists, stimulates, and suggests means whereby an institution may improve its educational effectiveness;

(e) encourages sound educational experimentation and permits innovations;

(f) encourages and assists in an exchange of information among institutions and related groups;

(g) informs institutions of current needs and developments in broad educational areas or in the area of interest of the particular professional agency;

(h) evaluates an institution or program of study only with the specific authorization of the chief administrative officer of the institution or his officially designated representative;

(i) submits to the institution questionnaires and forms of such type not only to obtain information for the visiting examiners but also to stimulate the institution to evaluate itself (critical self-evaluation by the institution's own faculty and staff should precede the work of the external evaluators and should form a major part of the accrediting process);

(j) conducts an evaluation visit to the institution by experienced and qualified examiners under conditions that assure impartial and objective judgment;

(k) provides for adequate consultation during the visit between the team of visitors and the faculty and staff of the institution, including the chief administrative officer or his designated representative;

(l) provides the chief administrative officer with an opportunity to read and comment upon the report of the visiting team before the agency takes action on it;

(m) considers the report of the team in the presence of a member of the team, preferably the chairman;

(n) as a result of the accreditation visit, furnishes a written report to the chief administrative officer of the institution with comments on the institution's areas of strength, on the areas needing improvement, and on suggested means of improvement;

(o) charges for its evaluation services only a reasonable fee to be paid either at the time of the visit or pro-rated in small, yearly payments and does not make accreditation conditional upon the payment of any other sums of money.

12. The professional agency notifies the secretary of the commission on colleges and universities of the appropriate regional association when the agency plans to evaluate a program of study at an institution. Subject to the wishes of the institution, the regional association notifies the duly authorized official of a professional agency when it plans an evaluation of an institution offering a program in the agency's area of specialization.

Following the NCA meeting in May, 1964, NCATE adopted a set of principles to guide in any revisions in the Council's structure. In its August meeting the Council approved a revised constitution dealing only with structural changes. This proposal was subsequently presented to NCA and the constituent groups of NCATE for their reactions. In the revised constitution of NCATE, two changes were recommended:

1. The representation of AACTE on the Council was increased from seven to 10, thus increasing the Council membership from 19 to 22. It was further specified that AACTE "shall take the initiative for determining that those it elects are broadly representative of the various types of collegiate institutions and staff and faculty positions."

2. Provision was made for an "Advisory Assembly on Accreditation of Teacher Education":

> In order to enhance the responsiveness of the Council to all concerned, an organization to be known as the Advisory Assembly on Accreditation of Teacher Education shall be established and shall hold annual meetings. This assembly shall be broadly representative of all organizations concerned with the education of teachers.
>
> The Advisory Assembly on Accreditation of Teacher Education . . . shall appoint three (3) [members of the Council]. At least two (2) of these shall be faculty and staff members from institutions of higher learning. The Assembly shall take the initiative and responsibility for involving the various learned societies and professional associations in appointing its members. It is anticipated that this will assure the presence on the Council of members from various college teaching fields.

The Council would call the first meeting of the Advisory Assembly "which shall be organized within a framework similar to the Conference of One Hundred held on November 14–15, 1963, in Chicago." The Council would also "hold meetings periodically with representatives of institutions accredited by the NCATE to provide an opportunity for all accredited institutions to have a direct contact with the Council."

The proposed constitutional revision was criticized for not going far enough toward meeting the NCA guidelines. Most severely criticized was the proposed Advisory Assembly, which was characterized as too vague and ephemeral to give the assurance of representation and participation demanded by those outside the five constituent organizations.

In November, 1964, NCATE formulated and approved a further revision of the organization's structure, and submitted it to NCA and the constituent members for their reactions. In the new proposal, the provision for an advisory assembly was dropped and a new provision was added.

The Council shall include:

> Three (3) [selected] by learned societies, at least two (2) of whom shall be faculty and staff members from institutions of higher learning. The Council will choose the societies which are to name Council members, rotating the choices, so as to assure on the Council over a period of time the presence of scholars from the various disciplines involved in the education of teachers.

Under "Standards," there is this significant provision:

> The Council shall be responsible for the adoption of the standards it applies in the accreditation process. It shall arrange for the continuous evaluation and development of proposed standards for its consideration by an organization or organizations broadly representative of

teacher education institutions, working in consultation with other organizations concerned with teacher education.

Provision is also made for "meetings with representatives of accredited institutions and related organizations":

> The Council shall hold annual meetings with institutions accredited by the NCATE and other organizations having an interest in teacher education to provide them an opportunity to have a direct contact with the Council.
>
> The Council may invite to such meetings representatives of various organizations concerned with teacher education in order to enhance the value of this meeting as a forum for the presentation and discussion of ideas relating to accreditation of teacher education.

Under the second revision, there would be somewhat greater flexibility in amending the NCATE constitution. Except in a proposed amendment which would (1) eliminate a constituent organization, (2) reduce the number of Council members named by any constituent organization, (3) increase the total membership of the Council beyond 25, or (4) change the amendment process:

> . . . proposals for the amendment of this constitution, approved by a vote of at least three-fourths of the members of the Council, shall be referred to the constituent organizations for study and reaction, and will become effective upon a second approval by three-fourths of the members of the Council after consideration at a meeting held no sooner than six (6) months from the time of first approval. If the Council prefers, it may take the final vote by mail ballot after the second meeting.

The efforts of NCATE in the past two years to act on the recommendations of the National Commission on Accrediting, although sincerely and seriously undertaken, have served to emphasize two points. First, the structure of NCATE with the veto power of the five constituent members was unwieldy, thus making it extremely difficult and time consuming to change from the *status quo*. Second, the magnitude of the responsibility of NCATE and the limited financial resources and staff made it almost impossible for NCATE to plan constructively for improvements, providing for broad discussion of the issues, and at the same time to carry on its regular accrediting functions. It seems certain that no one associated with NCATE has played a deliberately delaying role. It has just been impossible to meet the challenges of NCA recommendations under existing operating conditions.

APPENDIX II

ALPHABETICAL DESIGNATIONS OF
ORGANIZATIONS AND AGENCIES

AAAS—American Association for the Advancement of Science
AAC—Association of American Colleges
AACTE—American Association of Colleges for Teacher Education
AAHPER—American Association for Health, Physical Education, and Recreation
AASA—American Association of School Administrators
AAU—Association of American Universities
AAUP—American Association of University Professors
ACE—American Council on Education
ACEI—Association for Childhood Education International
ACLS—American Council of Learned Societies
ACS—American Chemical Society
AHA—American Historical Association
ASCD—Association for Supervision and Curriculum Development
CCSSO—Council of Chief State School Officers
COGS—Council of Graduate Schools
ETS—Educational Testing Service
MLA—Modern Language Association of America
NASDTEC—National Association of State Directors of Teacher Education and Certification
NASM—National Association of Schools of Music
NCA—National Commission on Accrediting
NCATE—National Council for Accreditation of Teacher Education
NCTEPS—National Commission on Teacher Education and Professional Standards
NEA—National Education Association
NSBA—National School Boards Association, Inc.
SSRC—Social Science Research Council

APPENDIX III

COMPARATIVE DATA ON PROFESSIONAL ACCREDITING AGENCIES

ARCHITECTURE—National Architectural Accrediting Board

Accrediting Body Within Agency
National Architectural Accrediting Board.

Composition of Accrediting Body
Six members: two each from American Institute of Architects, Association of Collegiate Schools of Architecture, and National Council of Architectural Registration Boards.

Use of Institutional Self-Studies
Institution submits descriptive report on resources, operations, objectives, problems, and needs as result of four pages of questions.

Composition of Visiting Team
Three members: one from NAAB; two from the other sponsoring organizations. At least one is a faculty member or administrator of a school of architecture.

Function of Visiting Team
Supplements information submitted by the school; appraises the school and recommends accrediting action.

Use of Student Scores on Standardized Tests
None.

Nature of the Visiting Team Report
Report covering 19 items of information is drafted by the team chairman, signed by the team members, and submitted to the Board.

Action on the Report by the Accrediting Agency
National Architectural Accrediting Board takes action. Affirmative votes by at least four of the six members are necessary for accreditation.

Method of Setting and Reviewing Standards for Accreditation
The National Architectural Accrediting Board sets and reviews its own standards.

Interpretation of the Accrediting Standards
According to the Board, "facilities and activities of each school will be judged in terms of the purpose it seeks to serve." "It is clear that considerable divergence from average or optimal conditions may occur without detracting too greatly from the essential educational worth of a specific institution."

Quantitative Standards Required for Accreditation *
The Board is prohibited by its founding agreement from publishing the standards used in accreditation, but its statement of policy contains no

---

* It should be noted that quantitative factors, such as the presence, absence, or extent of student achievement, faculty effort and accomplishment, effective educa-

specific quantitative criteria and instead notes areas of the Board's concern. Eligibility is limited, however, to schools offering a five-year program beyond secondary school.

ART—NATIONAL ASSOCIATION OF SCHOOLS OF ART

Accrediting Body Within Agency
Committee on Admissions and Accreditation.

Composition of Accrediting Body
Three members elected by Association.

Use of Institutional Self-Studies
Institution completes wide-ranging 14-page questionnaire.

Composition of Visiting Team
Two to four members, appointed by the chairman of the Committee on Admissions and Accreditation. At least one is from a similar institution and two have served on previous evaluations of institutions.

Functions of Visiting Team
Aids the Association by evaluating the institution and recommending accrediting action and also gives guidance to institution in strengthening its program.

Use of Student Scores on Standardized Tests
None.

Nature of the Visiting Team Report
The report covering 13 items of information in the team's checklist is drafted by the team chairman, corrected by the team members, and transmitted to the Committee on Admissions and Accreditation.

Action on the Report by the Accrediting Agency
Recommendation of Committee on Admissions and Accreditation is presented to the Board of Directors which recommends action to the Association's member institutions at the annual meeting.

Method of Setting and Reviewing Standards for Accreditation
The Committee on Admissions and Accreditation drafts standards for approval by the Association's 13-member Board of Directors.

Interpretation of the Accrediting Standards
"In no other field is conformity to some pre-established pattern less desired. . . . Worthy goals must be identified and adopted by the school. The means of achieving them are within the discretion of each school. The results can only be evaluated in terms consistent with the objectives."

Quantitative Standards Required for Accreditation *
The Association is particularly interested in the educational philosophy

---

tional procedures, or adequate physical facilities, are taken into account by all accrediting agencies in many of their decisions regarding accreditation. Some accrediting agencies are more explicit than others in specifying in their published standards the minimum quantitative requirements they expect schools to meet in order to be eligible for accreditation. This heading identifies only these minimum quantitative requirements *in their published standards* and not additional ones that may be used in interpreting the published standards.

of the institution, but it does expect agreement on the awarding of credits and expects the curriculum to include general education, art history, studio study, and laboratory studies.

BUSINESS ADMINISTRATION—AMERICAN ASSOCIATION OF COLLEGIATE SCHOOLS OF BUSINESS

Accrediting Body Within Agency
(1) Undergraduate Accreditation Committee.
(2) Committee on Accreditation of Master's Programs.

Composition of Accrediting Body
(1) Undergraduate Accreditation Committee—Seven members.
(2) Committee on Accreditation of Master's Programs—Seven members.

Use of Institutional Self-Studies
Institution responds to 23 pages of questions on policies and operations. Involvement of many persons within the institution is suggested.

Composition of Visiting Team
Two to three members, all from member schools: one from a similar institution, one from another region, one from the Committee.

Function of Visiting Team
Fact finding and recommendation regarding accreditation.

Use of Student Scores on Standardized Tests
Institution is expected to summarize the results of any standardized or professional examinations given during or at the end of the student's program.

Nature of the Visiting Team Report
The chairman drafts the report covering suggestions for improvement and recommendations for accrediting action to the appropriate committee for action.

Action on the Report by the Accrediting Agency
The appropriate committee recommends action to the Executive Committee which submits any of its favorable recommendations to the Association for final action.

Method of Setting and Reviewing Standards for Accreditation
The Standards Committee recommends revisions in standards to the Executive Committee which recommends action on them to the membership of the Association.

Interpretation of the Accrediting Standards
"Schools seeking admission into the Association will be expected . . . to demonstrate more than perfunctory conformity to the quantitative aspects of each of the individual standards."

Quantitative Standards Required for Accreditation *
The Association expects that 40 percent of the business student's work will be related to business; that seven fields will be covered in the business curriculum, and that the business faculty will consist of at least five professors teaching not more than three courses or 12 hours a week.

CHEMISTRY—AMERICAN CHEMICAL SOCIETY

Accrediting Body Within Agency
Committee on Professional Training.

Composition of Accrediting Body
Nine members: college or university chemistry faculty members, balanced by field of training, type of institution, and geography.

Use of Institutional Self-Studies
Institution completes factual questionnaire; limited self-evaluation is expected.

Composition of Visiting Team
One "visiting associate" selected from among 150 highly regarded scientists and educators.

Function of Visiting Team
Acts only as an observer to verify material submitted by institution and determine the adequacy of the professional program in chemistry. Recommends accrediting action.

Use of Student Scores on Standardized Tests
None.

Nature of the Visiting Team Report
The visiting associate makes a detailed confidential report to the Committee on Professional Training, including his recommendation for accrediting action.

Action on the Report by the Accrediting Agency
The Committee acts after meeting with the department chairman and sometimes the visiting associate. It reports its accrediting decision to the Council of the Society.

Method of Setting and Reviewing Standards for Accreditation
The Committee on Professional Training adopts and revises accrediting standards with the assistance of department chairmen, other educators, scientists, and its visiting associates.

Interpretation of the Accrediting Standards
The Committee states that it will employ flexibility in interpreting its standards and will accredit experimental programs deviating from the standards if their scope, staff, and professional intent are adequate.

Quantitative Standards Required for Accreditation *
The Committee expects that accredited programs will, in general, have at least four faculty members in chemistry and will require at least a semester's work in each of several chemical fields, and will require certain numbers of hours of laboratory work in them.

DENTAL HYGIENE—AMERICAN DENTAL ASSOCIATION

Accrediting Body Within Agency
Council on Dental Education.

Composition of Accrediting Body
Nine members elected by ADA House of Delegates: three each nominated by ADA, American Association of Dental Examiners, and American Association of Dental Schools.

Use of Institutional Self-Studies
Institution completes factual 68-page pre-visit questionnaire.

Composition of Visiting Team
Three members: two Council members or consultants; one Council Staff member. Additional observers may attend from American Dental Hygienists' Association and state dental examination board.

Function of Visiting Team
Both counseling to strengthen the program and evaluation for accreditation.

Use of Student Scores on Standardized Tests
Information on state licensing examinations and National Board Examination failures is obtained.

Nature of the Visiting Team Report
The report covering 15 items of information is usually drafted by the staff member and submitted to the Council.

Action on the Report by the Accrediting Agency
The Council on Dental Education takes accrediting action.

Method of Setting and Reviewing Standards for Accreditation
The Council on Dental Education drafts standards and revisions in them for approval by the House of Delegates of the American Dental Association.

Interpretation of the Accrediting Standards
The Council states that it encourages inquiries regarding interpretation of its standards and that it desires experimentation rather than uniformity.

Quantitative Standards Required for Accreditation *
The standards list 20 subjects required in the curriculum and identifies the number of clock hours of instruction expected in each of them.

DENTISTRY—AMERICAN DENTAL ASSOCIATION

Accrediting Body Within Agency
Council on Dental Education.

Composition of Accrediting Body
Nine members elected by ADA House of Delegates: three each nominated by ADA, American Association of Dental Examiners, and American Association of Dental Schools.

Use of Institutional Self-Studies
Institution completes 80-page evaluation form.

Composition of Visiting Team
Four members: three members of the Council—usually one educator, one practitioner, and one dental examiner—plus one Council staff member. In addition, an observer from the state licensing board.

Function of Visiting Team
Serves as impartial judge on adequacy of the school for the school's officials and recommends accrediting action.

Use of Student Scores on Standardized Tests
Information on failure of state licensing examination obtained.

Nature of the Visiting Team Report
The report covering at least 11 items of information is drafted by the Council staff member and approved by the other team members for submission to the Council on Dental Education.

Action on the Report by the Accrediting Agency
The Council on Dental Education takes accrediting action.

Method of Setting and Reviewing Standards for Accreditation
The Council on Dental Education drafts standards and revisions in them for approval by the House of Delegates of the American Dental Association.

Interpretation of the Accrediting Standards
The Council states that it encourages inquiries regarding interpretation of its standards and that it desires experimentation rather than uniformity.

Quantitative Standards Required for Accreditation *
Among its 12 criteria, the only specifically quantitative standard is an admissions requirement of at least two academic years of college with courses in English, chemistry, biology, and physics.

ENGINEERING—ENGINEERS' COUNCIL FOR PROFESSIONAL DEVELOPMENT

Accrediting Body Within Agency
Education and Accreditation Committee.

Composition of Accrediting Body
Eighteen members: nine selected by the Committee itself; six nominated by ECPD technical societies; three appointed by ECPD non-technical societies.

Use of Institutional Self-Studies
Institution completes 21-page questionnaire.

Composition of Visiting Team
One member for each curriculum under evaluation. The chairman is the E&A Committee member serving as regional chairman or vice chairman; he selects the other members.

Function of Visiting Team
Assesses qualitative factors of the curriculums; examines materials; helps institution assess strong and weak points; recommends accrediting action.

Use of Student Scores on Standardized Tests
None.

Nature of the Visiting Team Report
Each member drafts a section for assembly by chairman and transmittal to E&A Committee. Report includes accrediting recommendation plus two types of suggestions for the school: (1) those pertinent to the accrediting recommendation, and (2) those not related to the recommendation.

Action on the Report by the Accrediting Agency
The Education and Accreditation Committee recommends accrediting

action to the Engineers' Council for Professional Development which takes final action.

Method of Setting and Reviewing Standards for Accreditation
The Council adopts standards upon the consensus of its constituent societies and often on the advice of one of them, the American Society for Engineering Education.

Interpretation of the Accrediting Standards
The Engineers' Council for Professional Development attempts to avoid rigid standards in order to prevent "standardization and ossification" and to encourage new developments and experimentation in engineering curricula.

Quantitative Standards Required for Accreditation *
The only specific quantitative standards specify the minimum length of five portions of the student's curriculum.

FORESTRY—Society of American Foresters

Accrediting Body Within Agency
Committee for the Advancement of Forestry Education.

Composition of Accrediting Body
Seven members: five forestry educators, one public forest agency representative, one private forest industry representative; appointed by president with approval of Society's Council.

Use of Institutional Self-Studies
Institution completes two-page questionnaire plus report forms on the forestry faculty.

Composition of Visiting Team
Two or occasionally three members: one member of the Committee for the Advancement of Forestry Education, often the executive or assistant executive secretary of the Society.

Function of Visiting Team
Factual observation, particularly of doubtful areas of the program.

Use of Student Scores on Standardized Tests
None.

Nature of the Visiting Team Report
Team prepares a factual account of conditions emphasizing factors of questionable strength or weakness, but without recommendations regarding accreditation.

Action on the Report by the Accrediting Agency
The Committee for the Advancement of Forestry Education recommends action to the Council of the Society.

Method of Setting and Reviewing Standards for Accreditation
Standards are drafted by the Committee for the Advancement of Forestry Education in cooperation with the Council of Forestry School Executives and are approved by the Council of the Society of American Foresters.

Interpretation of the Accrediting Standards
The Committee previously attempted to interpret its standards quantitatively on the basis of a score of 100 being a perfect score, but it has discarded this approach.

Quantitative Standards Required for Accreditation *
The "Bases for Accrediting Professional Forestry Education" contain several quantitative factors regarding field instruction, faculty duties, etc., that the Council deems desirable. It requires, however, that the faculty consist of at least seven qualified full-time staff members teaching at least one course in each of the five basic fields in the professional forestry curriculum or in closely related areas.

JOURNALISM—AMERICAN COUNCIL ON EDUCATION FOR JOURNALISM

Accrediting Body Within Agency
Accrediting Committee.

Composition of Accrediting Body
Twelve members from outside the Council: seven educators and five journalists.

Use of Institutional Self-Studies
Institution completes 30-page report form on many areas of operation and policy.

Composition of Visiting Team
One member for each sequence under evaluation.

Function of Visiting Team
Observes, evaluates, and recommends accrediting action.

Use of Student Scores on Standardized Tests
None.

Nature of the Visiting Team Report
Team members submit detailed evaluations of each sequence of the curriculum, together with accrediting recommendations, to the Accrediting Committee.

Action on the Report by the Accrediting Agency
The Accrediting Committee recommends action to the Council which takes final action.

Method of Setting and Reviewing Standards for Accreditation
Policies and standards are developed and revised by the Council and its Accrediting Committee.

Interpretation of the Accrediting Standards
"A school should be evaluated in terms of its stated objectives. . . . A school that claims to offer programs in the various phases of journalism should be judged on the basis of its claims," according to the Council.

Quantitative Standards Required for Accreditation *
The only specific quantitative standard of the Council is that three-fourths of the journalism student's curriculum be devoted to liberal arts outside of journalism.

LANDSCAPE ARCHITECTURE—American Society of Landscape Architects

Accrediting Body Within Agency
Committee on Education.

Composition of Accrediting Body
Seven members: four educators, three landscape architects in private or government practice.

Use of Institutional Self-Studies
Institution completes descriptive report of resources, objectives, operations, problems, and needs as the result of five-page School Evaluation form.

Composition of Visiting Team
Three members: two educators, one practitioner, appointed with the acceptance of the school.

Function of Visiting Team
Counsels and advises; makes suggestions, criticisms, and compliments; recommends accrediting action.

Use of Student Scores on Standardized Tests
None.

Nature of the Visiting Team Report
The chairman drafts a report of five parts from a checklist for the signatures of the team.

Action on the Report by the Accrediting Agency
The Committee on Education recommends accrediting action to the Board of Trustees which takes final action.

Method of Setting and Reviewing Standards for Accreditation
Standards are formulated by the Committee on Education, endorsed by the Board of Trustees, and adopted by the Society.

Interpretation of the Accrediting Standards
"The Accrediting Committee will not attempt to prescribe in areas of purely internal affairs and policies . . . except insofar as these can be demonstrated to interfere with the maintenance of minimum acceptable standards and reasonable conditions for teaching and research."

Quantitative Standards Required for Accreditation *
The specific quantitative standards cover the minimum number of instructors in landscape architecture, the student-faculty ratio, and the minimum number of hours required of students in three professional areas.

LAW—American Bar Association

Accrediting Body Within Agency
Council of the Section of Legal Education and Admissions to the Bar.

Composition of Accrediting Body
Thirteen members: officers of the Section and others elected by the Section, divided among lawyers, educators, and state bar examiners.

Use of Institutional Self-Studies
Institution submits annual factual information about operations and policies.

Composition of Visiting Team
One or occasionally more members: the Adviser to the Council or occasionally a team appointed by the Council.

Function of Visiting Team
Makes factual examination but no recommendations regarding accrediting.

Use of Student Scores on Standardized Tests
The percentage of success in bar examinations is considered an important factor in judging the effectiveness of the law school.

Nature of the Visiting Team Report
The Adviser to the Council reports on the school to the Council, but does not make a recommendation regarding accreditation.

Action on the Report by the Accrediting Agency
The Council recommends action to the Section which is open to any ABA member in good standing upon payment of Section dues. The Section recommends action to the House of Delegates which takes final action.

Method of Setting and Reviewing Standards for Accreditation
The House of Delegates authorizes all revisions in standards, but the Council adopts its own interpretation entitled "Factors Bearing on the Approval of Law Schools."

Interpretation of the Accrediting Standards
The standards, consisting of six brief items, are interpreted by the Council in 16 pages of "factors that identify areas of concern regarding accreditation."

Quantitative Standards Required for Accreditation *
The only quantitative standards specify the length of the law program and admission requirements. Quantitative factors include student-teacher ratio, percent of non-theory credits acceptable for admission, extent of library holdings and expenditures, and median faculty salaries.

LAW—Association of American Law Schools

Accrediting Body Within Agency
Executive Committee.

Composition of Accrediting Body
Six members: president and vice president of the Association plus four from faculties of member schools.

Use of Institutional Self-Studies
A questionnaire is now being developed by the Association.

Composition of Visiting Team
Three members: one law librarian, two faculty members or administrators appointed by the President of the Association with advice of the Executive Committee.

Function of Visiting Team
Observes strengths and weaknesses and recommends accrediting action.

Use of Student Scores on Standardized Tests
None.

Nature of the Visiting Team Report
The team reports to the Executive Committee its observations about the strengths and weaknesses of the school and makes a recommendation about membership in the Association.

Action on the Report by the Accrediting Agency
The Executive Committee recommends action to the member schools at the annual meeting.

Method of Setting and Reviewing Standards for Accreditation
The Executive Committee proposes membership requirements for approval of member schools. It implements these requirements in membership regulations unless a fourth of the members object and half disapprove of the regulations.

Interpretation of the Accrediting Standards
The Executive Committee will grant variances to the membership requirements for a period of six years to a school conducting an acceptable experiment in legal education.

Quantitative Standards Required for Accreditation *
Quantitative standards specify admission requirements, length of program, number of faculty, extent of library holding and expenditures, and seating capacity of the library.

LIBRARIANSHIP—American Library Association

Accrediting Body Within Agency
Committee on Accreditation.

Composition of Accrediting Body
Five members.

Use of Institutional Self-Studies
Institution submits 19-page library school report form on its operations and policies together with information on faculty members.

Composition of Visiting Team
Three to four members: one from the Committee on Accreditation; others representing education and the profession, based on various factors. Selected by chairman and secretary of Committee and commented on by the school before being appointed to the team.

Function of Visiting Team
Observes factors incapable of being judged from the documents that are submitted; makes suggestions about program and accrediting recommendation.

Use of Student Scores on Standardized Tests
None.

Nature of the Visiting Team Report
The chairman drafts a report using the school report form outline and including both suggestions for the school and recommendations to the Committee on Accreditation.

Action on the Report by the Accrediting Agency
The Committee on Accreditation takes action by at least a 3-to-1 or 4-to-1 vote.

Method of Setting and Reviewing Standards for Accreditation
The Committee on Accreditation develops standards and presents them to the Executive Board which submits them to the Council of the Association for approval.

Interpretation of the Accrediting Standards
The Committee holds to the principle of avoiding "rigidity and inflexibility which would hamper general progress in the education of librarians."

Quantitative Standards Required for Accreditation *
Standards aim to indicate "levels of achievement which contribute to continuing progress in the education of librarians." The only quantitative standard specifies the percent of professional library course work in the five-year curriculum.

MEDICAL RECORD LIBRARIANSHIP—AMERICAN MEDICAL ASSOCIA-
    TION in collaboration with the AMERICAN ASSOCIATION OF MEDICAL
    RECORD LIBRARIANS

Accrediting Body Within Agency
Council on Medical Education (AMA).

Composition of Accrediting Body
Ten members.

Use of Institutional Self-Studies
Institution submits five-page application questionnaire and assembles documents about the program for the use of the visiting team.

Composition of Visiting Team
Two members: one staff member from the American Association of Medical Record Librarians, one from the Council on Medical Education, American Medical Association.

Function of Visiting Team
Consultation and counseling as well as gathering information and recommending accrediting action.

Use of Student Scores on Standardized Tests
Registry examination scores from the American Association of Medical Record Librarians are usually available, but are not required and are not necessarily critical in the accrediting decision.

Nature of the Visiting Team Report
The report is usually drafted by the staff members from the American Association of Medical Record Librarians, approved by the other team member, and submitted to the Education and Registration Committee of the American Association of Medical Record Librarians.

Action on the Report by the Accrediting Agency
Education and Registration Committee of AAMRL recommends action to Committee on Allied Medical Services of the Council on Medical

Education (AMA) which recommends action to the Council. The Council on Medical Education takes final action.

Method of Setting and Reviewing Standards for Accreditation
The standards are developed by the Council on Medical Education in collaboration with the American Association of Medical Record Librarians and are approved by the House of Delegates of the American Medical Association.

Interpretation of the Accrediting Standards
The standards are titled and considered "Essentials of an Acceptable School."

Quantitative Standards Required for Accreditation *
The quantitative essentials specify admissions requirements and the number of clock hours to be devoted to required subjects in medical record librarianship.

MEDICAL TECHNOLOGY—AMERICAN MEDICAL ASSOCIATION in collaboration with the BOARD OF SCHOOLS OF MEDICAL TECHNOLOGY, AMERICAN SOCIETY OF CLINICAL PATHOLOGISTS

Accrediting Body Within Agency
Council on Medical Education (AMA).

Composition of Accrediting Body
Ten members.

Use of Institutional Self-Studies
Director of school completes five-page questionnaire on operations and policies and submits detailed statistical report including annual number of laboratory tests performed.

Composition of Visiting Team
Two members: one medical technologist from the American Society of Medical Technology; one pathologist from the American Society of Clinical Pathologists.

Function of Visiting Team
Consultation and counseling as well as gathering information and recommending accrediting action.

Use of Student Scores on Standardized Tests
Registry examination scores from the Board of Registry of Medical Technologists are usually available, but are not required and are not necessarily critical in the accrediting decision.

Nature of the Visiting Team Report
The two visitors independently submit their recommendations and point scores to the Board of Schools of Medical Technology of the American Society of Clinical Pathologists.

Action on the Report by the Accrediting Agency
The Board of Schools of Medical Technology recommends action to the Committee on Allied Medical Services of the Council on Medical Education (AMA), which recommends action to the full Council. The Council on Medical Education takes final action.

Method of Setting and Reviewing Standards for Accreditation
The standards are developed by the Council on Medical Education in collaboration with the Board of Schools of Medical Technology and are approved by the House of Delegates of the American Medical Association.

Interpretation of the Accrediting Standards
The standards are titled and considered "Essentials of an Acceptable School" and schools are evaluated quantitatively by point scores.

Quantitative Standards Required for Accreditation *
Quantitative essentials include admissions requirements, pre-admission course requirements, and the extent of laboratory materials available for use.

MEDICINE—Liaison Committee on Medical Education of the Council on Medical Education of the American Medical Association and the Executive Council of the Association of American Medical Colleges

Accrediting Body Within Agency
Liaison Committee on Medical Education of the Council on Medical Education of the American Medical Association and the Executive Council of the Association of American Medical Colleges.

Composition of Accrediting Body
Eight members: four from each of the two sponsoring Councils; chairmanship alternates yearly.

Use of Institutional Self-Studies
Institution and each department of the medical school submit information as result of objective style questionnaire.

Composition of Visiting Team
Four members: two from each organization, including one medical school administrator, one faculty member, one staff member of one of the Councils, and one member from either Council.

Function of Visiting Team
Observes, makes suggestions about program, and recommendations about accreditation.

Use of Student Scores on Standardized Tests
National Board Examination scores are available.

Nature of the Visiting Team Report
The team prepares a report containing comments on strengths and weaknesses, suggestions for improvement, and recommendations for action.

Action on the Report by the Accrediting Agency
Members of the two Councils vote before the Liaison Committee acts. In some cases, Liaison Committee must get concurrence of both Councils before taking final action.

Method of Setting and Reviewing Standards for Accreditation
The House of Delegates of the American Medical Association and the membership of the Association of American Medical Colleges approve accreditation standards.

Interpretation of the Accrediting Standards
The two organizations hold that high standards of medical education are nurtured where "there is not excessive concern with standardization."

Quantitative Standards Required for Accreditation °
The only specific quantitative standards specify three years of college as a minimum admission requirement and full-time instructors in five major clinical areas.

MUSIC—NATIONAL ASSOCIATION OF SCHOOLS OF MUSIC

Accrediting Body Within Agency
Commission on Curricula.

Composition of Accrediting Body
Eight members: past president of the Association; others, including chairman, elected by the Association.

Use of Institutional Self-Studies
Institution completes 15-page self-study questionnaire and also answers 60 questions about policies, operations, needs, and plans.

Composition of Visiting Team
One or occasionally two members: an administrator or faculty member chosen by the institution from among four names of former Association officers or Commission members nominated by the secretary of the Association.

Function of Visiting Team
Secures first-hand information for the Commission; interprets Association policies and philosophy to the institution; recommends accrediting action.

Use of Student Scores on Standardized Tests
Institution is asked to describe any standardized or professional placement examinations or other measures of progress used during or at the end of degree programs.

Nature of the Visiting Team Report
The visitors' report includes facts and evaluation of degrees and curriculum, training of faculty, etc., in terms of purposes of program, as well as suggestions and recommendations regarding accreditation.

Action on the Report by the Accrediting Agency
Commission on Curricula recommends accrediting action to the Executive Committee which recommends to the member institutions of the Association at their annual meeting.

Method of Setting and Reviewing Standards for Accreditation
Subcommittees of the Committee on Curricula recommend criteria to the Committee which recommends action to the members of the Association.

Interpretation of the Accrediting Standards
The Association has "no desire or intent to curb or restrict an administration or a school in its freedom to develop new ideas and to experiment or to expand its program."

Quantitative Standards Required for Accreditation °
The standards specify minimum levels of student competence in applied music, but the only quantitative standards specify the number of course hours in specific areas of music and eligibility is restricted to institutions with 25 music candidates in residence.

NURSING—NATIONAL LEAGUE FOR NURSING

Accrediting Body Within Agency
Collegiate Board of Review, Department of Baccalaureate and Higher Degree Programs.

Composition of Accrediting Body
Twelve members: three each from undergraduate, graduate, and public health nursing departments of accredited schools; chosen by Steering Committee of the Department of Baccalaureate and Higher Degree Programs.

Use of Institutional Self-Studies
Institution submits self-evaluation report based upon accreditation standards. Report can be in any form, but includes sheets on each nursing faculty member.

Composition of Visiting Team
Two or more members: faculty members from the same region but not the same state whose names are reported to the institution in advance of their appointment.

Function of Visiting Team
Six-day visit to supplement self-evaluation report and examine the entire nursing program in order to provide Board of Collegiate Review with a clear understanding of it. Does not make accrediting recommendation.

Use of Student Scores on Standardized Tests
Institution is asked to compare state and school mean scores of state licensing examination with the national mean.

Nature of the Visiting Team Report
The visiting team prepares primarily a factual description of the program, pointing out strengths and weaknesses, that supplements the school's self-evaluation report.

Action on the Report by the Accrediting Agency
The Collegiate Board of Review takes action by a vote of at least nine of its 12 members.

Method of Setting and Reviewing Standards for Accreditation
The Council of Member Agencies recommends standards for consideration by subcommittees of the Department Steering Committee for approval by the Steering Committee. The Collegiate Board of Review carries out the policies set by the Steering Committee.

Interpretation of the Accrediting Standards
The "Criteria for the Evaluation of Educational Programs" of the Department are stated as maximum objectives and no institution is expected to meet all of them completely.

Quantitative Standards Required for Accreditation *
None of the standards or criteria have any specific quantitative requirements.

OCCUPATIONAL THERAPY—AMERICAN MEDICAL ASSOCIATION in collaboration with the AMERICAN OCCUPATIONAL THERAPY ASSOCIATION

Accrediting Body Within Agency
Council on Medical Education (AMA).

Composition of Accrediting Body
Ten members.

Use of Institutional Self-Studies
Institution completes three-page application questionnaire and 13-page survey form covering objectives, teaching and evaluation methods, operations, and policies of the professional curriculum.

Composition of Visiting Team
Four members: a staff member of the American Occupational Therapy Association and the director of an accredited occupational therapy school, plus a staff member of the Council on Medical Education (AMA) and a physician.

Function of Visiting Team
Consultation and counseling as well as gathering information and recommending accrediting action.

Use of Student Scores on Standardized Tests
Registry examination scores from the American Occupational Therapy Association are usually available, but are not required and are not necessarily critical in the accrediting decision.

Nature of the Visiting Team Report
The staff member from the American Occupational Therapy Association usually drafts the report which is approved by the other members for transmission with recommendations to the Council on Education of the American Occupational Therapy Association.

Action on the Report by the Accrediting Agency
The Council on Education of the American Occupational Therapy Association recommends action to the Committee on Allied Medical Services of the Council on Medical Education which recommends action to the Council.

Method of Setting and Reviewing Standards for Accreditation
The standards are developed by the Council on Medical Education in collaboration with the American Occupational Therapy Association and are approved by the House of Delegates of the American Medical Association.

Interpretation of the Accrediting Standards
The standards are titled and considered "Essentials of an Acceptable School."

Quantitative Standards Required for Accreditation *
The quantitative essentials specify admissions requirements, length of program, and semester hours of instruction.

OPTOMETRY—American Optometric Association

Accrediting Body Within Agency
Council on Optometric Education.

Composition of Accrediting Body
Seven members: Director of AOA Department of Education; two each from Association of Schools and Colleges of Optometry and International Association of Boards of Examiners; two optometrists.

Use of Institutional Self-Studies
Institution completes questionnaire asking for extensive information and critical self-analysis.

Composition of Visiting Team
Three to five members selected on the basis of special abilities and experience in the areas that they are assigned to evaluate.

Function of Visiting Team
Observes, evaluates, and recommends accrediting action.

Use of Student Scores on Standardized Tests
The performance of graduates on national and state optometric board examinations is noted.

Nature of the Visiting Team Report
Each member of the team prepares a section of the report following an outline of strengths, weaknesses, and recommendations. Sections are consolidated by the chairman for submission to the Council on Optometric Education.

Action on the Report by the Accrediting Agency
The Council on Optometric Education considers the report and recommendations of the visiting team and takes final action regarding accreditation.

Method of Setting and Reviewing Standards for Accreditation
Standards and proposed changes in them are discussed by the Council in joint annual meetings with the Association of Schools and Colleges of Optometry and the International Association of Boards of Examiners in Optometry with the Council taking action.

Interpretation of the Accrediting Standards
"The Council intends to promote principles which will preserve the desirable individual qualities of institutions. . . . Well conceived experiments undertaken to improve educational methods are considered essential to the growth of institutions of higher education and will be encouraged."

Quantitative Standards Required for Accreditation *
The only specific quantitative standard concerns admission requirements to the school of optometry.

PHARMACY—American Council on Pharmaceutical Education

Accrediting Body Within Agency
American Council on Pharmaceutical Education.

Composition of Accrediting Body
Ten members: three each from American Association of Colleges of Pharmacy, American Pharmaceutical Association, and National Association of Boards of Pharmacy, plus one from the American Council on Education.

Use of Institutional Self-Studies
Institution completes application form requiring detailed information on operation and policies.

Composition of Visiting Team
Two to three members: one or two Council members and the Director of Educational Relations of the Council, plus representatives of the State Board of Pharmacy.

Function of Visiting Team
Observes, evaluates, suggests means of strengthening the school, and recommends accrediting action.

Use of Student Scores on Standardized Tests
The performance of graduates on pharmacy board examinations is noted.

Nature of the Visiting Team Report
The team report contains evaluations of strengths and weaknesses and recommendations regarding accreditation. Suggestions for improving the program are made orally by the team to the school's administrator rather than in the report.

Action on the Report by the Accrediting Agency
The American Council on Pharmaceutical Education considers the report and recommendations of the team and takes final accrediting action.

Method of Setting and Reviewing Standards for Accreditation
Proposed changes are sent to accredited schools, state boards of pharmacy, and governing bodies of the Council's sponsoring associations. Second draft is then given open hearing at the annual convention; final revisions are made by Council.

Interpretation of the Accrediting Standards
The Council aims to avoid forcing accredited colleges to adhere to an unvarying, inflexible curricular pattern.

Quantitative Standards Required for Accreditation *
The only quantitative requirements concern the length of program and the training of faculty.

PHYSICAL THERAPY—AMERICAN MEDICAL ASSOCIATION in collaboration with the AMERICAN PHYSICAL THERAPY ASSOCIATION

Accrediting Body Within Agency
Council on Medical Education (AMA).

Composition of Accrediting Body
Ten members.

Use of Institutional Self-Studies
Institution submits two-page application and 17-page questionnaire on

objectives, policies, operations, teaching methods, and plans for curriculum, plus individual faculty forms.

Composition of Visiting Team
Four members: a staff member of the American Physical Therapy Association and the director of an accredited physical therapy school, plus a staff member of the Council on Medical Education (AMA) and a physician.

Function of Visiting Team
Consultation and counseling as well as gathering information and recommending accrediting action.

Use of Student Scores on Standardized Tests
None.

Nature of the Visiting Team Report
The staff member from the American Physical Therapy Association usually drafts the report which is approved by the other members for transmission with recommendations to the Advisory Committee on Professional Education of the American Physical Therapy Association.

Action on the Report by the Accrediting Agency
The Advisory Committee on Professional Education of the American Physical Therapy Association recommends action to the Committee on Allied Medical Services of the Council on Medical Education which recommends action to the full Council.

Method of Setting and Reviewing Standards for Accreditation
The standards are developed by the Council on Medical Education in collaboration with the American Physical Therapy Association and are approved by the House of Delegates of the American Medical Association.

Interpretation of the Accrediting Standards
The standards are titled and considered "Essentials of an Acceptable School."

Quantitative Standards Required for Accreditation °
The quantitative essentials specify admissions requirements, student-faculty ratios, semester credits, and clock hours of instruction.

PSYCHOLOGY—AMERICAN PSYCHOLOGICAL ASSOCIATION

Accrediting Body Within Agency
(1) Committee on Evaluation.
(2) Education and Training Board.

Composition of Accrediting Body
(1) Nine members elected by Council of Representatives.
(2) Twelve members: six officers of the Association plus six members of the Council of Representatives.

Use of Institutional Self-Studies
Institution completes questionnaire forms on six areas of the program; limited interpretation or self-evaluation required.

Composition of Visiting Team
One member from the Committee on Evaluation plus additional members if needed.

Function of Visiting Team
Rates on five-point scale 17 characteristics of the program plus the faculty; evaluates strengths and weaknesses; and recommends accrediting action.

Use of Student Scores on Standardized Tests
None.

Nature of the Visiting Team Report
The visitor submits his rating sheets plus his general comments about strengths and weaknesses and his recommendations to the Committee on Evaluation. It is suggested that he draft his comments in the form of a letter that could be sent to the institution following final action.

Action on the Report by the Accrediting Agency
The Committee on Evaluation reviews the report and recommends action to the Education and Training Board which then recommends action to the Board of Directors of the Association which takes final action.

Method of Setting and Reviewing Standards for Accreditation
The Committee on Evaluation proposes standards to the Education and Training Board which recommends action on them to the Board of Directors of the Association.

Interpretation of the Accrediting Standards
The Committee tries to guard against standardization and the infringement of the independence of training institutions.

*Quantitative Standards Required for Accreditation **
The only specific quantitative standard calls for seven members on the psychology faculty, but time allocations in various areas of psychological training are suggested.

PUBLIC HEALTH—American Public Health Association

Accrediting Body Within Agency
Committee on Professional Education.

Composition of Accrediting Body
Twelve members appointed by the Executive Board of the Association.

Use of Institutional Self-Studies
Institution presently completes eight-page questionnaire plus cards for each public health member. Questionnaire currently (1965) being revised.

Composition of Visiting Team
Four members: the Director of Professional Education, American Public Health Association; a faculty member from a school of public health; a public health officer; and an educator from outside the public health profession.

Function of Visiting Team
Observes and evaluates strengths and weaknesses; suggests means of strengthening program; makes recommendations regarding accreditation.

Use of Student Scores on Standardized Tests
None.

Nature of the Visiting Team Report
The Committee drafts a report that covers strengths and weaknesses, suggestions about strengthening the program, and recommendations about accreditation.

Action on the Report by the Accrediting Agency
The Committee on Professional Education reviews the report and takes final action regarding accreditation.

Method of Setting and Reviewing Standards for Accreditation
Standards are developed and adopted by the Committee on Professional Education.

Interpretation of the Accrediting Standards
The standards are presently being revised (1965) as result of decision to accredit schools of public health rather than the degree programs in public health.

Quantitative Standards Required for Accreditation *
The standards are presently being revised (1965).

SOCIAL WORK—Council on Social Work Education

Accrediting Body Within Agency
Commission on Accreditation.

Composition of Accrediting Body
Fifteen members: nine full-time faculty members of accredited schools; three in educational work of National Association of Social Workers; and three selected from groups in the House of Delegates of the Council.

Use of Institutional Self-Studies
Institution undertakes comprehensive self-study as the result of five-page accrediting questionnaire listing 45 questions.

Composition of Visiting Team
Two members: a full-time faculty member from an accredited school plus one member of the Commission. Both must be acceptable to the school.

Function of Visiting Team
Analyzes submitted materials; supplements them by observation of many facts about school; evaluates program; and recommends accrediting action.

Use of Student Scores on Standardized Tests
None.

Nature of the Visiting Team Report
The report follows the outline of the "Manual" covering strengths, weaknesses, issues, questions related to accreditation, conclusions, and recommendations.

Action on the Report by the Accrediting Agency
The Commission on Accreditation takes final action on accreditation.

Method of Setting and Reviewing Standards for Accreditation
The Commission on Accreditation formulates all standards for adop-

tion by the Board of Directors, except those involving the curriculum which are developed by a standing curriculum committee, adopted by the Board of Directors, and applied by the Commission on Accreditation.

Interpretation of the Accrediting Standards
The Commission does not assume that *all* standards will be met, but it holds that deficiencies must not "jeopardize the achievement of objectives of professional social work education."

Quantitative Standards Required for Accreditation *
The only quantitative standard specifies the length of the professional program.

SPEECH PATHOLOGY AND AUDIOLOGY—AMERICAN SPEECH AND HEARING ASSOCIATION

Accrediting Body Within Agency
Education and Training Board of the American Boards of Examiners in Speech Pathology and Audiology.

Composition of Accrediting Body
Five members, four of whom are associated with educational institutions.

Use of Institutional Self-Studies
Institution answers nine pages of questions in "Outline of Information to be Provided by an Institution" about policies, operations, and plans.

Composition of Visiting Team
At least two members selected by the chairman of the Education and Training Board from roster approved by the American Boards of Examiners. The institution can request a change in the team.

Function of Visiting Team
Observes, evaluates strengths and weaknesses, makes suggestions to director of program, recommends accrediting action.

Use of Student Scores on Standardized Tests
Accrediting procedures currently being initiated (1965).

Nature of the Visiting Team Report
The report covers five items: strengths, weaknesses, factors of importance in addition to those submitted by the institution, suggestions for improvement, and recommendations regarding accreditation.

Action on the Report by the Accrediting Agency
The Education and Training Board drafts a summary of the report and recommends action to the Directors, American Boards of Examiners in Speech Pathology and Audiology, for final action.

Method of Setting and Reviewing Standards for Accreditation
The Education and Training Board develops standards, subject to review by the Directors of the American Boards of Examiners in Speech Pathology and Audiology.

Interpretation of the Accrediting Standards
The American Speech and Hearing Association is presently commencing accreditation (1965) and is developing its interpretation of the standards.

Quantitative Standards Required for Accreditation *
The only quantitative standards specify the minimum number of graduates per year from the professional program in speech pathology and/or audiology and the length of the professional program.

TEACHER EDUCATION—NATIONAL COUNCIL FOR ACCREDITATION OF TEACHER EDUCATION

Accrediting Body Within Agency
National Council for Accreditation of Teacher Education.

Composition of Accrediting Body
Nineteen members: for appointments by constituent members, see pages 52, 53 of text.

Use of Institutional Self-Studies
Institution submits up to 100-page report containing detailed information about its teacher education program as the result of suggestions in "Guide" and "Quantitative Data Summary" sheets.

Composition of Visiting Team
Five to nine members, none from the Council itself. Institution permitted to strike names from the suggested list. Team includes administrators and faculty members from teacher education programs and academic fields from institutions in other states plus representatives of state department of education and state education association.

Function of Visiting Team
Collects, validates, and reports information bearing on the total teacher education program; does not criticize, praise, give advice to the institution, or make recommendations regarding accrediting action.

Use of Student Scores on Standardized Tests
Scores on intelligence and achievement tests plus state and national examinations related to teaching are requested of the institution.

Nature of the Visiting Team Report
Members of the team report evidence of success or failure of parts of the program and describe the program on the basis of the Council's seven standards. The chairman compiles these into a report containing no recommendations for submission to the Visitation and Appraisal Committee.

Action on the Report by the Accrediting Agency
The Visitation and Appraisal Committee reviews the report and recommends action through one of its four subcommittees—one for multipurpose institutions and three for other institutions in three regions—to the Council for final action.

Method of Setting and Reviewing Standards for Accreditation
The Council adopts standards upon the recommendation of its Committee on Standards, consisting of four NCATE members and three non-members. The standards are reviewed annually by the Committee on Standards.

Interpretation of the Accrediting Standards
The Council is concerned with favorable conditions for producing

good teachers; thus it considers its seven standards as principles that should govern teacher education programs.

Quantitative Standards Required for Accreditation *
None of the seven standards has any specific quantitative requirements.

THEOLOGY—AMERICAN ASSOCIATION OF THEOLOGICAL SCHOOLS IN THE UNITED STATES AND CANADA

Accrediting Body Within Agency
Commission on Accreditation.

Composition of Accrediting Body
Nine members elected by the Association on nomination of the Executive Board.

Use of Institutional Self-Studies
Institution completes Association biennial report form and 48 pages of questionnaires or "schedules."

Composition of Visiting Team
Two members from the Commission on Accreditation.

Function of Visiting Team
Observes, evaluates, and recommends accrediting action.

Use of Student Scores on Standardized Tests
None.

Nature of the Visiting Team Report
The Committee submits a report on the institution containing recommendations for accreditation to the Commission on Accreditation.

Action on the Report by the Accrediting Agency
The Commission on Accreditation takes final action regarding accreditation.

Method of Setting and Reviewing Standards for Accreditation
The Commission on Accreditation develops standards for approval by the member institutions of the Association.

Interpretation of the Accrediting Standards
The Commission "does not treat its standards as definite rules and specifications to be applied in an exact and mechanical fashion," but instead to be administered "by way of stimulus and encouragement." Thus accredited institutions that inadequately meet certain standards are identified in the Association's list.

Quantitative Standards Required for Accreditation
The quantitative requirements for associate members are four faculty members and 25 students; for accredited members, six faculty members. The normal length of program is specified, as are teaching loads and library budgets.

VETERINARY MEDICINE—American Veterinary Medical Association

Accrediting Body Within Agency
Council on Education.

Composition of Accrediting Body
Ten members elected by the House of Delegates from 10 major areas of veterinary medical education and practice.

Use of Institutional Self-Studies
Institution supplies facts on "General Information" forms plus a variety of other materials, such as the dean's report, weekly schedule of classes for the year, etc.

Composition of Visiting Team
Five members: four from the Council, usually two educators and two practitioners, plus the staff consultant to the Council.

Function of Visiting Team
Observes, suggests means of improving program, and recommends accrediting action.

Use of Student Scores on Standardized Tests
None.

Nature of the Visiting Team Report
The staff consultant to the Council drafts a report covering the information submitted by the institution, observations regarding strengths and weaknesses, suggestions for improvement, and recommendations regarding accreditation.

Action on the Report by the Accrediting Agency
The Council on Education reviews the team report and takes final accrediting action.

Method of Setting and Reviewing Standards for Accreditation
The Council on Education develops standards for approval by the House of Delegates of the American Veterinary Medical Association.

Interpretation of the Accrediting Standards
"The aims and purposes of the Council are to promote active progress in veterinary medical education in the various schools and colleges, with full accreditation of them as the ultimate goal. In fulfilling this function, the Council will encourage and assist schools to meet requirements."

Quantitative Standards Required for Accreditation *
Quantitative standards specify admissions requirements and the length of the professional program. Instruction is expected in 16 subjects.

APPENDIX IV

ADDITIONAL INFORMATION ON REGIONAL
ACCREDITING ASSOCIATIONS

	Administrative Structure	Membership	Voting Power
New England	*Officers:* Pres., V.P., Sec. Treas. *Exec. Comm:* 3 officers, chairmen 3 standing comm., 3 members-at-large Committees: Inst. of Higher Ed., Independent Sec. Schools, Public Sec. Schools	Individual Institutional Associate	Colleges and universities— 2 voting delegates Secondary Schools— 1 voting delegate
Middle States	*Officers:* Pres., V.P., Sec. Treas. Secretary manages the Ass'n *Exec. Comm.:* 4 officers plus one from each member state	Individual and Institutional (Instit. includes state and local depts. of education)	In meetings, each del. has one vote. In a mail ballot vote, each instituti al member has one vote
North Central	*Officers:* Pres., V.P., Sec. and Treasurer *Executive Committee:* Pres., V.P., Treas., Editor of *Quarterly*, chairmen of three standing committees	Since 1916 two classes of members— indiv. and instit. *Inst.:* Univ., colleges, secondary schools *Indiv.:* Officers and 1. Comm. members 2. Honorary mem.	Each institutional member has one vote
Southern	*Officers:* President, President Elect, Exec. Sec., Treas. *Executive Comm:* 1. Pres., Pres. Elect, Immediate Past Pres., Exec. Sec. Treas. 2. Twelve elected members	Three classes: 1. Colleges and universities 2. Secondary schools 3. State depts. of education	Each institutional member has one vote
Northwest	*Officers:* Pres., 1st V.P., 2nd V.P., and Sec.-Treas. *Executive Committee:* 1. Elected officers 2. Chairmen of state comm. 3. Two at-large members 4. Four from higher institutions	Three classes: 1. Colleges and universities 2. Secondary schools 3. State depts. of education	Each institutional member has one vote
Western	*Officers:* Pres., V.P. and Executive Sec.-Treas. *Executive Committee:* Pres., V.P., Immediate Past Pres., Exec. Sec.-Treas., Chairman of Commission on Membership Standards, 6 elected members	Institutional Memberships Active Associate	Each active institutional member has one vote

Publications	Growth of Area	Major Changes
ew England Assn. *view* (published irregularly)	Area has remained constant	1885–1927 Individual membership only Since 1927 also institutional mem. 1936 representation changed 1952 changes made in reevaluation procedure
oceedings of annual meetings *st* of member institutions *formation* Bulletin	From Pennsylvania as original area to added states of New York, N.J., Delaware, Maryland, and D.C.	In 1945 associate membership for non-accredited institutions abolished
rth Central Association *Quarterly*	Membership increased from 6 to 15 states	Present constitution adopted in 1942
oceedings of annual meetings	Territory actually decreased as territories were transferred to North Central	Since 1954 provision has been made for affiliation of elementary schools
oceedings of annual meetings	From four to eight states (including Alaska)	California colleges and universities have not been accredited by NW since 1948; high schools since 1956
oceedings of annual meetings	Hawaii added	First constitution in 1931. Procedures for accrediting adopted in 1947. In 1950 a cooperative plan inaugurated for accrediting junior colleges

APPENDIX V

SUMMARY OF INFORMATION OBTAINED THROUGH QUESTIONNAIRES TO STATE DIRECTORS OF TEACHER EDUCATION AND CERTIFICATION

In the spring of 1964 a questionnaire on state procedures and practices in accreditation of teacher education, including reference to relations with national and regional accrediting associations, was addressed to an officer in the state department of education in each of the 50 states. The names of persons to whom the questionnaire was addressed were taken from the 1964 Directory of the National Association of State Directors of Teacher Education and Certification. It is a tribute to the professional dedication of these persons that all questionnaires were returned with rather complete answers on all questions in which the respondent felt he had helpful information to share. In many cases, supplementary documents were also included. The questionnaire was formulated with the assistance of the officers of NASDTEC, including the four regional chairmen.

A second inquiry was addressed to the 50 state directors of teacher education and certification in the fall of 1964. Replies from most of the states were promptly received.

Some information obtained from the responses to the questionnaire and to the later inquiry has been reported in a number of chapters of this report of the Study. In this appendix are presented further data obtained from the state directors with supplementary information for two topics. The following subheadings are used:

> Varying Patterns of State Accreditation of Teacher Education
> Accrediting Functions of State Universities
> Accrediting Activities of Other Agencies in the States
> Percent of New Teachers from Out of State
> MAT Programs
> Programs Leading to the Doctorate
> Questions Relative to the Effects of Accreditation

The data on accrediting activities of state universities and other agencies were obtained from other sources.* The remainder of the data and opinions reported in the following sections were obtained from the questionnaires or inquiries addressed to the state directors.

Answers submitted to questions relative to the effects of accreditation are statements of opinion. These data, which in some instances are tabulated, are reported with the question asked heading each section.

VARYING PATTERNS OF STATE ACCREDITATION OF TEACHER EDUCATION

What method is used in your state in accrediting teacher education programs? In answer to the question the following information was obtained.

---

* Theresa Birch Wilkins, "Accreditation in the States," in Lloyd E. Blauch, ed., *Accreditation in Higher Education*, Washington, Dept. of Health, Education, and Welfare, 1959, pp. 31–41.

274

Thirty-five states reported that one step is the establishment of criteria; 37 said they send teams to inspect institutions; 33 publish a list of accredited institutions; 34 states reported making a periodic review. Nine states reported that they rely completely upon the regional accreditation or else depend on regional standards for evaluating institutions. Three states reported using the standards recommended by NASDTEC and the U. S. Office of Education. Six states reported that they rely largely on NCATE standards.

Examples of practices in a number of states are given in the following paragraphs.

Arizona. The State Board of Education accredits institutions of higher education through the baccalaureate degree. The state legislature enacts statutes authorizing the State Board of Education to administer the statutes. The accreditation of teacher education is based on the standards of the national and regional accrediting associations. The accreditation is valid for five years.

Delaware. Institutions of higher education are accredited by the State Board of Education for offering teacher education programs. Under the school laws of Delaware no institution may offer a course or courses for the training of public school teachers without having first procured assent of the State Board of Education. Accreditation is based on data filed by the institutions and visits to the campuses. No period of time is set for required evaluation. Programs of teacher education are accredited through the sixth year.

Idaho. Supervision and control of certification of professional education personnel are vested in the State Board of Education. The Board approves the programs of education of such personnel in all institutions of higher education, both public and private, and accredits as teacher-training institutions those in which such programs are approved. In accreditation the Board honors programs in regionally accredited institutions of higher education for whatever period regional accreditation is given.

Indiana. The teacher-training and licensing commission of the State Board of Education is responsible for accrediting institutions of higher education for teacher education. The commission is composed of the state superintendent of public instruction and six members appointed by the governor. The administration of accreditation and certification rests with a teacher-training and licensing division appointed by the commission.

Iowa. The State Board of Public Instruction is the state accrediting agency for the entire program of public junior colleges and for teacher education in all colleges. Accreditation includes sixth-year programs and is valid for five years. Institutions file reports on each teacher education program in terms of Iowa standards. Non-NCATE-accredited institutions make a self-evaluation using NCATE *Standards and Guide*. Visits to campuses are a part of the accreditation process.

Massachusetts. Massachusetts does not accredit programs as the term is generally accepted. The Board of Education will accept for certification purposes (1) the degrees and courses of nationally and regionally accredited institutions, (2) colleges of which the degree-granting power has been approved by the Massachusetts Board of Collegiate Authority, and (3) colleges approved for certification purposes by the state board of the state in which the college is located.

Missouri. Regional accreditation is recognized as "satisfactory acceptance" for a teacher education program. Certificates to teach in the public schools of Missouri are granted by the State Board of Education. Although the state does not accredit programs, representatives of the state department visit and work with each college of the state in the development of teacher education programs.

North Carolina. Among legal responsibilities assigned to the State Board of Education are certification and regulation of the grade and salary of teachers and other school employees. Institutions that meet certain standards regarding resources, faculty, personnel policies, curriculum, and facilities are approved to provide teacher education. Approved institutions assume greater responsibility in the selection and retention of prospective teachers, in the preparation of teacher candidates, and in the recommendation of their graduates in teacher education for state certification. The approved-program approach was adopted by the State Board on September 6, 1962. All institutions must be under the approved program by September 1, 1966. The guidelines and standards for implementing the program were developed over a two-year period involving more than a thousand academicians, professional educators, public school personnel, and lay persons.

Oregon. NCATE-approved programs in elementary and secondary education are approved without evaluation by the state department of education. For non-NCATE-approved programs, accreditation of the institution by the Northwest Association is a prerequisite to evaluation by the state department. A visiting committee selected from a panel of persons nominated by professional groups recommends to the State Board of Education.

Texas. The State Board of Education accepts membership in the Association of Texas Colleges, an extralegal agency, or accreditation by the Southern Association, as prerequisite to the approval of an institution for teacher education.

ACCREDITING FUNCTIONS OF STATE UNIVERSITIES

Sometimes by law but usually custom, some state universities are given or assume the responsibility of evaluating higher institutions and programs within the state. In some instances, what the university does in this capacity is called accreditation; in others, the universities evaluate courses or curriculums to determine the acceptability of credit for transfer. In the latter situations, what the university does is referred to as "accept," "appraise," "approve," "classify," or "recognize." Several examples are given in the next five paragraphs.

Questions arising outside the state about the standing of graduates of Kansas colleges are referred to the state university whose practice and evaluations are used to determine the standing of any college. A long-standing policy of the university senate committee is to give automatic recognition to institutions accredited by North Central. All others must be inspected and evaluated annually by the university.

The committee on institutional relationships of the University of Minnesota senate is responsible for accreditation in the state. Junior colleges are accredited according to criteria established by the University. For degree-granting institutions, the criteria and procedures of the North Central Association are followed.

The University of Missouri committee on accredited schools and colleges accredits public and private junior colleges. A committee from the University faculty visits the institution seeking accreditation, inspects facilities and examines the administration, instruction, finances, records, and other pertinent features.

An institution not accredited by the Southern Association is visited by members of the University of Tennessee committee on admissions and advanced standing, who decide what credit, if any, will be allowed and under what conditions. The committee may then accredit the institution as a whole, certain departments, or certain courses with limitations on credit hours acceptable.

The University of Wisconsin performs an accrediting function through a standing committee on college accreditation which inspects and evaluates the work of institutions in the state primarily to determine what credits from the non-accredited institutions to accept.

ACCREDITING ACTIVITIES OF OTHER AGENCIES IN THE STATES

In a few states, agencies other than state boards of education, state departments of education, and state universities engage in accrediting or related activities. About half of these are legally authorized and the other half are voluntary. Among such agencies are: Iowa Committee on Secondary Schools and College Relations, Massachusetts Board of Collegiate Authority, Michigan Commission on College Accreditation, Collegiate Accrediting Commission of Mississippi, North Carolina College Conference, Ohio College Association, Oklahoma State Regents for Higher Education, and Association of Texas Colleges.

PERCENT OF NEW TEACHERS FROM OUT OF STATE

The state directors were asked: *What percent of those receiving a new teachers certificate completed their teacher education programs outside your state?* A tabulation of replies is:

	Number of States	States
More than 75%	3	Alaska, Delaware, New Mexico
50%–74%	6	Arizona, Colorado, Florida, Georgia, Hawaii, Idaho
25%–49%	7	California, Iowa, Kansas, Louisiana, New Jersey, Ohio, Rhode Island
Less than 25%	17	
No report	17	

Among the 17 states from which no report is available are some in which the state directors of teacher education indicated that the data requested had not been tabulated, and others because the data were not readily available. These 17 states include some of the more populous states such as Illinois, Indiana, Maryland, Minnesota, and Pennsylvania. The reports are largely based on the employment of new teachers for the school year 1963–1964.

MAT PROGRAMS

The 50 state directors of teacher education and certification were asked to give the number of masters of arts in teaching programs (MAT programs) in their states. For the purpose of this question, an MAT program, the directors were informed, is to be considered a formally organized program of at least two semesters' duration to provide preparation for teaching for those who are liberal arts graduates.

Twenty-four states reported the existence of 81 such programs. Replies from 14 states indicated that no programs of this kind were offered by the institutions of higher education of their states. No information in reply to this question was submitted by the remaining 12 states, although four of the 12 states answered other inquiries in the same communication, and hence can be presumed to know of no MAT programs in their states. Thus, there are at least 24 states in which one or more MAT programs are offered and 14 states in which no program of this type is available.

PROGRAMS LEADING TO THE DOCTORATE

In the first questionnaire mailed to the 50 state directors of teacher education and certification, to which there was a 100 percent response, 23 state directors indicated that their state accredits or approves teacher education programs beyond the sixth year (four undergraduate years and two graduate years). Those directors were then asked if this means that programs leading to the doctorate were approved or accredited by the official state accrediting agency.

If the states in which approval of doctoral programs is just being started are included, then 11 states do accredit or approve programs leading to the highest degree. The states are: Colorado, Delaware, Florida, Georgia, Idaho, Indiana, Kansas, New Jersey, New York, Ohio, and Washington. Six of the 23 states to which this question was addressed definitely replied in the negative. No replies were received from the remaining six.

QUESTIONS RELATIVE TO THE EFFECTS OF ACCREDITATION

To what extent does NCATE accreditation affect state department procedures in your state?

This question, like the others, was answered in a variety of ways and apparently with differences in interpretation of the question. Some respondents submitted a statement of state regulations or guides regarding NCATE. Where replies fitted a category appropriate for the answers of as many as four states, the tabulation is:

	Number of States
Graduates of NCATE-accredited institutions are automatically given at least provisional certification	16
Are more readily or speedily certified	6
NCATE-accredited institutions are automatically accredited by the state	5
NCATE accreditation has little effect	9
NCATE accreditation has no effect	6
NCATE accreditation serves as a guide for state accreditation	4

Some states which automatically grant at least provisional accreditation to graduates of NCATE-accredited institutions are not included in the 16 states in the first item above. Apparently the respondents in these states did not consider this an effect on state procedures.

Two states answered that NCATE affects state procedures to a great extent. Other replies given by those who completed the questionnaire in one or more states are: State department works closely with NCATE in the accreditation process; the state and NCATE support each other; NCATE gives moral support to the state; and "none, except that there is a natural 'spill-over.'" The response from one state was in part: "[State accreditation] has not yet been applied to out-of-state NCATE-accredited institutions since one finds a substantial number of such institutions do not require the amount of mathematics or science we feel is needed by elementary teachers."

What specific examples can you cite of improvements or adverse effects in your state of national accreditation of teacher education?
Thirty-six state replies were worded in a way which can be interpreted as a report of improvements from the point of view of the respondent. The replies from two states can be interpreted as reporting only adverse effects, while one additional reply included effects labeled as beneficial and effects labeled as adverse. Another report was "no adverse effects"; two responded "little or no effect," and one respondent indicated that the list and description of effects would be too long for the space allotted. The remaining seven replies to this question were "No comment."

No fewer than 35 different kinds of effects were listed, and of these it appears that no more than four were considered to be adverse effects by those who replied. In many instances specific institutions of higher education were named. While practically all were effects on institutions, the influence of the "thinking of the state advisory committee regarding certification requirements" was given in one reply, and support to the state agency in two replies. One respondent stated that national accreditation has enabled his department to keep up with its work load.

The effects which were in the replies of at least four states, with the number of states listing them are:

Number of States	Effect
9	Selection and retention policies have been improved
7	All-institutional teacher education committees have been appointed
7	Faculty members in Education have been added or better qualified staff members in Education appointed
7	Library and instructional materials centers have been strengthened
6	Curriculums and courses have been improved
6	Improvements have been made in student teaching (better qualified staff, director of student teaching appointed, student-supervisor ratio decreased)
4	Improvements have resulted from required self-study (greater awareness of teacher education on part of faculty)
4	Clear-cut administrative channels have been established

Other effects listed included improved admission to graduate programs and improved graduate programs; placing of more resources and interest in teacher education by nonaccredited institutions; appointment of better qualified staffs in academic departments; increased local and national prestige for institutions; improvement of faculty salaries, physical facilities, and secretarial assistance. Only one reply made specific reference to the facilitation of reciprocity among states, but this effect may have been implied in other responses.

The four effects which the respondents labeled as adverse or probably considered to be adverse were: national accreditation not based on quality; national accreditation sometimes aroused conflict between national and state accrediting agencies; experimentation has not been restricted nor has it been encouraged; and "hard" feelings are caused between institutions which achieve accreditation and those which are denied it. Each of these was listed once, except the last, which was given two times.

What in your judgment would be the effect in your state of the removal of the present accreditation of teacher education at the national level?

The replies to this question were classified in terms of the implied degree of gain or loss in the quality of teacher education programs and to the institutions offering the programs and in the availability of well-qualified teachers. In the tabulation where one or two categories seemed possible, the category least favorable to national accreditation was chosen. For example, a reply "little effect" was tabulated as "no effect," and where the effect reported was limited to the hampering of reciprocity, the reply was classified as a "moderate loss."

Effects	Number of States
Possible gain	1
No comment	3
No effect	7
Moderate loss	14
Very considerable loss	25
	50

This tabulation shows that 78 percent of the state directors of teacher education and certification would classify the removal of national accreditation as a loss and half of them as a very considerable loss. Only one state gave a reply in which the removal could be interpreted as a possible gain, using these sentences: "Accreditation at the national level does not seem to be as vital to the program as regional and state accreditation. National accreditation could lead to mediocrity if national standards are so low that they are within the reach of all institutions."

As verification of consistency of responses to different questions, the 11 states in the first three categories above were among the 13 states from which no improvements were reported in the preceding question.

A grouping of more specific responses to the question follows with a listing of effects reported from at least four states. Quite a number of states listed several effects. Also since a number of different responses were classified as "moderate loss," for example, the data below cannot be used to check the data above. A listing of several effects, each classified as moderate when given singly, was classified as a "very considerable loss" above.

Number of States	Effect
8	Reciprocity would be hampered (or impossible)
7	No (little, doubtful) effect
6	Serious (unfortunate, very bad, disastrous)
5	Moderate effect
5	Approved-program approach would be hampered (state would lose needed national guidance)
4	Programs would lose in quality at all levels
4	Profession of teaching would lose status

Other effects listed were: certification procedures would be thrown out of gear; institutions would lose incentive for self-study and improvement and from absence of visitors from other institutions; accredited institutions would lose prestige; non-accredited institutions would lose incentive for improvement; the state and regionals would function but not as effectively; progress would be stopped.

What in your judgment would be the effect in your state of the removal of the present accreditation of teacher education at the regional and state levels?

Separate questions were asked with respect to national, regional, and state accreditation. The answers with respect to national accreditation were tabulated above. Some thought the abolition of NCATE accreditation would be most disastrous; others, regional; the largest number, state.

The effects of the removal of regional accreditation are suggested in the following statements:

It would produce a chaotic condition among the institutions.

We would have to change our entire procedure for assessing course work which we can accept for certification purposes.

Without regional accreditation, substandard institutions would flourish.

Create a confusion among the colleges of our state.

Many new colleges not needed might attempt to organize on low standards.

Very bad.

It would remove our basis of a minimum-quality program.

Their removal would create a vacuum of dangerous proportions.

Limited to moderate effect.

Our certification system would be obsolete.

Relatively minor effect.

Would be unfortunate.

Here are some of the comments made by state officials about the effect of the removal of state accreditation:

Create anarchy among colleges . . . .

The education of teachers would become a stepchild again in colleges. . . . Credit counting would of necessity increase.

Would open door to marginal or substandard programs under private auspices.

Disastrous for teacher education.

It would wreck quality in the weaker institutions and in the basic private liberal arts colleges.

A complete destruction of the teacher-certification system . . . .

Would diminish the status of teacher education on college campuses with consequent lowering of professional competence of graduates applying for teaching positions.

Chaos.

Considerable retrogression.

Splintering of programs and the disappearance of quality preparation of teachers.

In some instances I am afraid the deterioration would amount to disintegration.

Politics would make it almost impossible for a state to operate alone.

How successful have the accrediting agencies been in achieving their goals?
Some thought NCATE had been most successful; others gave greatest credit to the states. The inclination was to credit the regional associations with relatively little influence on teacher education programs. In the words of the state director of an eastern state:

NCATE is having [a] tremendous impact in creating [an] institution-wide organization for policy making in teacher education; in raising the standards of student teaching programs; in developing "General Education" requirements that apply to all teacher education curricula; in careful examination of "teaching majors"; in focusing attention on standards and procedures for admitting students to teacher education programs; in encouraging the attention to study in graduate fields in teacher education.

According to one southern state:

State accreditation . . . is having more effect on teacher education than regional or national agencies. In the general improvement of teacher education, NCATE has been only one of several important groups and its specific contribution is not always easy to identify.

It was reported from another southern state that:

The goals are fairly well achieved in each case. Improvement results from each of the processes. Each group develops new interests in self-improvement. These may be pressures institutions voluntarily put themselves under to continue progress. I believe that all are needed to get the best possible program for preparing teachers.

What effects, in addition to those intended, does accreditation of teacher education programs have on colleges and universities in your state?
Here are some of the varied answers:

Full accreditation has a powerful public relations value which goes far when recruiting students. Facilitates entry into graduate institutions. Few people will make substantial gifts and bequests to non-accredited institutions. Fully accredited institutions attract more competent faculty.

Sometimes better cooperation among various groups within the college. Better understanding of one's own program and internal organization and operation.

The pressure brought about in meeting certain NCATE standards has resulted in some resentment from people in Letters and Science, but these problems are being worked out and they are yielding to the development of a more unified program of teacher education.

Increased public respect for the teaching profession.

Some undue fears are stimulated.

Accreditation of teacher education programs has a unifying effect on the faculty; accreditation procedures bring about a better understanding on the part of all involved; various faculty members receive stimulation and challenge from the others; the total faculty appears to become more knowledgeable of trends and developments and is highly motivated to have quality programs.

I suppose that, depending on one's point of view, one might find too much conformity, not enough experimentation, development of feeling of self-satisfaction, "now we've made it" air. I can't say I've observed these things [here] but could be.

Accreditation undoubtedly stifles innovation in some colleges. The better the college, the more likely it is to make a strong case for experimentation and win the flexibility it deserves. Some good institutions, however, do not make this effort for fear of being turned down.

To what extent is it possible to compare in a useful way the "products" of NCATE-accredited teacher education programs in your state and products of an institution which has been refused NCATE accreditation?
Most of the answers to this question were stated in the negative. A few were given in more affirmative terms.

While this is highly desirable, it seems almost impossible to accomplish. It would be a terrific, long-term research project. However, I would like to see someone try it.

It is possible . . . to make certain comparisons between the products of an NCATE-accredited teacher education program and those of an institution which has been refused NCATE accreditation. On file in the State Department are evaluations of each teacher within the state . . . , NTE examinations, and institutional transcripts of the teacher. The institution which was refused NCATE accreditation normally produces a product which appears inferior to the accredited institution.

In general . . . institutions not applying for accreditation are more limited in qualified staff in education, in providing excellent laboratory experiences in teacher education, in evaluation of the programs.

APPENDIX VI

THE CATALOG SURVEY OF UNDERGRADUATE COLLEGE AND UNIVERSITY PROGRAMS

The purpose of the catalog survey was to consider two basic questions concerning undergraduate teacher education. First, does there exist a common pattern of undergraduate teacher education programs? Second, are there any significant differences between National Council for Accreditation of Teacher Education (NCATE)-accredited programs and non-NCATE-accredited programs, and what are these differences?

THE POPULATION

The population for this study was determined by consulting two publications: (1) *Institutional Members, National Commission on Accrediting* (NCA), 1962–1963 and 1963–1964, hereafter referred to as the Blue Book; and (2) *National Council for Accreditation of Teacher Education* (NCATE), *Tenth Annual List,* 1963–1964, hereafter referred to as the White Book. The Blue Book lists 1,342 institutions which held membership in the NCA in 1962–1963 or 1963–1964. It should be emphasized that this does not represent a listing of accredited colleges and universities only, since NCA membership is open to members of seven national associations, not all of which require accreditation for membership. The White Book lists 408 colleges and universities in the continental United States which have been accredited by NCATE.

All institutions which did not offer a four-year program in teacher education were eliminated from the total list. The final listing included 962 institutions. These were then separated into three mutually exclusive categories: (1) multipurpose universities, (2) state and teachers colleges, and (3) liberal arts colleges. Two publications were consulted to aid in these classifications: (1) *A Manual on Certification Requirements for School Personnel in the United States,* edited by W. Earl Armstrong and T. M. Stinnett, and (2) *American Universities and Colleges, Ninth Edition,* published by the American Council on Education.

The following criteria were used to classify institutions as multipurpose universities, state and teachers colleges, or liberal arts colleges:

> Multipurpose universities were defined as those institutions offering several professional programs, such as law and engineering, in addition to teacher education and which also offered a doctoral degree. In several instances, institutions which included "university" in their names were not classified as multipurpose because of the limited nature of their programs.
>
> State and teachers colleges included institutions whose main purpose was teacher education but whose offerings may have also included a liberal arts degree program. Such institutions usually offered a master's degree program with an emphasis upon education.
>
> Liberal arts colleges were those institutions in which the main emphasis was placed upon liberal arts study but in addition it was possible for students to obtain teacher certification. For the main part, such institutions offered the bachelor's degree and in some cases a master's degree program.

The number of institutions in the population so defined is described in the table below:

Type of Institution	Total	Accreditation	
		NCATE	Non-NCATE
Multipurpose Universities	140	109	31
State and Teachers Colleges	251	197	54
Liberal Arts Colleges	571	102	469

THE SAMPLE

A 10 percent sample was selected, using a table of random numbers, from each of six categories of the population. The six categories are defined under Data Processing below. The number of institutions in the samples are shown in the following table:

Type of Institution	Total	Accreditation	
		NCATE	Non-NCATE
Multipurpose Universities	14	11*	3**
State and Teachers Colleges	25	20	5
Liberal Arts Colleges	57	10	47

* Catalogs could not be obtained from two universities.
** Four universities were actually studied.

Such factors as geographical distribution, church- or non-church-related schools, and men's or women's colleges were randomized by the procedure of selecting the samples.

DATA COLLECTION

The data of the study were collected from the latest catalogs of the sample institutions available at the University of Tennessee. In cases where catalogs were not available, special requests were sent to the institutions for their latest catalogs. No catalogs were consulted which were published before 1961, hence it is felt the data reflect the curriculums actually studied by students during the past four years.

DATA PROCESSING

The data collected as described above were transferred to IBM cards and processed by the IBM 1620. Such statistics as means, standard deviations, and frequencies for six categories of institutions were obtained. These six categories are: (1) NCATE multipurpose universities; (2) non-NCATE multipurpose universities; (3) NCATE state and teachers colleges; (4) non-NCATE state and teachers colleges; (5) NCATE liberal arts colleges; (6) non-NCATE liberal arts colleges.

Tests of the equality of two means were determined by use of the t distribution for 76 different variables. The means of each of the 76 variables of categories (1) and (2); (3) and (4); and (5) and (6), respectively, were compared. The results of these tests are shown in 76 tables prepared as a part of the survey, but not shown here.

ANALYSIS OF DATA

In the survey comparisons between pairs of the six categories of institutions were made of requirements for admission to the institution and to teacher education programs offered by the institutions, general education and professional education requirements, and major specialization requirements for prospective secondary school teachers and area specialization for elementary teachers. The results obtained are reported in Chapters 11 and 13, with the exception of area specialization for elementary teachers.

Although specializations are firmly established in secondary education, they are relatively new in elementary education and a large number of institutions do not offer such specializations. Many of the specializations arise in elementary education because liberal arts colleges usually require a major area of concentration for any student as part of a normal liberal arts program. Professional education is then elected by such students to satisfy state certification requirements.

The survey was conducted under the direction of Professor Donald J. Dessart of the Departments of Mathematics and Education of the University of Tennessee. As a paragraph on conclusions, Dessart writes:

On the basis of this study, one can conclude that there exist common patterns of teacher education in both elementary and secondary education in the institutions of the defined population. However, specializations in elementary education are apparently just beginning to evolve as indicated by the very small number of schools offering such specializations.

Few statistically significant differences were found in the mean requirements of NCATE and non-NCATE similar-type institutions; and such differences were not of a magnitude to indicate a real educational difference.

It should be pointed out that catalogs may not always provide a highly accurate description of an institution's actual program and policies—a factor which could not be treated in this Study. However, catalog analyses in conjunction with institutional visitations undoubtedly provide more valid conclusions than merely one of these methods of study.

APPENDIX VII

STATISTICAL INFORMATION RELATIVE TO ACCREDITATION IN TEACHER EDUCATION

A. Accreditation of Institutions of Higher Education by States and Type of Institution

The Ten States with the Largest Number of Institutions Accredited by NCATE

| | Number of Accredited Institutions | |
	Regional Association	NCATE
New York	71	22
Pennsylvania	72	21
Texas	44	20
Illinois	44	19
Wisconsin	28	19
Minnesota	23	17
Ohio	45	16
California	47	15
Kansas	22	15
Massachusetts	44	15

States with More than 50% of Institutions Regionally Accredited, also Accredited by NCATE

Arizona	3 out of 3		Nevada	1 out of 1
Arkansas	9 out of 16		New Mexico	4 out of 6
Colorado	7 out of 12		Oklahoma	13 out of 16
Indiana	14 out of 26		Oregon	8 out of 15
Kansas	15 out of 22		Utah	4 out of 5
Louisiana	9 out of 17		Washington	8 out of 15
Minnesota	17 out of 23		West Virginia	9 out of 15
Montana	5 out of 8		Wisconsin	19 out of 28
Nebraska	12 out of 16		Wyoming	1 out of 1

287

The number of regionally accredited institutions, as of January, 1964, is derived from W. Earl Armstrong and T. M. Stinnett in *A Manual on Certification Requirements,* 1964 edition, published by NCTEPS in cooperation with NASDTEC. The number of NCATE-accredited institutions is taken from the Eleventh Annual List (September 1, 1964, to August 31, 1965) published by NCATE.

In three states (Arizona, Nevada, and Wyoming) all institutions accredited by their regional association are also accredited by NCATE. These are states of small population and with no more than three regionally accredited institutions. Of the 18 states having more than 50 percent of their institutions regionally accredited, also accredited by NCATE, only Indiana and Wisconsin are among the 16 most populous states for which statistics are given by Conant in *The Education of American Teachers.* The rank order of the 18 states by percent of numbers of regionally accredited institutions also accredited by NCATE is:

	Percent
Arizona, Nevada, Wyoming	100
Oklahoma	81
Utah	80
Nebraska	75
Minnesota	74
Kansas, New Mexico, Wisconsin	68
Montana	63
West Virginia	60
Colorado	58
Arkansas	57
Indiana	54
Louisiana, Oregon, Washington	53

The seven states with less than 20 percent of the institutions regionally accredited, also accredited by NCATE, are:

Alaska	0 out of 1	Rhode Island	1 out of 7
Delaware	0 out of 2	South Carolina	1 out of 18
Hawaii	0 out of 2	Vermont	1 out of 7
	Virginia	5 out of 30	

By Types of Institutions

Armstrong and Stinnett (*A Manual on Certification Requirements*, 1964 edition) lists 1,173 approved teacher education institutions by types of institution. They classified these institutions, using as the basic source for determining classification the annual publication of the U. S. Office of Education, *Education Directory, 1962–1963*. The class, Teachers College, includes only separate, single-purpose institutions which have teachers college or college of education in their names or which are degree-granting normal colleges. Below in the left-hand column is the tabulation of Armstrong and Stinnett. The classification of the right-hand column is made by the authors of this Study. Quite a number of institutions have changed names and/or functions since the 1962–1963 *Directory* was prepared. Hence in some instances, as an example, Institution X may be classified in the left-hand column as a teachers college and as a public general college in the right-hand column.

	Number of Approved Teacher Education Institutions	Number of Institutions Accredited by NCATE
Teachers Colleges		
Public	35	14
Private	12	4
Universities		
Public	116	99
Private	145	51
Public General College	197	162
Private Liberal Arts College	580	92
Technical Schools	29	
Junior Colleges	50	
Unclassified	9	
	1,173	422

B. Production of New Teachers by NCATE-Accredited Institutions

The most recent complete report on *Teacher Supply and Demand*, published by the Research Division of the National Education Association, was dated 1962 and was based on 1961 graduates of colleges and universities. A new report on 1964 graduates is due in 1965.

According to the 1962 *Teacher Supply and Demand* report, of the total new teachers graduated in 1961 NCATE-accredited institutions produced 68.9 percent. Of all the graduates prepared for elementary school teaching, 71.3 percent were produced by NCATE-accredited institutions, while NCATE-accredited institutions produced 67.4 percent of the new teachers prepared for high school teaching.

For the purposes of this report institutions were classified as teachers colleges, general colleges, and universities. The table shows the percent of new teachers produced by type of institution.

Percent of New Teachers Produced

	Elementary	Secondary
Teachers Colleges	21.6	19.2
General Colleges	41.7	41.1
Universities	36.7	39.7

C. Membership in AACTE by Type of Institution and by States

	Percent
Primarily Teacher Education	14.0
Private Colleges	38.0
Enlarged Public Colleges	18.1
Universities—Medium scope	
Public	5.8
Private	5.2
Complex Universities	
Public	11.8
Private	6.5
Specialized Graduate Schools of Education	.6

These data were compiled by AACTE and based on the classification system proposed by Pattillo and Pfnister and the *USOE Directory, Part 3, 1962–1963*.

In 1963, the 11 states with the largest number of institutional members of AACTE were, in order:

New York	37	Texas	28
Illinois	33	Massachusetts	24
California	29	Michigan	21
Ohio	29	Missouri	21
Pennsylvania	28	Indiana	20
		Iowa	20

D.   Teacher Supply and Demand Projections*

According to a study of the teacher supply and demand relationship completed one year ago by the U. S. Bureau of Labor Statistics, the persistent shortage of qualified teaching personnel which has prevailed since 1945 will be considerably relieved by 1975. Indeed it is expected that in 1975 the total supply of secondary school teachers will be greater than the demand, a situation which may start as early as 1965.

In the past 20 years, since the end of World War II, there has been a shortage of qualified personnel for teaching in the elementary and secondary schools. According to estimates made by the U. S. Bureau of Labor Statistics, the need for pre-college level teachers will have reached its peak during this school year, 1964–1965, and in the next decade, the number of teachers needed each year will fall below this peak level. This conclusion reflects the drop in number of births for a few years after 1947, and subsequent lower rate of increase during the 1950's. Furthermore, it is projected that the supply of trained teachers will steadily increase to 1975.

The projections indicate that the teacher supply situation in the elementary schools, where the shortage has been most critical, will improve significantly in 10 years, and that an adequate supply (or surplus) will be available for the secondary schools. In the analysis of the projections, it is recognized that shortages in some parts of the country may persist and also in some subjects at the secondary school level, such as mathematics, science, and foreign languages.

Teacher Supply and Demand Projections

Average Annual Requirements for Growth and Replacement Needs in
Elementary and Secondary Schools 1960–1975
(In Thousands)

Year	Total	Elementary	Secondary
1960–1965	190	97	93
1965–1970	186	108	78
1970–1975	206	119	87

Illustrative Projected Average Annual Balance (Requirements Minus
Supply) of Elementary and Secondary School Teachers, 1960–1975
(In Thousands)

Year	Total	Elementary	Secondary
1960–1965	−33	−22	−11
1965–1970	+21	−12	+33
1970–1975	+41	−6	+47

* The data, including the two tables, in this appendix are based on a report, "A New Look at Manpower Needs in Teaching," Maxine G. Stewart, *Occupational Outlook Quarterly* (May, 1964), Vol. 8, No. 2. The *Quarterly* is issued by the Bureau of Labor Statistics, U. S. Department of Labor.

Among the assumptions on which these projections are based are: school attendance rates will continue to increase, particularly in secondary schools; college graduations will continue to increase as predicted by the U. S. Office of Education and those prepared to teach will continue to represent about one-third of all baccalaureate graduates; entrance requirements for teaching will not increase significantly; teaching salaries will remain in about the same position relative to other occupations; new education legislation will not change the total numbers enrolled at the pre-college level beyond the increases already reflected in the U. S. Office of Education projections; the teacher-pupil ratio will undergo no great change by 1975, since counter-balancing forces, such as offering small classes in advanced subjects and greater use of audiovisual aids, will prevail; the present estimated annual separation rate (leaving teaching for other occupations) of 8 percent will be maintained. It should be noted that the number of new teachers needed for replacement will be four times the number needed to take care of expanding enrollments. The projections also take into consideration the numbers who return to teaching and the numbers now teaching on emergency certificates. It is estimated that in 1964, 83,000 teachers were on emergency certificates, slightly more than two-thirds of them in the elementary schools.

APPENDIX VIII

SUGGESTED AREAS FOR ADDITIONAL RESEARCH

The need for research related to teacher education cannot be overstated.

Perhaps it will be a long time before a consensus is reached on a definition of good teaching, on the qualities of a good teacher, and on the preparation program which will be most effective in producing a good teacher. One inherent difficulty in all of these problems is the individualistic nature of them. Nevertheless modern methods of research, the new techniques, including new possibilities for both mass and individual instruction, and the tremendously improved methods of data processing make possible the finding of solutions to problems that a decade ago almost certainly were out of reach.

The quality of research in education has been and, unfortunately much of it continues to be, open to grave question. This has been true in part because too much of the research has been done by individuals without adequate financial support. Too often the major part of educational research done in the universities has been the work of graduate students for which a doctoral degree has been awarded. In these efforts, the students have not been inspired to dedicate themselves to a lifetime of research. There are many signs, however, that this situation is changing and that the means will soon be available whereby it can be changed.

National, regional, and state efforts to improve teacher education must have the guidance of research if they are to be successful. Efforts to improve the accreditation of teacher education must likewise have such guidance. Some of the issues for research which seem most pressing in relation to the findings of this Study are listed below.

Small and sometimes large efforts are already being directed to these problems. These efforts must be strengthened and supporting studies initiated. Individual effort should be fostered and large group studies undertaken. The research must become the responsibility of college and university staffs, government and private agencies. Some of the most promising efforts now under way are carried on by such groups as the National Merit Scholarship Fund and the American Institute for Research.

Recent efforts by scholars in the disciplines have already had a strong influence on the teaching of foreign languages, science, and mathematics. These groups must be provided further support and new ways must be found in which professors of education and psychology, professors in the other social sciences, and in the humanities and natural sciences can work as teams.

Research in education has been of several kinds: controlled experimentation with carefully isolated variables; data collection and interpretation; developmental studies of curriculum and evaluation instruments. Problems identified for supporting research in the improvement of accreditation of teacher education may require utilization of all of these methods and others.

Problems for Research

1. *Teacher education programs*

Experimental teacher education programs with carefully stated behavioral objectives should be established. These can then be evaluated to determine if the objectives are achieved. Those initiating the programs will, of course, have to make their own identification of the behaviors of a good teacher which they wish to develop. They will then identify factors of training, experience, and adjustment for individual differences which they hope will develop these behaviors.

Special attention should be given in this research to behavioral objectives and the achievement of them in student teaching separately, in the course sequence in professional education separately, and in liberal education and major or area of concentration specialization.

2. *Other factors contributing to success in teaching*

Few, if any, definitive studies are available on factors contributing to success in teaching. While research on the contribution of the undergraduate teacher education program to success in teaching involves the isolation of this factor from sociological and personal factors, modern methods of statistical analysis make this possible. Similarly, the teacher program factor might be isolated in research on other factors which may contribute to success in teaching, such as socioeconomic level in which the teacher grew up or participation in extracurricular activities.

3. *Development of tests to measure behaviors which reflect*

(a) knowledge of subject matter (both academic and professional),
(b) attitudes toward teaching,
(c) personality characteristics desirable in a teacher.

While tests are available to measure knowledge, attitudes, and personality, these usually are not measures of behavior. New and more imaginative tests are needed, particularly if test results are to be used as a factor in accreditation and/or certification. Appropriate academic groups with the assistance of psychologists expert in measurement should take the major responsibility for the development of these tests under item (a), and should be included among those responsible for tests under items (b) and (c).

Development of Rating Scales

There is a difference of opinion on whether the development of rating scales, or the use of them, can properly be called research. There is also a difference of opinion on the value of rating scales or the collection of opinions in general. Although the value of opinion analysis is down graded by some researchers, others view information of this kind helpful in particular kinds of decision making. The development of rating scales is proposed here in the belief that every possible source of information on quality programs of teacher education must be exploited.

It is suggested that rating scales to record observations of teaching effectiveness, observations of school or college atmosphere that contribute to teaching effectiveness, and opinions of school administrators of college teacher education programs could be useful in educational evaluation in many areas, and especially useful in accreditation and/or certification.

The educational community has too long assumed that teacher effectiveness cannot be measured, that college atmosphere would not lend itself to a rating scale, and that opinions of school administrators on teacher education programs of individual colleges would be subjective and biased. A concentrated attack on these problems should produce some highly valuable scales.

Collection on a Comprehensive Basis of Opinion

Ratings of Teacher Education Institutions,

Undergraduate and Graduate

The American Council on Education-sponsored study of graduate departments of universities, reported in Chapter 9, has established a pattern for institutional evaluation by opinions of leaders in the field. These procedures should be applied to teacher education at the graduate level, and, because of the importance of undergraduate preparation of teachers, to undergraduate programs separately.

THE NEW HORIZONS REPORT *

Reference to the *New Horizons* report is made in a number of chapters of the report of this Study. This review is included as an appendix in order to provide background for these references, to point out what at least one group in professional education believes accreditation should mean, and because of the strategic role assigned by the *New Horizons* report to accreditation and NCATE in particular.

The National Commission on Teacher Education and Professional Standards (NCTEPS or TEPS) was established by the NEA in 1946. Believing in 1958 that many of its original goals had been accomplished and that "momentum toward the achievement of others was adequate to promise their accomplishment in the foreseeable future," the TEPS Commission began to re-examine its purposes, goals, and procedures. The re-examination resulted in a proposal which ultimately became the Project on New Horizons in Teacher Education and Professional Standards. The Project, supported by the National Education Association, held its first meeting in August, 1959, and the report was published in 1961. Responsibilities were organized in five areas: (1) advancement of professional standards; (2) teacher education, both pre- and in-service; (3) accreditation; (4) certification; and (5) identification, selective admission, and retention of professional personnel. The chapters in the final *New Horizons* report are suggested by these areas. Margaret Lindsey of Teachers College, Columbia University, was the Director of the Project.

The report states:

> Accreditation of preparatory programs is the keystone which supports all other standards and their enforcement. It is the core of the Professional Standards Movement. (p. 115)

The profession's goal with respect to accreditation of preparatory programs is summarized as follows:

> To enter teaching or any other area of professional service the educator should have completed an approved program of preparation in an institution of higher education accredited by the NCATE. (p. 114)

It should be pointed out that this goal is not shared by all who would call themselves members of the profession of teaching. NCATE itself has not exerted pressure on institutions to become accredited and has never at any time given encouragement to or endorsement of such an ambitious goal for national accreditation of teacher education. Indeed, some of NCATE's most ardent supporters have stated that NCATE accreditation should be a real mark of distinction which not all teacher preparing institutions can hope to achieve.

In essence *New Horizons* is a stirring call to those in teaching and related activities to become professional and to act like members of a profession. Those in the profession are called upon to accept the responsibilities of a

---

* Margaret Lindsey, ed., *New Horizons for the Teaching Profession* (Washington, D. C., 1961).

professional and to be prepared to police their own ranks. The report identifies as the three essential processes of enforcement of professional standards: accreditation of preparatory programs, licensure of professional personnel, and rigorous application of professional standards of practice. Again all groups in the profession are directed to understand these obligations, to assist in defining them and in determining standards for them, and to support their enforcement.

The two chapters of greatest relevance for this Study are Chapter 4, "Preparation of Professional Personnel," and Chapter 5, "Accreditation of Professional Preparatory Programs." The emphasis of *New Horizons* on the need for experimentation with professional programs was reported in the chapter on Experimentation and Research of this Study. In Chapter 4 of the *New Horizons* report, through 82 pages, rationalization for the following conclusions about preparatory programs is given: (pp. 106-108)

1. Competence required of professional educators is achieved through a distinctive organization of learning experiences; it is not a by-product of becoming a well educated person.
2. For the professional educator, "control" of knowledge has value in the power it provides for mature quality of action.
3. The interrelatedness of general (or liberal) education, specialization in the teaching field, and professional education is recognized and the program designed to erase unnatural and unnecessary dividing lines.
4. Human variation and individual creativity are deliberately preserved; each student pursues an individually designed program.
5. Pre- and in-service education is a continuous process.
6. College teachers and special service personnel are professionally prepared for their roles, with graduate work including a period of full-time study and direct experience in roles which the educator is preparing to perform (e.g., college teaching under supervision). Teaching experience in elementary or secondary schools is a prerequisite for admission to graduate programs preparing college teachers of professional education and special service personnel for schools.
7. The preparing institution is held accountable for the graduate's competence to teach or to perform other services for which his program was designed. Evidence of competence is provided through qualitative reports of the student's total college program, including satisfactorily passing a comprehensive examination and demonstration of competence in an internship.
8. Preparation of professional personnel is the responsibility of the total teaching profession, with delegation of leadership to those especially qualified.

In Chapter 5 attention is given to the three levels of accreditation of teacher education (state, regional, and national). The brief analysis of these agencies as they act at this time and their influence supports in part many of the observations by this Study. Consideration is given in the chapter to the responsibility in the accreditation process of individual members of the profession, their professional organizations, the legal agencies, and the accrediting associations themselves. The chapter concludes with the statement:

> It is crystal clear that if the professional accrediting agency is to perform its service effectively, the profession must assume, more than it does at present, responsibility for the moral and financial support of NCATE.

Among key points made in the chapter are:

Concern with teacher preparation and with accreditation is "clearly and incontrovertibly" a professional responsibility shared by every classroom teacher.

Responsibility for developing and teaching understanding of accreditation is shared by the institutions, the associations, and the teachers.

Membership in professional organizations must be considered in terms of graduation from an accredited institution. (AASA is the only organization which has taken such action.)

Sound improvement of teacher education requires feedback by teachers and their associates.

Service on accrediting teams can and should be rendered by classroom teachers.

Continuous development and revision of accreditation standards is shared by the professional organization, individual member, and the legal agency.

State departments of education can implement the work of accrediting agencies, particularly NCATE.

In the foreseeable future all state-accredited institutions which prepare teachers will meet NCATE standards and be NCATE-accredited.

Groups, such as the Modern Language Association, the National Science Teachers Association, and others, should be encouraged to work with NCATE in determining standards which will be utilized by all accrediting agencies.

NCATE must receive adequate support to conduct the needed research, . . . to validate evaluating and measuring procedures.

A minimum of from 50 to 100 persons should be trained for visiting teams each year. (It is further implied that a number of these persons should be selected by learned societies and it is suggested by question that the learned societies might pay for their training.)

BIBLIOGRAPHY

BOOKS AND PAMPHLETS

AACTE. *Sourcebook on Accreditation of Teacher Education.* Washington: The Association, 1962.

American Council on Education. *Coordination of Accrediting Agencies.* Washington: American Council on Education, 1939.

Armstrong, W. Earl. *The Education of Teachers: Retrospect and Prospect.* Kirksville: Simpson Printing Company, 1964.

Armstrong, W. Earl, and Stinnett, T. M. *A Manual on Certification Requirements for School Personnel in the United States.* Washington: National Education Association, 1964.

Blauch, Lloyd E., ed. *Accreditation in Higher Education.* Washington: Government Printing Office, 1959.

Boroff, David. *Campus U. S. A.: Portraits of American Colleges in Action.* New York: Harper and Brothers, 1961.

Conant, James B. *The American High School Today.* New York: McGraw-Hill Book Company, 1959.

Conant, James B. *The Child, the Parent, and the State.* Cambridge: Harvard University Press, 1959.

Conant, James B. *The Education of American Teachers.* New York: McGraw-Hill Book Company, 1963.

Conant, James B. *Shaping Educational Policy.* New York: McGraw-Hill Book Company, 1964.

Conant, James B. *Slums and Suburbs.* New York: McGraw-Hill Book Company, 1961.

Deferrari, Roy J. *Memoirs of the Catholic University of America, 1918–60.* Boston: Daughters of St. Paul, 1962.

Deferrari, Roy J. *Self-Evaluation and Accreditation in Higher Education.* Washington: The Catholic University of America Press, 1959.

Donovan, George R. *Selected Problems in Administration of American Higher Education.* Washington: The Catholic University of America Press, 1964.

Gardner, John W. *Excellence: Can We Be Equal and Excellent Too?* New York: Harper and Brothers, 1961.

Huggett, A. J., and Stinnett, T. M. *Professional Problems of Teachers,* 2nd ed. New York: The Macmillan Company, 1963.

Introducing the New England Association. Published by the New England Association of Colleges and Secondary Schools, 1957.

Kelly, Fred J., et al. *Collegiate Accreditation by Agencies Within States.* U. S. Office of Education, Bulletin No. 3. Washington: Government Printing Office, 1940.

Kinney, L. B. *Certification in Education.* Englewood Cliffs: Prentice-Hall Inc., 1964.

Knight, Douglas M. (ed.). *The Federal Government and Higher Education.* Englewood Cliffs: Prentice-Hall, Inc., 1960.

Koerner, James D. *The Miseducation of American Teachers.* Boston: Houghton Mifflin Company, 1963.

LaGrone, Herbert F., Director. *A Proposal for the Revision of the Pre-Service Professional Component of a Program of Teacher Education*

(A Project to Improve the Professional Sequence in Pre-Service Teacher Education through the Selective and Planned Use of New Media). Washington: AACTE, 1964.

Lindsey, Margaret (ed.). *New Horizons for the Teaching Profession.* Washington: National Education Association, 1961.

Morris, Alvin E. *A Critical Analysis of Types of Quantitative Data Requested by the Professional Teacher Education Accrediting Agency and the Six Regional Accrediting Agencies.* Detroit: Wayne University Press, 1959.

NCTEPS. *Milestones in Teacher Education and Professional Standards.* Washington: National Education Association, 1964.

Nevins, John F. *A Study of the Organization and Operation of Voluntary Accreditation Agencies.* Research Monographs 22.3. Washington: Catholic University of America Press, 1959.

Reid, Robert H. *American Degree Mills. A Study of Their Operations and of Existing and Potential Ways of Controlling Them.* Washington: American Council on Education, 1959.

Ryans, David D. *Characteristics of Teachers: Their Description, Comparison, and Appraisal.* Washington: American Council on Education, 1959.

Selden, William K. *Accreditation, A Struggle Over Standards in Higher Education.* New York: Harper and Brothers, 1960.

Snavely, Guy E. *A Short History of the Southern Association of Colleges and Secondary Schools.* Reprinted from the *Southern Association Quarterly,* Vol. IX, November, 1945.

Wiggins, Sam P. *Battlefields in Teacher Education.* Nashville: George Peabody College for Teachers, 1964.

Zook, George F. and Haggerty, M. E. *The Evaluation of Higher Institutions.* Chicago: University of Chicago Press, 1936.

ARTICLES

"Accreditation," *Journal of Health, Physical Education and Recreation,* 34:35, 36. April 1963.

Anderson, G. L., and Ertell, M. W., "Extra-Institutional Forces Affecting Professional Education," National Society for the Study of Education, *1961 Yearbook,* Part II, 235–253.

Armstrong, W. Earl, "Regional and Professional Accreditation," *Liberal Education,* 48:234–242. May 1962.

Blackman, E. B., "Accreditation and General Education," *North Central Association Quarterly,* 37:303–306. September 1963.

Bowles, Frank H., "The Place of the Regional Association in the Future Educational Scene," Middle States Association, *Proceedings,* 1957: 24–36.

Breuhaus, B. A., "Accreditation Enhances Quality," *NEA Journal,* 49:52–53. April 1960.

Broudy, Harry S., "Conant on the Education of Teachers," *Teachers College Journal,* 35:132–138. January 1964.

Brown, Bob Burton, "Issues in the NCATE Controversy," *American Teacher Magazine,* 48:10. December 1963.

Burns, Norman, "Accrediting and Educational Diversity," *North Central Association Quarterly,* 35:257–258. April 1961.

Burns, Norman, "Accrediting Enters a New Phase," *North Central Association Quarterly*, 27:293–296. January 1953.

Burns, Norman, "Role of Accrediting in the Improvement of College Education," *Junior College Journal*, 24:545–551. May 1954.

Burns, Norman, "Some Thoughts on the Theory and Practice of Accrediting," *North Central Association Quarterly*, 28:205–214. October 1953.

Burns, Norman, "Tasks of Accrediting in Higher Education Today," *North Central Association Quarterly*, 34:220–225. January 1960.

Camille, Sister Mary, "NCATE Criteria, Policy and Implications," National Catholic Education Association, *Bulletin*, 59:232–240. August 1962.

Cartwright, William H., "Securing Teachers of High Quality," *Teachers College Journal*, 35:127–132. January 1964.

Case, J., "While School Keeps: Recommended Changes in Structure of NCATE," *Saturday Review*, 46:70, 71. March 23, 1963.

Chase, F. S., "Teacher Education for the Next Decade," *School and Society*, 92:140–142. March 21, 1964.

"Conant's Impact on Teacher Education," *Phi Delta Kappan*, XLV, No. 9:425–499. June 1964.

Davis, B. H., "Accreditation: A Cooperative Venture," AAUP *Bulletin* 48:3. March 1962.

Dickey, F. G., "Accreditation and Excellence," AACTE *Yearbook*, 128–134. 1962.

Elam, S., "Will Wisconsin Accredit NCATE?" *Phi Delta Kappan*, 44:154–159. January 1963.

Engbretson, Wm. E., "The Influence of Accreditation Programs and the TEPS New Horizons Project on Teacher Education," *Teachers College Journal*, XXXIII, No. 6:151–155. May 1962.

Farr, S. David, "Evaluation and Selection Instruments in Teacher Education Programs," University of Buffalo, *CRP Project No. S. 005*. February 1964–August 1964.

Fleege, U. H., "Catholic Institutions Accredited by NCATE," National Catholic Education Association *Bulletin*, 59:231–232. August 1962.

Gilman, Richard C., "Basic Issues in Teacher Education," ACCTE *Sixteenth Yearbook*, 50–56.

Goldthorpe, J. Harold, "Office of Education Relationships to Accreditation," *Higher Education*, 11:51–54. December 1954.

Grieder, C., "Accrediting Agencies Create Distorted Image," *Nations Schools*, 65–66. March 1960.

Hangartner, C. A., "NCATE and the Large University," National Catholic Educational Association *Bulletin*, 59:240–241. August 1962.

Hill, Alfred T., "Small Colleges Win Accreditation," *School and Society*, 87:117–119. November 14, 1959.

Hill, Alfred T., "What is a Non-Accredited College?" *Educational Record*, 38:348–354. October 1957.

Humphrey, B. J., "Survey of Professional Education Offerings in NCATE Accredited Institutions," *Journal of Teacher Education*, 14:406–410. December 1963.

Kinney, Lucien B., "Designing Accreditation," *Journal of Higher Education*, 26:25–30, 57–58. January 1955.

Kirk, R., "To Educate the Educators," *National Review*, 15:24–25. June 16, 1963.

Kline, Clarice, "The Place of Accreditation in Insuring Expertness," *Journal of Secondary Education*, 38, No. 5:313–318. May. 1963.

Koerner, James D., "The Education of Teachers," *Vital Speeches*, 29:412–416. April 15, 1963.

Koerner, James D., "How to Teach Teachers," *Atlantic Monthly*, 211:59–63. February 1963.

Koerner, James D., "Merely Training in Pedagogy," *N.E.A. Journal*, 48:18. April 1959.

Koerner, James D., "Speaking Out: Teachers Get the Worst Education," *Saturday Evening Post*, 236:8. June 1963.

Koerner, James D., "Teacher Education: Who Makes the Rules?" *Saturday Review*, 45:78–80. October 20, 1962.

Koerner, James D., "What Shall We Teach?" *Vital Speeches*, 25:716–721. September 15, 1959.

Ladd, Edward T., "The Proper Place of Accreditation," *Journal of Secondary Education*, 38:296–305. May 1963.

Lander, R., "What NCATE Means to the Teacher," *N.E.A. Journal*, 52:30, 31. February 1963.

McCormally, John, "The Root of Opposition to Federal Support," *Education Digest*, 27 No. 4:32–33. December 1961.

Meder, A. E., Jr., "Absolute Importance of Regional Accreditation," *School and Society*, 91:108. March 9, 1963.

Meder, A. E., Jr., "Accrediting Procedures of NCATE," *School and Society*, 91:192–193. April 20, 1963.

Millis, J. S., et al, "Accreditation: Burden, Luxury or Necessity?" *Liberal Education*, 46:76–81. March 1960.

Nyquist, Ewald B., "National and Regional Developments in Cooperative Evaluation and Accrediting Activities," *Journal of English Education*, 44:533–538. May 1954.

Ohles, J. F., "Accreditation Story," *Teachers College Journal*, 34:30–34. October 1962.

Pattillo, Manning M., "Recent Developments in Accrediting," *North Central Association Quarterly*, 27:290–292. January 1953.

Pattillo, Manning M., "Accreditation in the Public Interest," *Educational Record*, 36:120–128. April 1955.

Pattillo, Manning M., "A General Accrediting Agency," *Journal of Higher Education*, 27:141–146. March 1956.

Pfnister, Allan O., "A Regional Accrediting Agency Experiments in the Training of Consultants for Higher Educational Institutions," *Educational Record*, 40:62–68. January 1959.

Pinkham, Fred O., "The State University and the National Commission on Accrediting," National Association of State Universities, *Proceedings:* 1954, pp. 35–46.

"Place of Accreditation in Insuring Expertness," *Journal of Secondary Education*, 38:280–318. May 1963.

"The Professor and Accreditation," AAUP *Bulletin*, 47:146–150. June 1961.

Pulliam, A. Lloyd, "Form and Substance in the Accreditation of Teacher Education," *Liberal Education*, XLVIII, No. 4 (December 1962).

Pullias, Earl V., "Some Special Responsibilities of Accrediting Agencies," *Educational Record*, 39:340–347. October 1958.

Romine, S. A., "A Look to the Future," *North Central Association Quarterly,* 35:175–180. October 1960.

Romine, S. A., "How A Free Society Meets Its Educational Needs," *North Central Association Quarterly,* 37:186–190. Fall 1962.

Selden, William K., "Accrediting—What Is It?" AAUP *Bulletin,* 42:629-635. December 1956.

Selden, William K., "The National Commission on Accrediting: Its Next Mission," *Educational Record,* 38:152–156. April 1957.

Selden, William K., "Basic Issues in Accreditation of Teacher Education," *Liberal Education,* 47:536–546. December 1961.

Selden, William K., "Not Two Cultures but 102," *Teachers College Record,* 65:50–56. October 1963.

Selden, William K., "Relative Unimportance of Regional Accreditation," *Journal of Teacher Education,* 13:319–325. September 1962.

Selden, William K., "The Three Basic Principles of Accrediting," *School and Society,* 87:308–310. June 20, 1959.

Selden, William K., "What Is an Accredited College?" *NEA Journal,* 47:43, 44. January 1958.

Selden, William K., "Where Do We Go From Here?" *Exceptional Children,* 24:203–205. January 1963.

Selden, William K., "Why Accredit Teacher Education?" *Journal of Teacher Education,* 11:185–190. June 1960.

Selden, William K., and Land, William G., "The Forgotten Colleges," *North Central Association Quarterly,* 35:271–273. April 1961.

"Statement of Policy Relative to the Accrediting of Institutions of Higher Education," *North Central Association Quarterly,* 33:19–30. June 1958.

Stiles, Lindley J., "The Role of Liberal Arts Colleges in Teacher Education," *The Educational Forum,* XXVIII, 171–177. January 1964.

Stiles, Lindley J., "The University of Wisconsin Plan for Teacher Education," *School and Society,* 90:189–191. April 21, 1962.

Stiles, Lindley J., "Wisconsin vs. NCATE," *School and Society,* 91:236. Summer 1963.

Stone, Jas. C., "Insuring Expertness Through State Accreditation of Teacher Education Institutions," *Journal of Secondary Education,* 38, No. 5:306–312. May 1963.

Stoope, J. A., "Education for Education," *Pennsylvania School Journal,* 111:206–210. January 1963.

Stuit, D. B., "Accreditation: Its Problems and its Future," *Teachers College Record,* 62:629–641. May 1961.

Turbeville, Gus, "How We Got Accredited," Association of American Colleges *Bulletin,* 43:428–434. October 1957.

Upton, Miller, "Quality in Higher Education," *North Central Association Quarterly,* 37:307–314. Spring 1963.

VanDyke, L. A., "Time for Reappraisal," *North Central Association Quarterly,* 37:163–165. Fall 1962.

"Who Should Set the Standards?" *Time,* 81:61–62. November 15, 1963.

"Why Teachers Can't Teach," *Life,* 54:4. March 22, 1963.

Wilker, Arthur V., "Some Questions for Small Colleges," *College and University Business,* 22:19–21. January 1957.

INDEX